# Poor Women in Rich Countries

# POOR WOMEN IN RICH COUNTRIES

## The Feminization of Poverty Over the Life Course

Edited by

**Gertrude Schaffner Goldberg**

OXFORD
UNIVERSITY PRESS

2010

OXFORD
UNIVERSITY PRESS

Oxford University Press, Inc., publishes works that further
Oxford University's objective of excellence
in research, scholarship, and education.

Oxford New York
Auckland Cape Town Dar es Salaam Hong Kong Karachi
Kuala Lumpur Madrid Melbourne Mexico City Nairobi
New Delhi Shanghai Taipei Toronto

With offices in
Argentina Austria Brazil Chile Czech Republic France Greece
Guatemala Hungary Italy Japan Poland Portugal Singapore
South Korea Switzerland Thailand Turkey Ukraine Vietnam



Published by Oxford University Press, Inc.
198 Madison Avenue, New York, New York 10016
www.oup.com



Library of Congress Cataloging-in-Publication Data

Poor women in rich countries : the feminization of poverty over the life
course / edited by Gertrude Schaffner Goldberg.
p. cm.
Includes bibliographical references and index.
ISBN 978-0-19-531430-4
1. Poor women—Developed countries—Cross-cultural studies. 2. Women
heads of households—Developed countries—Cross-cultural studies.
3. Poverty—Developed countries—Cross-cultural studies. I. Goldberg, Gertrude S.
HQ1155.P66 2010
305.48′96942091722—dc22
2009014124

9 8 7 6 5 4 3 2 1
Printed in the United States of America
on acid-free paper

*To my fellow authors whose knowledge, insight, and commitment to social justice have made possible this work and my two previous cross-national studies.*

*Gradgrind's School*

| | |
|---|---|
| Schoolmaster, Mr. McChoakumchild: | *Girl number twenty, isn't this a prosperous nation, and aint you in a thriving state?* |
| Girl Number Twenty, Sissy: | *I said I didn't know. I thought I couldn't know whether it was a prosperous nation or not, and whether I was in a thriving state or not, unless I knew who got the money, and whether any of it was mine.* |

– Charles Dickens, *Hard Times*

# ACKNOWLEDGMENTS

My indebtedness to other scholars grows longer with each new study that I undertake. The second wave of the women's movement was a major impetus for studying poverty and inequality from the perspective of women. Sociologist and social worker Diana Pearce coined the phrase and the idea of feminization of poverty in the late 1970s that led to research on this phenomenon in the United States. My colleagues and I at Adelphi University School of Social Work, stimulated by one of our student's questions—whether feminization of poverty exists outside the United States—began to investigate that question. In time we gathered enough data, even in the 1980s, to be able to publish *The Feminization of Poverty: Only in America?*—an exploration of the phenomenon in seven industrialized countries. We were quite inexperienced in cross-national study and were not knowledgeable about some of the countries. At that time, data on women's poverty was hard to come by in some countries, much less permitting reliable international comparisons.

By the time of our second cross-national study, *Diminishing Welfare*, there was much more comparative data. The Luxembourg Income Study (LIS) has enabled all three of our studies to make some cross-national comparisons and, with the passage of time, to include more countries and more variables. I am fortunate that Ann Morissens, co-author of this volume's chapter on Sweden, helped me to access detailed data from LIS on the poverty of both lone mothers and lone elderly women. As this book demonstrates, I also owe much to the theorists, the giants on whose shoulders we stand: the women and men whose work on the welfare state stimulated and challenged my quest for knowledge.

In this, as in my previous two cross-national studies, Helen Lachs Ginsburg, Professor Emerita of Economics at Brooklyn College, City University of New York and my long-time collaborator in scholarship and social reform, has generously shared her knowledge and encouraged my efforts. Her comparative work, *Full Employment and Public Policy: The United States and Sweden*, published in the early 1980s, inspired my research. Helen Ginsburg not only co-authored a chapter in *Diminishing Welfare* but read and critiqued parts of that manuscript and the present one as well. I also thank Marguerite G. Rosenthal, Professor Emerita of Social Policy, Salem State College and co-editor of *Diminishing Welfare*, for sharing that project and the intellectual growth that it stimulated and for her careful reading and commentary of this manuscript. Dr. Eleanor Kremen, co-editor and co-author of the first of these international works and, for many years, my colleague at the Adelphi University School of Social Work, did much to stimulate my initial thinking about the feminization of poverty in international perspective. Finally, as the dedication to this book manifests, I thank all of the co-authors, the collaborators on this and previous studies who have made them possible.

Were I not to mention the National Jobs for All Coalition (NJFAC) whose principal goal is full employment at living wages, I would be leaving out an important stimulus to all my thinking. I have learned a great deal from my fellow workers in this effort to understand the evil of unemployment that exists chronically and now acutely in most, if not all, industrial countries. We believe that living-wage jobs for all is the approach to inequality and poverty that, along with public income support, best approaches economic justice and social welfare in the broadest sense of that term. Along with Helen Ginsburg, I thank NJFAC stalwarts Sheila D. Collins, Professor of Political Science, William Paterson University; Philip Harvey, Professor of Law and Economics, Rutgers School of Law; and June Zaccone, Associate Professor Emerita of Economics, Hofstra University.

I thank my colleagues at the Adelphi University School of Social Work for their encouragement and interest in this project and particularly the Assistant to the Doctoral Program, Stacey Avella, for her editorial work on the manuscript. I am grateful to Adelphi's President, Dr. Robert A. Scott, for hosting a cross-national conference, Social Policy as if People Matter, November 2004—a dialogue that kindled my interest in further international research. I also thank Dr. Maud Edgren-Schori of Stockholm University, co-chair of that conference.

The Columbia University Seminar on Full Employment, Social Welfare, and Equity has been an intellectual stimulus to my thinking about full employment and public policy, including their impact on the poverty of women. I thank the Columbia University Seminar Program and its director, Professor Robert Belknap, for a grant that helped us to undertake the research and publication of *Poor Women in Rich Countries* as well as two previous books.

Gertrude Schaffner Goldberg
New Canaan, CT
June 2009

# CONTENTS

# CONTRIBUTORS

**Patricia Evans**
Professor
School of Social Work
Carleton University
Ottawa, Canada

**Gertrude Schaffner Goldberg**
Professor of Social Policy
and Director, Ph.D. Program
School of Social Work
Adelphi University
Garden City, New York

**Kumiko Hagiwara**
Lecturer of Sociology of Gender
and Labor
Tsuru University
Yamanashi, Japan

**Kimiko Kimoto**
Professor of Sociology
Graduate School of Social
Sciences
Hitotsubashi University
Tokyo, Japan

**Ute Klammer**
Professor of Political Sciences and
Social Policy
University of Duisburg-Essen
Essen, Germany

**Claude Martin**
Directeur de recherche au Centre
national de la recherche
scientifique—CNRS (senior research
fellow at CNRS)
University of Rennes
Chair of Social Care at the École des
Hautes Études en Santé Publique
(French School of Public Health)
France

**Jane Millar**
Professor of Social Policy
Pro-Vice-Chancellor for Research
University of Bath
Bath, United Kingdom

**Ann Morissens**
Research Associate
Higher Institute for Labour Studies
Katholieke Universiteit Leuven
Leuven, Belgium

**Enrica Morlicchio**
Associate Professor of Sociology
Department of Sociology
University of Naples
Naples, Italy

**Diane Sainsbury**
Professor Emerita
Department of Political Science
University of Stockholm
Stockholm, Sweden

**Elena Spinelli**
Senior Lecturer in Social Policy and Social Services
School of Social Work
La Sapienza University
Rome, Italy

# Poor Women in Rich Countries

# 1

# REVISITING THE FEMINIZATION OF POVERTY IN CROSS-NATIONAL PERSPECTIVE

*Gertrude Schaffner Goldberg*

## Introduction

This is a cross-national study of the feminization of poverty or the predominance of women among the poor. It asks whether this phenomenon, first identified in the United States, occurs in other rich countries. Is it an international phenomenon? To answer this question, the study investigates the condition of women in eight developed nations in Europe, North America, and Asia: Canada, France, Germany, Italy, Japan, Sweden, the United Kingdom, and the United States. This research was completed just prior to the economic crisis of 2008. Most of its findings pertain to the period prior to that, but some authors have referred to effects of the financial collapse and severe recession.

Feminization of poverty, a term coined by Diana Pearce (1978), can be viewed both narrowly and broadly. Pearce focused on women who support themselves and their families, women who are "poor in their own right" (1978, p. 28). Using that approach, our earlier cross-national study concluded that feminization of poverty had occurred in the United States because the proportion of single-mother families among all poor families had increased from just over one-fourth (28%) in 1960 to three-fifths (60%) in 1987—a very substantial majority and a very substantial increase (Goldberg, 1990b).[1]

This book not only revisits the question of the feminization of family poverty but extends the inquiry over the life course to the many elderly women who live alone. It asks whether the poverty of the lone elderly is also feminized. It should be noted that the terms lone, single, sole, or solo mother are used interchangeably in this work. Different countries tend to favor one or more of these designations.[2] Lone elderly women is used to refer to older women who are without partners and who live alone.

Focusing solely on single women, however, fails to tap the gender-related poverty of married women and the likelihood that many of them would join the ranks of the poor if they were on their own. Others, already poor, would probably be more so if they were to become single. This research concentrates on single mothers and single, elderly women but also considers the actual and potential poverty of married or partnered women. In the narrower sense of the term, feminization of poverty is a measure of both the risk of poverty and the composition of the poor. It depends on the proportion of women in a particular population group who are on their own and the difference between their poverty rates and that of other individuals or families in that group. The term feminization of poverty, which implies a trend toward women's predominance among the poor, applied to the United States in the late 1980s: single-mother families had grown from a minority of all poor families with children to a substantial majority within about a quarter of a century.

In the study already cited, feminization of poverty in the narrower sense of the term had not occurred in four other capitalist democracies. Single-mother families did not predominate among poor families because the two necessary conditions for this phenomenon were not met: a rate of single-mother poverty substantially higher than that of other families with children and a high rate of single motherhood (Goldberg & Kremen, 1990). Paradoxically, U.S. single mothers had a lower poverty rate in the mid-1980s than a quarter century earlier but nonetheless remained at much higher risk than either two-parent or single-father families. Thus, the continuing high poverty rates of lone mothers and the near tripling (2.7) of their numbers resulted in the feminization of family poverty in the United States.

Single mothers were quite poor in Japan and Canada, but there were few of them at the time of the study, particularly in Japan (Axinn, 1990; Goldberg, 1990a). Thus poverty was not feminized in these two countries. On the other hand, Sweden shared with the United States a relatively high rate of single motherhood.[3] It made little sense, however, to speak of the feminization of poverty in a country where the poverty rates of all groups were then quite low. In France, neither the rate of poverty nor of single motherhood was high enough for poverty to be feminized. Insufficient data made it difficult to draw conclusions about the two remaining countries in the study, Poland and the former Soviet Union, although we did observe that because women were more likely to be employed in lower-paying occupations and sectors, their poverty might well have been greater than men's (Kremen, 1990; Wojciechowski, 1990).[4]

In recent decades, lone motherhood has risen swiftly in most developed countries (Algava, Le Minez, & Bressé, 2005; Curtin, 2005; Martin & Kats, 2003). In fact, one reason for undertaking the present study is that, with the increase in single motherhood, feminization of poverty might have occurred in some other countries.

With the exception of the United States, the country studies in this volume do not provide trend data on the extent to which poverty is feminized. However, if poverty were now found to be feminized in Canada, France, Japan, and Sweden, feminization would have occurred since single-mother families were not the majority of poor families in these countries in the mid- to late 1980s. Because single motherhood has risen in Germany and the United Kingdom, two countries included in this study but not in the previous one, that would probably also be the case—if single mothers were now the majority of all poor families.

In the chapters that follow, the term feminization of poverty is used, as in the literature generally—both to pertain to the extent to which single women predominate among various groups of the poor and in the more general sense of the potential poverty of many partnered women. Strictly speaking, it means feminized poverty and, unless specifically noted, it does not refer to a trend in that direction.

## Solo Mothers: How Different?

It is true that single mothers have been found to have higher poverty rates than married mothers (Algava et al., 2005; Christopher, 2002; Kilkey & Bradshaw, 1999).[5] However, these statistics obscure the poverty of married women. For example, such figures give no indication of how income is distributed within the family (Glendinning & Millar, 1987; Sen, 1999). In the mid-1990s, mothers' share of couples' total income in seven wealthy nations averaged less than one-third (calculated from Daly & Rake, 2003, p. 126).[6] Nearly half of all women in Italy had no personal income, including income from the state. Without state benefits, that was the case for more than a quarter of women in France, Germany, and the United Kingdom, and a fifth in the United States (Daly & Rake, 2003, pp. 122–123).[7]

Married and single women alike are subject to the general inequalities of the highly segregated labor markets and the related gender gaps that exist everywhere, albeit in differing degrees. A wife's small income that keeps the family out of poverty or in modest comfort can become a path to poverty if she has to support herself as a divorcée or widow. As Daly and Rake express it, "For those women currently part of couples, and hence presumably 'protected' from poverty by a male income, the reality is that they remain just a husband or partner away from poverty" (2003, p. 115). Over two decades ago, Hilda Scott estimated that between two-thirds and three-fourths of American women of working age would be poor if they were obliged to support themselves and just one dependent. Scott referred to "the threat [of poverty] that hangs over the majority of women" (1986, pp. 3–4).

As the principal caregivers in their families, married women suffer disadvantages in the labor market that lower their earnings, skill acquisition, and occupational mobility. Women who are confined to the domestic sphere while caring for their children are only able to take part-time jobs, less taxing ones, or sporadic employment, and are potentially poor because of their reproductive roles.

Why, then, do we spotlight lone mothers? One reason is that the way a society treats them is an indication of its policies toward women, generally. As Lister puts it, "the kinds of state support solo mothers receive can be seen as a measure of the strength or weakness of the social rights of women with families" (1997, p. 194). Millar (1992, p. 149) has argued that "examining the situation of lone mothers, where the consequences of the economic inequalities between men and women are so clearly seen, also casts light on the nature and causes of these inequalities." Solo mothers "bear the brunt of the economic, social and psychological costs of sexist discrimination and condemnation" (Brush, 2002, p. 171). Christopher has pointed out that "the economic status of single mothers is an important bellwether for the extent to which mothers can form autonomous, solvent households independent of men" (2002, p. 61).

## Elderly Women

The economic disadvantages of women follow them into old age and are exacerbated by the likelihood of their being single and alone for a longer time than men. As Daly and Rake (2003, p. 109) point out, "sex differences in longevity mean that it is women who are affected most by the income risks associated with the loss of a partner." Recent, cross-national study has found that elderly women who live alone have higher poverty rates than all elderly women or the elderly as a group (Smeeding & Sandström, 2005). Smeeding and Sandström conclude that gender, living arrangements and, to a lesser extent, older age (among those already elderly) all tend to increase the risk of poverty.

Focusing on the disadvantages of lone, elderly women calls attention to the straitened circumstances that may await many older women who are still married as well as those who have been single earlier in life. In our earlier cross-national study we called attention to the predominance of women among the elderly poor in the United States. However, this is the first cross-national study that looks systematically at the conditions of both lone mothers and lone, elderly women, thus presenting an international, life-course perspective on women without partners.

## Feminized Poverty Factors: Single Mothers

Our earlier research identified five factors that contribute to feminized family poverty (Goldberg & Kremen, 1990). Three of these pertain to the level of poverty. A fourth, demographic factor determines the size of the group that is at risk of poverty. Minority race and ethnicity, demographic factors derived from analysis of the women's poverty in the United States, affect both poverty rates and the size of the population at risk. The present study observes these four factors in eight countries:

**Labor market conditions**—women's labor force participation; unemployment, occupational segregation, wages (actual levels and the gender wage gap); substandard, contingent, or precarious work; and the level of employment and unemployment.

**Equalization policies**—reduction of women's inequality in the labor market through affirmative action, pay equity, and anti-discrimination and minimum wage laws; and social welfare benefits such as child care that permit women to participate in the labor market on a less unequal footing.[8]

**Social welfare**—income support to compensate parents for the costs of child-bearing and child-rearing through such measures as paid parental leave and family allowances; supplementation of low wages and other forms of social assistance such as subsidies for housing, food, and other necessities; and benefits specifically for lone mothers such as guaranteed child support.

**Demography**—size of the female population at risk; marital status of single mothers (widowed, divorced/separated, never married); and minority race, ethnicity, and/or immigrant status.

## Feminized Poverty Factors: Single, Elderly Women

For single, elderly women, social welfare and demographic factors are the most important conditions. Labor market and equalization measures play a lesser current role but are important earlier in their lives, influencing the amount of some social welfare benefits.

Market income alone—earnings, private pensions, and savings—would leave most elderly people poor. Wu's study of 15 developed countries found that about two-thirds of the elderly would be poor without social security income (2005). If unemployment were lower or labor market conditions better, more of the elderly who are able and want to work might be employed. Equal opportunity policies are additional factors. Many older people might be employed if age discrimination were reduced. Of great importance, too, is the general availability of work or the levels of employment and unemployment.

This study seeks data on the proportions of older people who are employed, the barriers to wage work for those who would like it, and equal opportunity measures that protect older workers. Elderly women would benefit from affirmative action and pay equity, particularly those who suffer the disadvantages of both gender and minority race or ethnicity. With increase in the eligibility age for public pensions in the United States, equal opportunity policies and the availability of jobs in the economy are becoming more important for older people. Increase in the minimum wage would also improve the lot of lower-wage, elderly workers.

Services like elder care that enable frail older people to remain in their own homes are important to identify and compare cross-nationally. The former are important, not only for older women but are also means of reducing the burdens of the younger women who care for them, enabling them to pursue other, economically and socially rewarding roles.

Demographic factors contribute to the predominance of elderly women among the poor and to their poverty. However, earlier study has found that the preponderance of older women in the various subgroups of the elderly is not as great as their proportion among the poor in these groups (Smeeding & Sandström, 2005). Marital status among single women is related to access to private and public pensions and to past and present employment (Muller, 1999). It is also a factor in the quality and quantity of social supports (Goldberg, Kantrow, Kremen, & Lauter, 1986) and in the extent of social exclusion. As with single mothers, minority race and ethnicity increase the risk of poverty among older persons in the United States (Muller, 1999).

## Timing of the Study

In addition to the increase in single parenthood and the aging of populations, there are some important reasons for undertaking this investigation at this time: trends in social policy, the labor market, and demography as well as recently expanded conceptions of poverty or disadvantage and new theoretical perspectives on the welfare state.

### Social Policy

Allusions to dismantling, retrenchment, and restructuring of the welfare state have been part of the social policy discourse for several decades. Nonetheless, the extent and type of change are still matters of debate. One conclusion is that change has not been radical "but rather [there is] a 'frozen' welfare state landscape" (Kleinman, 2002, p. 58). On the other hand, if new problems arise or former ones increase, then a "frozen" landscape may be a form of retrenchment, particularly if national output expands and these potential resources for meeting social need are unused (Goldberg & Rosenthal, 2002). Others emphasize that nations face new risks, different from the industrial hazards to which welfare states responded in the decades following World War II, and they view some welfare regimes, notably the social democratic or Nordic, as better positioned to meet them than other regime types (Taylor-Gooby, 2004).

Paul Pierson (1994, 1996) hypothesized that welfare states are hard to cut back because they develop vested interests in their maintenance. Pierson concluded that cutbacks were minimal in Britain and the United States under the two leading conservatives of the age, Ronald Reagan and Margaret Thatcher. Later, emphasizing that radical retrenchment has been implausible because welfare states "continued to command extensive political protections." Pierson identified three types of welfare state change: cost containment that restrains future rates of growth rather than cost-cutting or reduction of current outlays; recommodification that reduces social support to workers outside the market, but largely confined to the United States and the United Kingdom; and "recalibration" or adaptation of "old" welfare states to new social and economic conditions (2002, p. 9).

Some other scholars have found clear evidence of retrenchment. Korpi and Palme (2003) studied changes in replacement rates in sickness, work accident, and unemployment insurance in 18 countries from 1975 until 1990 and found that cutbacks had occurred in these three social insurances in a number of countries. Goldberg and Rosenthal and their colleagues (2002) applied additional retrenchment criteria to Pierson's—changes in employment assurance that were an important component of welfare states in the post–World War II era; achievement of goals such as reduction of poverty and inequality; and the extent to which increased needs owing to demographic and labor market changes are met. They also examined a wider sample of countries and studied retrenchment over a longer period of time that included the repeal of the public assistance entitlement in the United States and Swedish policy changes in the 1990s. Their conclusion was that both retrenchment and welfare state restructuring had occurred. Retrenchment was marked in the United Kingdom and the United States, Pierson's star witnesses for minimal regress (Goldberg, 2002c; Millar, 2002).

Social policy toward single mothers has changed considerably in some countries. "In recent years," writes Jane Millar (2004a, p. 1), "many countries have reviewed the support available to lone parents, and introduced policies intended to support, or to compel, lone parents to participate in paid work, or to undertake other work-related activities, such as training." Activation policies that seek to increase employment of welfare recipients are compulsory in the United States and voluntary to varying degrees in a number of countries, including the United Kingdom (Millar, 2004a; Skevik, 2005).

Social security or old age insurance has been under attack and subject to cutbacks in a number of countries. Sweden has moved from a defined benefit to a defined contribution (Ginsburg & Rosenthal, 2002). Cuts in German pension rights occurred several times during the 1990s (Bäcker & Klammer, 2002). The shift in emphasis from state to private pensions in Britain has been shown to disadvantage older women (Ginn & Arber, 1999). Privatization of social security seems to have been laid to rest, at least temporarily, in the United States, but there have been cuts in benefits in the form of reduced replacement rates and an increase in the retirement age.

Restructuring and welfare state expansion are also evident. Japan and Germany, two countries strongly identified with the male breadwinner model (Kimoto, 2004; Lewis with Hobson, 1997), have moved toward broader child care provision. In Japan, the total fertility rate dropped to an alarming 1.52 in 1990 (Martin & Kats, 2003, p. 4). Reversing earlier welfare state retrenchment, Japan responded to this threat to economic growth and national survival by enacting measures to reduce the unmitigated family responsibilities of women that were seen as a cause of declining fertility (Kimoto, 2004; Peng, 2002). Changes in social policy came in the form of long-term care insurance, expanded public child care, new parental and family leaves, and support services for workers with family responsibilities. In Germany, nursing home insurance was added in the early 1990s amidst general welfare state retrenchment (Bäcker & Klammer, 2002; Gottfried & O'Reilly, 2002; Ostner, 1998).

Restructuring has taken place along with retrenchment in the United States. The United States expanded its Earned Income Tax Credit (EITC) for working-poor families with children at the same time that it repealed its entitlement to public assistance for poor women and children. Tax credits for working families in the United Kingdom are similar to the EITC in the United States. The supply of child care in the United States increased in the late 1990s, but this was far short of need, despite the change in public assistance policy that made employment mandatory for single mothers (Gornick & Meyers, 2003; Helburn & Bergmann, 2002).

In the 1990s, trends in the social services were different for child and elder care. In Sweden, publicly financed child care expanded and came even closer to a universal right. Elder care moved in the opposite direction: cutbacks led to targeting those in greatest need and an increase in privately financed care (Szebehely, 1998, pp. 277–278). In Italy, too, the two types of services moved in opposite directions, with child care continuing to "strive towards universalism" and the possibility that for the over-75s, the situation would worsen (Trifiletti, 1998, p. 198). In France, child care expanded, but the system of care for the elderly remained a minimalist, targeted benefit for the poor alone (Martin, Math, & Renaudat, 1998). Whether these trends are continuing into the first decade of the twenty-first century is a question addressed by this research.

## Labor Market Conditions

The most advanced welfare states have been full employment states. Indeed the two forms of provision—public income support and services as well as jobs—are closely linked in a number of welfare state formulations (Beveridge, 1945; Ginsburg, 1983; Goldberg, 2002a; Korpi, 1978). As Korpi wrote of the Swedish model: "The full employment policy... has probably been the most important part of the policy package.... Social policies directed towards decreasing want and improving economic security have of course also been valuable but would probably not have been sufficient" (1978, pp. 107–108).

Cutbacks in employment—increased unemployment and underemployment—should be seen side by side with whatever retrenchment, slowed growth, or restructuring that has occurred in social policy (Goldberg, 2002a). "The return of unemployment on a mass scale since the 1970s," wrote Korpi and Palme, "must be described as a basic regress of welfare states, a crushing of one of their central parts" (2003, p. 429).

High unemployment reduces the coffers for income transfers, particularly if financing is largely through payroll taxes. It also burdens the welfare state with the cost of unemployment compensation and the need to address the social problems created by unemployment (Brenner, 1995; Jin, Shah, & Svoboda, 1995; Paugam, 1996). For single mothers, unemployment is particularly threatening because they are much less likely than other families to have that important bulwark against unemployment: more than one family breadwinner.

Unemployment tends to differ less by gender than some other economic indicators (OECD, 2007, pp. 32–37). However, hidden unemployment, such as dropping out of the labor market when one becomes jobless and therefore not being counted as unemployed, is larger for women than men. Moreover, unemployment is more prevalent and a bigger problem for single mothers than for women or mothers, generally. For example, in 2004, the unemployment rate of U.S. single mothers was 6 percentage points higher than married mothers (U.S. Bureau of Labor Statistics, 2005). Probably this difference also reflects the high proportion of minority women among U.S. single mothers.

High unemployment rates for women as well as men are formidable labor market barriers, whatever the direction of the gender gap. Unemployment rates of 10.9%, 10.8%, and 10.1% for German, French, and Italian women (2005), respectively, were hardly conducive to an escape from poverty for many women in those countries (OECD, 2007). Lone mothers are more likely to escape poverty if they are employed rather than full-time caregivers; thus chronic, mass unemployment can signal poverty for them. Trends in women's unemployment are mixed: steadily high in France, Germany, and Italy, and they have increased in Sweden and Japan but are still relatively low in the latter (U.S. Bureau of Labor Statistics, 2008).

Contingent or nonstandard work that gives employers greater flexibility in hiring, firing, and wages and fringe benefits was already looming when feminization of poverty was first viewed cross-nationally. The greater likelihood of women being contingent workers was also recognized. The term "precarious work" has gained prominence in Europe and Canada in recent years. As Evans points out, precarious employment is a term used "to capture the shift from full-time and more or less permanent jobs to those that are increasingly characterized by some or all of the following dimensions: temporary, part-time, irregular hours of work, low wages and few, if any, benefits" (2005, p. 3). Atkinson (1998) includes in the definition lack of training and prospects for internal promotion. Precarious work more than doubled in Italy between 1996 and 2004, currently employing almost two-fifths of the work force. In northern Europe, though the magnitude is less, about one-fifth of the French work force consists of temporary workers, and stagnation in Germany in the early years of the century has increased precarious work there, too (Fumagalli, 2005).

The male breadwinner model—in which men are employed full-time and women provide full-time family care—is breaking down, even in former bastions such as Germany and Japan (Gottfried & O'Reilly 2002; Peng, 2002). Households with full-time housewives are now the minority in Japan (Kimoto, 2004). Precarious employment, however, has often been the new role for women, along with significant, remaining responsibilities in the home. In the 1990s, nonregular work increased in Japan; according to figures for 2002, women were the overwhelming majority in nonregular positions (Kimoto, 2004).

As the availability of regular work for men has declined, increasing numbers of women have become earners, with governments differing in the extent to which child care is socialized, commercialized, or provided by family members.[9] The dual earner family that has become the norm in a number of countries puts the single earner family, hence the great majority of lone mother families, at an economic disadvantage.

## Demographic Trends

Recent years have seen changes in population characteristics of both groups of single women. One of these, as noted, is an impetus for this study. Single motherhood is increasing in most developed countries to the extent that some writers have suggested that it is a phase in the female life course (Ford & Millar, 1998). The average increase in single parenthood in ten wealthy countries, mostly in the last 15–20 years of the twentieth century, was 60% (calculated from Martin & Kats, 2003, p. 12).[10] These changes make feminized poverty more likely in countries where lone mother poverty is high.

Immigration is a demographic trend that must be considered in relation to feminized poverty. Between 1993 and 2003, the foreign population, as a percent of the total population of the United States grew by almost one-half and was about 12% of the population. Growth was more modest (13.0%) in Canada, which has the largest proportion of immigrants in the study, approaching one-fifth of its population. Immigration has risen considerably in the United Kingdom and Japan although immigrants are still a very small portion of their populations. The foreign-born population of Italy more than doubled but was still below 4%. In France and Sweden the proportion of foreign-born people actually decreased (OECD, 2005).

Such data, however, can overlook the children of the foreign born. The uprising of second-generation Arab youth in France in 2005 and what it implies about social exclusion and other forms of social deprivation argue for taking immigrants and their children into account in this study (for the uprising, see Ireland, 2005).

In a comparative study of migrants' social rights, Morissens and Sainsbury found "major disparities between how migrant and citizen households fare in welfare states and that the discrepancies widen for migrants of colour" (2005, p. 637). The average poverty rate for citizen households in the six countries was 8%, compared to 26% for migrant households and 32% for ethnic minority migrant households in five of these countries (calculated from Morissens & Sainsbury, 2005, p. 644).[11] This study seeks more comparative data on the condition of immigrant women.

Between the late 1980s and the early 2000s, the elderly have increased as a proportion of the population in five of the eight countries in our study—from a high of 65% in Japan to a low of 13% in Canada (OECD, 1991, pp. 6–7, 2004, pp. 6–7).[12] In Germany, according to one study, the projected, "tremendous growth" of the elderly population and "the anticipated explosion of need for long-term-care services and the financial burden entailed in paying for them" led to the introduction of mandatory long-term care insurance (Geraedts, Heller, & Harrington, 2000, p. 375). With the growth of the older population in most countries, the proportion of single, elderly women in the population is increasing as well.

## Theoretical Perspectives

A rich body of conceptual work on the welfare of state emphasizing reduction of both class and gender inequality has been developed since our earlier study (Esping-Andersen, 1990, 1999, 2002; Lewis, 1997; Ireland, 1997, 2003; O'Connor, Orloff, & Shaver, 1999; Sainsbury, 1996, 1999). Most of this work is cross-national and quite relevant to this study.

In 1990, Esping-Andersen published a typology of welfare regimes based on de-commodification or the extent to which benefits are provided irrespective of the market status of recipients. He used the term, "regime," in order "to denote the fact that in the relation between state and economy a complex of legal and organizational features are [sic] systematically inter-woven" (1990, p. 2).[13] Esping-Andersen identified three regime types in order of the extent of de-commodification: social democratic, corporate/conservative, and liberal.

Feminist scholars were critical of the de-commodification scheme, for it addressed inequality of social class but not gender (Lister, 1997; O'Connor et al., 1999; Orloff, 1993; Sainsbury, 1996, 1999). Esping-Andersen, subsequently, added the criterion of de-familialization "to capture policies that lessen individuals' reliance on the family, that maximize individuals' command of economic resources independently of familial or conjugal relationships" and that "encourage women's full-time, lifelong participation in the labour market by lessening the familial burden" (p. 45). Several years earlier, Ruth Lister had suggested enlarging the criteria for regime types: "welfare regimes might … also be characterized according to the degree to which individual adults can uphold a socially acceptable standard of living independently of family relationships, either through paid work or through social security provisions" (Lister, 1997, p. 173).[14] One infers from Lister's formulation that it is not only a matter of whether welfare regimes lessen reliance on the family or facilitate continuous, full-time employment but whether they enable lone women to escape poverty. Even if women were freed from enough familial responsibilities to work continuously, year-round, full-time, the handicap of a single, woman's income might well persist. Also of interest, in view of the potential poverty of many partnered women, is Lister's subsequent addition to her formulation, namely that economic independence be "either inside or outside a couple relationship" (2003, p. 172).

Sainsbury and her colleagues examined the interplay between gender equity and basic features of the three regime types and concluded that "gender cuts across and fragments welfare state regimes." Of particular interest to this study is the finding that "the countries with policies that allow solo mothers to form an autonomous household with little risk of poverty [do not] crystallize into a cluster corresponding to a particular welfare state regime" (1999, pp. 245–248). In their comparative study of the effects of the welfare state on gender relations, Daly and Rake concluded that typologization "underplays differences among countries … [and] is ill-suited to deal with the context-rich and complex information necessary for a gender-focused analysis" (2003, p. 167).

It is important to point out that partnered mothers as well as single mothers benefit from de-familialization policies. Both are aided by policies that enable mothers to participate in the labor market by assuming some of their responsibilities for child care, that provide opportunities for employment, education, and retraining, that contribute to the desegregation of labor markets and to pay equity, and that enable mothers to nurture the very young without economic ruin. Indeed, lone mothers have been found to do best where benefits and care services for mothers are universal (Sainsbury, 1996).

Single mothers will not necessarily escape poverty through the replacement of the traditional male breadwinner model with a family ideal such as the "dual-earner-dual-carer society." Gornick and Meyers credit British sociologist Rosemary Crompton (1999) for giving the label "dual-earner-dual-carer" to a transformed society "that recognizes the rights and obligations of women and men to engage in both market and care work as well as the needs of children for intensive care and nurturance during the earliest years" (Gornick & Meyers, 2003, p. 12). Such a model could do more to encourage fathers to continue to be dual carers after divorce, to continue to share the support of children, and to equip mothers better for self-support. However, in societies that approach this model, single mothers are still disadvantaged by a single income; thus there is need for government policies that make up for that loss.

The goal of autonomy for women may sound like extreme individualism. It may seem to resemble the "self-sufficiency" rhetoric of U.S. welfare reform that forces single mothers to be self-supporting in an economy plagued by low-wage work. It could be said to overlook the interdependence that has always existed in the family and that is particularly important in this age of economic restructuring when families need not only women's reproductive work but their market incomes. Feminist scholar Zillah Eisenstein (2005) calls attention to the concurrence of women's "liberation" through paid work and the decline in the family wage that makes such "liberation" an economic necessity.

Traditionally, interdependence in the family did not count economically for women. Even though families and employers depended on mothers for reproductive work, they were treated as dependents because they were not breadwinners. Currently, even if a woman combines care work and part-time work or full-time employment at low wages, she may well lack sufficient income to support herself.

The labor market and income support and services from the state are potential routes to independence from the family, but each may be insufficient and controlling or exploitative. Dependence on income transfers could result in trading one form of control or dependency for another: "state patriarchy" for family patriarchy (Boris & Bardaglio, 1983). Or, as U.S. welfare rights leader Johnnie Tillmon put it, welfare is "like a supersexist marriage. You trade in *a* man for *the* man" (1972). That, of course depends on whether recipients are protected by constitutional rights of privacy, whether they maintain all civil and political rights, and what legal recourse they have if benefits are denied. Wary of government, Scandinavian feminist Birte Siim (1988) nonetheless recognizes that "in the modern state, there is no alternative to women's dependency on the state" (p. 175). Siim distinguishes between women as clients of the welfare state and as consumers of its services, the latter being a less dependent relationship and one more prevalent in Scandinavia than elsewhere.

Whether the state is "woman-friendly" (Hernes, 1988) depends on the extent of women's political mobilization and power, their participation and influence at various levels, from the shop floor to parliament. As Ruth Lister points out, women's entry into the public sphere through paid work outside the home can "encourage politicisation and open up political processes and the wider 'public' sphere (particularly through trade unions). It can also provide access to the kinds of skills needed for advancement in conventional forms of politics" (2003, p. 138). In another respect, women's employment can deter active citizenship. Particularly for actors with limited financial power, time is a critical resource. This is a problem, particularly for lone mothers because it means adding to their demanding, dual roles in the home and the labor force still another, as active democratic citizens. Reservations about true independence notwithstanding, this study asks whether and how lone women—as single mothers or at the end of the life course—are able to escape poverty.

## Choice of Study Countries

The eight countries in this study are, for the most part, the usual suspects but nonetheless very good ones. They are located on three continents. They have all undergone change in social policies but to varying degrees. They represent the full range of the reigning welfare state typologies (Esping-Andersen, 1990, 1999). Sweden is an example of the more advanced, social democratic regime; Germany, France, Italy, and Japan have been categorized as conservative; and Canada, the United Kingdom, and the United States are designated as liberal regimes. Further, these countries vary greatly in size and population diversity. Although they differ in wealth, they are among the world's richest countries. They also vary in the extent to which they use these resources to reduce the poverty of vulnerable groups of women—and not in relation to their wealth. Their conceptions of women's and men's roles are still another dissimilarity.

### Recent Trends

The countries in this study experienced some very significant changes in recent years. Most sweeping is German reunification: the transformation from socialism to capitalism and from dictatorship to political democracy of the five Länder of the former German Democratic Republic (GDR). Initially, women in East Germany seemed to be big losers, both of jobs and of benefits such as child care and parental leave (Goldberg, 1991; Rudolph, Appelbaum, & Maier, 1991). The cost of reunification was a big strain on the public budgets of the Federal Republic of Germany (Bäcker & Klammer, 2002).

Although neither its economic nor political system has been revolutionized, Sweden, changed in ways that were hardly predictable prior to the 1990s. As Ginsburg and Rosenthal wrote: "Swimming against the tide on a continent plagued with high unemployment, Sweden had a jobless rate of less than 2 percent and a seemingly secure welfare state as recently as 1990. Since then, Sweden has experienced mass unemployment…, along with extensive social welfare cutbacks" (2002, p. 103). Many of the lost jobs were in the care services for which Sweden had received justifiable praise, and women who provided those services were among the big job losers. Determining how single mothers and single elderly women have fared—given the losses of benefits, services, and jobs—is one task of this study. Even though unemployment is lower and 4% is said to be an "interim" goal, the government has not set another benchmark (Ginsburg & Rosenthal, 2004). In 2005 and 2006, the unemployment rate of Swedish women was in the 7% range (U.S. Bureau of Labor Statistics, 2008).

Although Sweden's regress was late, sudden, and its permanence in question, the regress of Britain and the United States was early and protracted. Under almost two decades of conservative rule (1979–1997), changes in Britain's welfare state were less drastic than Thatcherite rhetoric, but neo-liberalism nonetheless brought substantial increases in poverty and inequality, especially among women and children, and the near doubling of "workless" households or those without an adult in paid work (nearly one-fifth by the mid-1990s) (Millar, 2002). "New" Labour under Prime Minister Tony Blair was more market-minded than old Labour, but its rhetoric was much more social-minded than the conservatives who preceded it. Britain's new Labour recovery, if short of some of its lofty, anti-poverty goals, is nonetheless a reality (Millar, 2004b; Taylor-Gooby & Larsen, 2004, on falling short of goals).

The United States had 12 years of conservative government (1981–1993) with concomitant increases in poverty and inequality. Rhetoric absent from the White House since the 1930s demonized government and lionized the "free" market. As in Britain, cutbacks were less severe than the rhetoric but nonetheless hard on the neediest. Next followed two terms under new Democrat Bill Clinton (1993–2001) who had spent years leading his party to the middle and away from "big government" (Burns & Sorenson, 1999). Under Clinton, unemployment dropped significantly—fueled largely by a stock market boom (Pollin, 2003). Inequality continued to rise, and real wages still lagged below the level of the early 1970s. Under the banner of welfare "reform," the new Democrat assented to the repeal of the 60-year-old social assistance program for single mothers and their children. Along with forced employment and lifetime limits to welfare came increased subsidies for the working poor and more child care, albeit nowhere near the need for it. With George W. Bush (2001–2009), came harsh conservatism — a return to the rhetoric and reality of regression (Goldberg, 2002c, 2004).

Canada's regress was late and relatively short. It moved from deficit laggard in 1994 to one of the few nations with a budgetary surplus and, moreover, willingness to spend it on social welfare. Ten years later, both labor market conditions and social provision had improved (Evans, 2005). The picture changed, however, with the election of a conservative government in 2006.

Unemployment has been severe and prolonged in France, Germany, and Italy with differences among them in the extent to which social policy has followed suit. Japan's economic stagnation has been accompanied by higher unemployment but nowhere near European levels, and after years of stubbornly resisting welfare expansion, Japan appears to be moving in that direction under the duress of a severe decline in fertility.

## Conceptions of Deprivation

Income deficiency continues to be a principal measure of social deprivation, but in recent years, broader concepts, encompassing both social and economic factors, have gained more attention (Sen, 1999; Wagle, 2002). Social exclusion, for example, is a concept that includes economic deprivation and a range of social disadvantages as well.

Social exclusion was first formulated and applied to conditions in Europe (Edgren-Schori, 2004; Saraceno, 2002), but it has crossed the Atlantic. American scholars, Alfred Kahn and Sheila Kamerman, who edited a book on the social exclusion of children, define it as "the process by which individuals and groups are wholly or partly closed out from participation in their societies because of low income as well as constricted access to employment, social benefits and services, and other aspects of cultural and community life" (2002, p. 13). As Holden writes, "Social exclusion offers a wider concept than poverty in addressing the needs of the poor or marginalized, dealing as it does with the need for inclusion and participation rather than simply increased income" (Holden, 2003, p. 310). A Social Exclusion Unit, established by the British government in 1997, is charged with tackling a combination of linked problems—unemployment, poor skills, low incomes, poor housing, high crime environments, bad health, and family breakdown (Millar, 2004b).

Quality of life is a multidimensional approach to well-being, and its absence another, broader concept of deprivation. Quality of life has been used in studies of the well-being of former recipients of public assistance in the United States. Indicative of its multidimensionality are five components used in one such study: economic resources; employment and working conditions; support services and programs; housing and social support; and friendship networks (Hollar, 2003; see also Altman & Goldberg, 2007).

Nobel laureate Amartya Sen believes that his "freedom perspective" is generically similar to quality of life because it, too, "concentrates on the way human life goes ... and not just the resources or income a person commands" (1999, p. 24). Sen uses the term "social functionings" to refer to a range of conditions, from being adequately nourished to very complex personal states such as "being able to take part in the life of the community and having self-respect" (1999, p. 75). In rejecting income as a sole measure of poverty, Sen points out that similar incomes generate different outcomes because individuals differ in their capacity to convert economic resources into functionings. Employment is an important component of social functioning in Sen's conception, and as he and others have emphasized, it can contribute more to well-being than income (Beveridge, 1945; Goldberg, 2002b). At the same time, employment at low wages under oppressive working conditions is a form of deprivation. Without relief of family responsibilities, it is especially oppressive.

In this study we give material deficiency its full due. We consider the multidimensional approach to deprivation important but recognize that data pertaining to quality of life are less easy to come by than those about income. Nonetheless, we have to pay some attention to noneconomic dimensions such as social isolation and discrimination and stigma.

Our study emphasizes not only cash benefits but also provision of goods and services. Care services are particularly important for both the younger and older women who are the focus of this study. Access to adequate care is clearly related to the quality of life and to social functioning. The absence of socially provided care can be impoverishing, interfering with earning a living and costly for those who are obliged to purchase it. Health care is not a substantial extra cost in other industrial countries, but in the United States, many are not insured, and even the elderly who are covered by Medicare have large out-of-pocket costs. Quality and affordability of housing should also be considered. Because housing consumes a large proportion of income, housing subsidies that reduce the burden on cash income are to be considered. In this regard, it is interesting to point out that in Britain, poverty rates are calculated with and without housing costs.[15] Employment in a number of its dimensions—availability, wages, compatibility with family responsibilities—is an important focus of this study; its absence can be impoverishing beyond income loss (Beveridge, 1945; Sen, 1999).

### The Poverty Standards

The definition of poverty differs among countries. In each of the eight countries studied, the standard will be one by which the nation itself measures its poverty. In summarizing the results of the study, the concluding chapters use comparable data on poverty from international sources such as the Luxembourg Income Study (LIS); Eurostat, the statistical office of the European Union; and, in the case of labor market data, the Organisation for Economic Co-operation and Development (OECD).

For purposes of comparison, the standard will usually be less than half the median disposable income (MDI) in each of the countries. Although this is a standard that prevailed in Europe for a number of years, the emerging norm—and one used by Eurostat—is higher: less than 60% of MDI. The 50% standard is a compromise between the emerging European poverty level and the low U.S. standard that is thought to be less than 40% of MDI. In Chapter 10, the poverty rates from the international data sets are sometimes presented by all three relative poverty standards: less than 40%, 50%, and 60% of MDI, but at other times only the 50% standard, the norm for this study, is used. A brief appendix to Chapter 10 points out some of the difficulties in using both international databases that are necessary for comparative purposes and official statistics from individual countries that often differ from the international sources.

## Expected Outcomes

This study focuses on the poverty of women in eight wealthy nations representing a variety of welfare regimes, size, level of economic resources, extent of recent change, and geographic diversity. The spotlight is on two groups of single women, lone mothers and lone, elderly women and on the potential for economic independence of both lone and partnered women.

As noted, Diane Sainsbury and her colleagues found that the countries that allow solo mothers to form an autonomous household with little risk of poverty did not "crystallize into a cluster corresponding to a particular welfare state regime" (1999, pp. 247–248). This research extends the analysis to lone, elderly women asking what countries permit them an autonomous escape from poverty, whether these are the same regimes that offer similar opportunities for younger women, and whether they form a cluster corresponding to a particular welfare regime type.

This study raises some political questions. In each of the countries some attention needs to be paid to the power resources of women generally and of the two groups of single women, particularly. What role do organized labor and progressive political parties play in advancing the condition of women? What is the strength of movements for women's equality, and in what countries are they most influential? To what extent do they emphasize civil and political rights of citizenship, social or economic rights, or both (Lister, 2003; Marshall, 1963/1973; O'Connor et al., 1999)? To what extent are women's movements committed to defending and expanding the welfare state and to the well-being of poor women and those disadvantaged by minority race and ethnicity as well as immigration? Is there solidarity among women based on the recognition that the status of single women is a bellwether for the condition of all? To what extent do poor women participate in efforts to change their condition?

A careful look at the recent past might be expected to provide some insight into the future. In this case, the task of drawing such inferences was rendered very difficult because just as the book was nearing completion, a severe economic crisis with worldwide ramifications erupted in the United States. For most, if not all, of the countries in this study, a serious recession—perhaps the worst since World War II—was looming. The final chapter will spell out implications of the study for the future condition of women as if the crisis had not occurred. This will be followed by a brief consideration of some ways in which the changed economic conditions may be expected to alter these predictions.

## Notes

1 The study also found that among all poor families (with and without children), feminization had also occurred: from 23% in 1960 to 52% in 1987.

2 For example, lone mother is the term used most frequently in the chapter on Italy; single mother in Japan; solo mother in Germany and Sweden; both single and lone mother in Canada and France; and solo, sole, and lone mother in the United Kingdom. Although single mother is the term used in the United States, the U.S. chapter uses lone mother as well, and the first and concluding chapters use all of these terms. In some countries the term single mother may pertain only to never-married mothers, but in the United States, single mother

is the general term, and never married refers to one of the marital statuses of single mothers and of the lone elderly as well.

It should be noted that for all but the authors of chapters on Canada, the United Kingdom, and the United States, these terms in English are, of course, foreign-language versions. For example, Germans refer to *alleinerziehende Mutter*, literally "a mother bringing up her children alone." The French refer to *les familles monoparentales* or "one-parent families."

3 Swedish single parents (probably including a small proportion of single fathers) were about 20% of all families with children, according to a study published by the Swedish Ministry of Health and Social Affairs (Eriksson, 1987). However, a recent compilation of data by the U.S. Bureau of Labor Statistics, which drew on surveys from the various countries, reported that the proportion of single-parent households in Sweden was considerably lower—15% in 1990. The U.S. figure of 24% in 1990 matches better with our figures (Martin & Kats, 2003, p. 14).

4 Single motherhood was relatively high in the Soviet Union (Kremen, 1990), but not in Poland (Wojciechowski, 1990).

5 In Christopher's study (2002b, p. 70), single mothers, on average, had rates 3.68 times that of married mothers (mid-1990s). It should be noted that this multiple is misleading in the case of Sweden. Single mothers were four times as likely to be poor as married mothers, but their actual poverty rate was only 4.4%, far below the 26% average poverty rate for the countries in that study.

6 The average is not weighted for population.

7 State benefits reduced the share of women without any personal income by between three-fourths and one-half in France, Germany, Sweden, and the United Kingdom but only by 6% in the United States (Daly & Rake, 2003, p. 123).

8 Child care can also be seen as social welfare or income support.

9 There has been some move away from the male breadwinner model in Germany, but in important respects it persists. For example, despite the introduction of long-term insurance, "the norm of home-based care is strong" (Daly & Rake, 2003, p. 140). According to Ute Klammer whose research and publication interests include the reconciliation of work and family life: "It is true that many young families do not live the 'strong breadwinner model' anymore (or to be more precise, they only live it for a much shorter time, when children are small). But the main institutional incentives for the breadwinner model (such as the joint taxation of couples by which one-earner families are highly subsidised, or widow's pensions, or the free insurance of housewives in their husbands' health insurance) have hardly changed" (personal communication, November 20, 2005).

10 Between 1990 and about 2000, the proportion of single-parent households increased in Sweden, France, Germany, Japan, Canada, the United States, and the United Kingdom—from lows of 7% and 11% in the United Kingdom and the United States, where it was already high, to about 40% or more in Germany, France, and Sweden. Canada, on the low end of single parenthood in the late 1980s, increased its rate by 20%.

11 The six countries were the United Kingdom, United States, Germany, France, Denmark, and Sweden. Data were not available for all migrant households in the United Kingdom and for ethnic minority migrant households in Germany. However, in both countries, the poverty rates for one of the two

migrant measures were considerably higher than for citizen households (Morissens & Sainsbury, 2005).

12 The percentage of persons 65 years and older in the population remained the same in Britain and dropped 2%–3% in the United States and Sweden where it was highest among the eight countries at the earlier date. The U.S. drop is related to the rise in immigration in which younger people predominate.

13 Esping-Andersen preferred "welfare regime" to welfare state because the latter was too conventionally associated with "social-amelioration policies" (1990, p. 2).

14 Lister (1997, p. 234) points out that in 1994, McLaughlin and Glendinning "put forward the same concept of 'defamilialisation' and virtually the same definition of it totally independently."

15 In 1994–1995, 18% of the population were poor before housing costs and 23% were poor with them (calculated from Millar, 2002).

## References

Algava, E., Le Minez, S., & Bressé, A. P. (2005). Les familles monoparentales et leurs conditions de vie. *Études et Résultats, 389*(Avril), 1–12.

Altman, J. C., & Goldberg, G. S. (2007). The quality of life paradox: A study of former public assistance recipients. *Journal of Poverty, 11*(4), 45–69.

Atkinson, A. B. (1998). Social exclusion, poverty and unemployment. In A. B. Atkinson & J. Hills (Eds.), *Exclusion, employment and opportunity, CASE/4* (pp. 1–20). London: Centre for Analysis of Social Exclusion, London School of Economics. Retrieved from http://sticerd.lse.ac.uk/dps/case/cp/Paper4.PDF. Accessed May 23, 2009.

Axinn, J. (1990). Japan: A special case. In G. S. Goldberg & E. Kremen (Eds.), *The feminization of poverty: Only in America?* (pp. 91–106). New York: Praeger.

Bäcker, G., & Klammer, U. (2002). The dismantling of welfare in Germany. In G. S. Goldberg & M. G. Rosenthal (Eds.), *Diminishing welfare: A cross-national study of social provision* (pp. 211–244). Westport, CT: Auburn House.

Beveridge, W. (1945). *Full employment in a free society.* New York: W. W. Norton.

Boris, E., & Bardaglio, P. (1983). The transformation of patriarchy: The historical role of the state. In I. Diamond (Ed.), *Families, politics, and public policy: A feminist dialogue on women and the state* (pp. 70–93). New York: Longman, Green.

Brenner, H. (1995). Political economy and health. In B. Amick, A. R. Tarlow, & D. C. Walsh (Eds.), *Society and health* (pp. 211–246). New York: Oxford University Press.

Brush, L. D. (2002). Changing the subject: Gender and welfare regime studies. *Social Politics, 9*(Summer), 161–186.

Burns, J. M., & Sorenson, G. J. (1999). *Dead center: Clinton–Gore leadership and the perils of moderation.* New York: Scribner.

Christopher, K. (2002). Welfare state regimes and mothers' poverty. *Social Politics, 9*, 60–86.

Crompton, R. (Ed.). (1999). *Restructuring gender relations and employment: The decline of the male breadwinner.* London: Oxford University Press.

Curtin, J. S. (2005). Japan, land of rising poverty. *Asia Times,* February 11. Retrieved from http://www.atimes.com/atimes/Japan/GB11Dh01.html. Accessed May 23, 2009.

Daly, M., & Rake, K. (2003). *Gender and the welfare state: Care, work and welfare in Europe and the USA.* Cambridge, UK: Polity Press.

Edgren-Schori, M. (2004). *Social exclusion: A European perspective.* Paper presented at the Conference, Social Policy as if People Matter, Adelphi University, Garden City, NY, November 11–12. Retrieved from http://www.adelphi.edu/peoplematter/pdfs/Schori.pdf. Accessed August 6, 2009.

Eisenstein, Z. (2005). A dangerous liaison: Feminism and corporate globalization. *Science & Society, 69*, 487–518.

Eriksson, I. (1987). *Some facts about single parents in Sweden.* Stockholm: Ministry of Health and Social Affairs.

Esping-Andersen, G. (1990). *The three worlds of welfare capitalism.* Princeton, NJ: Princeton University Press.

Esping-Andersen, G. (1999). *Social foundations of post-industrial economies.* New York: Oxford University Press.

Evans, P. M. (2005). (Not) taking account of precarious employment: Workfare policies and lone mothers in Ontario and the UK. Unpublished paper, Ottawa, Ontario, School of Social Work, Carleton University.

Ford, R., & Millar, J. (1998). *Private lives and public responses: Lone parenthood and future policy.* London: Policy Studies Institute.

Fumagalli, A. (2005). *Some points on European precarity and how to fight it: The proposal of new flexicurity.* Paper given at the 11th Workshop on Alternative Economic Policy in Europe, Brussels, September 23–25.

Geraedts, M., Heller, G. V., & Harrington, C. A. (2000). Germany's long-term-care insurance: Putting a social insurance model into practice. *The Milbank Quarterly, 78*(3), 375–401.

Ginn, J., & Arber, S. (1999). Changing patterns of pension inequality: The shift from state to private sources. *Ageing & Society, 19*, 319–342.

Ginsburg, H. L. (1983). *Full employment and public policy: The United States and Sweden.* Lexington, MA: Lexington Books.

Ginsburg, H. L., & Rosenthal, M. G. (2002). Sweden: Temporary detour or new directions? In G. S. Goldberg & M. G. Rosenthal (Eds.), *Diminishing welfare: A cross-national study of social provision* (pp. 103–148). Westport, CT: Auburn House.

Ginsburg, H. L., & Rosenthal, M. G. (2004). *The current status of the Swedish welfare state.* Paper presented at the Conference, Social Policy as if People Matter, Adelphi University, Garden City, NY, November 11–12. Retrieved from http://www.adelphi.edu/peoplematter/pdfs/Sweden.pdf. Accessed August 6, 2009.

Glendinning, C., & Millar J. (1987) *Women and poverty in Britain.* Brighton: Wheatsheaf Books.

Goldberg, G. S. (1990a). Canada: Bordering on the feminization of poverty. In G. S. Goldberg & E. Kremen (Eds.), *The feminization of poverty: Only in America?* (pp. 59–90). New York: Praeger.

Goldberg, G. S. (1990b). The United States: Poverty amidst plenty. In G. S. Goldberg & E. Kremen (Eds.), *The feminization of poverty: Only in America?* (pp. 17–58). New York: Praeger.

Goldberg, G. S. (1991). Women on the verge: Winners and losers in German unification. *Social Policy, 22*(Fall), 35–44.

Goldberg, G. S. (2002a). Diminishing welfare: Convergence toward a liberal model? In G. S. Goldberg & M. G. Rosenthal (Eds.), *Diminishing welfare: A cross-national study of social provision* (pp. 321–372). Westport: Auburn House.

Goldberg, G. S. (2002b). Introduction: Three stages of welfare capitalism. In G. S. Goldberg & M. G. Rosenthal (Eds.), *Diminishing welfare: A cross-national study of social provision* (pp. 1–32). Westport, CT: Auburn House.

Goldberg, G. S. (2002c). More than reluctant: The United States of America. In G. S. Goldberg & M. G. Rosenthal (Eds.), *Diminishing welfare: A cross-national study of social provision* (pp. 33–73). Westport, CT: Auburn House.

Goldberg, G. S. (2004). *People matter less: Further to the Right in a second Bush term.* Paper presented at the Conference, Social Policy as if People Matter, Adelphi University, Garden City, NY, November 11–12. Retrieved from http://www.adelphi.edu/peoplematter/pdfs/Goldberg.pdf. Accessed May 23, 2009.

Goldberg, G. S., Kantrow, R., Kremen, E., & Lauter, L. (1986). Single, elderly childless women and their social supports. *Social Work, 31*, 104–112.

Goldberg, G. S., & Kremen, E. (Eds.). (1990). *The feminization of poverty: Only in America?* New York: Praeger.

Goldberg, G. S., & Rosenthal, M. G. (Eds.) (2002). *Diminishing welfare: A cross-national study of social provision.* Westport, CT: Auburn House.

Gornick, J. C., & Meyers, M. K. (2003). *Families that work: Policies for reconciling parenthood and employment.* New York: Russell Sage.

Gottfried, H., & O'Reilly, J. (2002). Reregulating breadwinner models in socially conservative welfare systems: Comparing Germany and Japan. *Social Politics, 9*, 29–59.

Helburn, S. W., & Bergmann, B. R. (2002). *America's child care problem: The way out.* New York: Palgrave Macmillan.

Hernes, H. M. (1988). The welfare state citizenship of Scandinavian women. In K. B. Jones & A. G. Jónasdóttir (Eds.), *The political interests of gender: Developing theory and research with a feminist face* (pp. 187–213). London: Sage.

Holden, C. (2003). Decommodification and the workfare state. *Political Studies Review, 1*, 303–316.

Hollar, D. (2003). A holistic theoretical model for examining welfare reform: Quality of life. *Public Administration Review, 63*(January/February), 90–104.

Ireland, D. (2005). Why is France burning: The current Franco-Arab rebellion is the anguished scream of a lost generation. *The Nation, 281*(November), 29–30.

Jin, R. L., Shah, C. P., & Svoboda, T. J. (1995). The impact of unemployment on health: A review of the evidence. *Canadian Medical Association Journal, 153*, 529–540.

Kahn, A. J., & Kamerman, S. B. (Eds.). (2002). *Beyond child poverty: The social exclusion of children.* New York: The Institute for Child and Family Policy at Columbia University.

Kilkey, M., & Bradshaw, J. (1999). Lone mothers, economic well-being, and policies. In D. Sainsbury (Ed.), *Gender and welfare state regimes* (pp. 147–184). London: Oxford University Press.

Kimoto, K. (2004). *Labour conditions for women in contemporary Japan: Where do the problems lie?* Paper presented at the Conference, Social Policy as if People Matter. Adelphi University, Garden City, NY, November 11–12. Retrieved from http://www.adelphi.edu/peoplematter/pdfs/Kimoto.pdf. Accessed May 23, 2009.

Kleinman, M. (2002). *A European welfare state: European Union social policy in context.* Houndmills, Basingstoke, Hampstead: Palgrave.

Korpi, W. (1978). *The working class in welfare capitalism: Work, unions and politics in Sweden.* London: Routledge and Kegan Paul.

Korpi, W., & Palme, J. (2003). New politics and class politics in the context of austerity and globalization: Welfare state regress in 18 countries, 1975–95. *American Political Science Review, 97*, 425–446.

Kremen, E. (1990). Socialism: An escape from poverty? Women in European Russia. In G. S. Goldberg & E. Kremen (Eds.), *The feminization of poverty: Only in America?* (pp. 157–182). New York: Praeger.

Lewis, J. (Ed.). (1997). *Lone mothers in European welfare regimes: Shifting policy logics.* London: Jessica Kingsley Publisher.

Lewis, J., with Hobson, B. (1997). Introduction. In J. Lewis (Ed.), *Lone mothers in European welfare regimes: Shifting policy logics* (pp. 1–20). London: Jessica Kingsley Publisher.

Lister, R. (1997). *Citizenship: Feminist perspectives.* New York: New York University Press.

Lister, R. (2003). *Citizenship: Feminist perspectives* (2nd ed.). New York: New York University Press.

Marshall, T. H. (1963/1973). *Citizenship and social development.* Westport, CT: Greenwood Press.

Martin, C., Math, A., & Renaudat, E. (1998). In J. Lewis (Ed.), *Gender, social care and welfare state restructuring in Europe* (pp. 139–174). Aldershot, UK: Ashgate.

Martin, G., & Kats, V. (2003). Families and work in transition in 12 countries, 1980–2001. *Monthly Labor Review 126*(9), 3–31.

Millar J. (1992) Lone mothers and poverty. In C. Glendinning & J. Millar (Eds.), *Women and poverty in Britain: The 1990s* (2nd ed.) (pp. 149–161). Brighton: Harvester/Wheatsheaf.

Millar, J. (2002). Diminishing welfare: The case of the United Kingdom. In G. S. Goldberg & M. G. Rosenthal (Eds.), *Diminishing welfare: A cross-national study of social provision* (pp. 149–180). Westport, CT: Auburn House.

Millar, J. (2004a). *Lone mothers and their children: Work and welfare.* Paper presented at the Conference, Social Policy as if People Matter, Adelphi University, Garden City, NY, November 11–12. Retrieved from http://www.adelphi.edu/peoplematter/pdfs/Millar.pdf. Accessed May 23, 2009.

Millar, J. (2004b). *Where are we now? Country report: The United Kingdom.* Paper presented at the Conference, Social Policy as if People Matter, Adelphi University, Garden City, NY, November 11–12. Retrieved from http://www.adelphi.edu/peoplematter/pdfs/United.pdf. Accessed May 23, 2009.

Morissens, A., & Sainsbury, D. (2005). Migrants' social rights, ethnicity and welfare regimes. *Journal of Social Policy, 34*, 637–660.

Muller, C. (1999). The distinctive needs of women and minorities. In R. N. Butler, L. K. Grossman, & M. R. Oberlink (Eds.), *Life in an older America* (pp. 97–120). New York: The Century Foundation Press.

O'Connor, J. S., Orloff, A. S., & Shaver, S. (1999). *States, markets, families: Gender, liberalism and social policy in Australia, Canada, Great Britain and the United States.* Cambridge: Cambridge University Press.

OECD. (1991). *OECD in figures: 1991 edition.* Paris: Author.

OECD.(2004). *OECD in figures: 2004 edition.* Paris: Author.

OECD. (2005). *OECD in figures, 2005 edition: Statistics of the member countries.* Paris: Author. Retrieved from http://213.253.134.43/oecd/pdfs/browseit/0105061E.PDF. Accessed August 6, 2009.

OECD. (2007). *OECD in figures 2006–2007 edition.* Paris: Author. Retrieved from http://www.oecdobserver.org/news/fullstory.php/aid/1988/OECD_in_Figures_2006–2007.html. Accessed May 23, 2009.

Orloff, A. S. (1993). Gender and the social rights of citizenship. *American Sociological Review, 58*(3), 501–518.

Ostner, I. (1998). The politics of care policies in Germany. In J. Lewis (Ed.), *Gender, social care and welfare state restructuring in Europe* (pp. 111–138). Aldershot, UK: Ashgate.

Paugam, S. (1996). Poverty and social disqualification: A comparative analysis of cumulative social disadvantage in Europe. *Journal of European Social Policy, 6*, 287–304.

Pearce, D. (1978). The feminization of poverty: Women, work and welfare. *The Urban and Social Change Review, 11*(1 and 2), 28–38.

Peng, I. (2002). Social care in crisis: Gender, demography, and welfare state restructuring in Japan. *Social Politics, 9*, 411–443.

Pierson, P. (1994). *Dismantling the welfare state: Reagan, Thatcher, and the politics of retrenchment.* Cambridge: Cambridge University Press.

Pierson, P. (1996). The new politics of the welfare state. *New Politics, 48*, 143–179.

Pierson, P. (2002). Retrenchment and restructuring in an age of austerity: What (if anything) can be learned from the affluent democracies? *Cadernos de Saúde Pública, 18*, 7–11. Retrieved from http://www.scielo.br/scielo.php?script=scI_arttext&pid=S0102–311X2002000700002&lng=en&nrm=iso. Accessed May 23, 2009

Pollin, R. (2003). *Contours of descent: U.S. economic fractures and the landscape of global austerity.* London: Verso.

Rudolph, H., Appelbaum, E., & Maier, F. (1994). Beyond socialism: The uncertain prospects for East German women in unified Germany. In N. Aslanbeigui, S. Pressman, & G. Summerfield (Eds.), *Women in the age of economic transformation: Gender impact of reforms in prost-socialist and developing countries* (pp. 8–23). London: Routledge.

Sainsbury, D. (1996). *Gender, equality and welfare states.* Cambridge: Cambridge University Press.

Sainsbury, D. (1999). Gender, policy regimes, and politics. In D. Sainsbury (Ed.), *Gender and welfare state regimes* (pp. 245–276). London: Oxford University Press.

Saraceno, C. (2002). Social exclusion: Cultural roots and variations on a popular concept. In A. J. Kahn & S. B. Kamerman (Eds.), *Beyond child poverty: The social exclusion of children* (pp. 37–74). New York: The Institute for Children and Families at Columbia University.

Scott, H. (1986). Women and the future of work. Unpublished paper, Cambridge, MA.

Sen, A. (1999). *Development as freedom*. New York: Anchor Books.

Siim, B. (1988). Toward a feminist rethinking of the welfare state. In K. B. Jones & A. G. Jónasdóttir (Eds.), *The political interests of gender: Developing theory and research with a feminist face* (pp. 160–186). London: Sage.

Skevik, A. (2005). Women's citizenship in the time of activation: The case of lone mothers in "needs-based" welfare states. *Social Politics, 12*, 42–66.

Smeeding, T. M., & Sandström, S. (2005). Poverty and income maintenance in old age: A cross-national view of low income older women. No. 398, Luxembourg Income Study Working Paper Series. Syracuse, NY: Maxwell School of Citizenship and Public Affairs, Syracuse University.

Szebehely, M. (1998). Changing divisions of carework: Caring for children and frail elderly people in Sweden. In J. Lewis (Ed.), *Gender, social care and welfare state restructuring in Europe* (pp. 257–283). Aldershot, UK: Ashgate.

Taylor-Gooby, P. (Ed.). (2004). *New risks, new welfare: The transformation of the European welfare state.* Oxford: Oxford University Press.

Taylor-Gooby, P., & Larsen, T. P. (2004). The UK—A test case for the liberal welfare state? In P. Taylor-Gooby (Ed.), *New risks, new welfare: The transformation of the European welfare state* (pp. 29–82). Oxford: Oxford University Press.

Tillmon, J. (1972, Spring). Welfare is a women's issue. *Ms.* Retrieved from http://www.msmagazine.com/spring2002/tillmon.asp. Accessed May 23, 2009.

Trifiletti, R. (1998). Restructuring social care in Italy. In J. Lewis (Ed.), *Gender, social care and welfare state restructuring in Europe* (pp. 175–206). Aldershot, UK: Ashgate.

U.S. Bureau of Labor Statistics (USBLS). (2005). Employment characteristics of families in 2004. *News.* USDL 05–876. Washington, DC: Author.

U.S. Bureau of Labor Statistics (USBLS). (2008). Civilian unemployment rates approximating U.S. concepts by sex, 1960–2007 (percent). Washington, DC: Author. Retrieved from ftp://ftp.bls.gov/pub/special.requests/ForeignLabor/lfcompendiumt08.txt. Accessed May 23, 2009.

Wagle, U. (2002). Rethinking poverty: Definition and measurement. *International Social Science Journal, 54*(171), 155–165.

Wojciechowski, S. (1990). Poland: A country of conflicts. In G. S. Goldberg & E. Kremen (Eds.), *The feminization of poverty: Only in America?* (pp. 183–200). New York: Praeger.

Wu, K. (2005). The material consequences of how social security keeps older persons out of poverty across developed countries. No. 410, Luxembourg Income Study Working Paper Series. Syracuse, NY: Maxwell School of Citizenship and Public Affairs, Syracuse University.

# 2

# SWEDEN: THE FEMINIZATION OF POVERTY?

*Diane Sainsbury and Ann Morissens*

## Introduction

As noted in the introduction, this book's predecessor, *The feminization of poverty: Only in America?* (1990), concluded that low levels of poverty were the main explanation for the failure of the feminization of poverty to emerge in Sweden. In revisiting this issue, our chapter initially presents the specific matrix of Swedish policies that has contributed to low poverty rates with special emphasis on women's employment and social rights. It then describes the challenge to the Swedish welfare state in the 1990s—an era of economic crisis and retrenchment—and the major policy responses. The main part of the chapter offers an analysis of the economic situation of solo mothers and single elderly women in the middle of the first decade of this century (mid-2000s), taking 1990 as benchmark for comparison. Central to our analysis is the question of whether policy changes since 1990 have led to a feminization of poverty in Sweden.

With the growth of the welfare state in the rich industrial countries during the postwar decades, scholarly attention came to concentrate on explanations of welfare state expansion and eventually on identifying the distinctive features of different countries' policies. To clarify important distinctions, analysts developed social policy models and the concept of welfare regimes. Feminist researchers, noting that the models and concepts were gender blind, formulated alternatives, such as gender policy models and gender policy regimes. What, then, are the distinctive characteristics of Swedish policies as identified by welfare and gender policy regimes? How have they enhanced women's employment and social rights? And do Swedish policies still prevent the feminization of poverty?

## Distinctive Policy Characteristics

A distinctive feature of the Swedish welfare regime has been full employment as an overarching goal. As put by Gøsta Esping-Andersen, "the right to work has equal status to the right to income protection" (1990, p. 28). The emphasis on employment entailed not only keeping the unemployment rate low (until 1990 usually under 2%) but also promoting the employment of people not in the labor market. Accordingly, the backbone of Swedish policy has been active labor market policies rather than passive measures such as unemployment compensation or other cash benefits to the unemployed that are the principal approach in many other countries. Since the late 1950s the Swedes have developed an arsenal of measures, which have included training and retraining programs, training allowances, geographical mobility grants, and sheltered employment for the handicapped.

Originally, active labor market measures were aimed at men, but in the late 1960s women became eligible. By the late 1970s almost half of the participants in many labor market programs were women. The programs were a major contributing factor to the rise in Swedish women's labor market participation rate and closing the gender gap in paid employment. Between 1960 and 1990 women's labor market participation rate rose from 50% to 85%, and women comprised nearly half of the work force. In effect, the full employment policy has been a central component of equalization policies.

Also of major significance, the gender policy regime has encouraged women to become earners and men to become carers. The main policies included individual taxation, the expansion of child care, generous parental leave, and anti-discrimination legislation. The 1971 tax reform eliminated joint taxation of earnings, reduced tax deductions for wives that privileged single earners in married-couple families, and taxes were constructed so that a married woman's earnings contributed more to family income than if her husband increased his hours of work. Government subsidies for the construction and operating costs of child-care centers aimed at affordable, high-quality care. The parental leave scheme accorded extensive rights to both mothers and fathers and safeguarded their jobs (Sainsbury, 1999). In addition to promoting women's and mothers' employment, these gender equality policies decreased women's economic dependency in the family. Around 1990 Swedish women had a higher share of total labor market earnings and contributed a higher portion to family income than in most countries (Gornick, 1999, pp. 226–228).

The Swedish welfare regime has also distinguished itself through social rights covering the entire population. The inclusive coverage has stemmed from citizenship or permanent residence as a basis of social entitlement, and this was reflected in Sweden's first major social insurance scheme—the 1913 old age and disability insurance. It broke with earlier schemes that were limited to employees such as those in Germany and those based on a means test as in Britain and Denmark. The Swedish scheme established the principle of individual entitlement to a pension regardless of sex, marital status, labor market participation, or income. Likewise the introduction of child allowances in the mid-1940s immediately extended benefits to all children. A final example is parental benefits that have been available to working parents and those who are not in the labor force. In sum, programs whose principle of entitlement is citizenship or permanent residence led to more encompassing coverage than those based on work performance or need established through means-testing.

Citizenship or residence as the basis of social entitlement has been to the advantage of women. This basis of entitlement neutralizes the influence of marital status on social rights by conferring the same rights on married and unmarried persons as well as on husbands and wives; it provides individual rights and eliminates the need for rights derived on the basis of dependent status in the family. Individualization of social rights has become a hallmark of Swedish welfare state policies in contrast to countries where family relationships and marital status determine entitlements. Neutralizing the impact of marital status on social rights also has enhanced the rights of solo mothers.

Since the 1950s social reforms have assigned increasing importance to labor market participation as a basis of entitlement, supplementing benefits based on citizenship/residence. This resulted in a two tier system of income maintenance programs, with benefits based on citizenship providing basic security or an income floor and benefits based on paid work providing income security. The full employment policy and gender equality policies not only closed the gap in paid employment of women and men but also narrowed the gender gap in access to social benefits based on labor market participation (Sainsbury, 2000, p. 90). Women's access has also been facilitated by modest earnings thresholds and contribution requirements with eventually no contribution requirements for public pensions, health insurance, sickness benefits, and parental benefits. Furthermore, since the 1980s nearly all part-time employees worked enough hours to qualify for benefits based on labor market status. Differences in women's and men's access to work-related benefits have declined, but earnings-related benefits present a problem since they reproduce gender pay differentials in women's and men's benefits.

An additional characteristic has been the provision of a wide variety of public social services available to the entire population. The scope of service provision is reflected in the fact that expenditures for public services and cash benefits or transfers have amounted to approximately equal portions of the GDP, 20%–25%, whereas many other welfare states have been heavily biased toward cash benefits. A major policy thrust has been to make medical services, transportation, education, day care, and family services into public goods. In other words, although cash benefits have increasingly become attached to labor market participation, the entitlement to services has been based on residence and thus universal.

The service sector of the Swedish welfare state has been important to women in two ways. The expansion of social services has provided women with new job opportunities. In 1990, approximately half of the female work force was employed in the public sector, and two-thirds of all public employees were women (SCB, 1990, p. 134). Second, the availability of services, such as child care and elder care, have enabled women to reconcile family responsibilities and paid employment; and in contrast to many countries, the labor market participation rate of mothers has been higher than that of other women. A downside of this development, however, has been a concentration of women in low-paid service jobs, contributing to gender segregation of the labor market and wage differentials between the sexes. On the other hand, as seen in the share of women occupying top posts, it has been much easier to advance to such positions in the public sector than in the private sector. In addition, women in routine service jobs have generally had higher pay than their counterparts in other countries (SOU 2004: 43, p. 203). Women's higher pay has largely been the result of the unions, which have given priority to improving the wages of low income earners in the collective bargaining process. The political clout of the unions has been enhanced by the high degree of membership in Sweden, and by the mid-1980s women's unionization rate (85%) was on a par with men's (SCB, 1988, p. 226).

A final regime trait has been the stress on egalitarian outcomes and the redistributive impact of welfare state policies. In the early 1980s, disposable income was more equally distributed in Sweden than in most industrial countries, and the reduction of inequality in the market income through transfers and taxes has been impressive (Mitchell, 1991, p. 127). Inequality in disposable income has since inched upward, but the redistributive capacity of welfare policies has remained strong. Lastly, it needs to be underscored that the redistributive impact of welfare policies also consists of benefits in kind such as medical services, education, child care, transportation that is not captured in disposable income.

**Policies and poverty.** The Swedish policy model has implications for combating poverty. Long before workfare came into vogue in the 1990s, employment was viewed as the major panacea to poverty. However, employment and equal access to paid work was seen as a right, not an obligation. Furthermore, the model has underlined the preventive rather than the curative nature of social policies, that is, policies should prevent rather than alleviate poverty. Its universal bent has also underlined that policies should encompass the entire population rather than be targeted to the needy. Sweden has not had an official poverty line; instead emphasis has been on a social minimum as a right of all residents. Public assistance—or "welfare," in U.S. parlance—provides a social minimum in the event that other provision is inadequate.

Swedish policies have resulted in low poverty rates for the population as a whole and for vulnerable groups—solo mothers, the elderly, and families with several children. Even more striking in a cross-national perspective has been the Swedish gender poverty gap—the ratio of women's poverty to men's. There have been small differences in women's and men's poverty rates; women have had a lower poverty rate than men in Sweden, whereas in most countries men have had a lower poverty rate than women (Casper, McLanahan, & Garfinkel, 1994; Sainsbury, 1999).

On the basis of the poverty rates of the working-age population across eight countries in the 1980s, Lynne Casper et al. (1994) argue that Swedish women's high employment explained their low poverty rate, but this does not explain why women have a lower poverty rate than men in Sweden. A more recent study (Christopher, England, McLanahan, Ross, & Smeeding, 2001) notes the importance of social benefits. Because of their lower earnings, working women had a higher pretransfer poverty rate than working men in the early 1990s, and cash benefits played a crucial role in lifting these women out of poverty. The Swedish transfer system has reduced the pretransfer poverty rates of women and men to the advantage of women.

The expansion of social insurance and other cash benefits diminished the importance of public assistance in terms of beneficiaries as a proportion of the population and share of social spending. Insurance benefits and other cash transfers have played a major role in poverty reduction. This development has caused social policy analysts to conclude that assistance and means-tested benefits had been marginalized by universalism and the availability of other benefits. However, a cross-national analysis of the impact of assistance and other means-tested benefits in lifting people out of poverty revealed that the poverty reduction effectiveness of these benefits was greater in Sweden than in several other countries, including the United Kingdom, which has assigned major significance to combating poverty through means-tested benefits (Sainsbury & Morissens, 2002). In other words, the importance of social assistance in alleviating poverty in a country representing the social democratic welfare regime should not be written off. In contrast to many other countries, assistance has provided adequate benefits; the social minimum has generally been pegged at approximately 60% of the median income adjusted by family size. In short, it has been the combination of the full employment policy, the two tier system of income maintenance policies, and adequate social assistance benefits that has accounted for the low Swedish poverty rates, and they, together with gender equality policies, have prevented a feminization of poverty.

## The Challenge of the 1990s

The 1990s were a turbulent decade that put unprecedented strains on the Swedish welfare state. Sweden experienced its most severe economic downturn since the 1930s depression. During three consecutive years—1991 to 1993—the GDP fell, and more than a half million jobs disappeared: a loss of one out of every nine jobs. Within the span of a few years Sweden went from full employment to mass unemployment. In turn, rising unemployment (from 1.6% in 1990 to 8% in the mid-1990s) increased social expenditures and created a huge hole in government revenues. A budget surplus of 5.4% of the GDP in 1989 was transformed into a deficit of 12.3% in 1993 (Kautto, 2000, p. 33).

Mass asylum seeking in the early 1990s created added pressure. Between 1991 and 1994 nearly 180,000 asylum seekers arrived in Sweden, when unemployment was at its height (Palme et al., 2002a). For the decade as a whole, the number of immigrants totalled half a million. Already in 1968 the government declared that Sweden was a country of immigration, and Sweden has a high proportion of foreign born in its population, roughly 12% in the mid-2000s, which is similar to the United States and Germany. Contrary to these two countries, however, immigrants in Sweden have much stronger social rights (Sainsbury, 2006).

In coping with the financial crisis, governments, irrespective of their political complexion, cut social spending. A center-right coalition government headed by the conservative Moderate Party entered office in 1991 on a platform of revamping the welfare system. The government focused on social security spending, with the largest cuts hitting pensions and housing subsidies. When the Social Democrats returned to power in 1994 their major priority was to put public finances in order and balance the budget. To achieve this, they embarked on a budget consolidation program that assigned nearly equal weight to tax hikes to increase revenues and cuts to lower expenditures. The cuts were much more far-reaching than those introduced by the previous government and involved all policy areas; reductions in the expenditures of the Ministry of Social Affairs amounted to approximately 50% of the budget cuts. The program resulted in a remarkable turnaround, and the budget was balanced by 1998 (Kautto, 2000, pp. 42–45).

With the return of a surplus in the budget, benefit levels were raised but seldom to their precrisis level, and expansive reforms resumed. Even during the 1990s there were improvements in family policy through the introduction of the so-called daddy month and a law requiring the municipalities to guarantee a place in child care for all children (1994). The provision of child care has increased since 1990 so that it approximates a universal social right, and class differences in utilization have diminished (Bergqvist & Nyberg, 2000). Among the most important recent reforms of the Social Democratic government were a legislated national minimum for public assistance (1998); introduction of a ceiling on child-care fees paid by parents (2000); increases in child allowances (2000 and 2001); a second "daddy month" (2002); free preschool for all 4- and 5-year-old children (2003); a new allowance (*äldreförsörjningsstödet*) for elderly people not meeting requirements for the basic guaranteed pension (2003); improved access to survivor benefits for children irrespective of their parents' pension rights (2003); and raising the income ceiling of parental benefits (2006).

Furthermore, the availability of child care was nearly universal in 2005 (SV, 2007). Eighty-eight percent of children aged 1–5 had day care, and 7% were at home with parents on paid parental leave—or 95% had some form of public-sponsored care. The reform lowering fees for child care also established the right to a place in child care for unemployed parents (good for solo mothers who have a higher unemployment rate) and for a sibling whose parent is home caring for another child on paid parental leave. The reform further increased utilization and leveled class differences. Solo mothers have continued to utilize child care more than married or cohabiting parents, 96% compared to 87% for children aged 1–5. Immigrant parents had the same utilization rate as Swedish born parents. Moreover, three-fourths of children aged 6–9 were utilizing some form of after-school care, but it fell to 16% for children aged 10–12. That only 16% of children aged 10–12 are in after-school care is seen as a major problem. There was no difference in utilization for singles or couples in care for children aged 6–9, but single parents had a slightly higher utilization rate for children aged 10–12.

Social Democratic campaign promises in the 2006 election included more resources for elder care and improved replacement rates in unemployment insurance and parental leave. However, the center-right parties won the election primarily because they pledged to create more jobs and increase employment by lowering taxes and employers' payroll taxes. They also proposed to lower replacement rates and emphasized overutilization of benefits and fraud. The first steps of the new government were to lower income taxes, reduce unemployment benefits and the income ceiling for sickness benefits and benefits to care for a sick child, and raise employees' contributions for unemployment and sickness insurance. By cracking down on benefit fraud, the government budget for 2007 estimated it would save 2 billion crowns.

The lasting effects of the decade of retrenchment were, first, a downsizing of social insurance schemes by reducing replacement rates from generally 90% to 80%. The second was the end of full employment as a defining feature of the Swedish welfare regime. Neither the labor market participation rate nor the unemployment rate has returned to its pre-1990 level. The Social Democratic government set an employment rate of 80% and an unemployment rate of 4% as its goals in 1998, but these goals had not been reached by the mid-2000s (Nyberg, 2005a). Nevertheless, active labor market measures retained their importance in employment policy. Third, the pension reform, agreed to by all the political parties after years of negotiations, shifted financial responsibility for pensions from the state to the private sector. The state remains responsible for a basic guaranteed pension and an earnings-related pension, but benefits of the earnings-related pension were reduced. The scheme changed from a defined benefit to a defined contribution pension, and benefits based on the best 15 years of earnings out of 30 were replaced by pensions calculated on all earnings during 40 years. Both of these changes adversely affect women, but generous child-care credits were introduced to counteract the negative effects for mothers. The major innovation was a universal, mandatory private pension, which is supposed to make up the difference in retirement income previously provided by the state. The reform, introduced in 2003, will be fully phased in by 2019. Fourth, the social minimum was strengthened by establishing a national standard, but in the process it became less generous (Nelson, 2004, p. 41). Finally the most difficult change to gauge has been the privatization of public services, hospital care and medical services, education, and child and elder care. Privatization has proceeded unevenly across the counties and municipalities for different types of services (Palme et al., 2002a; Palme et al., 2002b). In elder care, substantial privatization has occurred, the provision of public services and the number of places in institutional care have declined, and the fees paid by the elderly have increased. Privatization of child care has been more limited, with the main increase in parental cooperatives rather than for-profit provision (Bergqvist & Nyberg, 2000).

## Changing Welfare State Outcomes?

How have the changes of the 1990s affected economic well-being, the redistributive capacity of welfare state policies, and the incidence of poverty in Sweden? And have they led to a feminization of poverty?

The failure to achieve full employment meant that the labor market participation rate in the mid-2000s was 8–9 percentage points lower than in 1990. As a result, a larger proportion of the population was now outside the labor market, had no earnings, and was not covered by social insurance schemes.[1] Both women's and men's labor force participation rates fell during the 1990s, but the lower rates did not alter the small difference in women's and men's employment. In 2000 the difference in Swedish women's and men's employment rates (4%) was the smallest in the European Union (EU) (SOU 2004: 43, p. 198). Overall, the number of working hours of employed women has increased since 1990. Women's part-time employment continued to decline, and women's short part-time work (1–19 hours) remained approximately 2% of all employed women.

Instead, generational differences in employment have emerged, with young people (16–24) experiencing the largest drop (roughly 20 percentage points), but the drop in their employment has been offset by an increased enrollment in secondary and higher education. The second major change has been the growing gap in the employment rates of first generation immigrants and the native born—59% versus 75% in 2004. Immigrants' unemployment rate was also much higher than the native born (Halleröd, 2004, pp. 7–9, 11; Nyberg 2005a, p. 24).

**Disposable income and redistributive capacity of policies.** Although there was no return to full employment, average disposable income had reached the same level as in 1991 by the end of the decade. Since then disposable income has grown, and by 2003 it was 15% higher in real terms than in 1991. However, the improvement was not equally shared by all the population. For the bottom income decile the increase in disposable income was only 6% during 1991–2003, while the income of the top decile increased 24% (SR, 2006, pp. 96–98).

Inequality in disposable income, as measured by the Gini coefficient, has increased 14% since 1990. However, welfare state policies remained robust in reducing income inequality. During both years transfers and taxes achieved roughly a 50% reduction in market income inequality.[2] What has changed is the degree of inequality in market incomes, with inequality peaking in 2000. Despite the increase in market inequality, Sweden still had the second lowest inequality in disposable income among the OECD countries in the early 2000s (HE 21 SM0601, 2006, pp. 17, 11).

Welfare state policies have also continued to reduce the inequalities in the average incomes of women and men in the working-age population. In 2002, the ratio of women's average market income to men's was .653, but the ratio of women's average disposable income to men's was .785, and both of these ratios had improved slightly in comparison to those for 1991 (Nyberg, 2005b, p. 61). In other words, without welfare state policies (cash benefits and taxation), women's share of income would have been 65% of men's instead of nearly 80% in the early 2000s. Nevertheless, as in all the countries in this book, women continue to be at an economic disadvantage compared to men because of the gender division of labor in the family and society.

**Poverty and low income.** According to official Swedish statistics, the poverty rate has remained quite low. Taking a disposable income below 50% of the median adjusted for family size as the poverty line, the poverty rate of the entire population increased from 3.4% in the early 1990s to 4.5% in 2004, with highest rates in 2000 and 2002 (4.8% and 4.9% respectively) (HE 21 SM0601, 2006, p. 30).[3] Nor was there a reversal of the gender poverty gap so that women's poverty rate was higher than men's during the 1990s and 2000s. However, using the EU poverty line of 60% of the median equivalent income, a reversal occurred in the late 1990s but in the mid-2000s the difference between women's and men's poverty rates was tiny (HE 21 SM0601, 2006, p. 29; Halleröd, 2004, p. 16).

A frequent gauge of low income, often employed as a proxy for poverty, is utilization of public assistance. As in the case of poverty rates, differences between women and men have been small; and men became a majority among the recipients of social assistance for the first time in the late 1960s (Korpi, 1973, p. 77). During the 1990s, the number of recipients rose to their highest levels during the postwar period: to 8.2% of the population in 1996 and 8.1% in 1997—the years with the heaviest cuts in other

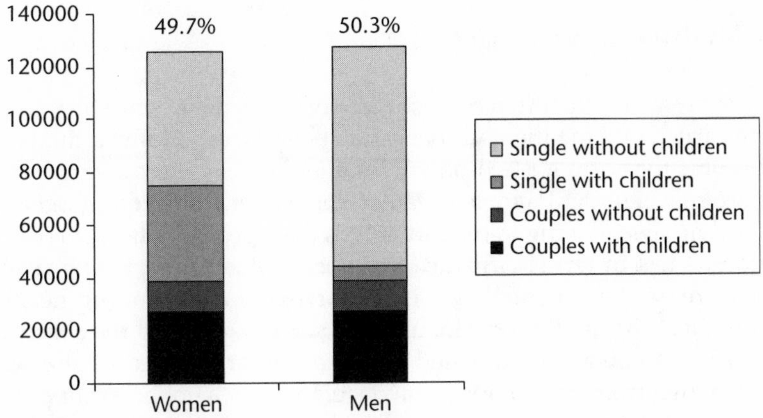


**Figure 2.1.** Use of social assistance by sex and household type, 2005.
*Source*: SS, 2006, p. 19.

social benefits. However, by 2001 the number of recipients as a percentage of the population was below the 1990 level, and their numbers have continued to decline. Long-term utilization also peaked in the mid-1990s and subsequently dropped but not to the 1990 level. Figure 2.1 shows the razor-thin difference between women's and men's use of social assistance in 2005; women totaled 49.7% and men 50.3%.

In summary, despite the economic crisis and high unemployment of the 1990s, welfare state policies performed well in reducing poverty and income inequality, especially during the years of zero growth, the highest unemployment rates and the worst budget cuts. Still these accomplishments conceal worrisome trends. The first is the fact that not all groups have shared equally in the return of economic growth and prosperity. Second, the relatively low poverty rate for the entire population masks the higher rates of singles, young people, solo mothers, immigrants, and people poorly covered by the major social insurance schemes.

We now turn to the situation of solo mothers and subsequently elderly women—and immigrants in both these categories. For both groups, we examine how welfare state policies have contributed to their economic well-being, the impact of the 1990s and their situation in the mid-2000s. To illuminate the impact of gender relations on economic well-being, we also consider the situation of solo mothers compared to mothers in two-parent families. Mothers in two-parent families have increasingly become earners but still assume more caring responsibilities than fathers, so that their contribution to family income is generally lower. In a similar vein, we compare the situation of single elderly women to single elderly men and elderly women in couples.

## Solo Mothers

Single-parent families often confront economic hardship since they consist of one earner, making them vulnerable to poverty, especially as dual earners become the norm for two-parent families. Solo mothers and their families are especially vulnerable because women generally command lower wages than men. Owing to the difficulties they face, solo mothers provide a rigorous test in terms of justice and social citizenship. Rising divorce rates increase the potential risk of a married woman finding herself a solo mother. The quality of solo mothers' social rights and the absence of stigma and disadvantage attached to single motherhood reduce the penalties of exiting from an unhappy marriage. In this way policies supporting solo mothers have implications for equality within the family (Hobson, 1994, p. 176). The growing number of dual earner families increases their incomes relative to those of single-parent families, making benefits more important in narrowing the income gap between families. In short, the strength of solo mothers' social rights is a barometer of equality not only within families but also among families and children generally.

The proportion of single-parent families and mother-headed families has gradually increased over the years primarily because of divorce and separation. In the mid-2000s single-parent families constituted 25% of all families and mother headed families slightly over 20% (Table 2.1). In Sweden the concept of illegitimacy was legally abolished and the rights of children born outside marriage strengthened at an earlier date than in most countries (Therborn, 1993, pp. 253–259). Never-married and cohabiting mothers have also suffered relatively little disrepute for quite some time. Widespread cohabitation—roughly one-third of the two-parent families with children under 18 were not married in the mid-2000s (SCB, 2005, p. 22)—and the legal parity of cohabitation and marriage in many instances have further reduced stigma. Cohabitation also inflates statistics on unmarried mothers, but unmarried mothers are not necessarily solo mothers.

TABLE 2.1 Families and Children[a] by Type of Family in Sweden, 1990 and 2004, Percentages

| | 1990 | | 2004 | |
|---|---|---|---|---|
| | Families | Children | Families | Children |
| Single-parent families | 19 | 15 | 25 | 22 |
| Mothers | 16 | 13 | 21 | 18 |
| Fathers | 3 | 2 | 4 | 4 |
| Two-parent families | 81 | 85 | 75 | 78 |

[a]Children under 18 living at home.

*Sources*: SCB, 1994, p. 12; SCB, 2005, pp. 13, 20; own calculations.

Historically the main policy focus has been on remedying the weak economic position of solo mothers and their children. Already in the late 1930s a system of advanced maintenance allowances for single mothers with low incomes was introduced. The reform guaranteed the payment of child support allowances to the mother, which the state then tried to collect from the father. In the early 1960s the allowance became a social minimum for the child/children of a solo mother, irrespective of her income; and, unlike child allowances, it was indexed against inflation. The allowance and tax benefits were the only measures specifically aimed at solo mothers, and several tax benefits were abolished with the introduction of individual taxation. Instead they have primarily benefited from universal family policy reforms from the late 1930s onwards. Family support measures—child allowances, housing allowances, and parental benefits, especially temporary paid leave to care for a sick child—have generally formed a much larger share of the income of solo mothers than of two-parent families. Finally, solo mothers have tended to utilize social assistance much more than two-parent families. In 1990 roughly 25% of solo mothers received assistance payments, but usually for short spells. All in all, social transfers have made a sizable contribution to solo mothers' income and have decreased the income differences between single-parent and two-parent families. In the early 1990s solo mothers' income after transfers and taxes was 40% higher than their market income (Gähler, 2001, p. 55).

Social transfers have also played a major role in keeping solo mothers and their children out of poverty. In 1992, the *pretransfer* poverty rate of solo mothers was 44%. However, social benefits lifted over 90% of the pretransfer poor mothers out of poverty, reducing the poverty rate to 3.7% (Morissens, 1999, p. 50). In other words, without social transfers the poverty rate of Swedish solo mothers and their children would be nearly on a par with the poverty rate of solo mothers in the United States, which was 47% in 1994, as reported by Christopher et al. (2001, p. 208).

Despite the importance of social benefits, earnings have constituted the mainstay of solo mothers' income. Traditionally solo mothers have had a higher employment rate than married mothers and have more often worked full time. The main policy promoting their employment has been public child care. A larger share of the children of solo mothers has been in municipal day care; and because of their lower family incomes, solo mothers have usually paid lower day care fees than married or cohabiting parents (Sainsbury, 1996, pp. 85, 100).

**The 1990s and 2000s.** The high unemployment and benefit cuts of the 1990s hit solo mothers very hard. Although unemployment was spread across the entire work force, single parents experienced more than their share of unemployment. Even before the economic crisis, unemployment was higher for single parents than most other groups; in the late 1990s, 30% of single parents had been unemployed during part of the year, and they were also unemployed for longer periods than other types of households (Lundborg, 2000, pp. 28–31). The difficult position of solo mothers in the labor market was further reflected in higher rates of temporary employment, holding down two jobs, working while looking for another job, and withdrawal from the labor market (SCB, 1998, p. 103).

Since cash transfers have been a major component of solo mothers' income, benefits cuts have potentially far-reaching consequences for their economic well-being. The most serious cuts included child allowances (during 1996–1997), housing allowances, and the conversion of advanced maintenance allowances to maintenance support.[4] In the early 1990s most solo mothers (between 80% and 90%) collected these three sorts of allowances (SD, 1996, p. 41). To make matters worse, the cuts in these allowances coincided with the lowest replacement rates for parental benefits, sickness compensation, and unemployment benefits during the decade.

Given these negative developments it is hardly surprising that the average disposable income of solo mothers fell sharply during the 1990s and did not recover during the decade. Recovery occurred later than for most other groups and has been sluggish. The increase in solo mothers' average disposable income between 1991 and 2004 was a mere 4%, while the increase for two-parent families was 17% (Table 2.2). The poverty rate of solo mothers has also increased, peaking in 2000 and subsequently remaining higher than in the early 1990s. Solo mothers have a higher poverty rate than two-parent families, whose poverty rate has also risen slightly during the past decade.

The worsening of solo mothers' economic well-being, presented in Table 2.2, can be traced to changes in employment, benefits, and taxation. Although solo mothers' employment rate began to rebound in the late 1990s, it did not return to its pre-1990 level. Compared to earlier, a smaller proportion of solo mothers had earnings as their principal source of income; the percentage fell from 75% in the late 1980s to roughly 60% in 2000. Simultaneously, the contribution of benefits to solo mothers' disposable income has eroded. The three benefits of special importance to solo mothers—child allowances, housing allowances, and maintenance payments—declined for all solo mothers and especially for those with low incomes between 1991 and 2002 (Ds 2004:41, pp. 138–139). At the same time data from the Luxembourg Income Study (LIS) for 2000 indicate a pronounced increase in the poverty rate of solo mothers whose principal source of income is social transfers. Finally, changes in taxation have also negatively affected solo mothers' disposable income. In the early 1990s the tax advantages of solo mothers were abolished (Skevik, 2006, p. 249), making the tax claw back for solo mothers substantially higher a decade later (Gähler, 2001, pp. 54–57).

Figure 2.2 presents the income packages of single-parent and two-parent families, using LIS data. The income package is comprised of market income (earnings and returns from capital), social benefits (both means-tested benefits and other transfers), and private transfers (child support and other income from individuals, usually relatives). As expected, benefits make up a much larger part of solo mothers' income package compared to

TABLE 2.2 Median Disposable Income[a] and Poverty Rates[b] by Family Type, 1991–2004

| Type of Family | 1991 | 1995 | 1998 | 1999 | 2000 | 2001 | 2002 | 2003 | 2004 | % change since 1991 |
|---|---|---|---|---|---|---|---|---|---|---|
| | | | | | **Median Disposable Income** | | | | | |
| Solo mothers | 107.1 | 98.5 | 96.8 | 103.6 | 105.9 | 109.6 | 108.7 | 109.6 | 110.9 | 3.6 |
| Cohabitating/Married parents | 135.1 | 121.1 | 129.3 | 134.5 | 144.0 | 148.4 | 152.0 | 153.6 | 157.5 | 16.6 |
| | | | | | **Poverty Rates** | | | | | |
| Solo mothers | 5.4 | 5.0 | 8.0 | 6.0 | 9.2 | 6.9 | 8.5 | 7.2 | 7.2 | 33.3 |
| Cohabitating/Married parents | 2.5 | 2.9 | 3.5 | 3.8 | 3.2 | 3.4 | 3.8 | 3.4 | 3.9 | 56.0 |

[a]Median Disposable Income is adjusted by family size and in thousands of Swedish crowns, 2004 prices.
[b]Poverty is defined as less than 50% of Median Disposable Income.

*Source*: Income Distribution Survey, 2004; HE 21 SM0601, pp. 19–20, 28–29.

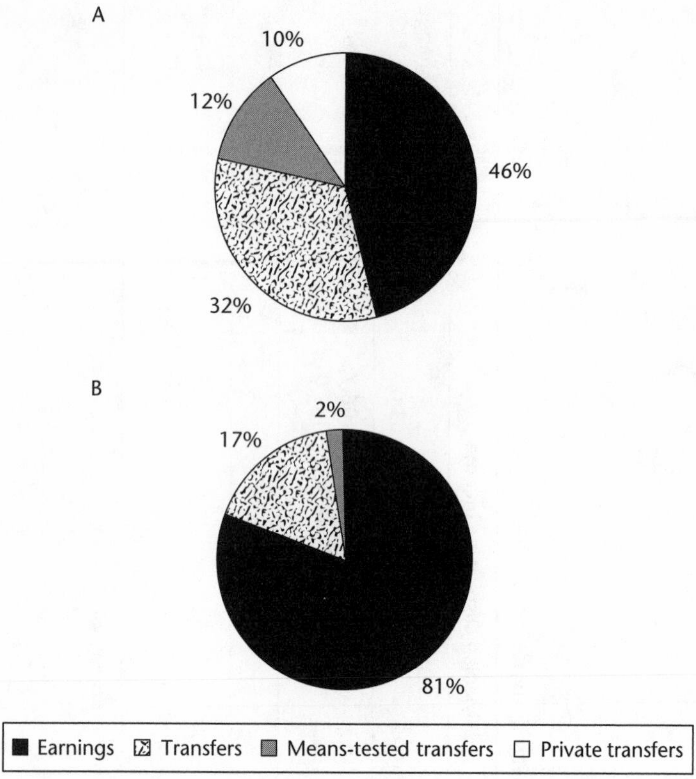


**Figure 2.2.** (A) Income package of solo mothers, 2000. (B) Income package of couples with children, 2000.
*Source*: LIS.

the two-parent income package; the benefits component has been roughly twice as large as for two-parent families. Still benefits have accounted for approximately 20% of the income of two-parent families and especially boosted their income in the mid-1990s. Benefits also play a larger role for families with young children (0–2 years) and three or more children. In 2000 social transfers continued to be of major importance in lifting solo mothers above the poverty line, and without them Swedish solo mothers would have a poverty rate similar to U.S. solo mothers (Tables 10.1 and 10.11, in this book).

The income package of solo mothers displayed steady erosion in the earnings component from the late 1980s until 2000. It declined from 56% in the late 1980s (Hobson, 1994) to 44% in the mid-1990s but rose to 46% in 2000. Rising unemployment in the 1990s resulted in a sharper deterioration in the labor market situation of solo mothers compared to other mothers (Björnberg, 1997, pp. 243–247). In 1990, solo mothers and cohabiting mothers had similar employment rates, but as the decade progressed, solo mothers' rate fell behind that of cohabiting mothers. Overall, the number of hours of paid work decreased for solo mothers and increased for mothers in couples. The discrepancy between solo and cohabiting mothers' employment has widened income inequality between single-parent and two-parent families. Equally important, the employment rate of fathers in two-parent families has remained very high since 1990, and fell only marginally during the decade (Ds 2004: 41, pp. 133–136). In the early 1990s solo mothers' average disposable income was nearly 80% of two-parent families' income but had dropped to 70% in the mid-2000s (calculated from HE 21 SM0601, 2006, pp. 19–20).

The developments since 1990 have contradictory consequences for cohabiting mothers who are exiting an unhappy relationship. The higher poverty rates of solo mothers and the drop in solo mothers' disposable income in relation to two-parent families represent a larger risk of financial hardship. Conversely, cohabiting mothers have strengthened their attachment to the labor market, making an exit less hazardous. The improved availability of child care and its lower costs also facilitate an exit. Furthermore, as discussed later, divorced mothers are at less risk of poverty than never-married mothers.

**Which solo mothers are at risk of poverty?** Solo mothers are not a homogeneous group, and certain mothers are more vulnerable than others. Just as the poverty rate of the entire population obscures solo mothers' higher risk of poverty, the poverty rate of all solo mothers fails to indicate which solo mothers are most vulnerable to poverty. To identify the factors associated with a high risk of poverty for solo mothers we utilize LIS data from 1995 and 2000.

As already indicated, and confirming earlier research, mothers without earnings run a much greater risk of being poor than those who have paid work. Swedish solo mothers without employment were twice as likely to have an income under the poverty line than those with earnings in 1987, but both had low poverty rates (Hobson, 1994, p. 181). Ann Morissens found that the poverty rate of solo mothers without employment was 6% in 1992, while employed solo mothers experienced little poverty (1999, p. 55). In 2000 solo mothers whose principal source of income was earnings had a poverty rate of 4%. By contrast, solo mothers with an income consisting primarily of benefits were nearly six times more likely to experience poverty. It appears that at the end of the decade benefits were less effective in lifting mothers above the poverty line, and employment was of increasing importance to solo mothers' economic well-being.

Two crucial factors illustrating the employment difficulties associated with solo motherhood are the age of the children and the number of the children. They both exert greater influence on solo mothers' employment compared to cohabiting mothers. Table 2.3 details the impact of children's age on mothers' employment. The same pattern is evident for solo and

TABLE 2.3 Mothers' Employment by Type of Family and Age of Youngest Child, 2004, Percentages

| | In the Workforce | | | | | | | Not in the Workforce | |
|---|---|---|---|---|---|---|---|---|---|
| Age of Child | At Work | | | Absent from Work[a] | | Unemployed | Total | Total | Studying |
| | Part Time | Full Time[b] | Total | Parental Leave | Total | | | | |
| Solo mothers | | | | | | | | | |
| –1 | 2 | 5 | 7 | 37 | 37 | 2 | 46 | 54 | 5 |
| 1 | 15 | 17 | 32 | 9 | 14 | 13 | 59 | 41 | 16 |
| 2–3 | 20 | 28 | 48 | 1 | 8 | 8 | 64 | 36 | 23 |
| 4–5 | 22 | 32 | 54 | 1 | 14 | 7 | 75 | 25 | 15 |
| 6–12 | 19 | 40 | 59 | 0 | 13 | 7 | 79 | 21 | 12 |
| 13–17 | 16 | 47 | 63 | 0 | 13 | 6 | 82 | 18 | 7 |
| 0–17 | 18 | 40 | 58 | 1 | 13 | 7 | 78 | 22 | 11 |
| Cohabiting/Married mothers | | | | | | | | | |
| –1 | 6 | 7 | 12 | 53 | 55 | 1 | 68 | 32 | 2 |
| 1 | 22 | 22 | 44 | 21 | 28 | 5 | 77 | 23 | 6 |
| 2–3 | 27 | 27 | 54 | 11 | 22 | 3 | 79 | 21 | 8 |
| 4–5 | 30 | 32 | 62 | 7 | 18 | 3 | 83 | 17 | 7 |
| 6–12 | 30 | 37 | 67 | 3 | 16 | 3 | 86 | 14 | 6 |
| 13–17 | 26 | 45 | 71 | 1 | 15 | 3 | 89 | 11 | 4 |
| 0–17 | 27 | 35 | 62 | 6 | 19 | 3 | 84 | 16 | 6 |

[a] In addition to parental leave, absence from work includes sick leave, vacation, and other reasons.
[b] Full time is defined as 35 hours or more.

*Source*: SCB, 2005, pp. 179–180, based on labor force survey data.

cohabiting mothers—employment increases with the age of the child/children—but in all age categories, cohabiting/married mothers had a higher employment rate. Neither solo nor cohabiting mothers are likely to work when their child is an infant, but roughly 50% are working once their child is 2 years old.

A disconcerting feature in the table is that solo mothers have lower utilization of paid parental leave with earnings-related benefits than cohabiting mothers. These results suggest that cohabiting mothers have a stronger labor market attachment before childbirth, which is necessary for benefits that replace earnings. These mothers are also guaranteed their job after leave. More solo mothers compared to cohabiting mothers were out of the labor market during the first year after the birth of their child and entitled to only minimum flat-rate parental benefits. In our exploratory probe using the LIS data, young children (3 and under) produced the highest poverty rate among solo mothers. However, the poverty rate fell when the youngest child was between 3 and 6 and was well below average for children above the age of 6.

Table 2.4 presents the effects of the number of children on mothers' employment. The employment rates of solo and cohabiting mothers with one and two children are nearly the same, except solo mothers were more likely to have full-time jobs. Interestingly, mothers with two children had higher employment rates than mothers with only one child. A major drop occurs in the employment rate of mothers with three or more children, and it was more pronounced for solo mothers. According to the LIS data, solo mothers with one child had a slightly higher poverty rate than those with two children, perhaps reflecting the importance of employment. Generally the poverty rates were similar for mothers with one to three children with a sharp increase for mothers with four or more children, but it was not as high as mothers with young children. On the other hand, the number of children has a more enduring impact on employment and poverty status than young children.

Other factors influencing solo mothers' poverty rates, but without the same powerful effects as family composition, were the mother's education, age, and marital status. Education influences job opportunities, and in the 1990s solo mothers had lower educational attainment levels than married mothers (Björnberg, 1997, p. 243; SD, 1996). However, as shown in Table 2.3, a larger percentage of solo mothers outside the labor market was studying. One of the positive developments of the 1990s was that solo mothers improved their educational credentials (Palme et al., 2002b, p. 67). Our exploratory calculations reveal that mothers with only primary education had a higher poverty rate; otherwise differences in poverty rates by levels of education were small. Using the higher, 60% poverty line, however, we found that as educational attainment increased, low income decreased. Second, there was a marked difference in the poverty rates of younger (under 35) and older solo mothers in 2000, which reflects a trend toward higher poverty among young people during the past decade. Between 1990

TABLE 2.4 Mothers' Employment by Type of Family and Number of Children,[a] 2004, Percentages[b]

| | Employed | | | | Unemployed | Not in the Workforce | |
|---|---|---|---|---|---|---|---|
| | Part Time | Full Time[c] | Total | % Employed Full Time | | Total | Studying |
| Solo mothers | 18 | 40 | 58 | 69 | 7 | 22 | 11 |
| 1 child | 17 | 43 | 61 | 71 | 6 | 21 | 10 |
| 2 children | 21 | 50 | 71 | 70 | 4 | 11 | 6 |
| 3 + | 19 | 30 | 49 | 61 | 9 | 29 | 13 |
| Cohabiting/ Married mothers | 27 | 35 | 62 | 56 | 3 | 16 | 6 |
| 1 child | 22 | 41 | 62 | 66 | 3 | 15 | 5 |
| 2 children | 30 | 41 | 72 | 57 | 1 | 6 | 2 |
| 3+ | 27 | 28 | 56 | 50 | 4 | 22 | 8 |

[a]Children under 18 living at home.
[b]In contrast to Table 2.3, this table does not include mothers who are absent from work, and thus the percentages do not add up to 100%.
[c]Full time is defined as 35 hours or more.

*Source*: SCB, 2005, pp. 179–180, labor force survey data.

and the 2000s, the age for getting established in the labor market rose from approximately 20–21 to 26–27 for men and 29–30 for women (SR, 2006, pp. 70–71). Finally, never-married mothers had a poverty rate which was nearly three times higher than that of divorced and separated mothers.

Immigration has increased ethnic diversity in Swedish society. How important are immigrant origins and the ethnic dimension for solo mothers' economic well-being? Divorce rates have been higher among immigrant than among Swedish couples (Björnberg, 1997, p. 254), and the number of mother-only families has increased among immigrant households with children. In the mid-2000s mother-only families were more prevalent among immigrant families than among Swedish families, 30% compared to 20%, and slightly over 20% of solo mothers were first generation immigrants (SCB, 2005, pp. 14, 23).

Immigrant solo mothers, according to the 2000 LIS data, had a substantially higher poverty rate than Swedish born solo mothers. Their higher poverty rate appears to be related to immigrants' employment difficulties and family composition. In the 1990s, there was a serious deterioration of immigrants' employment rate, which had begun to slide in the 1980s as the form of immigration changed from immigrant workers to refugees and family reunions. Immigrants' employment rate has risen since the mid-1990s, but in the mid-2000s the gap between the employment rates of immigrants and native born Swedes began to widen again (Halleröd, 2004, p. 11).

As can be observed in Figure 2.3, mothers not born in Sweden have had higher unemployment rates than Swedish mothers. The rates were especially high for mothers coming from non-OECD countries, and for solo mothers from these countries their unemployment rate was over 40% in

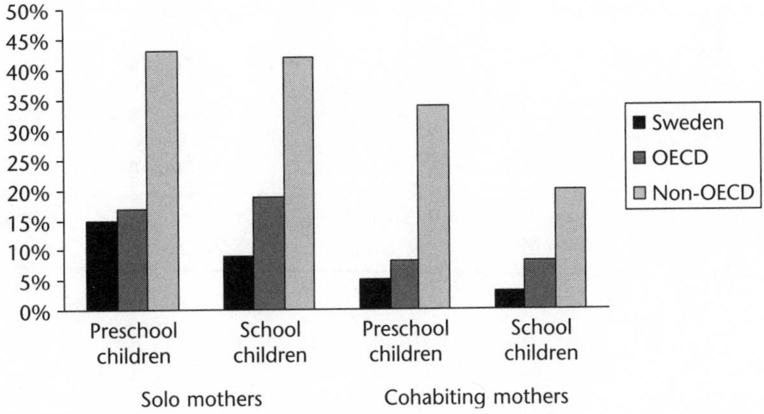


**Figure 2.3.** Unemployment of mothers by country of origin and age of children, mid-1990s.
*Source*: Björnberg, 1997, p. 255.

the mid-1990s. Besides lower labor market participation rates and higher unemployment rates, Ulla Björnberg (1997) found that in the mid-1990s, immigrant mothers were more often underemployed or in temporary employment than Swedish born mothers.

At the end of the 1990s, the disposable income of immigrant solo mothers had fallen more sharply than that of Swedish born solo mothers (Gähler, 2001, p. 97). The income package of immigrant solo mothers in 2000 also revealed a smaller earnings component and a larger benefit component than other solo mothers. Means-tested benefits formed a larger component for immigrant solo mothers compared to other solo mothers, but other transfers predominated in their benefit income and were on a par with Swedish born solo mothers.

In the mid-2000s immigrant solo mothers were slightly overrepresented among the mothers with young children; they constituted 25% of solo mothers with children 0–5 years but approximately 20% of solo mothers with children 0–17. Immigrant mothers, especially from Africa and Asia, were more likely to receive minimum flat rate benefits during parental leave, whereas most Swedish born mothers got earnings-related benefits. Even if mothers from Africa and Asia received earnings-related benefits, they were much lower than Swedish mothers, reflecting earnings differentials (Duvander & Eklund, 2006, p. 54). Lower parental benefits contribute to the precarious situation of immigrant mothers with young children and the likelihood of their falling below the poverty line.

Immigrant families also tend to have more children than Swedish born parents (Table 2.5), and as we have seen, solo mothers with three or more children had lower employment and higher unemployment rates and were more likely to be outside the labor market. Although the vast majority of families with three or more children have Swedish born parents,

TABLE 2.5 Number of Children[a] by Type of Family and Birthplace of Parents, 2004, Percentages

| | Parents Born in Sweden | | Parents Born Abroad | |
|---|---|---|---|---|
| Number of Children | Solo Mothers | Two-Parent Families | Solo Mothers | Two-Parent Families |
| 1 | 56 | 36 | 54 | 37 |
| 2 | 34 | 47 | 30 | 38 |
| 3 | 8 | 14 | 10 | 16 |
| 4 + | 2 | 3 | 5 | 9 |
| Average number of children | 1.54 | 1.85 | 1.69 | 2.02 |

[a]Children under 18 living at home.

*Source*: SCB, 2005, pp. 21–23; own calculations.

immigrants stand out in terms of having four or more children, which was the cut-off line for higher poverty rates among solo mothers. Immigrant mothers were 40% of all solo mother families with four or more children.

In summary, the LIS data revealed that poverty rates are highest among solo mothers who have low or no earnings, young children, four or more children, and are of foreign origins. Solo mothers confront a maternity penalty in terms of employment; their employment rate is lower than mothers in two-parent families. The age and number of children have a larger impact on solo mothers' employment and, in turn, their poverty rate than these factors have on the poverty rates of two-parent families. Immigrant solo mothers also face an immigration/ethnicity penalty in employment and poverty. Immigrant women and men, especially from the non-OECD countries, have lower employment rates than Swedish born women and men, and immigrants from the non-OECD countries have higher poverty rates than other immigrants and the native born. All immigrants, however, are vulnerable to poverty during their first 10 years in Sweden (HE 21 SM0601, 2006, p. 32). Furthermore, the poverty rate of Swedish born people has largely stabilized since the late 1990s, while immigrants' poverty rates have risen (Table 2.6).

The failure to restore full employment has exacerbated both the maternity and immigration/ethnicity penalties. In a tight labor market, employers have less leeway in choosing whom to hire. The shrinkage of employment in the 1990s gave employers greater possibilities to select from many job applicants and not to hire people who in their eyes are less attractive as workers. Solo mothers have much higher absentee rates, especially to care for a sick child, than mothers and fathers in two-parent families. Employers have complained that immigrants are unfamiliar with the Swedish way of doing things and seem to prefer employing Swedes. At the same time, employment has become more important since benefits lifted fewer solo mothers above the poverty line. In short, since 1990, the economic situation of solo mothers has become more precarious, while the situation of immigrant solo mothers has deteriorated even more.

## Single Elderly Women

In an international context, the economic situation of single elderly women has also been a source of the feminization of poverty. Pension reform has been a major trend across nations during the past two decades as policy makers have attempted to reduce the amount of public resources devoted to retirement income. These reforms have led to much speculation about differences in women's and men's future pensions, but the 2003 reform has only marginally affected the retirement income of current pensioners. Instead their income has largely been determined by the 1946 reform introducing flat rate pensions for all citizens and the 1959 reform that complemented citizen pensions with earnings-related benefits through

TABLE 2.6 Poverty Rates[a] by Country of Origin, 1991–2004

| | 1991 | 1995 | 1998 | 1999 | 2000 | 2001 | 2002 | 2003 | 2004 |
|---|---|---|---|---|---|---|---|---|---|
| Swedish born | 2.7 | 3.1 | 3.4 | 3.3 | 3.7 | 3.6 | 3.8 | 3.6 | 3.3 |
| Foreign born | 6.6 | 6.8 | 7.9 | 8.0 | 8.9 | 8.9 | 9.4 | 8.3 | 10.0 |
| Born in non-OECD countries[b] | 9.7 | 8.2 | 10.7 | 11.1 | 11.5 | 11.5 | 12.5 | 10.3 | 12.6 |

[a] Poverty is defined as less than 50% of Median Disposable Income.

[b] Here the OECD countries refer to Australia, Austria, Belgium, Canada, Denmark, Finland, France, Germany, Greece, Iceland, Ireland, Italy, Japan, Luxembourg, New Zealand, Netherlands, Norway, Portugal, Spain, Switzerland, United Kingdom, and the United States. Turkey and the more recent members are excluded.

*Source*: HE 21 SM0601, 2006, p. 32.

the supplementary pension system (ATP). The ATP reform reduced the income differences between the working-age population and pensioners, and the two reforms largely eliminated poverty among seniors.

The ATP scheme, however, introduced gender differentiation in benefits, whereas the citizen or basic pensions provided equal benefits to women and men. The most disadvantaged women were homemakers without paid employment and thus no ATP benefits. To compensate these women and those with only a few years of earnings, a special pension supplement was introduced. In addition, these pensioners were eligible for an income tested housing allowance and received tax exemptions so that they paid no income tax unless they had other income. In this way the transfer and tax system provided an adequate disposable income above the poverty line. Over the years pensioners without ATP benefits have decreased, as women entered the labor market. In the early 1990s slightly less than 25% of female pensioners had only the basic pension (compared to 5% of male pensioners) (SCB, 2004, p. 16).

As ATP was phased in, the male–female differential in pension income grew, even though more women received supplementary pension benefits. The average pension income of elderly women (65 and over) was only 60% that of elderly men in 1990. Despite predictions that that gap would narrow as a result of women's greater labor market participation, it was still 64% in the early 2000s. Instead of women's not having ATP benefits, the prime vulnerability is increasingly having low supplementary pension benefits. As in the case of women's and men's market income in the working-age population, taxation and other social transfers reduce the inequalities in women's and men's pension incomes, and the gender gap has been smaller for disposable income. Elderly women's disposable income amounted to 90% of elderly men's in 1990 (Sainsbury, 1996, p. 165).

**The 1990s and 2000s.** Even more than solo mothers, pensioners' economic well-being is affected by benefit income because pensions account for nearly 80% of their income. During the worst years of the economic crisis, pensions were frozen at a lower rate (1993–1999), and all pensioners except those with minimum benefits (only a basic pension and a special supplement to compensate for not having ATP benefits) paid higher taxes on retirement income because of the budget consolidation program. Nor have they benefited from the recent tax reductions on earnings.

Despite this, pensioners have been proclaimed the "winners" of the 1990s. The main reason is that the disposable income of pensioners as a group increased between 1991 and 2002 by 21%, which was higher than the increase for the working-age population. Most of this increase occurred through the higher pension income of new beneficiaries as the oldest pensioners with lower benefits died. Quite a different picture emerges if we follow the individual income development of the elderly who were pensioners in 1991. They experienced a meager rise of less than 2% (SCB, 2004, p. 6).

These two developments have affected the poverty rates of the elderly in different ways (Table 2.7). First, the low poverty rate of all the elderly shows no sign of increasing, which is in line with the improvement of pensioners' disposable income as a group. The drop in the poverty rate of younger, single pensioners, both female and male (aged 65–74) after 1991 can also be explained by new beneficiaries with higher pension income. The meager rise in disposable income of the elderly who were pensioners since 1991 is mainly discernible in the poverty rates for 2000 and 2001 of single elderly women and men over 75.

The relatively low poverty rates of the elderly in Table 2.7 are not solely the result of new beneficiaries with higher pension incomes but are also the outcome of government policies. To protect the most vulnerable pensioners—mostly women without ATP—pensioners' housing allowances were successively made more generous and the special supplement raised. Efforts to shield the most vulnerable pensioners resulted in a 40% increase in their disposable income between 1991 and 2002 and a 14% decrease for pensioners with the highest benefits (SCB, 2004, p. 37). Harmonization of the old and new pensions systems also brought improvements to pensioners with minimum benefits. The basic pension was converted into a guaranteed pension, which is taxable, but it provided higher benefits after taxes than the basic pension. A change in indexation of pensions from prices to wages has also proved advantageous to pensioners since inflation has been low and wages have risen in the 2000s (Ds, 2006, p. 13).

Table 2.7 also reveals higher poverty rates for both single women and men generally and specifically for pensioners who are 75 and older whose poverty rate has increased since 1991. By contrast, nearly all couples are above the poverty line, and the poverty rate of the oldest couples has declined. The pension income of the elderly is either stable or declines over the years; the death of a partner entails a loss of both income and the advantage of economy of scale. Pensioners with low ATP benefits—both women and men—are especially vulnerable. The earnings-related benefits of the supplementary scheme introduced not only gender but also class differentiation in pension income. Nevertheless, given women's greater longevity compared to men, the composition of the poor who are 75+ is predominantly women.

Elderly immigrants' pension and disposable incomes are generally lower than that of the Swedish born population (SCB, 2004, p. 61), but published statistics provide no information of the poverty rates of elderly immigrants. According to the LIS data for 2000, elderly immigrants had a higher poverty rate than all the elderly, and immigrant women had a higher rate than immigrant men. Immigrants' lower pension income stems from poorer earnings and, in many cases, fewer years of employment in Sweden. Furthermore, immigrants' basic pension rights were negatively affected when Sweden joined the EU. The eligibility requirement for a full basic pension was raised to 40 years of residence (compared to 10 previously), and this became the requirement for the guaranteed

TABLE 2.7 Poverty Rates[a] of the Elderly by Sex and Household, 1991–2004

| | 1991 | 1995 | 1998 | 1999 | 2000 | 2001 | 2002 | 2003 | 2004 |
|---|---|---|---|---|---|---|---|---|---|
| All 65+ | 3.3 | 1.8 | 2.1 | 2.8 | 3.8 | 4.1 | 3.5 | 3.0 | 2.8 |
| Single women | | | | | | | | | |
| 65–74 | 6.8 | 2.6 | 3.7 | 4.3 | 4.6 | 6.3 | 3.8 | 3.1 | 2.6 |
| 75+ | 5.2 | 3.0 | 3.6 | 5.5 | 8.4 | 8.2 | 6.4 | 6.3 | 6.2 |
| Single men | | | | | | | | | |
| 65–74 | 6.6 | 1.9 | 2.3 | 4.6 | 2.6 | 2.7 | 6.9 | 4.3 | 4.6 |
| 75+ | 5.7 | 3.1 | 4.8 | 3.8 | 7.1 | 6.7 | 6.6 | 4.4 | 7.3 |
| Couples | | | | | | | | | |
| 65–74 | 0.7 | 1.1 | 0.5 | 0.8 | 1.3 | 1.5 | 1.3 | 1.3 | 0.7 |
| 75+ | 1.1 | 0.4 | 0.8 | 0.7 | 0.9 | 1.3 | 1.2 | 0.8 | 0.7 |

[a] Poverty is defined as less than 50% of Median Disposable Income.

*Source*: HE 21 SM0601, 2006, pp. 28–30.

pension in the new system. The new rules deprived non-EU immigrants arriving in Sweden after the age of 25 of minimum pension benefits, except for recognized refugees; and elderly immigrants started showing up in the assistance statistics and were double the number of Swedish born in 2000. Their numbers fell and equaled those of the Swedish born after 2003, when the government introduced the new allowance to insure minimum benefits for all residents who failed to qualify for the guaranteed pension (SS, 2001, p. 12; SS, 2006, p. 23). Equally important, application for the new allowance has involved a standard administrative procedure rather than the former detailed scrutiny of resources by welfare workers; research has documented elderly immigrants' painful encounters with the local welfare authorities (Songur, 2002).

## The Politics of Reforms and Its Limits

Several features of reform politics in Sweden have worked to the advantage of solo mothers so that they have not been completely marginalized in the policy process. First, because poverty rates have been low, poverty has not been a political issue in Sweden. Instead political mobilization has revolved around issues of economic inequality and economic disadvantage, and since the late 1960s gender equality has been on the policy agenda. Importantly, these issues have generated broader mobilization and alliance building compared to the poverty issue in many countries.

Second, solo mothers have had important political allies. The plight of solo mothers was a major political concern of the Social Democratic Women's Federation, from its official founding in 1920, and a single mother was president of the Federation in the 1950s and 1960s. Union women have also championed issues, which have benefited solo mothers, such as equal pay and the expansion of public child-care centers. Nor have solo mothers been without clout in the corridors of power. Members of parliament and of the cabinet have indirectly or directly experienced solo motherhood. Among the most influential were Gustav Möller, Minister of Social Affairs (1932–1951) and Ulla Lindström, Minister of Family Affairs (1957–1966). Möller, a major architect of the Swedish welfare state, was brought up by an impoverished widow who died when he was 14, and his childhood experiences were instrumental in shaping his beliefs in the superiority of universal policies and that social benefits should be provided as a general right of citizenship (Tilton, 1990, pp. 112–124). Lindström's policy initiatives included appointing inquiry commissions on abortion liberalization and extending services to families. Women's parliamentary representation increased from 14% in 1970 to 47% in 2006; women MPs have frequently acted as watchdogs to insure that legislation has accommodated the interests of solo mothers (Winkler, 2002; Hobson & Takahashi, 1997).

Third, the individual political resources of solo mothers and elderly women do not indicate that they are socially excluded or marginalized. In contrast to most of the population, elderly women increased their organizational involvement during the 1990s—a period of membership decline in organizations. Many were members of the two pensioners' associations that have strong ties to the political parties. Solo mothers' membership in organizations was above the average, and they were primarily involved in unions, housing associations and parents' organizations (SCB, 2003, pp. 35, 38, 68, 153, 156, 177, 203).

Since 1990, however, the limits of reform politics for solo mothers and elderly single women have become more apparent. The hegemony of universal policies has militated against selective measures tailored to alleviate the financial hardships of solo mothers. For example, the 2005 inquiry commission on gender equality policies, composed of feminist activists, proposed a special tax allowance for single mothers, but the proposal fell on deaf ears. A cornerstone of the universal model is that everyone should contribute to its financing. Policy makers are reluctant to make exceptions in fear of spurring other groups to claim that they too should be eligible for deductions. On the other hand, without much fanfare, the Social Democratic government introduced measures to safeguard the economic standard of pensioners with the lowest benefits, most of whom were women.

The second limitation rests in the contradictory outcomes of the politics of care since 1990: an impressive expansion of child care and a serious contraction of elder care. In contrast to elder care, child care became a major political issue during the 1990s. The drop in women's representation in parliament after the 1991 election and the victory of a right-center government that called for sweeping changes in the welfare system and cuts in the public sector prompted a widespread mobilization of women and a resurgence of the women's movement (Bergqvist, Olsson Blandy, & Sainsbury, 2007). The right-center election victory also led to a further politicization of child care, as the government proposed to introduce a child-care allowance under the banner of freedom of choice for families. Women on the left rallied to the defense of public child care, emphasizing its importance as a gender equality issue. Party divisions in the government resulted in a compromise policy package that introduced a child-care allowance, a universal guarantee of a place in public child care, and the "daddy month" in the parental leave scheme (Bergqvist, 2007). The politicization of child care elevated its importance in party competition and electoral politics, and the parties upgraded the issue. In the run-up to the 2002 election the Social Democrats proposed a ceiling on public child-care fees and strengthened the right of unemployed parents to a place in public child care—a move that further broadened the constituency of support for public child care.

The politics of elder care reform has differed on several counts. It has been more difficult to increase public awareness that elder care is a gender equality issue, even if feminist researchers and publicists framed the issue in these terms during the 1990s (Stark, 1993; Stark & Regnér, 1997; Szebehely, 1998). Furthermore, public child care which has been framed as an investment in children and future human capital, whereas elder care has been portrayed as an economic burden without future returns. Pension reform has also overshadowed the issue of elder care; and social policy analysts have repeatedly heralded pensioners as winners during the 1990s (SCB, 2006), diverting attention from the oldest female pensioners' low retirement income and from care of elderly relatives as a growing source of women's unpaid work. Nevertheless, the issue of adequate elder care is a ticking political bomb ready to explode as the baby boomer generation become pensioners and require care.

## Conclusion

The findings of this chapter suggest that Sweden is at a crossroads. So far policies have reduced poverty, and according to official statistics, poverty rates are fairly low. Most impressive is the Swedish record of low poverty rates when economic distress was at its worst in the mid-1990s. Furthermore, during the 1990s and 2000s the differences between women's and men's poverty rates and utilization of assistance have been very small, often microscopic. Demographics work against a feminization of poverty in the working-age population provided that poverty rate differences are minimal because males outnumber females. Moreover, poverty among families with children remains lower than several other groups. As long as policies remain child oriented, solo mothers should reap substantial advantages. Decision makers have also introduced new social policy measures to protect those who are most vulnerable to poverty. They have included measures to improve the situation of the elderly with low benefits, a new allowance for persons who are not eligible for a guaranteed pension, enlarging children's access to survivor benefits so that they are not contingent upon parents' pension rights, and increases in minimum flat rate benefits in the parental leave scheme. In keeping with the Swedish model, the measures have had a universal thrust.

Still there are unsettling trends. First and foremost, welfare state policies were more effective in reducing poverty in the mid-1990s than in the 2000s. This is true for immigrants (Morissens & Sainsbury, 2005), solo mothers, and the most elderly whose poverty rates have increased in the 2000s. At least in 2000, according to LIS data, transfers did a poorer job in lifting solo mothers above the poverty line compared to earlier. A major issue here is whether this is the result of policy decisions. A goal of the former Social Democratic government was to reduce the number of people utilizing assistance by half, and the numbers have gone down. The national standard for the social minimum also became less generous in 1998.

Demographics also operate in the opposite direction with regard to poverty reduction among the elderly where women form the majority, and the female majority increases with age. Although the poverty rates of single elderly men and women are both high, more elderly women are single, while most elderly men live in couples, and couples are much less likely to experience poverty. On a further pessimistic note, the disposable income of single elderly women aged 75 or older and of solo mothers was highly skewed in the mid-2000s; nearly 90% had a disposable income below or at the average for all households (HE 21 SM0601, 2006, p. 24). So far Swedish policies have generally warded off poverty if it is defined as less than 50% of the median disposable income, but many solo mothers and elderly women have a disposable income between 50% and 70% of the average. They are at risk if a more ambitious measure of financial well-being like that of the current EU poverty line is used.

Lastly, a more imminent prospect than the feminization of poverty is the ethnicization of poverty. All available data indicate that immigrants have higher poverty rates—including immigrant solo mothers and elderly women—and that immigrants of color are more vulnerable. In the mid-2000s immigrants' poverty rate had not been held in check, while that of the native born had. In fact, the increase in the poverty rate of the entire population may be the result of immigrants' higher poverty rate. However, immigrant women had a lower poverty rate than immigrant men in the early 2000s so that the ethnicization of poverty may not be a new source of the feminization of poverty.

## Notes

1 In the mid-2000s roughly 20% of the working-age population were not in the labor market, approximately 10% had no earnings from work and 7%, compared to 5% in 1992, were not covered by the social insurance schemes (SR. Summary, p. 3).

2 We can measure the impact of transfers and taxes by calculating the net redistribution scores as follows ($R = [G-G^*]/G$), where $G$ is the Gini coefficient of market income before transfers and taxes and $G^*$ is the Gini coefficient of disposable income (Mitchell, 1991, p. 122). The scores were 0.50 in 1991 and 0.49 in 2004 (calculated from HE 21 SM0601, 2006, p. 17). These scores were only slightly lower than 0.53, the value of $R$ reported by Mitchell for 1979 (p. 129).

3 Although the 60% poverty line is increasingly used because of EU membership, we use the 50% of median equivalent disposable income poverty line here since we are interested in changes over time and cross-national comparisons. This has been the most commonly used poverty line in previous analyses and comparative studies.

4 In 1997 advanced maintenance allowances (bidragsförrskott) were converted into maintenance support (underhållsstöd). The most important changes were de-indexing the amount of support (previously 40% of the basic amount) and strengthening the financial obligations of the absent/other parent. De-indexation has eroded the real value of the amount of support (down 14% in 2004), and the proportion of children of single parents receiving maintenance

fell from 90% to 60%, which was slightly higher than the proportion in the 1980s (Ds 2004: 41, p. 354; Sainsbury, 1996, p. 85).

## References

Bergqvist, C. (2007). The debate about child-care allowances in the light of welfare state reconfiguration: The Swedish case. In M. Haussman & B. Sauer (Eds.), *Gendering the state in the age of globalization: Women's movements and state feminism in post-industrial democracies* (pp. 245–262). Lanham, MD: Rowman & Littlefield.

Bergqvist, C., & Nyberg, A. (2000). Welfare state restructuring and child care in Sweden. In S. Michel & R. Mahon (Eds.), *Child care policy at the crossroads: Gender and welfare state restructuring* (pp. 287–307). New York: Routledge.

Bergqvist, C., Olsson Blandy, T., & Sainsbury, D. 2007. Swedish state feminism: Continuity and change. In J. Outshoorn & J. Kantola (Eds.), *Changing state feminism* (pp. 224–245). Basingstoke: Palgrave Macmillan.

Björnberg, U. (1997). Single mothers in Sweden: Supported workers who mother. In S. Duncan & R. Edwards (Eds.). *Single mothers in an international context* (pp. 241–267). London: University College London Press.

Casper, L. M., McLanahan, S., & Garfinkel, I. (1994). The gender-poverty gap: What we can learn from other countries. *American Sociological Review, 59*, 594–605.

Christopher, K., England, P., McLanahan, S., Ross, K., & Smeeding, T. M. (2001). Gender inequality in poverty in affluent nations: The role of single motherhood and the state. In K. Vleminckx & T. M. Smeeding (Eds.), *Child well-being, child poverty and child policy in modern nations: What do we know?* (pp. 199–219). Bristol: The Policy Press.

Duvander, A. Z., & Eklund, S. (2006). Utrikesfödda och svenskfödda föräldrars föräldrapenningsanvändande. In P. de los Reyes (Ed.), *Om välfärdens gränser och det villkorade medborgarskapet* (SOU 2006:37) (pp. 33–68). Stockholm: Ministry of Justice.

Esping-Andersen, G. (1990). *The three worlds of welfare capitalism.* Cambridge: Polity.

Ds 2004:41. (2004). *Ekonomiskt utsatta barn.* Stockholm: Ministry of Health and Social Affairs.

Ds 2006:13. (2006). *Var det bättre förr? Pensionärernas ekonomiska situation i början av 2000-talet.* Stockholm: Ministry of Health and Social Affairs.

Gähler, M. (2001). Bara en mor—ensamstående mödrars ekonomiska levnadsvillkor i 1990-talets Sverige. In Å. Bergmark (Ed.), *Ofärd i välfärden* (SOU 2001:54) (pp. 15–99). Stockholm: Ministry of Health and Social Affairs.

Gornick, J. C. (1999). Gender equality in the labour market. In D. Sainsbury (Ed.), *Gender and welfare state regimes* (pp. 210–242). Oxford: Oxford University Press.

Halleröd, B. (2004). The fight against poverty and social exclusion: Non-governmental expert report no. 1–2004, Sweden. http://ec.europa.eu/employment_social/spsi/docs/social_inclusion/sv_network_en.pdf. Accessed July 29, 2009.

HE 21 SM 0601. (2006). Statistiska meddelanden. Serie HE—Hushållens ekonomi, *Inkomstfördelningsundersökningen 2004.* Stockholm: Statistics Sweden.

Hobson, B. (1994). Solo mothers, social policy regimes and the logics of gender. In D. Sainsbury (Ed.), *Gendering welfare states* (pp. 170–187). London: Sage Publications.
Hobson, B., & Takahashi, M. (1997). The parent-worker model: Lone mothers in Sweden. In J. Lewis (Ed.), *Lone mothers in European welfare regimes* (pp. 121–139). London: Jessica Kingsley Publishers.
Kautto, M. (2000). *Two of a kind? Economic crisis, policy responses and well-being during the 1990's in Sweden and Finland* (SOU 2000:83). Stockholm: Ministry of Health and Social Affairs.
Korpi, W. (1973). *Fattigdom i välfärden* (2nd ed.). Stockholm: Tiden.
Lundborg, P. (2000). Vilka förlorade jobbet under 1990-talet? In J. Fritzell (Ed.), *Välfärdens förutsättningar: Arbetsmarknad, demografi och segregation* (SOU 2000:37) (pp. 11–50). Stockholm: Ministry of Health and Social Affairs.
Mitchell, D. (1991). *Income transfers in ten welfare states.* Aldershot: Avebury.
Morissens, A. (1999). Solo mothers and poverty: Do policies matter? A comparative case study of Sweden and Belgium. LIS Working Paper No. 210, http://www.lisproject.org/publications/wpapers.htm. Accessed July 29, 2009.
Morissens, A., & Sainsbury, D. (2005). Migrants' social rights, ethnicity and welfare regimes. *Journal of Social Policy, 34*, 4, 637–660.
Nelson, K. (2004). The formation of minimum income protection. LIS Working Paper No. 373, http://www.lisproject.org/publications/wpapers.htm. Accessed July 29, 2009.
Nyberg, A. (2005a). *An evaluation of the gender dimension to the national action plan for social inclusion 2005—The Swedish National Report.* Stockholm: The National Institute for Working Life.
Nyberg, A. (2005b). Har den ekonomiska jämställdheten ökat sedan början av 1990-talet? *Forskarrapporter till Jämställdhetspolitiska utredningen* (SOU 2005:66) (pp. 11–82). Stockholm: Ministry of Employment, Communications and Industry.
Palme, J., Bergmark, Å., Bäckman, O., Estrade, F., Fritzell, J., Lundberg, O., et al. (2002a). Welfare trends in Sweden: Balancing the books for the 1990s. *Journal of European Social Policy, 12*, 4, 329–346.
Palme, J., Bergmark, Å., Bäckman, O., Estrade, F., Fritzell, J., Lundberg, O., et al. (2002b). *Welfare in Sweden: The balance sheet for the 1990s* (Ds 2002:32). Stockholm: Ministry of Health and Social Affairs.
Sainsbury, D. (1996). *Gender, equality and welfare states.* Cambridge: Cambridge University Press.
Sainsbury, D. (1999). Gender and social democratic welfare states. In D. Sainsbury (Ed.), *Gender and welfare state regimes* (pp. 75–114). Oxford: Oxford University Press.
Sainsbury, D. (2000). Välfärdsutvecklingen för kvinnor och män på 1990-talet. In Å. Bergmark (Ed.), *Välfärd och försörjning* (SOU 2000:40) (pp. 87–128). Stockholm: Ministry of Health and Social Affairs.
Sainsbury, D. (2006). Immigrants' social rights in comparative perspective: Welfare regimes, forms of immigration and immigration policy regimes. *Journal of European Social Policy, 16*, 3, 229–244.
Sainsbury, D., & Morissens, A. (2002). Poverty in Europe in the mid-1990s: The effectiveness of means-tested benefits. *Journal of European Social Policy, 12*, 4, 307–327.

SCB. (1988). *Inequality in Sweden 1975–1985*. Stockholm: Statistics Sweden.

SCB. (1990). *Offentliga sektorn: Utveckling och nuläge*. Stockholm: Statistics Sweden.

SCB. (1994). *Fakta om den svenska familjen*. Stockholm: Statistics Sweden.

SCB. (1998). *Sysselsättning, arbetstider och arbetsmiljö 1975–1995*. Stockholm: Statistics Sweden.

SCB. (2003). *Föreningslivet i Sverige*. Levnadsförhållanden Rapport 98. Stockholm: Statistics Sweden.

SCB. (2004). *De äldres ekonomiska välfärd – inkomster, utgifter och förmögenheter*. Stockholm: Statistics Sweden.

SCB. (2005). *Barn och deras familjer 2004*. Stockholm: Statistics Sweden.

SCB. (2006). *Äldres levnadsförhållanden: Arbete, ekonomi, hälsa och sociala nätverk 1980–2003*. Stockholm: Statistics Sweden.

SD. (1996). *Ensamföräldrarna–en utsatt grupp?* Stockholm: Ministry of Health and Social Affairs.

Skevik, A. (2006). Lone motherhood in the Nordic countries: Sole providers in dual-breadwinner regimes. In A. L. Ellingsæter & A. Leira (Eds.), *Politicising parenthood in Scandinavia* (pp. 241–264). Bristol: The Policy Press.

Songur, W. (2002). *Välfärdsstaten, sociala rättigheter och invandrarnas maktresurser: En jämförande studie om äldre invandrare från Mellanöstern i Stockholm, London och Berlin*. Stockholm: Department of Political Science, Stockholm University.

SOU 2004:43. (2004). *Den könsuppdelade arbetsmarknaden*. Stockholm: Ministry of Industry, Employment and Communications.

SR. (2006). *Social rapport 2006*. Stockholm: National Board of Health and Social Welfare, www.socialstyrelsen.se. Accessed September, 6 2006.

SS. (2001). *Ekonomiskt bistånd årsstatistik 2000*. Stockholm: National Board of Health and Social Welfare, www.socialstyrelsen.se. Accessed September 6, 2006.

SS. (2006). *Ekonomiskt bistånd årsstatistik 2005*. Stockholm: National Board of Health and Social Welfare, www.socialstyrelsen.se. Accessed September 8, 2006.

Stark, A. (1993). A scheme for analyzing work—a tentative approach. Paper presented at the "Out of the margin. Feminist perspectives on economic theory" International Conference 2–5 June 1993, Amsterdam, The Netherlands.

Stark, A., & Regnér, Å. 1997. Arbete—vem behöver, vem utför, vem betalar? En analysmodell med genusperspektiv. In A. Stark (Ed.), *Ljusnande framtid eller ett längt farväl? Den svenska välfärdsstaten i jämförande belysning* (SOU 1997:115) (pp. 37–98). Stockholm: Ministry of Labour Market Affairs.

SV. (2007). *Barns omsorg 2005: Omsorgsformer för barn 1–12*. Stockholm: The Swedish National Agency for Education, www.skolverket.se. Accessed January 28, 2008.

Szebehely, M. (1998). Changing divisions of carework: Caring for children and frail elderly people in Sweden. In J. Lewis (Ed.), *Gender, social care and welfare state restructuring in Europe* (pp. 254–283). Aldershot: Ashgate.

Therborn, G. (1993). The politics of childhood: The rights of children in modern times. In F. G. Castles (Ed.), *Families of nations: Patterns of public policy in western democracies* (pp. 241–291). Aldershot: Dartmouth.

Tilton, T. (1990). *The political theory of Swedish social democracy*. Oxford: Clarendon Press.

Winkler, C. (2002). *Single mothers and the state: The politics of care in Sweden and the United States*. Lanham, MD: Rowman & Littlefield.

# 3

# FEMINIZATION OF POVERTY IN FRANCE: A LATENT ISSUE

*Claude Martin*

## Introduction

To what extent is poverty gendered in France? Do the available data for the past decades show that poverty is feminized? And is women's poverty an issue in the public and political debate? In the French case, this last question is problematic. At first glance, it is tempting to answer positively, as gender inequalities are regularly pointed up and condemned, whether about salary, division of domestic labor, working conditions, or violence (INSEE, 1995; Milewski, Dauphin, Kesteman, Letablier, & Meda, 2005). But, in fact, political attention focuses much more on some other fragile social groups: young people, immigrants, or lonely and excluded men (Smith, 2004). Even though political attention to poverty and social exclusion pays scant attention to lone mothers and lone elderly women, a detailed analysis of recent trends shows a deterioration in their condition. Furthermore, there is an important difference in public concern for these two groups. Whereas lone parents have been identified as vulnerable for a long time, that is much less the case for lone elderly women whose economic situation improved noticeably during the past decades.

The French situation is thus apparently paradoxical, for we have to underscore, at the same time, an important reduction of poverty between 1970 and 1990, an improvement in the economic situation of the female elderly, and a real conquest of the labor market by women during the same period. Nonetheless there has been a decline in the economic situation of lone mothers and the development of job insecurity and precariousness despite their increased activation rates. The global financial crisis that erupted in 2008 is, of course, affecting the economic condition of a much wider group in the population. Women could be among the big losers, and their higher risk of poverty could be even less noticed amidst the general increase in economic insecurity.

Before presenting the data concerning these two groups, it is first necessary to describe the economic context and to emphasize that feminized poverty has been mainly an issue of family policy.

## Poverty and Precariousness

The poverty rate depends on the overall condition of a country's economy. The diagnosis of the French economy in the past decade is subject to debate, in particular the past few years. According to official national statistics (INSEE), income inequality and poverty declined during the past 30 years, as did the gap between male and female salaries. Over the same period, the gender gap in the labor market was also significantly reduced: 3.9 million women joined the labor market, compared to only 422,000 men. This means that 90% of the jobs created during this period went to women. During this time, too, the poverty of older people fell considerably.

There is controversy over recent employment trends in France and an alleged recovery. According to INSEE, the French statistical office, around 150,000 new jobs were created in 2005. INSEE also reported a decreasing unemployment rate between 2005 and 2007: from 9.7% in February 2006 to 8.0% in July 2007, the lowest since 1983. However, women still had a higher level of unemployment (8.5% compared to 7.4% for men).

The improvement in the unemployment rate has been contested by experts. In fact, determination of the actual rate of unemployment was postponed until after the election of spring 2007. To aid the conservative candidate's chances, the conservative government claimed that the unemployment rate fell significantly before the election. In any case, even the government's lower figure was still one of the highest rates of unemployment in Europe.[1] Moreover, this indicator does not say anything about the real situation of the labor market, that is, about the growth of precariousness or job insecurity. In fact, poverty has stayed the same since 1990, and precariousness is growing dramatically (Maurin & Savidan, 2007, 2008). The economist, Pierre Concialdi (2006, p. 20), recently made this pessimistic assessment of labor market trends:

> From the beginning of the 1980s, temporary employment or part-time jobs increased drastically: five times more temporary jobs, four times more fixed-term contracts (*Contrat à durée determinée*), three times more apprenticeships, professional training, unpaid work experience (*stages*) and "protected" jobs (*emplois aidés*),[2] and the people affected by underemployment more than

> doubled. In all, the amount of precarious employment increased by 2.5 million between 1983 and 2005, which represents more than 60% of the new salaried jobs in the period (4 million).

If we consider the situation in 2003, about 4 million people had precarious jobs, representing 16% of the labor force. And if we add the unemployed (2,656,000 people in 2003 or about 10% of the active population) to this precarious group, what Castel (2006) terms the "précariat"[3] included 6.6 million people (see also Castel, Fitoussi, Freyssinet, & Guaino, 1997).

And the picture is still grimmer, in particular for women, if we go beyond the International Labour Organization's (ILO's) very restricted definition of unemployment. The ILO definition does not include "discouraged" unemployed workers (760,000 people of whom 56% were women in 2001); the "unavailable" unemployed who cannot take a job immediately, mainly because of care responsibilities (220,000 workers, of whom two-thirds are women); and those who worked very few (but more than 1 hour during the week previous to the employment inquiry), which means that they are excluded from the statistics of unemployment because they are considered as employed, even if they were working only 1 hour during the week of reference (994,000 people of whom three-fifths are women) (Maruani, 2006).[4] Also not counted were underemployed people, people who work part-time but would like to work more (almost a million women or 8.6% of all women in the labor market, compared to 323,000 men or 2.4% of male workers) (Maruani & Méron, 2008). In this deteriorated labor market, the more vulnerable are young people, women, generally, and lone mothers, particularly, for whom the disadvantages are multiple.

Thus precariousness is a common experience of a sizable part of the French population. Many of them are afraid to be fired from their jobs in this context of massive unemployment; many others have an income just above the poverty threshold. France is also discovering the phenomenon of the "working poor" (Clerc, 2008). "In 2005, 3.7 million workers earned less than the poverty threshold, because they were alternately working and unemployed (1.2 million), had a part-time job (1.3 million), earned insufficient income even with a full-time job (e.g., self-employed, child minders, concierge, apprentice)" (Clerc, 2008, p. 30). One of the main causes of the problem is part-time jobs, and these are almost exclusively women's jobs. To earn more than the poverty threshold in 2005, a single person had to work at least 132 hours per month at the minimum wage (SMIC) (see Glossary).

In regard to the employment "recovery," Florence Jany-Catrice notes that the majority of the new jobs created during the 1990s were unskilled (more than 6% per year between 1994 and 2002). In 2003, there were 5.3 million of these jobs, 80% of them held by women, half of whom were working part-time, mainly involuntarily (e.g., as housekeepers, child minders, elderly carers, employees in catering services, cashiers, salespeople, etc.). Forty percent of these jobs were paid less than half the median salary. Most were incompatible with parental responsibilities (fragmented hours of work, late in the evenings or very early in the mornings, week-ends, etc.).

So, if the number of people in poverty decreased significantly between 1970 and 1990 (from approximately 6 million to 3.9 million people[5]), since 1990, the poverty rate has been stable, still affecting 3.7 million people in 2003. Since 2004, however, poverty has risen—up to 4.2 million people in 2006 or a poverty rate of 7.1%.[6] That same year, 3.5 million people were receiving one of the nine different French minimum incomes. Of these, 1.28 million people were beneficiaries of the *revenu minimum d'insertion* (RMI), the principal minimum income (see Glossary for definitions of income support programs). This was twice the number whose incomes had to be supplemented by the RMI in 1990.

In this context—a deteriorating labor market in which women are disproportionately affected—feminized poverty should be a very central issue in France. However, this is not really the case. Nonetheless, the economic and social inequality of lone parents is certainly more visible than that of lone elderly women.

## The Family as a Pillar of the French Welfare System

The French welfare state is generally considered one of the Bismarckian welfare regimes that are based on social insurance (Esping-Andersen, 1990; Palier & Martin, 2007). Nevertheless, compared to the archetypical German welfare system, the French regime is also characterized by a strong and explicit family policy. It has even been said that the "family issue" is the basis of the French social security system, just as poverty is a cornerstone of the Anglo-Saxon welfare state, workers' status that of Germany's *Sozial Staat,* and citizen's social rights that of the universal social-democrat welfare system (Merrien, 1990). In France, family benefits may be understood as a social wage, a supplement to workers' salaries, a means of reducing inequality, and as one of the main pillars of the social welfare system (Friot, 1998). Initially focused on the fertility issue, French family policy goals moved dramatically since World War II. Looking backwards, one is inclined to differentiate four main phases that do not necessarily indicate real turning points, but rather a progressive reframing of family policy goals and a process of cumulative change:

- 1945–1965: The "Golden Age" of French family policy with strong incentives to promote fertility and subsidize the cost of children. This was the time of a universal and intense family policy that absorbed more than half of social security expenditures in the mid-1950s.
- 1965–1975: The "Women's Rights" revolution, with fundamental reforms of Civil Law concerning marriage (*réforme des régimes*

*matrimoniaux* in 1965), parental rights, and obligations (*autorité parentale* in 1970), descent (*filiation* in 1972), divorce (1975), abortion rights (1975).

- 1975–1990: Equity emphasis, with, as Lionel Stoléru (1977) stated, the "rediscovery of poverty in a rich country"; the recourse to means testing in family allowances and the creation of different minimum incomes to fight social exclusion, one for single parents, the *allocation de parent isolé* (API) and the other, RMI to supplement incomes below a defined threshold with different measures of training to facilitate return to the labor market.
- 1990–2008: Regulating unemployment and facilitating compatibility of work and family responsibilities (mainly for women) by means of policies such as subsidized child care, development of the number of declared child minders, and a flat-rate paid parental leave (Le Bihan & Martin, 2008; Lewis, Knijn, Martin, & Ostner, 2008).

So, part of women's claims and rights were dealt with through family policy (Villac, 1992). The central role of family policies in the French welfare system has had an impact on the economic situation of lone mothers and lone elderly women. For the former, the main turning point is unquestionably the creation of the API in 1976, a minimum income for those parents (almost exclusively mothers) with sole responsibility for one or more children, which was initially conceived as a maternal salary. For lone elderly women, the main policy instrument has been the creation, in 1935, of the *pension de reversion* that made it possible for an insured male worker to claim that half of his pension be provided to his wife in case of death, after her 55th birthday. This "indirect pension," based on a male breadwinner model, was reformed and improved in 1971 (*Loi Boulin*), and finally, in 1988, widowhood insurance was inaugurated. Then, despite continuing gender inequality, the development of female employment and lifetime professional careers improved the economic conditions of elderly women.

## Lone-Parent Families and Lone Mothers as Vulnerable Households

The percentage of lone-parent families increased in most European countries over the past two decades (Bradshaw et al., 1996; Chambaz, 2000; David, Eydoux, Martin, & Millar, 2004; Kiernan, Land, & Lewis, 1998; Lewis, 1997). This is particularly the case in France (INSEE, 1994; Lefaucheur & Martin, 1993, 1997). As a percentage of all families with children under 25 years, old, lone-parent families increased from 10% in

TABLE 3.1 Lone Mothers and Fathers as Percent of All Lone Parents in France and the United Kingdom

| | Divorced/Separated Mothers | Widowed Mothers | Never-Married Mothers | Lone Fathers |
|---|---|---|---|---|
| France | 48 | 9 | 29 | 14 |
| U.K. | 48 | 3 | 45 | 4 |

*Source*: INSEE, 1999.

1982 to 13.2% in 1990, 17% in 1999, and 20% in 2005.[7] In 2005, 1.76 million families were lone-parent families with at least one child under 25, in which 1486 were lone mothers' households. As in many other European countries, lone-parent families are mainly lone-mother households (85%), and the significant increase in their number is due to the increase in divorce (Martin, 1994). Between 1980 and 2003, the number of divorces for 100 marriages (registered the same year) grew from 22% to 43%, which means that the rate of divorces almost doubled during this period. In comparison, the increase in the United Kingdom was much smaller: from 38% to 45% over the same period. The percentage of lone parents who are fathers decreased from 20% in 1968 to 15% in 2005, due to the reduction in the number of widowers with children. Approximately half of French lone mothers are divorced or separated, approximately a third has never been married, and one in ten is a widow. By contrast, in the United Kingdom there is almost the same number of never married as divorced and separated mothers (Table 3.1).

In contrast to the United Kingdom and the United States, the absolute numbers and the percentage of teenage mothers is comparatively low in France. Three percent of lone mothers are below the age of 24, and 41% are in the 40–49 age group. The percentage of never married, lone parents (including mothers and fathers) doubled during the past two decades (from 15% to 32% between 1982 and 1999), but the fact remains that the majority of all French lone parents lived as couples before becoming lone parents.

The number of children living in a lone-parent household is another way to estimate the magnitude of this phenomenon. In 2005, 2.84 million children (under 25 years old) were living in a lone-parent household or 17.7% of all French children under 25 (compared to only 7.7% of in 1968).

Race and ethnicity are not systematically recorded in the French system of statistics. In 2004, approximately one lone-parent family in ten was an immigrant (or person born in a foreign country) (Tavan, 2005). In absolute numbers, it means that about 30,000 households are composed of an immigrant father with children, and 167,000 households are composed of an immigrant mother with children or 12% of the immigrant households. Thus, lone parenthood is less frequent in immigrant households. We also have information concerning the "overseas departments" (*départements d'Outre-mer*—DOM: Guadeloupe, Martinique, Guyane, La Réunion, Mayotte, and Saint-Pierre et Miquelon), where single mothers are generally younger and never married, and have a higher level of poverty and dependence on social assistance than single mothers in mainland France.[8]

## Poverty Trap

Lone-parent families are much more vulnerable to poverty than two-parent families (Duncan & Edwards, 1997). In 2004, 29% of poor families with children were headed by lone parents, and 92% of these poor lone parents were lone mothers. In 2005, 27% of lone-parent families were poor, compared to 12% of couples with children. Despite their high level of poverty and a rate more than twice that of partnered families, lone mothers were not the majority of poor families with children (CERC, 2004).

The poverty of lone mothers stems from their position in the labor market (Algava, Le Minez, Bressé, & Pla, 2005). Approximately two-thirds of both lone mothers and married mothers were working in 2004, and in the following year, the rates were 68% for lone mothers and 72% for partnered mothers (Chardon, Daguet, & Vivas, 2008). So, at first glance, the situation of lone mothers does not seem so different from that of partnered mothers. But, in fact, lone mothers are two times more likely to be unemployed, and a majority of them for more than 1 year (Table 3.2). Among young mothers less than age 35, the unemployment rate of lone mothers is twice that of those who are partnered (32% vs. 16%).

Lone mothers have lower levels of education than partnered mothers (26% without any degree, compared to 20% for partnered mothers; 23% with a university degree, compared to 30% for partnered mothers). Thus, lone mothers are more often low-skilled or blue-collar workers, and they are also more likely to have precarious jobs. In 2004, almost 10% of lone mothers had a fixed-term contract job, compared to 7% of partnered mothers. They are also more frequently in "protected jobs" or apprenticeships (4.3%) than partnered mothers (1.7%) (Chambaz & Martin, 2001; Eydoux, Letablier, & Georges, 2007). If lone mothers are less frequently working part time than partnered mothers (26% compared to 34% in 2005), they are nevertheless much more likely to experience underemployment. More than two-fifths (44%) of lone mothers working part time would like to work more hours, compared to 20% of partnered mothers working part time. Yet, lone mothers have a lower level of inactivity than partnered mothers, and the same is true when we compare lone fathers with partnered fathers. This demonstrates the importance of employment and earnings for these parents who usually have sole responsibility for supporting their children.

Lone mothers are also confronted with nonstandard work time that is particularly problematic because they usually have to manage work

TABLE 3.2 Employment, Unemployment, and Long-Term Unemployment of Lone Parents[a] Compared to Partnered Parents,[a] 2004

| | Lone Parents | Partnered Parents | Lone Mothers | Partnered Mothers | Lone Fathers | Partnered Fathers | All |
|---|---|---|---|---|---|---|---|
| Employment rate | 68.3 | 78.8 | 66.8 | 67.9 | 78.7 | 89.7 | 77.9 |
| Unemployment rate | 14.4 | 6.9 | 15.0 | 8.3 | 10.4 | 5.6 | 7.5 |
| Rate of long-term unemployment (more than a year) | 55.4 | 38.3 | 57.1 | 38.3 | 37.6 | 38.5 | 41.1 |
| Inactivity rate | 17.3 | 14.3 | 18.2 | 23.8 | 10.9 | 4.8 | 14.5 |

[a] These parents are with children less than 18 years old.

*Source*: INSEE, 2004.

and care responsibilities by themselves. In 2004, 8% of lone mothers were working at least some nights during the previous month; 26%, some evenings; 27%, some Sundays and holidays; and 50%, some Saturdays. Seven percent were shift workers, and 26% had hours that varied from one day to another (Eydoux et al., 2007). These constraints may explain why many young lone mothers remain at home (Martin, 2006).

Of course, the economic situation of lone-parent families varies depending on their position in the labor market. In 2001, 23% of lone parents, almost all lone mothers, were not receiving any salary, compared to only 4% of couples with children. Another 23% of lone parents were earning a salary lower or equal to the SMIC (minimum wage), compared to only 7% of couples with children.

Given the decline in the quality and quantity of employment, it is not surprising that the already critical economic situation of lone parents has deteriorated during the past two decades. For example, between 1984 and 1989, when the percentage of households living under the poverty threshold decreased from 11.1% to 10.3% for all households, it increased from 13.3% to 18.9% for lone mothers. In 1995, according to Lucile Olier and Nicolas Herpin (1997), almost one lone-parent family in five was living under this poverty threshold. At that time lone mother families were the most vulnerable type of households, even more vulnerable than large families. At the beginning of the twenty-first century, the disposable income of lone-parent households was 25% less than that of other households with dependent children.

TABLE 3.3 Poverty Rates[a] by Household Type and Labor Market Status, 2004

| Type of Households | Poverty Rate |
|---|---|
| Households with householders less than 65 | 6.9 |
| People living alone | 12.5 |
| Couples with or without children | 5.5 |
| Active man, inactive woman with one child | 8.0 |
| Active man, inactive woman with two children | 5.8 |
| Active man, inactive woman with three or more children | 10.2 |
| Active man and woman with one child | 2.6 |
| Active man and woman with two children | 2.7 |
| Active man and woman with three or more children | 4.8 |
| Lone-parent families | 12.2 |
| Lone fathers (active and inactive)[b] | 7.2 |
| Inactive lone mothers | 25.0 |
| Active lone mothers | 9.9 |
| All individuals | 6.2 |

[a] Poverty is defined as less than 50% of Median Disposable Income.

[b] Numbers of fathers are too small to distinguish between active and inactive. A large majority of them are active.

*Source*: INSEE-DGI, 2004.

The poverty of lone mothers is directly linked to their participation in the labor market (Table 3.3). While 10% of active lone mothers were poor, that was the case for 25% of inactive lone mothers. Compared to the situation of couples with one or two children, which are the most common numbers of children in lone-parent families, lone mothers always have a higher risk of poverty.

The number of lone parents receiving a minimum income is another way to estimate the precariousness of these households. In 2003, around 480,000 lone parents were receiving a minimum income or income support: 189,000 were receiving the benefit for lone parents, API,[9] and 290,000 were receiving the minimum-income benefit, RMI (Hennion, Nauze-Fichet, Cazin, & Donné, 2006; Nivière, Dindar, & Hennion, 2006). Lone-parent families represent more than one-fourth of all the beneficiaries of the RMI. In case of nonpayment of alimony, lone mothers (generally) can also receive a specific benefit to compensate for this nonpayment: the *Allocation de soutien familial*—ASF (see Glossary). The number of recipients of this guaranteed child support increased dramatically during the past decade, from 113,500 in 1994 to 686,000 in 2004, for a total cost of €1 million.

Social transfers play a very important role in reducing poverty in France. Laurent Caussat and colleagues estimate that as a result of the benefits for young children the income of dual career couples with young children increased by 7.6% in 2000, but these benefits increase the income of lone-parent households with young children by much more, 47%, the API (lone-parent benefit) contributing 15% of this increase (Caussat, Le Minez, & Pucci, 2003).

Some more recent data complete this picture (Table 3.4). For couples with children, poverty was reduced 65% by transfers in 2001, and the rate for lone-parent families was just slightly higher, 67% or by two-thirds. Family transfers play the largest role in poverty reduction for couples and their children (44%), while housing transfers are especially important for lone-parent families, cutting their poverty rate by just over half.

Even with these different types of support, it is once again important to emphasize the deterioration of the social and economic situation of lone-parent families. For example, we can call attention to the increasing number of them dependent on a minimum income. The number of API recipients rose from 163,000 in 1998 to 206,000 in 2005, an increase of 24%, with the bigger rise during the last 3 years (13%) (Table 3.5).

The rise is even greater for lone parents' receipt of the RMI. In December 2003, 260,000 lone-parent families were receiving the RMI. If we consider 1994 as the point of departure, the number of lone parents receiving the RMI between then and 2003 increased by 53% (Clément, Mathieu, & Mahieu, 2005, Figure 3.1). This trend in RMI use is even more important for lone-parent families than for the total population, as shown in Figure 3.2. While the number of RMI recipients in the total population

TABLE 3.4 Rate of Poverty[a] of Lone-Parent Households before and after Social Transfers, Compared to Other Households, 2001

| | Before Social Transfers | After Family Transfers | And after Minimum Income | And after Housing Transfers | After All Social Transfers |
|---|---|---|---|---|---|
| Lone-parent families | 41.7 | 33.2 | 29.1 | 14.0 | 13.9 |
| Couples with dependent children | 17.9 | 10.0 | 9.3 | 6.2 | 6.2 |
| All households with dependent children | 20.5 | 12.6 | 11.5 | 7.1 | 7.1 |
| All households | 15.8 | NA | NA | 6.1 | NA |

[a] Poverty is defined as less than 50% of Median Disposable Income.

*Source*: Algava et al., 2005.

TABLE 3.5 Number of API[a] Recipients (in Thousands) and Percent Increase between 1998 and 2005

| API | 1998 | 1999 | 2000 | 2001 | 2002 | 2003 | 2004 | 2005 | 1998–2005 |
|---|---|---|---|---|---|---|---|---|---|
| Number in thousands | 163 | 168 | 170 | 177 | 181 | 189 | 197 | 206 | |
| Percent increase | | 3.1 | 1.2 | 4.1 | 2.3 | 4.4 | 4.2 | 4.6 | 26.4 |

[a] *allocation de parent isolé*

*Source*: CNAF-2006.

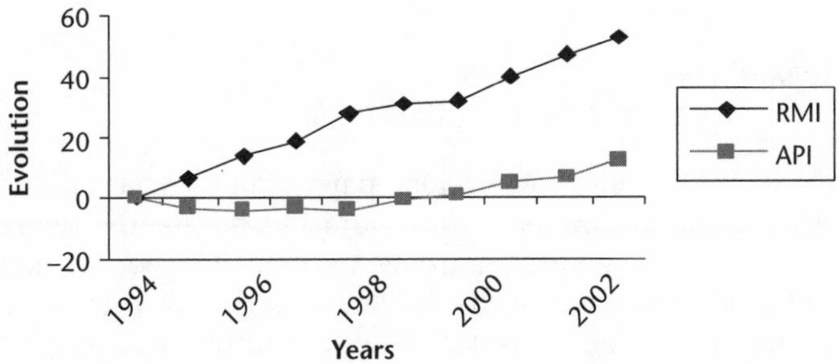


**Figure 3.1.** Evolution of lone-parent families receiving API and RMI (base 100 in 1994).
*Abbreviation*: API, *allocation de parent isolé;* RMI, *revenu minimum d'insertion.*
*Source*: Clément, Mathieu, & Mahieu, 2005.

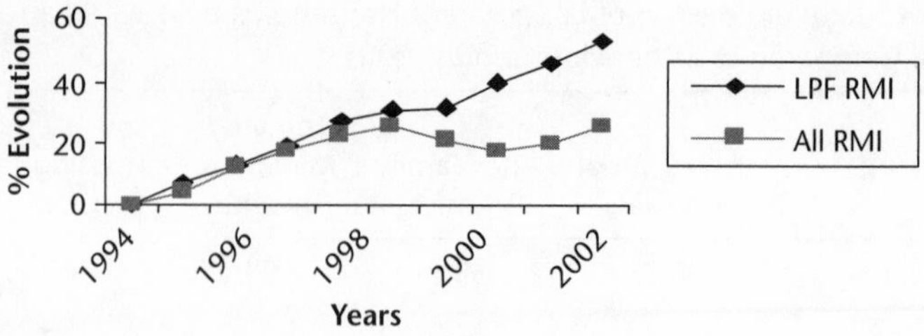


**Figure 3.2.** Evolution of lone-parent families receiving RMI compared to all RMI recipients.
*Abbreviation*: LPF, *lone parent families;* RMI, *revenu minimum d'insertion.*
*Source*: Clément, Mathieu, & Mahieu, 2005.

decreased between 1998 and 2002, the number of lone-parent families using it increased.

Child care for children under 3 years, an important component of family policy in France, plays a crucial redistributive role, with a special impact on lone-mother households (DREES, 2000; Leprince & Martin, 2003; Le Bihan & Martin, 2008). This policy is twofold. On the one hand, the objective is to facilitate work/family balance by the development of public services, but, mainly nowadays, with some specific benefits to help parents recruit child-care assistants and child minders (AFEAMA, AGED, and PAJE, see Glossary) (Fagnani, 2000; Martin, Math, & Renaudat, 1998). On the other hand, the availability of a low-paid, flat-rate parental leave facilitates exit from the labor market of nonqualified and unemployed mothers with young children, a group that includes many young lone mothers (Périvier, 2003; Piketty, 2005). Almost all children from 3 to 6 years old have access to preschool, and so do about 35% of the 2 to 3 year olds.[10] Children under 3 are also cared for in public *crèches* and in other settings (*halte-garderie* or parental crèches).[11]

### Policies toward Lone-Parent Families: From a Protective to an Activating Welfare State

Since the mid-1970s, policy toward lone-parent families has pursued three main objectives: to guarantee a minimum income for the poorest (and often also the youngest) single parents; to make it easier for mothers to work by offering extensive child-care facilities; and to provide a benefit (advanced maintenance) in case of nonpayment of child support. As in other European countries, policy has taken a new turn in the past decade, with the main focus on employment and activating policies (Knijn, Martin, & Millar, 2007). In this section, we focus on minimum-income policy and its evolution.

In the mid-1970s, French family policies were significantly reformed to support the more fragile households (Le Gall & Martin, 1987; Martin, 1997a, 1997b; Martin-Papineau, 2003). As mentioned before, a new allowance, the API or lone-parent allowance, was created in 1976 to guarantee a minimum income for all lone-parent families whose resources were under a specified threshold. We may consider this new policy a real turning point in French family policy in the sense that the objective became more and more to support the poorer families. Other minimum incomes and means-tested benefits were created at the same time, such as the minimum income for handicapped people (*allocation adulte handicapé*) and the new school year allowance (*allocation de rentrée scolaire*), to give different types of support to more disadvantaged groups.

The creation of the API took place in a specific context. At the time, the political debate defended this measure as a mean to facilitate "free choice" for mothers, between employment and staying home, so that there was no social discrimination between women who worked outside the home and those who devoted themselves exclusively to domestic and caring tasks. Simone Veil, Minister of Health at the time, presented this measure in the Parliament as addressed primarily to housewives who have lost access to income, due to the death or the departure of their partner or breadwinner. Amendments extended the access to pregnant and abandoned women and then to men (hence the name "single *parent* benefit"). This system had two other objectives: avoiding recourse to social assistance for children and preventing abortion.[12] During the debate in the Assembly, some critics expressed concern over the risk of fraud. But the main problem obviously was access to the labor market when the right to receive the API came to an end,[13] and some amendments tried to support access to professional training for these beneficiaries.

While the consensus on the creation of the API was quite evident during the debates in the Parliament and the Senate, the implementation of this measure and the increase in the number of its beneficiaries—which rapidly exceeded the 53,000 initially anticipated—caused much criticism from some experts and politicians (Bichot, 1992; Dumont, 1986; Sullerot, 1984). Thus, the lone-parent allowance was strongly criticized in the mid-1980s. Some argued that it had "perverse effects." For example, the beneficiaries of the API were suspected of hiding the existence of a new partner or even "scheduling" a new birth to continue to receive the benefit. The economic dependency of these lone parents, mostly lone mothers, was firmly condemned (Sullerot, 1984), and some proposals to abolish the API were formulated, but never implemented. One of the main issues was the risk of increasing the economic dependency of these women on the State. This issue of disincentive to work then retreated with the appearance of the "new poverty" issue.

Contrary to what happened in the United States and the United Kingdom, where many lone mothers were regarded as dependent on the welfare state because they were not working, lone parenthood was not considered a major social problem in the decade from 1985 to 1995. No significant reform happened during that period. The political agenda was more concerned about social exclusion of single men (without a family) than about lone-parent families. The issue of "dependence on welfare" reappeared at the end of 1995 in the introduction to the "Juppé plan" for social welfare reform. Two parliamentary reports were devoted to this problem,[14] both with quite strong moral and reproving components. However, once again, no reform was adopted.

At the end of the 1990s, most of the social policy reform debate was over the way to finance the *Allocation de parent isolé* and to bring together the API and the RMI to obtain a more coherent policy toward the most fragile households. During the "Conference on Family Issues" of 1998, some reform proposals concerning minimum incomes emerged. The Thélot-Villac report (1998) suggested financing the API with income taxes, along with the RMI. The objective was to reduce the weight of this allowance on payroll taxes. Two successive official reports also suggested merging the API and RMI into a single allowance (Fragonard, 1993; Join-Lambert, 1998): 45% of the ex-beneficiaries of API were indeed receiving RMI, a frequent trajectory for those who received API up to the legal limit (see Box 3.1).

**Box 3.1: Differences between API and RMI**

There is quite an important difference between these two minimum incomes. First, the API benefit is higher than RMI: for example, an adult with one child will receive €755 plus €100 to help with housing but only €670 in the same situation with the RMI scheme. The proposal was therefore to bring the RMI up to the level of the API. Second, the difference is also a symbolic one. API is conceived as a replacement income or as a "maternal salary" without any obligation to enter or return immediately to the labor market. So, going from the API to the RMI is perceived as a failure by the recipients. API is a benefit whose main objective is to give the claimant an opportunity to take care of her/his child for a specified period of time. Almost 60% of API cases ended at the legal period for receipt of the benefit (12 months or until the third birthday of the youngest child). If the API ends before the legal period, it is due to the reconstitution of a couple in almost 25% of the cases. Those cases in which the beneficiaries are living as a couple again are mainly young people with few children.[15] The suspension of the API was due to an increase of incomes in only 11% of the cases (Chaupin & Guillot, 1998). For beneficiaries of RMI, the end of the benefit is due to the resumption of work in only half the cases. The other terminations are mainly due to a modification in the family situation. Most of those who return to the labor market find a part-time job of less than 30 hours a week.

To avoid the work disincentive of minimum-income benefits, it has been possible, since 1988, to combine the API or RMI with an earned income (a *mécanisme d'intéressement* or incentive to reenter the labor market without an immediate cancellation of the benefit).[16] The whole earned income can be drawn concurrently with the benefit during the first 3 months. Then, for the following 9 months, 50% of the earned income is taken into consideration in determining the benefit. This mechanism works only when the earned income is lower than €670 (which is less income than full time at the SMIC). So it concerns only poorly paid or part-time jobs. In August 1998, almost 30% of the 220,000 lone parents on RMI (66,000 lone-parent families) were also earning an income. This gives an indication of how many lone parents were "working poor." In 1999, 132,000 people receiving the RMI (12% of the beneficiaries) were taking advantage of this welfare to work incentive, including 13% of the lone-parent families receiving the RMI (Rastier & Maingueneau, 2006).

In 2000, the API was paid to 169,000 beneficiaries (about 12% of lone-parent families) at an overall expenditure of €716 million. Sixty-one percent of the beneficiaries were under 30 years of age, and almost all of them were lone mothers. Overall, however, the visibility of the problem of lone-parent families was still relatively weak. The issue was more general—that of all poor households. It is furthermore remarkable and significant that the report from the National Observatory on Poverty and Social Exclusion in 2000 made no mention of lone-parent families (*Observatoire national de la pauvreté et de l'exclusion sociale*, 2000). This is in line with the fact that practically no new extensive research has been undertaken on these households over the last decade, whereas the problem of single and homeless men has received a lot more attention.

The work incentive was still considered too weak, even if many beneficiaries preferred to have a job rather than to receive a minimum income. So the reforms at the end of the 1990s concerned all the French minimum incomes and not only the API. The objective was to maintain a minimum income and to sustain all the motivations of the beneficiaries to return to the labor market. Jean-Michel Belorgey's report, *Minima sociaux, revenus d'activité, précarité* (2000), confirmed the suggestion of merging the API and RMI, with an increased rate for recipients caring for a child. It also suggested revising the scale of the RMI benefit to take a better account of the cost of a child in the household and to extend the time when the beneficiary could combine the benefit with a salary. These proposals were still on the political agenda at the time of the right-wing political turn of May 2002.[17]

One of the projects of the right-wing government of Jean-Pierre Raffarin most clearly directed toward a work requirement or workfare was the establishment of a "minimum activity income" (*Revenu minimum d'activité*—RMA) (approved by the Senate in May 2003) and the decentralization of the administration of the RMI. It is no longer a question of lone-parent families, even if this measure will have an impact on them. The main difference from the previous bills is that the rationale of workfare was emphasized by the Raffarin government. Hence, for example, the Minister of Social Affairs, Employment and Solidarity indicated in October 2002 that it was a matter of "trying to see how to require, even if this is sometimes symbolic, a job in exchange for an income" (Dollé, 2003).[18]

The rationale of the RMA is a right to government support with the obligation to accept a job or lose the support. This logic of *contrepartie* (accepting a job offer in return for social assistance) had already been an important part of the political debate before creating the RMI in 1988. It is also precisely the sense of the logic of workfare that is being adopted in several European countries and the United States. The difference between France and the United Kingdom in regard to workfare is that French policy is not particularly aimed at lone mothers, since a majority of them already work, but at all beneficiaries of a minimum income, including some lone mothers, who, after the termination of the API, are paid the RMI. They are affected by this policy although it is not necessarily aimed at them, contrary to the United Kingdom where single mothers represent a considerable percentage of "socially assisted persons."

A return to a less punitive orientation and/or an activation policy was adopted in 2005 to promote employment of the minimum-income recipients: the *contrat d'avenir*, adopted inside the *loi de programmation pour la cohésion sociale* in March.[19] If we consider the RMI recipients concerned by these two specific contracts in September 2006, the numbers are 9200 RMA and 44,700 *contrats d'avenir*. If we add the beneficiaries of the different programs (*mesures d'intéressement*, RMA, and *contrat d'avenir*), they totaled 158,300 people in September 2006, with an increase during the previous year (September 2005–September 2006) of 8.8% (Rastier & Maingueneau, 2006).

The successive right-wing governments of Jean-Pierre Raffarin (May 2002–May 2005) and Dominique de Villepin (May 2005–May 2007) decided to accentuate the activation policies, with the objective of reducing the high level of unemployment in France and the number of recipients of the various minimum incomes (e.g., employment premium or *prime pour l'emploi*, tax credits and the welfare to work incentives or *mécanismes d'intéressement*). The system that allowed minimum-income recipients to combine a salary with the RMI (which had been possible from the inception of the RMI in 1988) and with the API from 1998 onward was reformed in 2001. The possibility of combining a salary and a minimum income was extended for a period of 6 months. For the following three trimesters, only half of the recipient's salary is counted in calculating the amount of the minimum income.[20]

The number of minimum-income (API or RMI) recipients affected by these "welfare to work" and workfare incentives and who combine a salary with a minimum income was more or less stable from 2000 to 2005: between 12.5% and 13.5% for RMI recipients and between 5% and 6% for API recipients. In 2005, this system included 143,000 people receiving the RMI and 11,500 people receiving the API.[21]

The decentralization of the RMI after the law of December 18, 2003, had the same objective: to increase the efficiency of the administration of the minimum-income programs. But the results are still uncertain. The RMA was not successful (very few beneficiaries along with substantial resistance of the local administrations that implement this measure), and it is doubtful that the local authorities (mainly left-wing elected representatives) have increased their pressure on the recipients. Thus, it is difficult to argue that France is pursuing a real workfare strategy, compared, for example, to the United States. If it was the intention of the successive right-wing governments, it has not really been implemented. We still need more precise and local evaluation to know more about the direct impact on the users (Le Bihan, Martin, & Rivard, 2006). The process of reform has continued after the 2007 elections, as we will indicate in our conclusion.

## Poverty of Lone Elderly Women: A Less Visible Issue

The poverty of lone elderly women is less visible in the French political debate than lone-mother poverty. This relative invisibility is linked to the fact that the risk of poverty for this category of people is much smaller than for lone parents. Nevertheless, the economic condition of this group of women appeared recently as an issue in the Presidential campaign that ended with the election of Nicolas Sarkozy in April 2007. When considering the level of women's pensions, and in particular the level of the "indirect" pension that widows are receiving after the death of their husbands (*pension de réversion*), both main candidates (Ségolène Royal and Nicolas Sarkozy) promised an increase of these pensions to compensate for the important gender inequality in the older population.

The number of lone elderly women is a first source of inequality. Owing to the gap between the average life expectancy of men and women (77 years at birth for men and 84 for women) and the fact that women tend to marry men older than they, the percentage of women living alone is much larger than that of men. In 2004, 20% of women were living alone at 60 years of age, 32% at 70, and 52% at 80. It goes up to 57% for those 85 and 86 years old. The percentages for men are much lower: 12% at 60 years old, 13% at 70 years old, and 19% at 80 years old. These figures reveal a huge difference in the late life trajectories of women and men. Many more women than men are getting older alone (INSEE, 2005).[22]

When we consider women 65 years and older, 46% are widows, 42% married, 7% nonmarried, and 5.5% divorced. Even though the proportion still remains small, the number of divorces for people aged more than 65 is five times more than it was in 1970. Both social class and gender play a role in the disadvantage of some older women. Because life expectancy is lower for the less skilled or more disadvantaged population, women of this class are more likely to be confronted with widowhood and loneliness at an earlier age (Delbès & Gaymu, 2005).

In all, 2 million French women over 65 were living alone in 2004. In the last employment inquiry, only 50,000 were still in the labor market after 65, that is, 0.25%. In the last census, in 1999, a majority of these elderly women were or had been *employees* (a large category that includes relatively low-skilled wage workers in the private and public sector, mainly office workers and workers in services) (42%); factory workers (23%); less frequently, farmers (11%); middle-class professionals (12%); and executives (3)%.

The percentage of immigrant elderly people is a bit lower than for the total population: in 2004, 7% of the elderly persons aged 75 and older were immigrants, while immigrants represented 8.1% of the total population (Borrel, 2006). This lower level of female immigrants in the older age groups is a result of the predominance of male workers in the older waves of immigration. Since 1974, immigration has been mainly of women for family reunification.

## Level of Income and Risk of Poverty

The standard of living of elderly people (more than 65 years of age) has increased considerably (by 40%) since the mid-1970s, and this evolution went hand-in-hand with a reduction of the inequalities among elderly households (Baclet, 2006). In fact, poverty of the elderly as a whole declined, mainly because of women's increased access to full pensions that, in turn, is related to women's increased participation in the labor force. The median income of the households where the adult householder is more than 65 years old went up from €11,000 in 1975 (constant 2001€) to €15,600 in 2001, an increase of over 40%. This standard of living decreases with age because the older members of the group are mainly lone women who have worked little or not at all. Their resources are small because they consist mainly of indirect pensions from their husbands (*pension de reversion*). The younger they are, the longer and more complete their careers are likely to have been, and consequently the higher their personal pensions. Nevertheless, the gender inequality remains important due to the greater likelihood that women work part time and to the difference in the salaries of men and women (Bonnet, Buffeteau, & Godefroy, 2006).

Some elderly people are receiving a minimum income called *minimum vieillesse*. Created in 1956, this benefit guarantees a minimum income for people aged 65 and over[23] whose resources are below a certain level. In 2005, the *minimum vieillesse* for a single person was €660 per month[24] (and €810 for a couple). Since the beginning of the 1960s, the number of recipients declined steadily, due to the extension and improvement of pensions. This reduction was approximately 5% per year between 1983 and 2003. Since 2003, the number of people receiving the *minimum vieillesse* stabilized at 600,000 of whom 60% are women. Half of the women receiving the elderly minimum income are 80 years old and over whereas only 20% of male recipients are in that age range.

TABLE 3.6 Mean Level of Pensions (Per Month in Euros), by Gender and Age, 2001

| Age | 65–69 | 70–74 | 75–79 | 80–84 | 85+ | Total 65+ |
|---|---|---|---|---|---|---|
| Women | | | | | | |
| Personal pension (droits directs) | 666 | 619 | 587 | 566 | 506 | 606 |
| Reversion benefit | 101 | 151 | 206 | 252 | 280 | 175 |
| Minimum vieillesse | 7 | 8 | 10 | 13 | 24 | 11 |
| Indirect advantages[a] | 31 | 30 | 30 | 33 | 25 | 30 |
| Total pension | 805 | 808 | 833 | 864 | 835 | 822 |
| Men | | | | | | |
| Personal pension (droits directs) | 1393 | 1374 | 1373 | 1392 | 1187 | 1372 |
| Reversion benefit | 4 | 7 | 10 | 15 | 19 | 8 |
| Minimum vieillesse | 6 | 7 | 8 | 9 | 18 | 8 |
| Indirect advantages[a] | 63 | 68 | 73 | 71 | 63 | 67 |
| Total pension | 1466 | 1456 | 1464 | 1487 | 1287 | 1455 |

[a] Bonus for children, bonus for a third party assistance, bonus for a dependent partner.

*Source*: Ministry of Social Affairs, 2001.

In 2001, retired women (more than 65) were receiving a mean pension of €606 per month, based on their own contributions during their working life (*droits directs*). This level of pension is less than half of the mean pension for men of the same age (€1372) (Table 3.6). This gap stems mainly from the difference in their respective careers: While 85% of men have a full working life, this is the case for only 37% of women; while men, on average, contribute toward their pensions for 169 trimesters, women, on average, only contribute for 119. Even when women have a full working life, their personal pensions are 35% less than those of men who work and contribute a comparable length of time (Burricand & Deloffre, 2006). As Table 3.6 shows, men aged 65 and over, on average, have monthly incomes from pensions 77% more than women of the same age.

As for the *pension de reversion*, not surprisingly, it is provided to 36% of female pensioners (more than age 65), compared to only 4% of male pensioners. This gap between men's and women's careers and levels of pensions is getting smaller over the generations. Women are more and more likely to have full working lives, so their contributory personal pensions are increasing. Table 3.6 presents the level of these pensions and their composition for men and women in 2001. As shown, the level of the personal pension is getting bigger for the younger generations, and the level of the *pension de reversion* is getting smaller. Nevertheless, the younger generations of women receive on average a lower total pension than the older ones, because the rise in *droits directs* is less than the reduction in the *reversion*.

The increase in the number of separations and divorces will augment this gender gap. Because lone mothers are much more vulnerable to

TABLE 3.7 Distribution of Total Pensions of Women and Men, 60–69 Years Old, 2004, Percentages

| Euros | Less Than 700 | 700–900 | 900–1100 | 1100–1300 | 1300–1600 | 1600–2000 | More Than 2000 |
|---|---|---|---|---|---|---|---|
| Men | 8 | 8 | 10 | 12 | 20 | 17 | 26 |
| Women | 36 | 15 | 13 | 9 | 10 | 9 | 8 |
| Total | 22 | 8 | 11 | 12 | 14 | 13 | 17 |

*Source*: Burricand & Deloffre, 2006.

TABLE 3.8 Poverty Rates[a] by Age of Householder, 1975 and 2001

| Age | 1975 | 2001 |
|---|---|---|
| 65–69 | 13.0 | 3.8 |
| 70–74 | 14.4 | 3.1 |
| 75+ | 21.0 | 4.1 |

[a] Poverty is defined as less than 50% of Median Disposable Income.

*Source*: INSEE, 2005, p. 120.

unemployment and low wages, they will certainly face a much more precarious economic situation and small pensions in their late life.

In 2001, the mean, total pension of women aged 65–69 years old was €805, compared to €1466 for men. The distribution of these pensions is very unequal: just over half of female pensioners was receiving a pension smaller than €900 (compared to only 16% of men) (Table 3.7).

The economic situation of the elderly has improved during the past decades; their poverty rate is half that of the younger population (less than 65). In 1975, the situation was the reverse: the risk of poverty for people more than 65 years old was double that of the younger population. It means that the poverty rate of the people living in a household where the householder was more than 65 at the beginning of the period was between 3.4 and 5.1 times what it was at the end of the period, depending on the age group (Table 3.8).

In 1975, people living in a household where the householder was more than 75 years old had a poverty risk of 21%. In 2001, this risk of poverty for the same group was one-fifth the former rate. But this situation varies drastically depending on the composition of the household. The poverty rate of people 65 or older was 3.5% in 2001, but 6.7%, almost double, for women of that age living alone. Women over age 65 who live alone are three-quarters of the poor people in that age group. The poverty of the lone elderly is clearly feminized.

Table 3.9 shows that age, gender, and marital status are important determinants of poverty. First, the poverty rate is much higher for younger

TABLE 3.9 Number and Percent of People in Poverty[a] by Gender and Age, 2004, in Thousands

| | Women | | Men | |
|---|---|---|---|---|
| | Number | Poverty Rate | Number | Poverty Rate |
| Less than 18 | 520 | 8.1 | 503 | 7.4 |
| 18–24 | 237 | 9.7 | 210 | 8.5 |
| 25–34 | 222 | 5.6 | 220 | 5.6 |
| 35–44 | 281 | 6.5 | 258 | 6.1 |
| 45–54 | 304 | 7.2 | 245 | 6.1 |
| 55–64 | 151 | 4.6 | 190 | 6.0 |
| 65–74 | 89 | 3.2 | 31 | 1.3 |
| 75 and more | 133 | 4.8 | 42 | 2.5 |
| Total | 1936 | 6.4 | 1699 | 6.0 |

[a] Poverty is defined as less than 50% of Median Disposable Income.

*Source*: INSEE, 2004.

people. Second, there is a large gender gap: in the 65–74 year age range, a woman has a poverty risk 2.5 times that of a man and twice the risk for those 75 years and older. To recall, the poverty rate for inactive lone mothers the same year was 25%, which means a risk five times that of a woman 75 years old or more and 3.7 times that of the higher-risk elderly women, that is, older women living alone whose poverty rate is 6.7%.

This improvement in the economic situation of seniors is threatened by labor market decline. Indeed, the risk of poverty for aged people has been increasing since the end of the 1990s, due to forced early retirement. France is characterized by a very low level of employment of 55–64 year olds, called "senior workers" (with a reduction of 43% over the period 1971–2001) (Guillemard, 2003). When workers (in particular in the private sector) lose their jobs around their fifties, their chances of getting back in the labor market are extremely weak, even when the economy is in recovery. So, senior workers are particularly vulnerable to unemployment. That is the reason why a majority of men and women among the young pensioners (less than 70 years old at the end of the 1990s) have experienced unemployment and/or inactivity before becoming eligible for pensions. This phenomenon will have an impact on the level of pensions in the next 5 years.

Another problem contributes directly to the relative disadvantage of lone elderly women: the risk of incapacity, chronic diseases, or dependence. This "risk of dependence"—that is, the need to receive help for daily tasks (meals, washing, housekeeping, dressing, etc.)—has only very recently been recognized by the public authorities. This risk is directly linked to aging, and, given the gender gap, also to gender (Gisserot & Grass, 2007). Dependence goes hand-in-hand with poverty and loneliness. So it is important to emphasize that gender inequalities go beyond the strict economic dimension.

In France, the number of dependent elderly people needing help with daily tasks is about a million. Between 1997 and 2002, a social assistance scheme for poorer and more dependent elderly was implemented: the *prestation spécifique dependence*—PSD (see Glossary); but there were only 150,000 recipients at the end of the period. To make sure that public intervention was secondary to family solidarity local authorities were allowed to recover the expenditure for this social benefit from inheritances. This public response was absolutely insufficient (covering only 15% of the people in need of care and support) and very much criticized by professionals in this sector (Martin, 2003; Martin et al., 1998).

In January 2002, the socialist government of Lionel Jospin created a new scheme called the *Allocation personnalisée à l'autonomie (APA)*. This scheme is almost a universal one: every person in need of support above a defined level of dependence (dependence means incapacity and need of support in daily living, as assessed on a six-level national scale called *Autonomie gérontologique—Groupe iso resource—AGGIR*—see Glossary) is allowed to receive this allowance. But there is a system of co-payment so that the level of support depends on the level of income. Thus, above a certain level of income, the beneficiary receives very little, but below an income of €914 per month, there is no user fee. Seventy-three percent of the beneficiaries are paying such a fee at a mean level of about €110. The maximum APA varies depending on the level of dependence. For the higher level of dependence, the maximum APA benefit is about a thousand euros per month. The median level of the allowance is about €500 per month. This allowance covers part of the cost of the care package proposed by a medico-social team. In June 2008, 1,100,000 people were receiving the APA allowance to help them buy social services for these daily tasks (Espagnol, 2007). Approximately 60% of the recipients are living at home (40% in institutions), 80% are more than 75 years old, and 75% are women.

Even if this new scheme does not cover all needs, it is a very important turn for elderly dependent people (Le Bihan & Martin, 2007). Respite care is still missing, which leaves a heavy burden on the shoulders of women—wives, daughters, and daughters in law—with crucial problems of work/life balance for these female carers. The dramatic increase of the cost of this policy for local authorities will certainly bring new reforms in the coming years. President Nicolas Sarkozy has already suggested the development of voluntary and private insurance to cover these costs.

In summary, according to the available data and the review of social policies, the poverty of lone-aged women is not a central issue in France. Aged people are universally considered the main beneficiaries of the *Trente Glorieuses* (30 glorious years). So, except for the proposal to increase the lowest pensions, which will mainly concern elderly women, there is no specific measure to combat the poverty of this group. Still a latent problem?

## Some Closing Remarks

### Recent Developments

The campaign for the presidency in 2007 was a forum for different assessments of the French economic situation. Each candidate formulated a very different diagnosis of the main challenges for the near future. On the one hand, the Conservative candidate, Nicolas Sarkozy, held that France was going in the right direction after 10 years of neo-liberal public policies (tax reduction, mainly in favor of the well-off; important economic help for business and enterprises; opposition to assisting the underprivileged).[25] Further, he claimed that conservative policies had significantly reduced unemployment. On the other hand, Ségolène Royal, the socialist candidate, and François Bayrou, the centrist, were very critical of the results of the last 10 years of conservative policies. The large increase in inequality was one of the main issues of this political controversy.

Nevertheless, strictly speaking, the issue of poverty was almost absent from that presidential campaign, except to mention it "compassionately." As Martin Hirsch stated regarding the attitude of the main presidential candidates: "They don't know if speaking about poverty and about measures to fight against it, will attract voters or, on the contrary, chase away those who think that government already does more than enough for poor people and not enough for them. This leads towards 'a compassionate approach to poverty'" (Hirsch, 2007, p. 66); that is, just speaking about the deserving poor sympathetically, considering them as victims but without proposals or intentions of doing anything about poverty.

If we consider the amount of research on poverty, it is obvious that the poverty of women gets little attention, except as the traditional task of women scholars and gender studies, themselves small in comparison to the output in many other European countries.[26] Lone-parent families and lone mothers are also subjects that have been almost abandoned in the past 20 years. The call for projects to address the situation of these households was much more frequent in the beginning of the 1980s than it is 25 years later. So, the issue is as absent in the political debate as it is in the academic debate. In fact, poverty, in general, is usually not considered in terms of gender. For the elderly as well, gender is not on the agenda. Poverty concerns mainly other social groups: youth, immigrants, and lone, socially excluded men.

When considering policies to fight precariousness and poverty, the trend is clearly toward an activating welfare state. The new measures do not concern lone parents exclusively, but these households are included in the target group. Activation policies may be a greater burden for them because of the problem for a single parent of combining family responsibility and employment. Getting them into the labor force is considered the only solution to avoid welfare dependence, even if this does not necessarily mean avoiding poverty. So activation does not look like a solution but more of a political choice or a credo (Knijn et al., 2007). If France was once one of the countries where social assistance efficiently protected people against poverty, we are clearly going backward or toward a more liberal direction (Paugam, 2006).

For President Nicolas Sarkozy, elected in May 2007, the main political objectives are (at least until the financial crisis of October 2008) a reduction of government regulations to free the entrepreneurial spirit, to facilitate business initiative, and to increase opportunity for those who wish "to work more, to gain more." Among the numerous propositions of Sarkozy during the presidential campaign, the most important was the promise to reduce income taxes drastically, by 4% of GDP—which would be reducing taxes twice as much as Margaret Thatcher and in half the time that it took during the conservative revolution in Britain of 1985 to 1995. The economist, Thomas Piketty (2007) considered this promise both populist and dangerous. But it gives an indication of current and future public policies that will certainly significantly increase inequality and poverty, particularly among the working poor.

In a report delivered in May 2005, Martin Hirsh, a left-wing high civil servant, suggested the creation of a new scheme, *revenu de solidarité active—RSA,* to replace the different minimum-income schemes and the *prime pour l'emploi.* What Hirsh proposed was to include in this program all people with an income lower than a poverty threshold of less than 60% of the median disposable income, whether working or not. Such a scheme would assure to any worker, on a permanent basis, an income higher than the 60% poverty threshold (about €800 per month). The estimated total cost of this would be high—between €6 and €8 billion per year.

The right-wing government of Prime Minister François Fillon (since May 2007) has the task of implementing, on a much smaller scale, the proposal of Martin Hirsch, who has agreed to lead the new *Haut commissariat aux solidarités actives contre la pauvreté (*High Commission for Active Solidarity against Poverty*).* The project has been considerably reduced and implemented on an experimental basis in about 25 *départements* (local authorities in charge of social programs), for recipients of API and RMI who already have a *contrat aidé* (about 90,000 recipients). Beginning in January 2009, the RSA became available throughout the country. The additional cost of this new system is €1.5 billion more than the cost of the two minimum incomes (API and RMI) that it replaces. So, RSA is clearly the main social policy of the current right-wing government.

The RSA concerns not only the beneficiaries of the previous minimum incomes,[27] but also all working people with wages less than 1.2 SMIC. So this measure concerns a very large group of people: approximately 5 million households or approximately 10 million people (16% of the population of France). The objective is to complement low wages by a proportion of social income.[28]

The RSA has engendered controversies among experts. The criticism concerns the limitations of the scheme compared to Martin Hirsh's first proposition; its subsidy to enterprises for the wages of less skilled workers that could further pauperize work; the substantial cost to the government of paying part of a wage bill that business refuses to assume; the difficulty and possible injustice of distinguishing between the deserving and undeserving poor; and finally a policy that resembles workfare because it could force the unemployed to accept precarious work[29] (Clerc, 2008; Gadrey & Clerc, 2007). This new scheme is proposing to support at the same time people who don't work and are allowed to receive the same level minimum income as previously, and those who work at low incomes with an incentive to work because of the "make work pay" incentive or activation mechanism. In that sense, RSA seems close to the U.S. earned income tax credit scheme, except that the EITC provides nothing to those who don't work. The workfare logic is not as strong apparently but could emerge at the level of the local implementation.

In any case, these policies seem to have the same rationale: to promote a society of "full activity" but not full employment. As suggested by Robert Castel:

> Maybe we have to consider that it is the conception of employment that is being profoundly transformed, and also the relation between employment and non-employment. Can we still consider full employment and unemployment as opposites, employment in the full meaning of the expression and atypical forms of employment, *condition salariale* and "précariat?" Our hypothesis is that we are facing a downswing from classical employment towards forms of activity short of employment and that could ultimately lead to a society of full activity completely different from a society of full employment (2006, p. 417).

If we compare the French situation with other countries that have pursued neo-liberal policies, this diagnosis could be softened. French activation or "welfare to work" policies are still far from the hard workfare logic of U.S. policies. In France, this new activating policy is only beginning and still controversial. It facilitates the development of a very diverse rhetoric: from the harshness of workfare and punitive stigmatization of the poor to the softer one that could be defended as a real war against poverty. Leftist Martin Hirsh, who devised the RSA, intended to rescue a large group of people from poverty. It is still possible to consider this policy a social challenge and to wait for its results to evaluate it conclusively.

At the end of this report, we want to argue first that feminized poverty is a relatively latent phenomenon in France because some other groups are considered by public opinion to be even more burdened by poverty, in particular young people and young immigrants. This is the case, even though the precariousness of these two groups of women increased during recent years and will certainly grow in the near future. This, one should add, means growing inequalities among women themselves, depending on their cultural background, level of education, family, and professional careers. Third, the political debate around poverty is very confusing and combines very different perspectives that, in turn, lead toward divergent social and economic policies. But the context of the financial crisis, which is impacting drastically on the "real economy," will certainly affect the more fragile people, particularly lone women. They will be at the forefront of this transformation and probably will pay the price of more insecure employment, more economic uncertainty, and more poverty.

## Glossary to Chapter 3

**AFEAMA**: *Aide pour l'emploi d'une assistante maternelle agréée.* Introduced in 1991 to provide financial support to families employing a registered child minder. This benefit covers 40% of the cost (the total amount of the payroll taxes) and constitutes an incentive for not choosing unregistered child-care providers who were nearly as numerous as registered ones before the reform. Between 1994 and 2001, public expenditure on the AFEAMA increased by 177%.

**AGED**: *Allocation de garde d'enfant à domicile.* This was created in 1987 for parents hiring a domestic employee (without any specified qualifications) to care for their children under 3 years old. The incentive is a tax credit that covers a large part of the cost. The maximum tax credit for an employee in the home was boosted in 1994 from 13,000 francs (€1,900) to 45,000 francs (€6,700). That same year, AGED was extended to families with a child between 3 and 6. Consequently, the number of AGED recipients more than doubled between 1994 and 1996 (from 25,000 in 1994 to 54,000 in 1996). This allowance concerns mainly the well-off, dual career couples who may benefit from a significant tax reduction.

**AGGIR**: *Autonomie gérontologique—Groupe iso resource.* AGGIR is the French national scale to assess the level of dependency of the frail elderly.

**APA**: *Allocation personnalisée à l'autonomie.* Created in January 2002, this allowance is provided to dependent elderly people to buy services to help them in their daily life. It is a universal co-paid allowance delivered by local authorities.

**APE**: *Allocation parentale d'éducation* (APE). Created in 1985, the APE is a flat-rate parental leave (€500 a month).

**API**: *Allocation de parent isolé.* Created in 1976, the API is a minimum income for those parents (almost exclusively mothers) with sole responsibility for one or more children, which was initially conceived as a maternal salary. The amount of this allowance was €765 for a lone parent with one child in 2006.

**ASF**: *Allocation de soutien familial.* Created in 1984, the ASF is aimed at improving the system for child support enforcement. The benefit is given if the lone parent takes juridical action for the determination of the child maintenance against the other parent; it is served as an advance (on future child maintenance payments) in case of nonpayment of a child maintenance. The "Caisse d'allocations familiales" (CAF), the Social Security agency, may recoup those benefits from the "parent défaillant" or defaulting parent. The amount in December 2008 is about €85 per child per month.

***Minimum vieillesse:*** Created in 1956, this benefit guarantees a minimum income for people aged 65 and over whose resources are below a certain level (€660 per month in 2005).

**PAJE**: *Prestation d'accueil du jeune enfant.* Implemented in January 2004, this allowance replaces the previous schemes (APE, AGED, AFEAMA). It is composed of different elements: a universal basic allowance up to the third birthday of the child, a *complement du mode de garde (CMG)* for the parents of a child under 6 years old who want to work, and the *complement de libre choix d'activité (CLCA)* for the parents who want to reduce or stop their employment to care for their children up to their third birthday (it replaces the APE flat-rate parental leave). This CLCA may be paid after the birth of a first child for a 6 months period after the maternity leave. For a second child (or subsequent ones), it can be paid up to the third birthday of the youngest. The CLCA allows parents to stop working or to reduce their activity to part-time. Since July 2006, a new allowance has been added: the *complement optionnel de libre choix d'activité (COLCA),* for families with at least three children. It is €230 more than the CLCA and is provided for only 1 year. In 2007, 550,000 people were receiving CLCA and only 2300 COLCA.

**PSD**: *Prestation spécifique dépendance.* Implemented between 1997 and 2002, this allowance was for frail dependent and poor elderly people to pay for care services.

**RMA**: *Revenu minimum d'activité.* Implemented since 2003, RMA applies to beneficiaries receiving the RMI for over 2 years. Recipients are offered an employment contract with a private sector or nonprofit employer for a minimum of 20 hours per week, paid at the minimum wage (SMIC) per hour. The RMA provides a fixed rate benefit and a supplement to be paid by the employer.

**RMI**: *Revenu minimum d'insertion.* Created in 1988 and applied until January 2009, RMI was the main French minimum income that complemented the resources of people under a defined threshold. The amount depended on the composition of the household (e.g., €440 for a lone person).

**RSA**: *Revenu de solidarité active.* This minimum income replaced two previous minimum incomes (API and RMI) in January 2009. The beneficiaries are those who previously received API and RMI and working poor people who are paid less than 1.04 SMIC per hour. The objective is to complement the salary and to oblige those who receive just a minimum income to look for a job with the assistance of the public employment services.

**SMIC**: *Salaire minimum interprofessionnel de croissance.* This is the minimum salary paid per hour: in 2008, €8.71 as a gross wage, which means for a full-time job (151.67 hours with a 35 hour week) €1,321 gross salary per month or €1,037 take-home pay.

## Notes

1 The unemployment rate in the EU 27 was 7.1% in 2007.

2 In France "protected jobs" are jobs that receive some support from the State, either by payroll tax deductions granted by public authorities to the employers or by direct financial support granted by the State to pay the employee on fixed-term contracts. In France, there are different contracts of employment called *contrats aidés* or *emplois aidés;* they are mainly targeted to youth but also to the unemployed (e.g., *contrat d'avenir, contrat d'accompagnement dans l'emploi, contrat de professionnalisation, contrat d'apprentissage*).

3 We can call précariat this condition under which precariousness becomes a usual characteristic of the organisation of labor" (Castel, 2006, p. 422).

4 "A number of women are not registered as unemployed because they are 'naturally' trapped in the specific female and socially invisible form of privation of employment: as housewives …" (Maruani, 2006, p. 409).

5 Here as elsewhere in this chapter, poverty is defined as less than 50% of the median income.

6 With a 60% poverty threshold, which is the EU norm, 7.9 million people in France are poor in 2006, or 13.2% of the population. There were 7.6 million in 1996 (13.5%).

7 These figures are nevertheless difficult to evaluate because of the statistical definition of lone-parent households. For example, in France, where the national statistics bureau considers that a lone parent is living with his/her children under 25 but without a partner in his/her household, about 10% of the lone parents declared nevertheless that they live as couples (in different households, sometimes because of their professional activities). If we exclude these lone parents declaring that they live as couples, their number falls from 1,495,000 to 1,350,000 representing 15% of the families with children under 25 instead of 17% (Algava, 2002, 2003).

8 For example, 36% of the RMI recipients in the DOM are lone parents, compared to 24% in metropolitan France.

9 In 2004, the API benefit was €512 per month, plus €171 per child.

10 Preschool has been an important part of the French child-care system since the end of the nineteenth century. Since the mid-1970s, it has been a universal service, almost free of charge, available to children between 3 and 6, the age when they begin compulsory schooling (Martin & Le Bihan, 2009).

11 *Crèches parentales* are run by parents' associations. They were created after 1968 but were only officially recognized during the 1980s. The requirements are less stringent than for *crèches collectives*. They are smaller (between 10 and 15 children). Parents are present in the crèches between 6 and 8 hours per week. Two adults, at least one of which must have professional qualifications, are present with the children.

12 The law pertaining to *interruption volontaire de grossesse* (voluntary abortion) (IVG) had just been introduced by Simone Veil and adopted by the National Assembly (1975).

13 The beneficiary can receive the API for 1 year or up to the third birthday of the younger child.

14 Prime Minister Alain Juppé asked Charles de Courson and Gérard Léonard to prepare a preliminary report about fraudulent practices in social benefits (called the *commission anti-triche*). A second report proposing a reform of the API was given to the government in July 1996 by a RPR (right-wing party) parliamentary group under the direction of Laurent Catala, a high civil servant.

15 Sixty-five percent of the beneficiaries of API are less than 30 years old.

16 We suggest translating *mécanisme d'intéressement* as "welfare to work incentive" in this chapter.

17 Just before the changeover, a new tax mechanism called the "employment tax credit" was adopted. It is a tax credit for workers being paid a salary lower than 1.4 times the SMIC and having had a short period of employment during the last year. This tax credit is based on household income. Beneficiaries with children are paid a bonus, with the first child of a lone-parent family receiving a double bonus. This is consistent with the tax legislation that already recognized that children represent a greater burden for a single-parent than for a two-parent family.

18 This RMA system applies to beneficiaries receiving the RMI for over 2 years. Recipients are offered an employment contract with a private sector or non-profit employer for a minimum of 20 hours per week, paid at the minimum wage (SMIC) per hour. The RMA provides a fixed rate benefit of RMI (which corresponds to a single person with a fixed housing benefit) and a supplement to be paid by the employer. The employer pays the entire RMA but receives a grant equal to the fixed RMI benefit. Dollé (2003) points out that this measure means a deterioration of the employment contract, since the social protection of the worker benefiting from the RMA (social security contributions, unemployment insurance, pensions, etc.) will only be based on the payment made by the employer, not on the part corresponding to the RMI.

19 The *contrat d'avenir* is a 2 year contract (up to 5 years for those more than 50 years old) with 26 hours weekly paid at the minimum salary.

20 A recent law (March 23, 2006) has also created a premium for those who return to the labor market (€1000 limited to those who found a job for a minimum of 78 hours a month, after a minimum of four consecutive months of employment and of course, receipt of a minimum income—API or RMI). The government has also adopted a new measure: a flat-rate monthly premium (€150 for a single person and €225 for two or more people in the household) distributed after the return to employment (also with a minimum of 78 hours per month and after 3 months of work and for a maximum duration of 10 months). The administrative procedures had just been adopted before the Presidential elections in May 2007.

21 For the API recipients, it is necessary to distinguish between two main types of situations—the "long" or "short" API. The long one is for women who are pregnant or whose younger child is less than 3 years old; the short one is for those with older children, for a maximum of a year, after a separation, a divorce, or the death of a partner. The percentage of recipients of the "short API" who combine a salary and this minimum income is 8.5%, double that for the "long API" recipients (4.4%), which has to do, first with the problem of managing work and child care for those who have a young child and, second, with the youth of these mothers who are often still training or studying.

22 This gender gap will decrease in the next decades as elderly people are going to live much more often as couples than today (Gaymu, Festy, Poulain, & Beets, 2008).

23 This minimum age is 60 for the people unfit for work.

24 Sixty-five percent of the minimum salary the same year.

25 Nicolas Sarkozy used again a workfare perspective when he declared during the campaign: "I suggest that no minimum income could be offered without the obligation of a common interest activity" (Presidential campaign, 2007).

26 In France, there are only two main academic journals in this field: *Travail, genre et sociétés* and *Les cahiers du genre*.

27 API or RMI, who will still receive the same amount: €450 for a lone person and €675 for a couple.

28 For example, for a salary of €1000 per month, one could receive a €50 RSA (the basic RSA [€450] minus 40% of €1000 [€400]), and someone with a €500 salary could receive €250 of RSA (€450–€200 [500 x 40%]).

29 When an RSA beneficiary refuses two job offers consecutively, he/she will be excluded from the minimum-income schemes.

## References

Algava, E. (2002). Les familles monoparentales en France: Progression et diversité. *Population, 57, 4–5,* 733–758.

Algava, E. (2003). Les familles monoparentales: Des caractéristiques liées à leur histoire matrimoniale. *Etudes et résultats, 218,* février, 1–8.

Algava, E., Le Minez, S., Bressé, S., & Pla, A. (2005). Les familles monoparentales et leurs conditions de vie. *Etudes et résultats, 389,* avril, 1–12.

Baclet, A. (2006). Les seniors: Des revenus plus faibles pour les plus âgés, compensés par un patrimoine élevé. In INSEE. *Les revenus et les patrimoines des ménages* (pp. 25–37). Paris: INSEE.

Belorgey, J.-M. (Ed.). (2000). *Minima sociaux, revenus d'activité, précarité.* Paris: La Documentation Française.

Bichot, J. (1992). *La politique familiale: Jeunesse, investissement, avenir.* Paris: Editions Cujas.

Bonnet, C., Buffeteau, S., & Godefroy, P. (2006). Disparités de retraite entre hommes et femmes: Quelles évolutions au fil des générations? *Economie et statistiques, 398–399,* 131–148.

Borrel, C. (2006). Enquêtes annuelles de recensement 2004 et 2005. Près de 5 millions d'immigrés à la mi-2004. *INSEE première,* n 1098, août.

Bradshaw, J., Kennedy, S., Kilkey, M., Hutton, S., Corden, A., Eardley, T., et al. (1996). *Policy and the employment of lone parents in 20 countries.* Bruxelles: European Observatory on National Family Policies. European Commission. DG5.

Burricand, C., & Deloffre, A. (2006). Les pensions perçues par les retraités fin 2004. *Etudes et résultats, 538,* 1–12.

Castel, R. (2006). Au-delà du salariat ou en deçà de l'emploi? L'institutionnalisation du précariat. In S. Paugam (Ed.), *Repenser la solidarité: L'apport des sciences sociales* (pp. 415–433). Paris: PUF.

Castel, R., Fitoussi, J.P., Freyssinet, J., & Guaino, H. (1997). *Chômage: Le cas français.* Rapport au Premier ministre. Paris: La documentation française.

Caussat, L., Le Minez, S., & Pucci, M. (2003). Les aides aux familles ayant de jeunes enfants: Bilan de l'existant et première évaluation des réformes décidées en 2003 avec la prestation d'accueil du jeune enfant (PAJE). *Solidarité et santé, 3,* 67–92.

Chambaz, C. (2000). Les familles monoparentales en Europe: Des réalités multiples. *Etudes et résultats, 66,* 1–8.

Chambaz, C., & Martin, C. (2001). Lone parents, employment and social policy in France: Lessons from a family friendly policy. In J. Millar & K. Rowlingson (Eds.), *Lone parents, employment and social policy: Cross-national comparisons* (pp. 129–150). Bristol: Policy Press.

Chardon, O., Daguet, F., & Vivas, E. (2008). Les familles monoparentales. Des difficultés à travailler et à se loger. *INSEE premières, 1195,* 1–4.

Chaupin, S., & Guillot, O. (1998). Au sortir de l'Allocation de parent isolé. *Recherches et Prévisions, 50–51,* 17–26.

Clément, J., Mathieu F., & Mahieu, R. (2005). 1.5 million de familles monoparentales sont allocataires des CAF. *L'essentiel, 33,* janvier, 1–4.

Clerc, D. (2008). *La France des travailleurs pauvres.* Paris: Grasset.

Concialdi, P. (2006). La France précarisée: Un état des lieux. In M. Husson (Ed.), *Travail flexible, salariés jetables: Fausses questions et vrais enjeux de la lutte contre le chômage* (pp. 17–27). Paris: La découverte.

Conseil Emploi Revenus Cohésion Sociale (CERC). (2004). *Les enfants pauvres en France*. Rapport No. 4. Paris: La Documentation française.

David, O., Eydoux, L., Martin, C., Millar, J., & Séchet, R. (2004). *Les familles monoparentales en Europe*. Paris: Dossier d'études No. 54, CNAF.

Delbès, C., & Gaymu, J. (2005). L'histoire conjugale des 50 ans et plus. In C. Lefèvre & A. Filhon (Eds.), *Histoires de familles, histoires familiales* (pp. 339–356). Paris: INED. Les Cahiers de l'INED No. 156.

Direction de la Recherche, des Etudes, de l'Evaluation et des Statistiques (DREES). (2000). *Les modes de garde et d'accueil des jeunes enfants*. Document de travail, No. 1. Paris: Ministère de l'Emploi et de la Solidarité.

Dollé, M. (2003). Audition de Michel Dollé, rapporteur général du Conseil de l'Emploi, des revenus et de la cohésion sociale au Sénat, le mercredi 14 mai 2003 sur le projet de loi portant décentralisation en matière de revenu minimum d'insertion et créant le revenu minimum d'activité. http://www.senat.fr/rap/l02-304&-2/l02-304-24.html. Accessed July 29, 2009.

Dumont, G.F. (1986). *Pour la liberté familiale*. Paris: PUF.

Duncan S., & Edwards, R. (Eds.). (1997). *Single mothers in an international context: Mothers or workers?* London: UCL Press.

Espagnol, P. (2007). L'allocation personnalisée à l'autonomie au 31 décembre 2006. *Etudes et résultats, 569*, 1–8.

Esping-Andersen, G. (1990). *The three worlds of welfare capitalism*. Cambridge: Polity Press.

Eydoux, A., Letablier, M.T., & Georges, N. (2007). *Les familles monoparentales en France*. Rapport de recherche du Centre d'études de l'emploi, No. 36. Paris: CEE.

Fagnani, J., (2000). *Un travail et des enfants. Petits arbitrages et grands dilemmes*. Paris: Bayard.

Fragonard, B. (Ed.). (1993). *Cohésion sociale et prévention de l'exclusion*. Rapport de la Commission présidée par B. Fragonard, dans le cadre de la préparation du 11ème Plan. Paris: La Documentation Française.

Friot, B. (1998). *Puissances du salariat. Emploi et protection sociale à la française*. Paris: Editions La dispute.

Gadrey, J., & Clerc, D. (2007). Le RSA sert-il à quelque chose? *Alternatives économiques, 261*, 30–33.

Gaymu, J., Festy, P., Poulain, M., & Beets, G. (2008). *Future elderly living conditions in Europe*. Paris: INED.

Gisserot, H., & Grass, E. (2007). *Perspectives financières de la dépendance des personnes âgées à l'horizon 2025: Prévisions et marges de choix*. Rapport à Philippe Bas, ministre délégué à la sécurité sociale, aux personnes âgées, aux personnes handicapées et à la famille.

Guillemard, A.M. (2003). *L'âge de l'emploi. Les sociétés à l'épreuve du vieillissement*. Paris: Armand Colin.

Hennion, M., Nauze-Fichet, E., Cazin, S., & Donné, S. (2006). Le nombre d'allocataires du RMI au 30 septembre 2006. *Etudes et résultats, 541*, décembre. 1–12.

Hirsch, M. (2007). Combattre la pauvreté: Alternatives économiques. *Hors série spécial élections*, 2007, *28*, mars, 66–68.

INSEE. (1994). *Les familles monoparentales*. Portrait social, Collection *Contours et caractères*. Paris: INSEE.

INSEE. (1995). *Les femmes. Portrait social*. Collection *Contours et caractères*: Avec le service des droits des femmes. Paris: INSEE.

INSEE. (2005). *Les personnes âgées*. INSEE référence. Paris: INSEE.

Join-Lambert, M.T. (Ed.). (1998). *Chômage: Mesures d'urgence et minima sociaux*. Paris: La Documentation Française.

Kiernan, K., Land, H., & Lewis, J., (1998). *Lone motherhood in twentieth century Britain*. Oxford: Clarendon Press.

Knijn, T., Martin, C., & Millar, J. (2007). Activation as a common framework for social policies towards lone parents. In C. Martin & B. Palier (Eds.), *Reforming Bismarkian welfare systems* (pp. 638–652). Oxford: Blackwell.

Le Bihan, B., Martin, C., & Rivard, T. (2006). L'organisation du RMI et de son volet insertion dans neuf départements depuis la décentralisation. *Etudes et résultats, 535*, novembre, 1–12

Le Bihan, B., & Martin, C. (2007). Cash for care in the French welfare state: A skilful compromise? In C. Ungerson & S. Yeandle (Eds.), *Cash for care in developed welfare states* (pp. 32–59). London: Palgrave.

Le Bihan, B., & Martin, C. (Eds.). (2008). *Concilier vie familiale et vie professionnelle en Europe*. Rennes: Presses de l'EHESP.

Le Gall, D., & Martin, C. (1987). Les familles monoparentales. Paris: Editions sociales françaises.

Lefaucheur, N., & Martin, C. (1993). Lone parent families in France: Situation and research. In J. Hudson & B. Galloway (Eds.), *Lone parent families. Perspectives on research and policy* (pp. 31–50). Toronto: Thompson Educational Publishing.

Lefaucheur, N., & Martin, C. (1997). Single mothers in France: Supported mothers and workers. In S. Duncan & R. Edwards (Eds.), *Single mothers in an international context: Mothers or workers?* (pp. 217–239). London: UCL Press.

Leprince F., & Martin, C. (2003). *L'accueil des jeunes enfants en France: État des lieux et pistes d'amélioration*. Rapport pour le Haut conseil de la population et de la famille. Paris: La Documentation Française.

Lewis, J. (1997). (Ed.). *Lone mothers in European welfare regimes. Shifting policy logics*. London: Jessica Kingsley Publishers.

Lewis, J., Knijn, T., Martin, C., & Ostner, I. (2008). Patterns of development in work/family reconciliation policies for parents in France, Germany, the Netherlands and the UK in the 2000s. *Social Politics, 15*, 4, 261–286.

Martin, C. (1994). Diversité des trajectoires post-désunion. Entre le risque de solitude, la défense de son autonomie et la recomposition familiale. *Population, 6*, 1557–1584.

Martin, C. (1997a). *L'après-divorce. Lien familial et vulnérabilité*. Rennes: Presses universitaires de Rennes.

Martin, C. (1997b). L'action publique en direction des ménages monoparentaux. Une comparaison France/Royaume-Uni. *Recherches et Prévisions, 47*, mars, 25–50.

Martin, C. (Ed.). (2003). *La dépendance des personnes âgées. Quelles politiques en Europe?* Rennes: Presses universitaires de Rennes.

Martin, C. (2006). Le souci de l'autre dans une société d'individus. In S. Paugam (Ed.), *Repenser la solidarité: L'apport des sciences sociales* (pp. 219–240). Paris: PUF.

Martin, C., & Le Bihan, B., (2009). Public childcare and preschools in France: New policy paradigm and path dependency. In K. Scheiwe & H. Willekens (Eds.), *Childcare and preschool development in Europe: Institutional perspectives* (pp. 57–71). London: Palgrave Macmillan.

Martin, C., Math, A., & Renaudat, E. (1998). Caring for very young children and dependent elderly people in France: Towards a commodification of social care? In J. Lewis (Ed.), *Gender, social care and welfare state restructuring in Europe* (pp. 139–174). Aldershot: Ashgate.

Martin-Papineau, N. (2001). *Les familles monoparentales: Emergence, construction, captations d'un problème dans le champ politique français (1968–1988)*. Paris: L'Harmattan.

Maruani, M. (2006). Repenser la solidarité ... sans faire l'économie du genre. In S. Paugam (Ed.), *Repenser la solidarité. L'apport des sciences sociales* (pp. 397–414). Paris: PUF.

Maruani, M., & Méron, M. (2008). Emploi, salaire, chômage: La parité inachevée. In L. Maurin & P. Savidan (Eds.), *L'état des inégalités en France 2009* (pp. 201–208). Paris: Belin.

Maurin, L. & Savidan, P. (Eds.). (2007). *L'état des inégalités en France 2008*. Paris: Belin.

Maurin, L., & Savidan, P. (Eds.). (2008). *L'état des inégalités en France 2009*. Paris: Belin.

Merrien, F.X. (1990). Etats-providence: L'empreinte des origines. *Revue française des affaires sociales, 3*, 43–56.

Milewski, F., Dauphin, S., Kesteman, N., Letablier, M-T., & Meda, D. (2005). *Les inégalités entre les femmes et les hommes*. Paris: La Documentation française.

Nivière, D., Dindar, C., & Hennion, M. (2006). Les allocataires de minima sociaux en 2005. *Etudes et résultats, 539*, novembre, 1–8.

Observatoire national de la pauvreté et de l'exclusion sociale. (2000). *Les travaux de l'observatoire de la pauvreté et de l'exclusion sociale*. Paris: La Documentation Française.

Olier, L., & Herpin, N. (1999). Les familles monoparentales: Aidées mais fragilisées. In D. Bouget & B. Palier (Eds.), *Comparer les systèmes de protection sociale en Europe du Nord et en France: Rencontres de Copenhague* (pp. 315–334). Paris: DREES, collection MIRE.

Palier, B., & Martin, C. (Eds.). (2007). *Reforming the Bismarckian welfare systems*. Oxford: Blackwell Publishing.

Paugam, S. (Ed.). (2006). *Repenser la solidarité: L'apport des sciences sociales*. Paris: PUF.

Périvier, H. (2003). La garde des jeunes enfants: Affaires de femmes ou affaire dÉtat? *Lettre de L'OFCE*, no. 228. Paris: Presses de Science Po.

Piketty, T. (2005). Impact de l'Allocation Parentale d'Education sur l'activité féminine et la fécondité en France. In C. Lefèvre (Ed.), *Histoires de Familles, Histoires Familiales. Les Cahiers de l'INED*, no. 156, 79–109.

Piketty, T. Interview in *Les Echos* du 10 Avril 2007.

Rastier, A. C., & Maingueneau, E. (2006). Les dispositifs d'incitation à l'activité dans le système des prestations légales. *Recherches et prévisions, 85*, 64–70.

Smith, T. B. (2004). *France in crisis. Welfare, inequality and globalization since 1980*. Cambridge: Cambridge University Press.

Sullerot, E. (1984). *Pour le meilleur et sans le pire*. Paris: Fayard.

Tavan, C. (2005). Les immigrés en France: Une situation qui évolue. *INSEE première, 1042*, septembre, 1–4.

Thélot, C., & Villac, M. (1998). *Politique familiale. Bilan et perspectives*. Rapport à la ministre de l'emploi et de la solidarité et au ministre de l'économie, des finances et de l'industrie. Paris: La Documentation française.

Villac, M. (1992). Politique familiale et redistribution en direction des familles. *Recherches et prévisions*, CNAF, *28*, 1–11.

# 4

# GERMANY: POVERTY AS A RISK FOR WOMEN DEVIATING FROM THE MALE BREADWINNER NORM

*Ute Klammer*

## Poverty Research, Poverty, and the Institutional Background in Germany

### Poverty Research in Germany

Poverty research has a long-standing tradition in Germany and in the European Union (EU). Although the EU has always been reluctant to interfere in the social security protection systems of its member states,[1] the goal to combat poverty has been a common concern and field of politics in the EU for several decades.

In Germany, as in other European countries, there are several concepts for measuring poverty. Whereas for a long time the most widespread poverty concept in Germany defined the poverty line as 50% of the arithmetical mean of net equivalent household income, newer reports usually measure poverty at 60% of the net equivalent median household income, following the overall EU convention. Compared to the average income, the median's advantage—but also disadvantage—is that it is insensitive to changes in the income distribution at the lower and in particular upper end of the income distribution. It therefore does not adequately reflect the widespread trend toward a growing income inequality in society as long as the income of the person in the middle of the income distribution does not change very much. According to the most recent official poverty report in Germany (Bundesregierung, 2005), 60% of median income equaled €938/month for a single adult in 2003, whereas 50% of the average was €870/month.

The distribution of income and wealth has become more unequal in Germany in recent years. Today, the richest 20% (quintile) of the population possesses about two-thirds of the wealth of all private households, while the share of the poorest quintile share is –0.5%, which means that they are in debt (Bundesregierung, 2005). However, if one looks at the Gini coefficient as a measure for income inequality, inequality is still moderate in Germany compared to many other European countries and the United States. Further, using the 60% standard, Germany had the third lowest poverty risk in the EU in 2001, after Sweden and Denmark, with a rate of 11%, 4 percentage points below the EU average (Eurostat, 2004). Whereas the poverty risk for almost all household types was significantly lower than the EU average, the poverty risk for single parents in Germany was slightly above average (36% vs. 35%), a first indicator of the often difficult situation of single mothers. Germany, together with the Scandinavian countries and the Netherlands, also achieved the best results on duration of poverty, with "only" about 6% of the population staying in poverty during at least 2 consecutive years. In addition, social transfers managed to reduce market poverty in Germany by 28 percentage points (from 39% to 11%). Excluding pensions that are sometimes regarded as deferred primary income, transfers reduced the poverty risk by 10 percentage points, from 21% to 11% (Eurostat, 2004, p. 6). This can be taken as an indication of the extent to which poverty reduction in Germany depends on pensions and is thus biased toward the elderly.

The main sources for the following analysis of women's condition in Germany are the government's most recent, comprehensive report on poverty and wealth (Bundesregierung, 2005),[2] data from the social security administration and my own, co-authored evaluation of the data (Bothfeld, Klammer, Klenner, Leiber, Thiel, & Ziegler, 2005).

## Distribution and Development of Poverty in Germany

As Table 4.1 shows, the overall poverty risk rose by 1.4 percentage points or more than 10% between 1998 and 2003. With a poverty risk of 14.4%, women bear a higher risk of being poor than men. However, if we look at the *development* of poverty, the gap between women and men has diminished, due to a more than proportional rise in men's poverty in recent years. The trend is not toward increased predominance of women's poverty or a "feminization of poverty." One of the main reasons for men's increased poverty risk is the high level of unemployment and, in particular, the rising share of long-term unemployment in Germany. Due to this development, we can speak of a tendency toward a "feminization of male careers" in Germany, with more interruptions in male employment than in earlier decades.

The high impact of unemployment on poverty is obvious from Table 4.1: more than 40% of all unemployed persons have an income below the

TABLE 4.1 Poverty Rates[a] for Selected Groups of the Population, 1998 and 2003

| | 1998 | 2003 |
|---|---|---|
| Total population | 12.1 | 13.5 |
| Women | 13.3 | 14.4 |
| Men | 10.7 | 12.6 |
| Single parents | 35.4 | 35.4 |
| Couples with two children | 9.3 | 8.6 |
| Couples without children | 11.6 | 13.1 |
| Elderly persons (65+) | 13.3 | 11.4 |
| Unemployed persons | 33.1 | 40.9 |
| Self-employed persons | 11.2 | 9.3 |
| Persons with German nationality | 11.5 | 13.6 |
| Migrants | 19.6 | 24.0 |

[a] Poverty is defined as less than 60% of Median Net Equivalent Income; weights: new OECD equivalence scale (1/0.5/0.3); data source: EVS (*Einkommens- und Verbrauchsstichprobe [Income and Expenditure Survey]*).

*Source*: Bundesregierung, 2005, Appendix: 85–86, 90.

poverty line, and this group suffered the biggest increase in poverty during the last years. The increase can be explained by the rising share of long-term unemployment. The long-term unemployed receive lower or no benefits, and in addition general cuts in the benefit schemes have been implemented. The lack of employment can lead to social exclusion, particularly if one lacks compensating family and friendship networks; thus, unemployed men may be particularly vulnerable to social exclusion.

Besides unemployed people, single parents—and they are predominantly single mothers—are still one of the groups with the highest poverty risks. More than 35% live in poverty. However, it should be noted that the poverty risk of this group has not risen during the last years. Some improvements in the support systems that will be discussed later have stabilized the poverty of this group, albeit on a very high level.

Immigrants without German citizenship have a much higher poverty risk than persons of German nationality, and the gap has increased during recent years. With a poverty rate of 25.3% for women (22.7% for men), immigrants' poverty risk is almost twice as high as among those with German citizenship (13.6%). Problems of unemployment or underemployment and access to social security and different household structures (e.g., more children) contribute to this situation. In general, then, we can speak of two big shifts in poverty risk in Germany during the last decades: from the native German population to immigrants and from elderly people to children and young families, a trend that is broadly discussed as the "infantilization of poverty" in German poverty research.[3]

Elderly people today have a poverty risk below average in Germany. For today's generation of pensioners, the existing pension system has provided a relatively high average standard of living. As the analysis of the situation of elderly women will reveal, there are considerable differences between men and women and between different subgroups of the female elderly population. In addition, the different value of women's own and derived pensions has to be reflected. Finally, the foreseeable future trends reveal some light and much shadow as far as women's future pension claims are concerned.

## The Male Breadwinner Model and Its Differential Impact on West and East German Women

For a long time, social and family policy in (West) Germany, the Federal Republic of Germany (FRG), was focused on the breadwinner model of married couples and, as such, based on the expectation that women, particularly married women with children, would withdraw from the labor market permanently or at least temporarily. This model was strongly promoted and subsidized by state family policy through matrimonial tax splitting, premium-free health and long-term care insurance of nonemployed spouses, the derived system of survivors' pensions, and numerous other individual regulations in the tax and transfer system. In contrast, the expansion of public child-care infrastructure was neglected and progressed very slowly compared to many other countries of Europe (Klammer & Daly, 2003; Klammer, Klenner, Ochs, Radke, & Ziegler, 2000, pp. 336–340).

In East Germany, the former German Democratic Republic (GDR), a completely different gender model developed, with much higher labor market participation of women, including mothers. This was supported by a high level of public child care. Although the East German gender model never meant gender equality in the sphere of the private household, where women still had the main responsibility for housework and child care, it led to much more economic independence of women, whether married or solo mothers. For persons of working age, the gender pay gap was much less than in the FRG. Elderly persons of both sexes had very modest pensions compared to West Germany, but again with a relatively low gender gap. After reunification in 1990, however, the East German gender model had no major impact on the West German model and did not lead to a significant improvement in gender equality throughout Germany. Instead, the West German institutional framework was transferred to East Germany and confronted East German women with the established support for married couples and the breadwinner model. In combination with severe economic problems and a high rate of unemployment due to the economic restructuring process, solo mothers were affected much more than single elderly women, since most elderly women profited from their long years of employment when their pension claims were recalculated according to the West German system (for details see Klammer, 2005).

Concern over demographic trends and, in particular, the low birth rate (Germany currently ranks 181st out of 191 surveyed countries) has refocused attention on family policy in recent years, and it has become a key field of debate and policy in Germany since the late 1990s. During its first period in office the "Red-Green" government (1998–2002) mainly concentrated on increasing *monetary* benefits for families. Child allowance payments were increased several times, and the income limits for monetary benefits during parental leave were raised.

In addition the "Red-Green" government began to gear its policy toward making it easier for mothers to reconcile work with family. The emphasis was on facilitating and increasing the attraction of the "modified breadwinner model" with the wife working part time. The right to part-time employment was improved by the "Law on Part-Time Employment and Fixed-Term Contracts," as were the options for working part time during parental leave. A big pension reform in 2001 upgraded the rights of mothers in part-time employment (all three laws from 2001). This part-time policy, however, does not help most solo mothers to overcome poverty.

A central problem for many years is the low level of public child care, particularly in West Germany. There has been a right to a place for children above the age of 3 since 1996, but this does not extend to full-day care. Further, with coverage less than 3% in 2002, West Germany was near the back of the European pack when it comes to children *below the age of 3* (Table 4.2). In East Germany, many child-care facilities were closed down, but due to the considerable decrease of birth rates after reunification and the migration of many young people to West Germany, child care is still better and more comprehensive than in West Germany and in many other European countries.

In West Germany, many working parents complain that the opening hours of child-care facilities frequently do not cover normal working

TABLE 4.2 Children Covered by Public Child Care, 2002, Percentages

| | Children Age 0–2 | Children Age 3–6 (Below School Age) | Afternoon Places ("Hort") for School Children |
|---|---|---|---|
| Germany | 8.6 | 91.3 | 8.9 |
| West Germany | 2.8 | 88.9 | 4.6 |
| East Germany | 37.0 | 105.1[a] | 40.8 |

[a]More places available than children.

*Source*: Statistisches Bundesamt, 2004a.

hours and also that they provide insufficient flexibility in hours of service (Klenner, Pfahl, & Reuyß, 2003, pp. 268–285; Ludwig, Schlevogt, Klammer, & Gerhard, 2002, pp. 110–112).

In its second period in office (2002–2005), the Red-Green government declared the extension of state child-care facilities a high priority of family policy. A program with an expenditure of €1.5 billion was announced for the expansion of child-care facilities for children under the age of 3. An additional €4 billion were to be invested in extending the system of full-day schools (Schmidt, 2003), since most schools are still half day and thus a severe obstacle to mothers' full-time, sometimes even half-time, employment. In autumn 2004, a new law ("Tagesbetreuungsausbaugesetz") envisaged the further extension of public child care for children below the age of 3, with a focus on places for children who need particular support and on children of solo mothers and other working parents. However, the situation has not changed significantly for two main reasons: on the one hand, the Red-Green government hesitated to implement a *right* for parents to claim a child-care place for small children. On the other hand, the government cannot force municipalities to extend the number of child-care places. From the beginning researchers therefore had some skepticism about the actual extension of child care on the local level, due to the fact that most municipalities have severe budget constraints (Vesper, 2005).

After the change of government in 2005, when the Christian Democrats gained the majority of votes and a big coalition between Christian Democrats (CDU/CSU) and Social Democrats (SPD) took power, the support for families and the fight against poverty and social exclusion (in particular child poverty) remained on the agenda. Although the Christian Democrats always supported privileges for married couples and the idea of the male breadwinner family, it is the new Christian Democrat family minister Ursula van der Leyen who now pushes the extension of public child care and full-day schools with determination. On top of this she introduced a new parental leave benefit imitating the Scandinavian (in particular Swedish) approach. Under this scheme, since January 2007, parents who interrupt their employment to care for a new-born baby receive a parental leave benefit replacing 67% of their net income from work for up to 14 months out of which 2 months are reserved for the father, or second partner (solo mothers can take all 14 months). This new benefit is geared toward the working mother who only interrupts work for a short period after childbirth. Recent labor market reforms that increase the pressure for welfare mothers to seek work are akin to this effort to increase women's employment. At the same time, most privileges for the married male breadwinner family, such as the system of matrimonial tax splitting and derived benefits for nonworking spouses, remain untouched. These contradictory signals have repeatedly been seen as one of the main reasons why, compared to other European countries, women have still made so little headway in

TABLE 4.3 Employment Rate[a] of Mothers, Age 15–65, by Age of Youngest Child, 2004

| Age of Youngest Child | West Germany | | | East Germany | | |
|---|---|---|---|---|---|---|
| | Total | Full Time | Part Time | Total | Full Time | Part Time |
| 0–2 | 29 | 10 | 19 | 44 | 27 | 17 |
| 3–5 | 56 | 12 | 42 | 67 | 38 | 28 |
| 6–9 | 65 | 15 | 50 | 69 | 41 | 28 |
| 10–14 | 71 | 21 | 50 | 73 | 51 | 22 |
| 15–17 | 74 | 30 | 44 | 79 | 58 | 21 |

[a]At least 1 hour of paid work per week.

*Source*: Bothfeld et al., 2005, p. 175, based on data from the German Statistical Office.

West Germany in their efforts to attain equality in employment opportunities and income (e.g., Dingeldey, 2000, 2002).

In spite of some persisting advantages for the breadwinner model, it is no longer the norm or even the ideal for the majority. Surveys show that attitudes among both men and women are increasingly in favor of greater participation of women and—to a lesser extent—mothers of small children in the labor market (Statistisches Bundesamt, 2002, pp. 537–539). The actual employment rate of women in Germany has meanwhile reached about 60%, which is the European target set by the so-called Lisbon strategy for 2010. This rate of female employment puts Germany in the upper middle ranking of the 25 EU countries. In particular the employment rate of mothers has increased considerably. However, their labor market participation still depends very much on the age of the youngest child and the region. As Table 4.3 shows, mothers in East Germany (still) have a much higher activity rate than West German mothers, especially if the youngest child is of preschool age. The activity rate of East German mothers would be even higher if the unemployment rate were not so high.

The overall employment rates disguise the fact that there are still strong differences in men's and women's labor market participation in both working time and continuity. In West Germany, two-thirds of working mothers have part-time jobs—often with low salaries.[4] As a consequence, many women, particularly in West Germany, only contribute a small share to the household income and still depend economically on their husbands or male partners. At the turn of the twenty-first century, women with a male partner and two children only contributed 11% of the family's income (Engstler, & Menning, 2003). This has dramatic effects on their ability to support themselves in case of divorce or widowhood.

Lone mothers are a particularly disadvantaged group. Owing to insufficient child care, many of them cannot work and consequently live on welfare. If they get a job, it is often only a part-time job or a low-paid job that is not sufficient to overcome poverty.

## Solo Mothers: High Poverty Risk

### Empirical Findings

As in most other West European countries, the number and share of single parents has risen considerably during the last decades. In 2004, approximately 2.3 million single parents with more than 3.4 million children lived in Germany. This means that today almost every fifth family with children is a single-parent family. More than four-fifths of all single parents are single mothers. The share of solo fathers has not changed much since the mid-1990s (Bothfeld et al., 2005, p. 48). In addition, solo mothers on average live with more younger children than solo fathers. One reason is that single fathers tend to be divorced or widowed. Unmarried fathers of small children very rarely get custody of their children.

The employment rate of solo mothers is approximately 59%, about the same level as all women aged 15–65. However, the unemployment rate of solo mothers—approximately 20%—is well above average. Whereas married mothers often choose to stay at home for several years or to work in marginal part-time jobs, solo mothers are often, by necessity, closely attached to the labor market, either actually working or seeking work (Verband allein erziehender Mütter und Väter Bundesverband e.V. [VAMV], 2006, p. 7).

According to a 2002 study (Goebel, Habich, & Krause, 2002), almost one-third of all lone mothers lives below the poverty line (50% of arithmetic mean standard). This was reaffirmed by the Second Report on Poverty and Wealth in Germany (Bundesregierung, 2005) which again showed that solo parents are among the groups with the highest poverty risk. Measured by the 60% of the median standard, solo parents had a poverty risk of 35.4% in 2003, which was three times as high as that of couples with children. Although this report did not differentiate between solo mothers and fathers, the differences between solo mothers and fathers become obvious if one looks at welfare recipience (Table 4.4, p. 102). Before the system of social assistance was completely changed in 2005, more than one out of four single mothers, and every second single mother with three or more children, depended on social assistance. Compare the 6% poverty rate of single fathers and the 2.3% rate of partnered families with children.

### Different Groups of Single Mothers

Single mothers are not a homogeneous group. Some of the important differences stem from their marital statuses, whether they have never been married to the father of their child(ren), are divorced or separated or widowed. Whereas widowed mothers predominated among German single mothers in the 1950s and 1960s as a result of World War II, this gradually changed, and today divorced or separated mothers are the biggest group (60%). This is the situation in West Germany and the country as a whole.

TABLE 4.4 Social Assistance Receipt by Families with Children,[a] 2003, Percentages

| Single Mothers | | | | Single Fathers | Partnered Families with Children | All Families with Children |
|---|---|---|---|---|---|---|
| Total | One Child | Two Children | Three and More Children | Total | Total | Total |
| 26.3 | 22.0 | 30.5 | 51.0 | 6.1 | 2.3 | 3.7 |

[a]Children below 18 years.

*Source*: Statistisches Bundesamt, 2003, table A8.

TABLE 4.5 Solo Mothers[a] by Family Type, 2003, Percentages

| | Never Married | Widowed | Divorced/Separated |
|---|---|---|---|
| Germany | 32.4 | 7.3 | 60.3 |
| West Germany | 28.0 | 7.9 | 64.1 |
| East Germany | 47.1 | 5.1 | 48.1 |

[a]With children below 18 years.

*Source*: Statistisches Bundesamt, 2004b; Bothfeld et al., 2005, p. 49.

In East Germany, the share of divorced/separated mothers is smaller (48%), and an equal share (47%) has never been married to their children's father (see Table 4.5). This reflects the different role and higher financial independence of women in the former GDR.

Separation and divorce—the main reasons for becoming a single mother—usually have a very different impact on both spouses. Ninety-five percent of all divorced mothers, but only 23% of all divorced fathers, live with children in their household. On average, the woman suffers much bigger economic loss after separation and divorce. Although the majority of the women try to compensate for the financial loss by getting a job or increasing their working hours, their poverty risk doubles within the first year after separation (BmFSFJ, 2003, pp. 8–12; Bundesregierung, 2005, p. 83). The growing risk of poverty often goes along with health and emotional problems.

## Explaining Solo Mothers' High Poverty Risk

**Unemployment and lack of public child care.** In 2004, approximately 20% of all single mothers were registered as unemployed (VAMF, 2006, p. 7). One of the main reasons for their high unemployment is the previously noted lack of available and affordable public child-care facilities. The low supply of child care for children under the age of 3 years in West Germany has been criticized by the Organisation for Economic Co-operation and

Development (OECD) (OECD, 2004). Child care for children of kindergarten age is usually available, but often only half day or not flexible enough to cover unusual working times, so that it does not allow solo mothers to take a job if they do not have additional networks or care resources. Among solo mothers, 7.5% have a child aged 0–2 (VAMV, 2006, p. 7); they are particularly affected by the lack of child-care options.

Women who have been employed before the birth of a child can make use of the parental leave program which guarantees their job until the child is 3 years old. However, until December 2006 the cash benefit only replaced a small share of the former income and was not sufficient to prevent poverty in the absence of other income. Under the new scheme that replaces two-thirds of former income (for low income earners up to 100%), the situation of solo mothers who had been working before the child was born will improve in the future, at least for the first 14 months after the child is born. Solo mothers who were not employed before giving birth get the former benefit of €300 for 14 months. If they cannot get a job, the problems for both groups will increase in the second year since the old benefit was paid up to 24 months. However, since the majority of solo mothers are not caring for a child under 10 years, neither insufficient cash benefits during parental leave nor lack of public child care can be regarded as the main cause of their poverty (VAMV, 2006, p. 7).

**Insufficient income from work.** When it comes to the gender pay gap, Germany holds one of the "top" places among European countries. The German gender pay gap was about 23% in 2005, only "topped" by 3 of the then 25 members of the EU (Eurostat, 2005). The situation has hardly improved during recent years; in some branches and occupations the pay gap has even widened, in spite of efforts to incorporate gender equality in collective bargaining agreements. Evaluation of different data sources leads to the conclusion that after adjusting male and female income for such factors as differences in working hours, educational level, and professional experience, women in West Germany still earn between 12% and 32% less than their male counterparts, and in East Germany between 11% and 24% (Bothfeld et al., 2005, p. 244). The reasons for the low female labor market income have been analyzed in several scientific reports (Bothfeld et al., 2005; Deutscher Bundestag, 2002; Deutsches Jugendinstitut, 2005; Klammer et al., 2000). Whereas young women on average have higher formal qualifications than their male counterparts, they are still concentrated in a very limited range of "female" jobs with low salaries. Further, many of them work in small companies or branches in which jobs are not covered by collective bargaining agreements (e.g., in the service sector), and in addition part-time work and career interruptions reduce their actual income and future career and income prospects. Nor do women profit from overtime, nightshift, or seniority supplements to the same extent as men. So-called minijobs that generate an income of a maximum of €400 per month are highly subsidized in Germany by exemption from tax and social security contributions. Between 1991 and 2004, the share of women who work in minijobs with less than 15 hours per week rose from 6% to 13% (Bothfeld et al., 2005). The "incentives" concerning these jobs (tax exemptions, exemptions or reductions for social security contributions) were raised once more in 2003 to stimulate the creation of jobs in the low pay sector. In fact this has increased the labor demand in the field of minijobs, but partly because regular full-time or part-time jobs with access to social security have been split into minijobs by the employers. For many married women and "secondary earners" minijobs appear to be an attractive choice under the circumstances. But others work in minijobs because they cannot find a regular job. As working time surveys show, female part timers in West Germany on average would like to increase their weekly working time by 2.7 hours and female part timers in East Germany by 7.9 hours (Bauer, Groß, Lehmann, & Munz, 2004).

Employed solo mothers on average are employed 4½ hours per day, about 1 hour per day more than working mothers in couple households (Kahle, 2004). This is mainly due to a bigger share of full-time employed mothers among solo mothers. According to time-budget studies, solo mothers who are employed full time are the group with the highest combined hours from paid and unpaid work (Bothfeld et al., 2005, p. 233; Kahle, 2004). Policies that still support the male breadwinner model—part-time work for mothers and limited public child care—contribute to single mothers' difficulties in earning a sufficient living and their time stress. One year after divorce, women's poverty risk has doubled (BmFSFJ, 2003, pp. 8–12).

**Insufficient parental and welfare state support**. The so-called Düsseldorfer table has guidelines for the monthly amount an absent parent has to pay to the custodial parent for the children's subsistence. The amount differs according to the income of the absent parent and the age of the child; in early 2007, it ranged from €204 to €408 for children below age 6 and from €335 to €670 for children 18 and older. A critical factor in solo mothers' high poverty risk is that their children's fathers often do not pay all or part of the subsistence allowance they are officially obliged to pay. Approximately one of four eligible mothers does not receive these payments from their former husband or partner. Moreover, when the money is not paid, more than half the mothers eligible for child support and more than three-fourths who can claim subsistence payments for themselves do not pursue their rights in court (BmFSFJ, 2005).

Since 1980, a law (Unterhaltsvorschussgesetz) secures the payment of child support to the solo mother by a tax-financed benefit, in case the father is unknown or does not pay. At the end of 2004, 489,000 children living in solo-parent households received this benefit (BmFSFJ, 2006). This was about one-fourth of all solo-parent households (BmFSFJ, 2005; Klammer, 2005, p. 368). This benefit, however, is only paid for a maximum of 6 years and only until the child is 12 years old. Mothers with older children cannot claim the benefit.

**Insufficient cash benefits**. Poor solo mothers are usually eligible for cash benefits and other kinds of support from the state. Like all families they are eligible for the child allowance of €154 per child monthly (€179 for the fourth and further children, 2007).

Since 2005, solo mothers and other working parents who earn enough money for themselves, but are still needy because they have to care for children, can claim an additional monthly benefit of up to €140 per child. This benefit, which is limited to 3 years, was introduced to "make work pay."

Unemployed persons who had regular employment, a monthly income above €400 and contributed at least 1 year to the compulsory unemployment insurance fund have the right to an unemployment benefit with a net replacement rate of 60% (without children) or 67% (with children) during the first year of unemployment. However, for solo mothers (and other persons) who had a part-time or low-paid job the unemployment benefit can be too low to avoid poverty. Many solo mothers are not eligible for earnings-related unemployment benefits because they do not fulfil the conditions or their claim expired due to long-term unemployment. In January 2005 a major labor market reform ("Hartz IV") redefined the benefits for all long-term unemployed and needy persons. Under the new scheme (unemployment benefit type II, "ALG II"), unemployed, able-bodied, needy persons who actively seek work receive up to €345 per month (2007); in addition, the costs for housing (rent, including heating, etc.) are paid by the public authorities, provided the size and kind of the house is consistent with the rules. For each child a separate amount is paid (age 0–13, €207 per month and more for older children). Single parents can claim an additional benefit for their children (currently €124 a month for one child below 7 or two children below 16). In spite of these cash benefits, ALG II benefits usually do not lift recipients above the poverty line.

At the time of its introduction (January, 2005), 3.33 million households in Germany received benefits from the ALG II program; the number rose to 3.93 million by the end of 2005 (Graf & Rudolph, 2006, pp. 1–2) but has decreased since summer 2006 with the economic recovery. All mothers whose youngest child is below 3 years old are exempt from the obligation to actively seek work. They can claim the benefits even when they have an ongoing work contract but have chosen to make use of parental leave.

The new system of social protection for long-term unemployed persons that replaced the earnings-related unemployment and social assistance programs has led to a more precarious situation in many households with long-term unemployed persons. Single mother households did not lose ground, whereas the situation of couples often worsened because of a stricter means-testing in the family (Bothfeld et al., 2005, pp. 336–339). For many solo mothers who had been recipients of the former social assistance, their financial situation and access to active labor market measures even improved (Schulte, 2005, p. 1). The relative position of long-term unemployed solo mothers—compared to other groups of the long-term unemployed—therefore changed for the better. The picture looks different, however, if one applies a dynamic approach. As a first evaluation study of the new benefit system has shown (Graf & Rudolph, 2006, pp. 3–4), solo parents are the group least likely to earn enough to leave the ALG II benefit system. Out of the group of single parents who depended on the benefit in January 2005, 76% were still recipients after 1 year, and 70% had received the benefit through the whole year without interruption. Among couples with children, for example, 65% of the initial recipients still depended on the benefit at the end of the year, and 54% depended on it throughout the whole year without interruption. Solo mothers obviously have more problems overcoming poverty and returning to the labor market.

**Educational level of single mothers.** Being a solo mother is correlated with social class in Germany: girls and young women with poor educational backgrounds are much more likely to become solo mothers than those who are better educated. About one-fifth of all solo mothers has not finished any professional education (VAMV, 2006, p. 8). Consequently, their labor market prospects are low and have even decreased during the last decades with the trend toward a knowledge economy. The fact that a high proportion of single mothers lives below the poverty line is therefore *not only* a result of their marital status, but also of social class and other social factors correlated with poverty.

**Problems of single immigrant mothers.** Single immigrant mothers are 13.1% of all immigrant mothers, while the comparable figures for mothers of German nationality is higher, 18.3% (2004) (Deutsches Jugendinstitut, 2005, p. 44). Immigrant solo mothers, however, have particular burdens:

- On average they have more children than German solo mothers.
- Unless they have immigrated to Germany some years ago, their children need more support (time and money) to cope with the new situation.
- If they have suffered domestic violence shortly after migration, they often do not have social networks to support them; they need a longer time before they dare to leave their partners and often suffer from severe physical and psychic injuries.
- They often do not receive financial support from their former partner or his family, either because of the partner's own poor financial situation or because they are not informed of their rights, or (if a foreign marriage law is valid for them) because they do not have the right to claim payments from their former partner (Frings, 2005, p. 86).

The recent labor market reforms have increased the pressure to seek work for both single and partnered mothers. This conflicts with the gender model of certain groups of immigrants, such as traditional Muslims (Frings, 2005, p. 86). Even women who have been living in Germany for a long time, for example, from the Turkish migrations of the 1960s, have a very limited knowledge of German and are hardly able to support themselves and their children in case of separation and divorce. The government has launched a new, partly compulsory program for language courses to improve the integration and labor market chances for these immigrants.

Particular problems arise in cases where the residence permit of the women was linked to her husband. In these cases the woman can lose her right to stay in Germany after separation, in particular, if she has not lived with her husband in Germany for at least 2 years after marriage and if she doesn't manage to become independent from welfare within a year.

## Future Development

If one looks at the recent and foreseeable future developments for solo mothers, the picture is rather mixed. On the one hand, data on the development of poverty risks in Germany make clear that the *relative* exposure of solo mothers to poverty has not grown during the last years, although it has grown for some other groups in the population. This is partly the result of public policy and a certain focus on this vulnerable group. However, the improved position in relative terms cannot disguise the fact that single mothers are still one of the groups with a particularly high poverty risk in Germany and that the absolute number of poor single mothers is growing due to increasing divorce rates.

The increasing labor market participation of (West) German women will help to alleviate the poverty risk of single and divorced mothers in the future, as will the envisaged extension of public child care. The new parental leave scheme with an earning replacement benefit can help to prevent poverty during the first 14 months after the child is born, but only for those single mothers who are well integrated in the labor market before their child is born. Other developments, such as the reduced level of benefits for the long-term unemployed (ALG II), are reasons to assume that single mothers' poverty risk, like that of other groups affected by long-term unemployment, will remain high. Since men are also increasingly affected by unemployment and low wages, more women and their children will lack child support, even if it is not a matter of the father's refusal to pay. A currently discussed reform of the subsistence law (Unterhaltsrecht) which will give priority to children's right of subsistence over the mother's right to payments will reduce the monetary claims of single mothers in many of the cases where fathers have established a new family. As a result, if there is reason to talk about "feminization of poverty" in Germany, this still refers mainly to solo mothers.

## Lone Elderly Women

### Advantages and Disadvantages for Women in the German Pension System

Can we also speak of a "feminization of elder poverty" in Germany? Are elderly women—and in particular single elderly women—a disadvantaged group? The empirical findings seem to deny this. Although elderly women in Germany are affected by poverty more often than elderly men, they are, in contrast to their counterparts in many other countries—not affected by poverty more often than the population generally.

One could name several aspects of the German statutory pension system (Gesetzliche Rentenversicherung, GRV)—the main source of income for the elderly population in Germany—that even seem to favor women over men:

- Today, the majority of pensions and also the majority of pension expenditures within the GRV go to elderly women.
- Although women have a higher life expectancy than men, this is not taken into account in the calculation of GRV pensions. Accordingly, women on average get a higher "return on investment" for their contributions to the public pension system.
- Approximately 20% of the pension expenditures in the GRV system are spent on survivors' pensions, and the great majority of these pensions, for which no extra contribution has to be paid, go to widows.
- Women profit from tax-financed redistributive measures within the public pension system, such as benefits for the upbringing of children or for the care of elderly relatives.

Why is it nevertheless necessary to examine the financial situation of women in old age in greater detail, and in particular the situation of elderly single women?

- As far as the *overall poverty rate of elderly women* is concerned, the usual approach to measure poverty on a household basis leads by definition to the outcome that either all members of a household or nobody in the household are regarded poor. Women with low individual pensions are therefore not identified as being poor as long as they live with a well-off partner. Poverty research usually assumes that household income is pooled and evenly distributed among the household members, although empirical evidence for these assumptions is poor.

- The situation of *single elderly women* depends on their marital statuses, that is, whether they were never married, widowed, or divorced. The conditions of all three groups of single elderly women are directly influenced by the principles of the pension system.
- In spite of the aforementioned elements in the pension system that "favor" women, the dominant principles of the German pension system—in particular, the relatively strong orientation toward lifetime income from employment and the absence of a minimum pension—are oriented toward traditional male careers and leave most women with relatively low pensions of their own.
- As far as the "feminization of poverty" is concerned, it also has to be determined how recent reforms of the pension system might influence the *future situation of elderly women*. In particular, the pension reform implemented in 2001, together with some recent reforms, will have a significant impact on future pension claims.

## Pension Claims and Poverty Risks of Elderly Women

The government's second official report on poverty and wealth (Bundesregierung, 2005) reveals that the poverty rate of elderly women—measured by the 60% threshold—was 13.5%, compared to 9.8% for elderly men in 2003 (Table 4.6, p. 110) but also that the gap between elderly men and women has narrowed and that elderly people in general now have a lower poverty rate than the average population.

Since approximately 85%–90% of the income of elderly women consists of pension income,[5] the following sections will concentrate on income from the statutory (first pillar) and occupational (second pillar) pension schemes.

**Elderly women's own pension rights.** Almost all East German women and an increasing share of West German women are entitled to pensions of their own in the public pension system, GRV. However, many women have very low pensions of their own. In 2005, West German female pensioners on average received a monthly pension of their own of €458, less than half the average male pension. In East Germany, where, during the GDR-period, most women worked full time and wage differentials between women and men were lower, women on average have a pension of their own of €661 today, approximately 60% of an average male pension (BmAS, 2005, p. 93). If one looks at the historic development of pensions in West Germany, this relation between the level of female and male (own) pensions has not changed very much since 1960.

**Survivors' pensions.** Derived rights—namely survivors' pensions—still play a considerable role in women's old-age income. Approximately

TABLE 4.6 Poverty Rates[a] by Sex, Total Population, and Pensioners, 1998 and 2003

| | 1998 | 2003 |
|---|---|---|
| Female (total) | 13.3 | 14.4 |
| Male (total) | 10.7 | 12.6 |
| Female pensioners | 14.2 | 13.5 |
| Male pensioners | 9.7 | 9.8 |

[a]Poverty is defined as Less than 60% Median Equivalent Income.

*Source*: Bundesregierung, 2005, pp. 85ff.

4 million West German and another 960,000 East German women receive a widow's pension; 86% of all survivors' pensions in the public system go to women. On average, widows who are eligible receive a net monthly survivors' pension of €625 per month in West Germany and €556 in East Germany (BmAS, 2005, p. 95). Survivors' pensions are important means of avoiding poverty among older women who live alone. These benefits, however, do not carry the same rights as own pensions. First, they are means-tested, and if the claimant's own income or pensions are above a certain threshold, his or her survivors' pension is reduced. Second, a new marriage leads to the termination of the claim after a transition period of 2 years. Finally, survivors' pensions cannot be regarded as a reward for care work, because the level of the pension does not reflect the unpaid work of women but the work history of their husbands.

**Overcoming poverty through combining pensions.** The level of a single pension does not indicate anything about the poverty or well-being of the person who receives it. Approximately one-third of all female pensioners, most of them widows living alone, receive two or more pensions from the statutory pension program. On average, these elderly women received €1.053 per month from the GRV and reached a standard of living comparable to single elderly men, clearly above the poverty level. As a result it can be said that the group of elderly widows living alone are quite well protected by the German pension system—in particular those who chose the "modernized breadwinner model," combining a high male wage with female part-time employment.

**Women's access to occupational pensions.** In Germany, unlike some other European countries, occupational pensions—the "second pillar" of the pension system—are voluntary on the part of the employer. So far only a minority of elderly women in Germany has a claim to an occupational pension of her own, and the gap is only diminishing slowly. In 2003 only 19% of all elderly women who had worked in the private sector received an occupational pension, with an average monthly amount of €258. Men were almost three times as likely to have a pension, and their average benefit of €452 was also much higher (BmGS, 2005, pp. 7–8). Occupational

TABLE 4.7 Total (Gross) Monthly Income of Single, Elderly Women by Marital Status, in Comparison with Other Family Types, 2003, in €/Month

| | West Germany | East Germany | Germany |
|---|---|---|---|
| Women living alone—average | 1299 | 1253 | 1283 |
| - widows | 1311 | 1300 | 1309 |
| - divorced women | 1149 | 890 | 1081 |
| - never-married women | 1328 | 1023 | 1272 |
| Elderly married couples | 2454 | 2083 | 2381 |
| Own pension income of married women | 417 | 700 | 472 |

*Source*: BmAS, 2005, Appendix, pp. 40–42.

pensions therefore deepen the income gap between elderly women and men. This holds for West Germany; in East Germany hardly any of today's pensioners receives an occupational pension.

**Savings.** Concerning the "third pillar" of the German old-age security system—private savings for old age—there is still a lack of reliable gender specific data. However, earlier research has shown that if the husband or male partner saves for old age (e.g., in a pension plan), there is a higher probability that the female partner also saves for her old age (Bieber & Stegmann, 2000, pp. 180ff.).

**The situation of elderly women living alone.** Elderly women *who live alone* are not a homogenous group. Nearly four-fifths (78.8%) are widows; divorced and never-married women ("real singles") make up the remaining fifth (9.6% and 11.6%, respectively). The income and poverty risk of these three groups differ due to their (former) marital status, corresponding with different labor market behavior and the logic of the pension system.

As Table 4.7 shows, elderly women living alone are not necessarily worse off than married elderly women. On the one hand, the average income of elderly couples is approximately 86% higher than the income of elderly women living alone. If one looks at the own pension income of married women, on the other hand, the situation looks different. With an average personal income of €472, a married elderly woman is far below the poverty line. Twelve percent of all elderly married women do not receive any pension of their own, and another 24% have a pension of their own less than €250 per month (BmAS, 2005, p. 153). As a result of the male breadwinner model in (West) Germany, most of today's elderly women have a low personal income as long as their husband is alive.

As the data in Table 4.8 indicate, divorced elderly women have the worst economic status of the three subgroups of single elderly women, and widows have the highest. On average all three groups have incomes considerably higher than the poverty level for a single person. Another remarkable finding is that the differences among the three groups are not very big, particularly in West Germany.

TABLE 4.8 Average Monthly Income of Single Elderly Women and Men by Marital Status and Composition of Women's Income, 2003, in €

| | Married (Household Income of the Couple) | Living Alone (All Groups) | Widowed | Divorced | Never Married |
|---|---|---|---|---|---|
| Women | 2381 | 1283 | 1309 | 1081 | 1272 |
| Men | 2434 | 1677 | 1738 | 1602 | 1581 |
| Women's pension income | 2019 | 1148 | 1179 | 919 | 1130 |
| – own pension | 472 | 545 | 415 | 903 | 1130 |
| – derived pension | 1547 | 604 | 764 | (16) | – |
| Other income | 363 | 135 | 130 | 162 | 142 |
| Taxes and social security contributions | –252 | –112 | –113 | –89 | –128 |
| Total net income | 2129 | 1171 | 1196 | 992 | 1143 |

*Sources*: BmAS, 2005, Appendix pp. 40–42, Datasource ASID.

## Explaining Elderly Women's Situation

**Male norm as pension norm**. The main reason for the differences in men's and women's own pension claims is that old-age pensions in the German pension system mainly reflect the person's income level in each year of working life. Only a small share of today's female pensioners (in West Germany, below 5%) achieve the normative target of the system, 45 years of work with an average income.

The German pension system grants comparatively generous credits for child care and elder care. This holds particularly for women whose children were born since 1992 who, in old age, will receive an equivalent of three full insurance years per child, whether they have interrupted their career for child care or not. Periods for elder care are modestly taken into account since the implementation of the compulsory care insurance in 1995, but only where carers suffer an actual loss of income and insurance entitlements. In spite of these pension benefits for carers today there is—at least in West Germany—still a negative correlation between the number of children a woman has and her pension income (BmAS, 2005, p. 159; Klammer et al., 2000, p. 320).

Deficits in women's own pension claims are due to missing years in the labor market (time factor) and low income (income factor). According to AVID, an encompassing database on men's and women's working lives and pension claims, 83% of all West-German women born between 1936 and 1940 interrupted their careers to care for children and on average spent 10.3 years at home with their children below 18. Although these interruptions decreased in later cohorts, still 69% of West German women born between 1951 and 1955 spent some time as housewives (Klammer, 2007). In East Germany interruptions usually were and are shorter.

Another source of women's disadvantage, limited access to occupational pensions, stems from the smaller size companies in which they are employed and the minimum requirements for and the limited portability of occupational pensions (Klammer et al., 2000, pp. 314–316).

**Three groups of elderly women living alone.** As it has become clear, the differences between the incomes of the three groups of lone elderly women are not very big. Why?

- *Never-married women* had to work for their living; they therefore achieved much higher pension claims of their own than married women. But due to the gender pay gap, and so on, most get much lower pensions than single men.
- *Widows'* own pensions are low but only about one-third of their income, with survivors' pensions accounting for approximately 60% and other sources such as savings approximately 10%. Recall, however, that derived pensions are not equivalent to individual pension rights.
- Many *divorced women* lived in a breadwinner arrangement that causes a high poverty risk directly after divorce, but, in retirement they profit from the compulsory splitting of all pension claims built up by both spouses during marriage ("Versorgungsausgleich"). However, most divorces take place after a short marriage. Although the woman who stayed at home gets half of the pension claims accumulated during marriage, she will usually not be able to take up her career and to accumulate decent pension claims during the remaining years.

**Single elderly migrant women.** The problems described, in particular, the relatively low level and continuity of labor market participation and the low wages of migrant women, lead to a low level of own pension claims. In addition, many migrant women work in minijobs or in the shadow economy. Endeavors of the government to convert "black" jobs in private households to legal part-time work with social security contributions have not been very successful. Widows of men who immigrated to Germany in the 1960s and were employed for many years as industrial workers often get a decent survivors' pension, but this does not hold for other groups of immigrant women.

People from EU-member states can profit from favorable regulations (implemented in the early 1970s) that guarantee that all pension claims acquired in EU countries are taken into account when the pension is calculated. Germany also has bilateral agreements of a similar kind with a number of other countries. Migrants who come from countries without such an agreement with Germany are exposed to a higher poverty risk in old age.

**Future development.** Since 2001, the German pension system has been reformed considerably with changes that will have a significant effect on elderly women. The reform of 2001 introduced some improvements for mothers:

- Own pensions: Pension claims of employed parents with low income (but not "minijobs") will be upgraded, and nonworking mothers with at least two children will get a comparable supplement.
- Derived pensions: Introduction of a child bonus. Survivors' pensions for widows who have raised children replace 60% of the insured person's pension; childless survivors receive 55%. This improves the situation of former housewives and mothers relative to women who have longer work histories and higher income.

However, these new bonuses for mothers system have to be seen in the context of severe general cuts in the first pillar pension system:

- The pension reform of 2001 in combination with the more recent "RV-Nachhaltigkeitsgesetz" and changes in the taxation of pensions will lead to a decrease of the net replacement rate of a full pension from almost 70% to something like 52%.
- These cuts in the PAYG first pillar system imply that all the redistributive measures in the pension system from which mainly women profit—like pension credits for child care and elder care—will lose weight.
- Future pension adjustments will not cover the complete increase in the costs of living.
- Pensioners have to pay higher contributions than before for social care insurance.
- The official retirement age for both sexes will be raised from 65 to 67 over the next decades, with pension reductions in case of early retirement.

Owing to these cuts in the first pillar system Germans will have to increase their private savings and this is harder for women. In sum, feminist researchers assume that women are relatively disadvantaged through the reduced redistributive elements and the envisaged shift from first to second and third pillars of the pension system (Kerschbaumer & Veil, 2000).

**Measures to reform the second and third pillar.** The pension reform of 2001 has improved women's chances to claim an occupational pension by reducing the minimum requirements to 5 years work in the company instead of 10 years and reduction of the age when the employee can leave the firm without losing pension rights from 35 to 30; in addition, the portability of claims was increased in 2005 (Alterseinkünftegesetz). However, employers are still not obliged to offer an employer-financed occupational pension. Instead of introducing an obligation the government chose to give tax incentives or tax-financed subsidies for saving in special certified saving plans, including supplements for number of children (so-called Riester-, Eichel-, and Rürup-contracts).

It is too early to estimate the impact of these developments on the future incomes of elderly women. A positive development can be seen in the new obligation for insurances to offer gender neutral contributions to the subsidized saving contracts. Until 2005, women had to pay approximately 11%–15% more than men to get the same monthly payment in old age, due to their longer life expectancy.

To conclude, the recent developments in Germany give a mixed picture as far as the future poverty risks of women in old age are concerned. On the one hand, women will on average build up more own entitlements in the pension system due to their increased labor market participation. In addition, some improvements for mothers implemented by the pension reform of 2001 and in earlier reforms will lead to a relative improvement of the situation of mothers in old age. On the other hand, these changes go along with severe cuts in the whole first pillar system with its substantial redistributive elements from which mostly women benefited in the past. It is quite probable that the shift to greater reliance on second and third pillar systems will increase the overall poverty risk in old age and the poverty risk of elderly women as well.

## Gaps in Existing Knowledge

As pointed out, ample data are available on the development of poverty and the distribution of poverty risks among different subgroups of the German population. Data on the specific situation of the constantly growing migrant population is still limited.

As for the present discussion in German poverty research, there also is a certain discrepancy between theoretical concepts and available data. Whereas the government's second official report on poverty and wealth stresses the importance of Sen's capability approach to poverty (Sen, 1995, 1992), the data presented still focus on income. For future research the challenge will be to operationalize and measure poverty convincingly from the perspective of capabilities and chances for individual development.

## Political Resources: Support for Gender Equality?

Officially all political parties in Germany argue in favor of gender equality, and the EU exerts additional pressure on Germany to take action in this field, for example, through the European Court of Justice. However, in practice there is a lot of resistance to abolishing labor and social security laws favoring the male breadwinner model. The questionable distributive effects of the system of joint taxation of married partners have been revealed in a number of scientific studies (e.g., Deutscher Bundestag, 2002; Vollmer, 1998, 2006), and alternatives have been proposed (Deutsches Institut für Wirtschaftsforschung (DIW), 1999a, 1999b). Researchers and lobby groups such as the association of single mothers and fathers (VAMF) have demanded equal tax treatment of married, unmarried, and single parents for years. However, the system has hardly been changed and is still defended by many (mostly conservative) politicians and lawyers. As Mantl (2006) has shown, the support for the model that can be traced back to the period of industrialization in Germany has survived during all subsequent historical phases. The recent support for an extension of public child care and the new parental leave scheme certainly reflects a moderate change of paradigm. Whether the recent changes will contribute to a sustainable decrease in the poverty risk of solo mothers is still not clear.

Support for improving the condition of elderly women has also been widespread but with an ambivalent focus. While the acknowledgment of care work in the pension system has been improved, the dominant logic of the pension system is still oriented toward continuous, full-time employment, and consequently, the pension gap between elderly men and women persists. The fact that today's single elderly women are *not* exposed to a high poverty risk mainly reflects the fact that most of them are widows who had a long-lasting, stable marriage with a continuously employed male partner. The increased labor market participation of women will work toward closing the gap in individual male and female pension claims, but recent changes in the pension system pose new poverty risks for women in old age.

The fact that single elderly women *at present* do not have a particularly high poverty risk (especially as widows) is one of the reasons why, in contrast to single mothers, they are currently not really the focus of any influential political party or lobby. Actually it is the growing concern about child poverty and its potential impact on the future development of the country that has helped single mothers to receive a lot of attention and some support from different political parties and interest groups. Different proposals about the extension of public child care and primary education, but also new cash benefits for carers that are being discussed in the political arena might contribute to an improvement of their still precarious situation.

## Summary and Conclusions

As in most European countries, recent labor market reform laws in Germany have increased the pressure on unemployed adults of both sexes to become employed. But promotion of women's employment has hardly been accompanied by a reduction in the benefits enjoyed by nonworking married women. Women deviating from the norm—in particular by being solo mothers—suffer a particularly high poverty risk.

The situation is different for elderly, single women. Although most of today's female pensioners have relatively small pensions of their own, the poverty risk of elderly women today is not above average. Most partnered elderly women live with a partner whose pension claims are sufficient to prevent poverty in the household. In case of divorce, women profit from the obligatory sharing of all pension claims that have been acquired during marriage. The majority of elderly women living alone are widows, many of whom add a (decent) survivor's pension to a (small) pension of their own. They do not deviate from the norm—and are therefore relatively well protected by the German social insurance system. Only a small minority of today's elderly women have never been married. In comparison with younger women without partners, most of them are childless and have been working for many years so that their own pension claim in most cases lifts them above the poverty threshold.

A look ahead, however, reveals some indication that the situation of elderly women might change for the worse: Whereas more women will build up their own pension claims due to their rising employment rates, the decreasing stability of marriage, in combination with the severe future cuts already enacted in the first pillar public pension system point to reduced security in old age for women, particularly. This might expose single elderly women to a high risk of poverty once again.

## Postscript

After the release of a new wave of data from the "AVID" datasource in November 2007, it has become clear that Germany will probably have to face a considerable return of poverty in old age in future decades, and the topic has returned to the public debate. The official presentation of data by the government and the pension insurance (e.g., Rische, 2007) stressed the point that people with full working careers will almost be able to cover the cuts in the public system by making use of the subsidized, voluntary "Riester pension" (if the interest rate reaches 5%!). But it also became obvious that people with low income, discontinuous careers, and who do not save for old age will have to bear an increasing risk of poverty even more because of the current economic crisis that is expected to have serious long-term effects on employment and income. West German women are expected to improve their relative and partly even their absolute position (due to their increasing labor market participation). Poverty in old age will mainly affect East Germans, but low incomes and discontinuous careers are also characteristic of some women and men in West Germany.

## Notes

1 Social protection systems were regarded as the province of the EU-member states for a long time (principle of subsidiarity). In recent years the EU level has increased its impact on members' labor market and social protection policy.
2 The government report is based on a number of independent scientific studies (commissioned by the government) on different aspects of poverty in Germany.
3 In spite of their high risk of poverty, the situation of immigrants cannot be analyzed in detail in this chapter. The situation of solo mothers and single elderly women differs very much according to the countries of origin of the immigrants and the period of migration.
4 East German mothers are far more likely to have full-time employment.
5 Married elderly women: 85%, widows: 90%, divorced women: 85%, single women: 89% (BmAS, 2005, Appendix C-41, database ASID).

## References

Bauer, F., Groß, H., Lehmann, K., & Munz, E. (2004). *Arbeitszeit 2003, Arbeitszeitgestaltung, Arbeitsorganisation und Tätigkeitsprofile.* Köln: ISO.

Bieber, U., & Stegmann, M. (2000). Sozialversicherungspflichtige Teilzeitbeschäftigung in den Sozialversicherungsbiographien der zukünftigen Rentnerinnen und Auswirkungen auf die Altersvorsorge. *Deutsche Rentenversicherung, 6,* June, 364–383.

BmAS. (2005). *Ergänzender Bericht der Bundesregierung zum Rentenversicherungsbericht 2005 gemäß § 154 Abs. 2 SGB VI (Alterssicherungsbericht).* Berlin: BmAS.

BmFSFJ. (2003). *Wenn aus Liebe rote Zahlen werden. Über die wirtschaftlichen Folgen von Trennung und Scheidung.* Berlin: BmFSFJ.

BmFSFJ. (2005). *UVG-Statistik 2004,* 204–2627–5, Berlin: BmFSFJ.

BmFSFJ. (2006). *Der Unterhaltsvorschuss. Eine Hilfe für Alleinerziehende.* Berlin: BmFSFJ.

BmGS. (2005). *Sozialbericht 2005.* Bonn: BmGS.

Bothfeld, S., Klammer, U., Klenner, C., Leiber, S., Thiel, A., & Ziegler, A. (2005). *WSI-FrauenDatenReport 2005.* Berlin: Sigma.

Bundesregierung. (2005). *Lebenslagen in Deutschland. Der 2. Armuts- und Reichtumsbericht der Bundesregierung,* Berlin: Deutsche Bundesregierung.

Deutscher Bundestag. (2002). *Bericht der Bundesregierung zur Berufs- und Einkommens situation von Frauen und Männern,* BT-Drucksache 14/8952. Berlin: Deutscher Bundestag.

Deutscher Bundestag (2006). *Siebter Familienbericht. Familie zwischen Flexibilität und Verlässlichkeit – Perspektiven für eine lebenslaufbezogene Familienpolitik.* BT-Drucksache 16/1360, Berlin: Deutscher Bundestag.

Deutsches Jugendinstitut. (2005). *Kommentierter Datenreport zur Gleichstellung von Frauen und Männern in der Bundesrepublik Deutschland.* München: DJI.

Dingeldey, I. (2000). Einkommensteuersysteme und familiale Erwerbsmuster im europäischen Vergleich. In I. Dingeldey (Ed.), *Erwerbstätigkeit und Familie in Steuer- und Sozialver sicherungssystemen. Begünstigungen und Belastungen verschiedener Erwerbsmuster im Ländervergleich* (pp. 11–47). Opladen: Leske & Budrich.

Dingeldey, I. (2002). Das deutsche System der Ehegattenbesteuerung im europäischen Vergleich. *WSI-Mitteilungen, 3*(March), 154–160.

DIW (Deutsches Institut für Wirtschaftsforschung). (1999a). *Alternativen zur Ehegattenbesteuerung aus verfassungsrechtlicher, steuersystematischer und ökonomischer Sicht*, Forschungsauftrag der Hans-Böckler-Stiftung, Berlin/Münster: Hans-Böckler-Stiftung.

DIW. (1999b). *DIW-Wochenbericht* 8.

Engstler, H., & Menning, S. (2003). *Die Familie im Spiegel der amtlichen Statistik.* Berlin: BmFSFJ.

Eurostat. (2004). Armut und soziale Ausgrenzung in der EU. *Statistik kurz gefasst, Bevölkerung und soziale Bedingungen, 16.*

Eurostat. (2005). http://www.eds-destatis.de/de/database.php?m=db. Accessed July 29, 2009.

Frings, D. (2005). *Arbeitsmarktreformen und Zuwanderungsrecht – Auswirkungen für Migrantinnen und Migranten*. Frankfurt, AM: M.A.R.E.

Goebel, J., Habich, R., & Krause, P. (2002). Einkommensverteilung und Armut. In Statistisches Bundesamt (Ed.), *Datenreport 2002* (pp. 586–596). Wiesbaden: Statistisches Bundesamt.

Graf, T., & Rudolph, H. (2006). Bedarfsgemeinschaften im SGB II 2005. Beachtliche Dynamik bei steigenden Empfängerzahlen. *IAB-Kurzbericht, 23* (2006).

Kahle, I. (2004). Alleinerziehende im Spannungsfeld zwischen Beruf und Familie. In Statistisches Bundesamt (Ed.), *Alltag in Deutschland, Analysen zur Zeitverwendung, Forum der Bundesstatistik, 43*, 175–193.

Kerschbaumer, J., & Veil, M. (2000). Ein paternalistischer Flickenteppich für Frauen. *Frankfurter Rundschau, 248*, (10/25/2000), 8.

Klammer, U. (2005). Soziale Sicherung. In S. Bothfeld, U. Klammer, C. Klenner, S. Leiber, A. Thiel, & A. Ziegler (Eds.), *WSI-FrauenDatenReport 2005* (pp. 307–382). Berlin: Sigma.

Klammer, U. (2007). Zeit und Geld im Lebensverlauf – Empirische Evidenz und sozialpolitischer Handlungsbedarf aus der Geschlechterperspektive. *Intervention, 4*, 1(spring), 145–174.

Klammer, U., & Daly, M. (2003). Die Beteiligung von Frauen an europäischen Arbeitsmärkten. In U. Gerhard, T. Knijn, & A. Weckwert (Eds.), *Erwerbstätige Mütter. Ein europäischer Vergleich* (pp. 193–217). München: Beck.

Klammer, U., Klenner, C., Ochs, C., Radke, P., & Ziegler, A. (2000). *WSI-FrauenDatenReport*. Berlin: Sigma.

Klenner, C., Pfahl, S., & Reuyß, S. (2003). Flexible Arbeitszeiten aus Sicht von Eltern und Kindern. *Zeitschrift für Soziologie der Erziehung und Sozialisation, 23*, 3, 268–285.

Ludwig, I., Schlevogt, V., Klammer, U., & Gerhard, U. (2002). *Managerinnen des Alltags. Strategien erwerbstätiger Mütter in Ost- und Westdeutschland*. Berlin: Sigma.

Mantl, E. (2006). Gute Mütter - gute Töchter. Konzepte - Visionen - Lebenswirklichkeit. Zur Kulturalität deutscher Erfahrungen seit 1870. In H. Bertram, H. Krüger, & C. K. Spiess (Eds.), *Wem gehört die Familie der Zukunft? Expertisen zum 7. Familienbericht der Bundesregierung* (pp. 235–257). Opladen: Barbara Budrich.

OECD. (2004). *Starting strong – Länderbericht Deutschland 2004: Die Politik der frühkindlichen Betreuung, Bildung und Erziehung in der Bundesrepublik Deutschland.* Paris: OECD.

Rische, H. (2007). Vorstellung der Studie "Altersvorsorge in Deutschland (AVID)," 3. Aktuelles Presseseminar der Deutschen Rentenversicherung Bund, Würzburg 20.-21,11,2007. www.deutsche-rentenversicherung.de. Accessed July 29, 2009.

Schmidt, R. (2003). *Rede vor dem deutschen Bundestag am 9.9.2003*. Available at http://www.bmfsfj.de/dokumente/Rede/ix_92921_9182.htm. Accessed July 29, 2009.

Schulte, J. (2005). Paare – gemeinsam arm dran. *Boecklerimpuls, 1*, 1.

Sen, A. (1992). *Inequality reexamined*. Oxford & New York: Clarendon Press.

Sen, A. (1995). Rationality and choice. *American Economic Review, 85*, 1, 1–23.

Statistisches Bundesamt. (2002). *Datenreport. Zahlen und Fakten über die Bundesrepublik Deutschland*. Bonn: Statistisches Bundesamt.

Statistisches Bundesamt. (2003). *FS 13 Sozialleistungen, R 2 Sozialhilfe*. Wiesbaden: Statistisches Bundesamt.

Statistisches Bundesamt. (2004a). *Kindertagesbetreuung regional 2002. Krippen-, Kindergarten und Hortplätze im Kreisvergleich*, Edition 2004. Bonn: Statistisches Bundesamt.

Statistisches Bundesamt. (2004b). *Leben und Arbeiten in Deutschland, Ergebnisse des Mikrozensus 2003*. Wiesbaden: Statistisches Bundesamt.

VAMV (Verband allein erziehender Mütter und Väter Bundesverband e.V.). (2006). *Schwarzbuch Hartz IV und Alleinerziehende*. Berlin: VAMF. www.vamv.de. Accessed July 29, 2009.

Vesper, D. (2005). Gibt es fiskalische Anreize für die Kommunen zum Ausbau der Kinderbetreuung? *DIW-Wochenbericht. 3*, 41–48.

Vollmer, F. (1998). *Das Ehegattensplitting*. Baden-Baden: Nomos.

Vollmer, F. (2006). Verfassungsrechtliche Fragen der Ehe- und Familienbesteuerung. In J. Althammer, & U. Klammer (Eds.), *Ehe und Familie in der Steuerrechts- und Sozialordnung* (pp. 73–92). Tübingen: Mohr Siebeck.

# 5

# THE UNITED KINGDOM: THE FEMINIZATION OF POVERTY?

*Jane Millar*

The United Kingdom is a highly industrialized and rich country with a well developed welfare state providing both cash transfers and services, the latter including health care and education that are free at the point of use. The population of approximately 60 million people includes 11.6 million children under 16, 38.6 million people aged between 16 and 64, and 9.6 million people aged over 65 (ONS, 2007). Employment rates are at high levels, at around 76% for people of working age, and registered unemployment has been steady at 5%–6% in recent years, although rising to 7% in early 2009. Most people own, or are buying, their own homes (over 70%), and this is likely to be their most important asset. Ownership of consumer goods is high, and there are very few households that do not have televisions, washing machines, central heating, and so on. Most households own cars; 44% have access to one car; 30% have access to two. But the United Kingdom is also a country with significant levels of economic inequality and poverty. The top 10% own more of the total income than the whole of the bottom 50%. Overall income inequality is now higher than it has been since the 1940s, and inequalities in wealth are even higher (Hills, 2004). There are estimated to be 13.5 million people living in poor households (defined as incomes of less than 60% of the median, after housing costs) in 2007/8. This means that 23% of the British population live in poverty according to this measure, including 31% of children, 21% of adult women, and 19% of adult men (DWP, 2009).

However, poverty is not simply a random misfortune that strikes indiscriminately. Poverty is more likely to be found among people who do not have jobs and where no one in the household has a job, who have long-term health problems or disabilities, who have large families, who are sole-parent families, who come from ethnic minority groups (especially Pakistani and Bangladeshi families), and who are elderly and live alone. In each case, it is women who have higher rates of poverty than men, and this has been true for many years, including the first systematic British poverty studies carried out over 100 years ago (Bradshaw, Finch, Kemp, Mayhew, & Williams, 2003; Glendinning & Millar, 1987). There are more poor women in the United Kingdom than there are poor men; women have a higher risk of poverty than men, and they stay poor longer.

This chapter summarizes the key data on women's poverty in the United Kingdom and explores the impact of recent policy on two key groups: sole mothers and lone elderly women. The focus here is on the past decade or so, from about the mid-1990s to the most recent evidence available to us. This is a particularly interesting period for both political and economic reasons. On the political front, the election of a Labour government in 1997, after almost 20 years of Conservative rule, meant a change in policy direction and a clear commitment to reducing social exclusion and poverty, especially pensioner poverty and child poverty. The government has set an explicit target to eliminate child poverty within the first 20 years of this century. The U.K. economic situation in the 1990s was very positive, with a strong and growing economy and high levels of employment. There was thus, both, political will to tackle poverty and the economic opportunity to do so. Ten years on, however, the outcomes have proved to be rather mixed, and—as we will argue in this chapter—the policy directions taken have not always recognized the specific situations and needs of women. The next section of this chapter sets out some key data about women's access to employment and income in Britain at the turn of the twenty-first century, including a discussion of main policy developments, before going on to examine the situations of sole mothers and lone elderly women in more detail.

## British Women at the Turn of the Twenty-First Century: Independence and Dependence

One of the major drivers of the feminization of poverty is that there are increasing numbers of women who live alone, forming their own single-person or single-parent households. In this section we explore the extent to which women are living alone; the capacity of women to support themselves and their dependent children through paid employment; the level of income poverty and material deprivation among women living alone; and the ways in which poor women manage and survive.

### Women in Households and Families

As noted earlier, the total population of the United Kingdom is almost 60 million,[1] with slightly more females (30.5 million) than males (29.3 million).

TABLE 5.1 People Living Alone by Sex and Age, Great Britain, 2007, Percentages

| | Women | Men |
|---|---|---|
| 16–24 | 2 | 3 |
| 25–44 | 8 | 14 |
| 45–64 | 14 | 15 |
| 65–74 | 30 | 20 |
| 75 and over | 61 | 35 |

*Source*: ONS, 2009a, Figure 2.7.

This difference is mainly accounted for by the fact that there are more elderly women than elderly men. In 2004 there were 2.8 million women aged 75 and above compared with 1.7 million men. As in many other countries, there has been a significant increase in sole mothers living in Britain over the past generation. In 1971, approximately 18% of all households were one-person households, and by 2005 this had increased to 29%. If we consider people, rather than households, just over 7 million people are living alone, representing approximately 12% of all people. Living alone has become more common across the life course, but as Table 5.1 shows, this varies considerably with age and sex. It is older people, particularly older women, who live alone, with about three-fifths of women aged 75 and above living alone, compared with just over a third of men of that age. For both age groups among the elderly, women are from 50% to about 75% more likely to live alone than men. Women live longer than men, and men tend to marry women younger than they are, so men are less likely to be widowed than women.

In addition, it is women, rather than men, who are increasingly living in sole-parent families. The proportion of sole-parent households with dependent children has increased from 3% in 1971 to 7% in 2005, and nine in ten of these parents are women. If we focus only on households with dependent children, 25% are sole-parent families, accounting for 1.9 million families with 3.1 million children. There is some variation in rates of sole parenthood by ethnic origin. Nonwhite ethnic groups make up 12% of the U.K. population, including just over 1% with mixed ethnic backgrounds. Rates of sole parenthood are relatively high among the Black Caribbean (57%) and the Black African (47%) populations, and relatively low among the Indian (13%), Pakistani (19%), Bangladeshi (18%), and Chinese (18%).

Widowhood is now a very uncommon route into sole parenthood for women, accounting for around 5% of the total. The three main groups among sole mothers are ex-married mothers (39% of the total), ex-cohabiting mothers (29%), and single mothers who have never lived with a partner (25%) (Marsh & Perry, 2003). These groups are somewhat different in their characteristics. The ex-married women are typically older, have larger families, and their children are more likely to be teenagers. The single mothers are typically younger with just one child of preschool age and tend to have less contact with the fathers of their children than formerly married women. Sole parenthood is not permanent—children grow up and leave home, people find new partners—and the median duration of sole parenthood is 5 years (Millar & Ridge, 2001).

There are thus two main points in the lifecourse when British women are very likely to form their own households. The first point is sole motherhood, and in these households the women also have responsibility for dependent (and sometimes also nondependent, older) children. As noted earlier, there are 1.9 million women in this situation in the United Kingdom today. The second point is older age, and for the current generation this generally means that they are widowed women (for younger generations, where marriage is less common, this may not continue to be the case). There are 2.5 million women aged 65 and above living alone.

Thus in total there are about 4.4 million women in the United Kingdom in these two groups of sole mothers and elderly women who form their own households. This is almost one-fifth (18%) of all adult women. For sole mothers, their economic situation depends on the resources they can command through their own wages, through government transfers in the tax and social security systems and through transfers from former partners and other family members. For elderly women, the potential sources of income are less likely to include own wages from work, but could include pensions based on their wages, pensions based on survivors' rights from their husbands, savings, government transfers, and family support. As we explore subsequently, being able to combine different sources of income is essential in avoiding poverty but is often difficult to achieve in practice. Current access to resources is also dependent on past access to resources, and for both sole mothers and elderly women this includes their past relationships with husbands and partners. In focusing on sole mothers and elderly women, it is important not to forget that marriage or cohabitation is still the experience and situation of the vast majority of British women. We therefore need to consider the extent to which women in general—and not just those forming their own households—have access to adequate incomes independently of their partners.

## Women at Work

Wages are the main source of independent income for most people, and so employment participation and opportunity are key factors in understanding patterns of poverty. Women's labor force rates rose in the second half of the twentieth century, and the employment rate is now at approximately 73% for women of working age (16–59) without dependent children, 68% for those with dependent children. As Table 5.2 shows the employment rate varies by age for both women and men, and, for women, whether or not there are children. Young women without dependent children

TABLE 5.2 Employment Rates of Working-Age People with and without Dependent Children by Age and Sex, 2008

| | 16–24 | 25–34 | 35–49 | 50–59/64[a] | All |
|---|---|---|---|---|---|
| Women, no children | 59 | 89 | 83 | 70 | 73 |
| Men, no children | 56 | 88 | 84 | 71 | 74 |
| Mothers | 34 | 61 | 74 | 74 | 68 |
| Fathers | 68 | 90 | 92 | 85 | 90 |

[a] Women, ages 50–59; men, ages 50–64.
*Source*: ONS, 2009a, Table 4.6.

have employment rates very similar to young men without children (59% and 56%) with many of these young people still in full-time education. Employment rates rise to 88%–89% for the peak working years up to age 50, and then down to 70%–71% for those aged over 50. Fathers typically have higher employment rates than men without children. Mothers have lower employment rates than women without children. Nevertheless six in ten mothers aged 25–34 are in employment, as are three-quarters of mothers aged 35–49, so being in paid work is now more common than not for British mothers.

The increase in women's employment is in part because the amount of time taken out of the labor market by mothers to care full time for their children has been steadily falling. In 1979, 24% of women who were in employment when they became pregnant returned to work within 9–11 months of the birth. By 1996 this had risen to 67%, including 24% who returned to full-time jobs. Most of these women went back to the same employer (86%), and they were less likely than women in the 1970s to have suffered downward occupational mobility on their return to work (Callender, Millward, Lissenburgh, & Forth, 1997). However, not all women are able to maintain paid employment at the same level after having children. Reviewing the employment experience of mothers, Dex (1999, p. 33) concludes that this is characterized by

> a polarization between higher status, higher waged women and the less educated and qualified ... the former group remain in their jobs, or only take a short break ... the latter group are likely to have longer breaks from work, more part-time weekly hours, more jobs with non-standard employment contracts and less job security.

This has obvious implications for the capacity of this second group of women to be able to achieve economic independence.

One of the main ways that British mothers manage employment and family is by moving into part-time employment when they have children. The extent of part-time working in the United Kingdom is a key difference between women and men, with 48% of employed women in part-time jobs compared with just 9% of employed men. It is also a key difference between women with and without dependent children, with 58% of employed mothers in part-time jobs compared with 33% of women without children. Other caring responsibilities—for elderly people or people with disabilities—are also associated with part-time work. There are 3.4 million women who are carers for other adults (most commonly parents or partners), and women carers have lower employment rates than women in general (at 65%). Of those carers who are employed, 46% work part time (Equal Opportunities Commission [EOC], 2006).

Overall, in spring 2004, there were about 5.8 million women in part-time work, including 1.9 million women working for less than 16 hours per week (Millar, Ridge, & Bennett, 2006). The median hours of work for women in part-time jobs is 20 per week. In general, women workers are concentrated in two main industrial sectors: public administration, education, and health (41%) and distribution, hotels, and catering (22%) (Bellamy & Rake, 2005). Part-time work is even more concentrated in the service sectors, is rarely found at management levels, and the jobs tend to be poor quality with little opportunity for training or advancement. There seems to be very little opportunity to move between part-time work and full-time work in the same organization, so mothers who work part time can tend to get trapped, and usually have to change employers if they want to change their hours of work. There is also some evidence of underutilization of skills among part-time workers, to some extent associated with downward mobility when women move into part-time jobs after having children. Manning and Petrongolo (2005) estimate that approximately 39% of women with a teaching qualification who are working part time are working in lower-level occupations, as are 23% of women with nursing qualifications.

From the economic independence and poverty perspective, part-time work is not a good option, either for current or for future prospects. Part-time work usually means lower pay. In 2008, median hourly gross earnings were £7.51 for women in part-time jobs, compared with £10.91 for women in full-time jobs and £12.50 for men in full-time jobs (Office for National Statistics, 2008). Approximately half of those working at the national minimum wage are women in part-time jobs (Bryan & Taylor, 2004). Low pay is associated with family poverty when there is only one earner in the family. Thus sole mothers who work part time rarely manage to avoid poverty, unless they can call on other sources of income (Gardiner & Millar, 2006). In two-parent families, mothers who work part time provide an essential part of weekly income, helping to keep their families out of poverty. In terms of individual future prospects, low pay usually means low pension entitlements and so poverty may continue into old age.

## Women's Incomes and Poverty Rates

Income is usually measured, and compared, on a household rather than an individual basis. Thus, for example, the U.K. poverty statistics count

TABLE 5.3 Median Individual Income by Sex and Age, £ Per Week, 2004–2005

| | Women | Men |
|---|---|---|
| 16–19 | 86 | 90 |
| 20–24 | 178 | 226 |
| 25–29 | 252 | 338 |
| 30–34 | 240 | 415 |
| 35–39 | 228 | 435 |
| 40–44 | 241 | 435 |
| 45–49 | 231 | 437 |
| 50–54 | 209 | 412 |
| 55–59 | 150 | 357 |
| 60–64 | 135 | 266 |
| 65–69 | 109 | 225 |
| 70–74 | 116 | 206 |
| 75–79 | 124 | 191 |
| 80–84 | 133 | 177 |
| 85 and over | 145 | 170 |

*Source*: ONS, 2007, Figure 5.3.

the number of individuals who live in households where the household income, adjusted for family size, is below a certain threshold (usually 60% of the median). However, as Glendinning and Millar (1987) pointed out some years ago, this aggregation of income ignores the issue of the distribution of income within the household unit. Inequalities within the family mean that women do not necessarily receive a fair share of family income, and women may also reduce their own consumption in order to protect that of children and partners. We start here, therefore, by considering individual income levels.

Table 5.3 shows median individual income by sex and age. Individual net income is the sum of wages, social security benefits, and other income for that person. Any family benefit, such as a child benefit, is assigned to the person who receives it (which is usually the mother), and any joint income is split equally between recipients. Overall the median individual income of women is 60% that of men, and, as the figure shows, at each age, women have lower individual income than men. The gap is smallest at the youngest age groups when incomes tend to be low in general as young people are studying or just starting in the labor market. The gap between women and men also narrows again in the oldest age groups, when people are generally reliant upon pension income (see further discussion in the section on single elderly women below). Very elderly women (80 and above) have slightly higher individual incomes than women aged 65–79, because the former are more likely to be widows with some personal pension entitlement in the form of survivors' benefits. It is in the prime working/family age range of 25–55 when the gap between women and men is largest. For example, women in their thirties and forties have individual incomes that are not much more than half of the average for men in the same age group. The impact of family responsibilities on income from employment is apparent in these figures—these are the women most likely to be working part time and hence with lower wages and lower individual incomes.

Women also have lower median incomes than men across all family types. For example, female sole parents have incomes that are 82% of those of male sole parents. However, it is among couples where the gaps between women and men are particularly large. Among pensioner couples women have median incomes of just 39% those of men. This is because these women have lower state and occupational pensions than their husbands. Among working-age couples with children women have individual incomes less than half (48%) those of men. This again reflects their much lower, and part-time, earnings and occurs despite the fact that they will usually be receiving some child benefit income. These differences within couples reinforce the aforementioned point about the importance of looking within the family unit to explore individual incomes. Women living in couples rarely have adequate incomes in their own right, and if the family is broken up by divorce, separation, or death, they may face a significant poverty risk. Jenkins and Rigg (2001) estimate that 35% of women becoming a sole parent also become poor. On the basis of data from the late 1980s/early 1990s, Jarvis and Jenkins (1998) found that, while men's income changes little when a couple separates, women's income on average falls by almost one-fifth. A more recent update of this analysis (Jenkins, 2008) shows that there is still a substantial difference in income levels between men and women postseparation but that the size of the reduction in women's income is now not so substantial. For women separating in the period 1998–2004, the average fall in income in the following year was 12%. Jenkins concludes that this reflects the recent rises in employment rates among sole mothers.

Women and men also tend to have different sources of income. Bellamy and Rake (2005) calculate the contribution of various sources of income to the total for women and men. On average, earnings (including from self employment) contribute 68% of the total for women and 81% for men. The main other sources for men are investment income and occupational pensions (13%), whereas for women the main other sources are tax credits and benefits (21%). Almost two-thirds of the women's tax credit/benefit income relates to children, so is being received by women in their role as mothers. Daly and Rake (2003), using data from the mid-1990s, find that 25% of women in the United Kingdom report that they have no personal income in their own right, and a further 8% have only benefit income (this would mainly be the child benefit, which is a weekly, flat-rate benefit paid for all dependent children in the United Kingdom and usually paid directly to the mother). These women are therefore completely, or almost completely, dependent upon partners for income.

TABLE 5.4 Poverty Rates[a] and Composition of the Poor by Family Type, Great Britain, 2007–2008

| | Composition % | Poverty Rate |
|---|---|---|
| Pensioner couple | 10 | 17 |
| Single pensioner | 7 | 21 |
| – women | –6 | 23 |
| – men | –1 | 15 |
| Single without children | 20 | 25 |
| – women | –8 | 26 |
| – men | –12 | 25 |
| Single with children | 18 | 50 |
| Couple without children | 10 | 12 |
| Couple with children | 35 | 23 |
| Total | 100 | 23 |
| Number | 13.5 million | |

[a] Individuals or families with incomes less than 60% the median equivalent income, after housing costs.

*Source*: DWP, 2009, Tables 3.3, 3.5.

Thus, on average, women tend to have lower earnings than men and lower individual incomes. Table 5.4 summarizes the situation as regards income poverty, from official government statistics, and using an income poverty line which counts the number of individuals living in households with an income, adjusted for household size and composition, of less than 60% of the median. Income is measured after housing costs, as this gives a clearer indication of disposable income after meeting this large fixed cost that is also very variable across different regions and households. The figures are for 2007/2008. Where available, the table shows the comparison between women and men. But it should be noted that a detailed gender breakdown of the data is not available in the published reports, notably for sole parents. This means that it is impossible to get a full picture of gender differences, a criticism made 20 years ago by Glendinning and Millar (1987) and again recently by Bradshaw and colleagues (2003). It is difficult to see how the issue of women's poverty can be given serious policy attention when the basic data are not routinely available.

Table 5.4 shows both composition and risk of poverty. Pensioner poverty has been falling in recent years (see further discussion in the section on lone elderly women below), and poor pensioners make up about 17% of the total of poor households, including 6% who are single women pensioners. Families with children make up over half of all poor people, 35% being couples and 18% being sole parents. We know from other sources that most of these sole parents are women. Thus, taking our two key groups—sole mothers and lone elderly women—together, these women make up over a quarter (3.2 million) of those living in poverty in the United Kingdom.

In terms of poverty risk, it is sole parents (and almost all are mothers) who have the highest poverty risk, at 50%. This is much higher than the poverty risk for any other group. As noted previously, pensioner poverty has been falling, and poverty rates for pensioners are now a little lower than those for people of working age. Single women pensioners have a higher risk of income poverty than single men pensioners (23% compared with 15%), but there is little difference in poverty risk for single people of working age.

Taking composition and risk together, the outcome is different for sole mothers and single elderly women. Sole mothers are a relatively small proportion of the population, and so, although their poverty risk is very high, they are not the largest group of working-age people in poverty. It is couples with children who make up the majority of poor British families. Among the elderly, however, single women do dominate the numbers because they have a slightly higher poverty risk than single men, and they are also more numerous.

There are also significant differences in rates of poverty for women in different ethnic groups (Bellamy & Rake, 2005). The poverty rates (in 1999/2000) varied from 20% of white women, 40% of Asian or Asian British women, 23% of Indian women, 64% of Pakistani/Bangladeshi women, 38% of Black or Black British, and 28% of Chinese women. Palmer and Kenway (2007) also found that for all ages, family types, and work status groups, people from ethnic minorities are more likely to be poor than white people. That study did not look separately at gender and poverty rates, but it did show that low employment among Bangladeshi and Pakistani women is a key factor in the high poverty rates for these families. Among the black Caribbean and black African populations, the high poverty rates are associated with high rates of sole parenthood. Despite these high rates of poverty, in general the government's policies to reduce child poverty and tackle social exclusion have not had a specific ethnic dimension. As Platt (2007) argues, policies to close the ethnic minority employment gap have not been integrated with the measures to tackle child poverty.

Bradshaw, Finch, Kemp, Mayhew, and Williams (2003) carried out their own analyses of the official income data and show that women who are single pensioners, or unemployed, Pakistani or Bangladeshi, or teenage heads of household or tenants are more likely to be poor than men with the same characteristics (the teenage heads of household are probably mainly teenage sole mothers). They also carry out a multivariate analysis and show that there is an independent impact of gender—even after taking account of a range of factors associated with higher poverty risk the odds of a woman being poor are still higher than for a man. Using a wider range of nonincome indicators, such as access to socially perceived necessities, access to financial and other services, and feeling safe in the local environment, they again found women more at risk of disadvantage than men (see also Pantazis & Ruspini, 2006). However, women were less likely to report that they were socially isolated or disengaged from their communities than were men. As the authors note this could be because women have more time available away from employment and use this to sustain relationships, or it may be that women are more likely than men to seek to sustain social relationships.

The experience of poverty also differs between women and men. Women are, in the main, responsible for domestic work and management, and in low-income families they are also usually responsible for financial management. The stress and strain of managing on a low income very often falls upon women, not only in sole-parent families, but also among couples with children (Bradshaw et al., 2003; Millar, 2003; Yeandle, Escott, Grant, & Batty, 2003). There is clear evidence that mothers seek to protect their children from poverty, not only at the level of trying to ensure adequate diets, heating, and clothing, but also in relation to trying to ensure their children have the same opportunities as other children to take part in educational and social activities (Middleton, Ashworth, & Braithwaite, 1997). Where income is limited, this can only be done at cost to their own consumption, and this "doing without" can have serious repercussions in terms of the mother's own physical and mental health. Tensions within families may also be heightened. High levels of debt are found among poor families. Poor housing conditions, unsafe neighborhoods, and lack of local amenities and services all contribute to the difficulties of surviving on low incomes (Lupton, 2003). As one Bangladeshi woman, quoted by Yeandle and colleagues (2003, p. 5), put it: "We have no peace of mind. We talk about it all the time. It is in your head all the time." Managing poverty can have a negative impact on women's physical and mental health. Ghate and Hazel (2002) found that parents living in deprived environments were three times as likely as adults in general to suffer emotional and mental health problems and that sole mothers were particularly likely to be living under such conditions for several years. Studies that have explored the dynamics of poverty over time also show that women are more likely than men to have experienced poverty at some time in their lives and are also more likely to experience recurrent and longer spells of poverty (Jenkins & Rigg, 2001; DWP, 2004). Over the 4 years from 2002 to 2005, about 9% of individuals were in households that were persistently poor, defined as having incomes below 60% of the median in 3 out of those 4 years. Those most likely to be persistently poor were sole parents (19%) and single pensioners (18%)—again the two key groups in relation to the feminization of poverty (ONS, 2009a, Table 5.19).

## Women's Independence: Recent Policy Developments

Gender equality legislation has been in operation in the United Kingdom since the 1970s, outlawing discrimination against women and requiring employers to have equal pay for work of equal value. The Equal Opportunities Commission has a mandate to investigate issues of sex discrimination and inequality related to gender, although a single body (the Commission for Equality and Human Rights) was established in 2007 to include gender, ethnicity, and disability. From 2002, central government departments were required to address a set of 19 "Gender Equality Public Service Agreement Targets," and the Women and Equality Unit (located in the Department of Trade and Industry) reported on these in 2006 (Women & Equality Unit, 2006). The "Gender Equality Duty" came into force in April 2007 and requires all public authorities in England, Wales, and Scotland to demonstrate that they are promoting equality for women and men and eliminating sexual discrimination and harassment.

There is, therefore, a commitment to gender equality as a general principle in U.K. politics and policy. Nevertheless, as we have seen, there are some significant inequalities between women and men in access to economic resources. In this section we briefly review some of the key policies, especially those introduced in recent years, in three main areas that are likely to have an impact on opportunities for economic independence—education and training, support for combining paid work and care work, and financial support for work. All these have an impact on current income and economic independence and also on incomes and living standards over time. We explore issues relating to pensions and living standards in old age in a later part of the chapter, when we look more specifically at the situation of lone elderly women.

**Education**. There is a strong link between educational attainment and income, especially for women. In general women have lower educational qualifications than men. But this is increasingly not the case, as younger women outperform younger men in both school and higher education. In 2003–2004, 44% of girls and 35% of boys obtained two or more "Advanced" level certificates, and 55% of university undergraduates were women. However, as Bradshaw and his colleagues (2003, p. 21) point out, "this advantage is not translated into well-paying jobs or careers." They blame subject specialization by gender for this, and there is indeed a significant gap between the subjects studied by gender. In universities there are very few women in technological areas and engineering, for example, and very few men in education courses. There are also big differences in vocational training courses; 98%–99% of those in plumbing, construction, automotive, and engineering apprenticeships are men, while over 95% of those in health, hairdressing, and child-care apprenticeships are women. The "New Deal" training programs, which are targeted at unemployed people and include a specific program for young people, have also tended to be divided along gender lines. As Rake (2000) points out, the programs with high levels of male participation have the highest budgets and the most extensive range of options, including training options. Where women are accessing training through the New Deal, this is often in traditionally female occupations. The occupational gender divide looks set to continue for many years to come, unless this gender divide in training is tackled. The government approach to tackling gender issues in education is summarized in the 2005 *Opportunity for All* report (DWP, 2005a), which includes a chapter on women. This includes identifying specific groups with low attainment for additional support and projects to try and encourage more girls to study subjects such as engineering. However, a recent review of skills (HM Treasury, 2007), which aims to set priorities for future policy, does not include any strategy for tackling gender differences in skills by subject or employment area.

**Combining paid work and family care work.** Increasing employment is a key target for the government, and especially there is a focus on increasing employment among parents, to reduce child poverty. The issue of "work/life balance" has come to the center stage in policy discussions, with a number of policy initiatives coming forward. Thus since 1997 there has been a rapid expansion in support for working families. This has included an increase in child-care provision and improved rights for reduced working time for employed parents.

The National Childcare Strategy, launched in 1998, provided the umbrella for an expansion of child-care services. Provisions have included guaranteeing free part-time (2.5 hours per day) nursery places for all 3- and 4-year-old children; the expansion of after-school clubs for older children; and the development of "Sure Start" programs providing health, social, and child-care services for preschool children living in poor neighborhoods. The total number of registered child-care places for children aged below 8 has doubled since 1997, and there are now 1.2 million places, one place for every five children. Further increases are planned over the next 5–10 years (HM Treasury, 2004). Help with child-care costs is available on an income-tested basis, although this does not pay full costs and is paid to only a relatively small number of families. The average cost for a full-time nursery place for a 2-year-old child in 2009 is £167 per week, rising to £226 in inner London (Daycare Trust, 2009). In December 2008 the average award of the Childcare Tax Credit was £68 a week, and there are 462,000 families in receipt, including 294,000 sole parents (HM Revenue and Customs, 2008). The Childcare Tax Credit is available to all who meet eligibility conditions, but the conditions are quite tight: low incomes, formal child care and in couples, both parents must be in work for at least 16 hours per week.

In terms of time to care, there have been a number of extensions to existing maternity and parental leave rights, and some new measures introduced. All women are entitled to 39 weeks of paid maternity leave (for the first 6 weeks paid at 90% of salary, then at a flat rate). Women with at least 26 weeks continuous employment with their employers are eligible to take another 13 weeks of unpaid leave. Men are entitled to 2 weeks statutory paid paternity leave and have the right to request up to 26 weeks unpaid leave. There is a right to 13 weeks unpaid parental leave for parents with children under the age of 5, for those who have been employed with the same employer for at least 12 months; and the right to request flexible working for parents with a child aged under 6 or with a disabled child under 18, and for those caring for a disabled adult. The introduction of the "Part-Time Workers Directive" in 2000 extended the same occupational pension rights, pay, and training opportunities to part-time workers as to their full-time colleagues.

In practice, of course, there may be limits to the impact of these provisions. Women part timers can claim the same rights as full timers only if there is a full-time colleague with whom they can make a direct comparison. For financial reasons some new mothers do not take their full statutory entitlement to maternity leave (Hudson, Lissenburgh, & Sahin-Dikmen, 2004). Workplace norms and expectations can make it difficult for people to request or take up flexible working. Survey data show that 17% of employees in 1 year requested flexible working, with women much more likely to do so than men (29% compared with 12%). Most of these women wanted to switch to part-time working. Approximately 20% had had their requests refused (Stevens, Brown, & Lee, 2004).

**Financial support for employment**. This has been an important area of government activity in recent years. "Making work pay" is at the center of the government's strategy to end child poverty, and there have been a number of significant policy developments in this area. The National Minimum Wage, introduced in 1999, has particularly benefited women, given (as we have seen) their concentration in low-paid employment. It is estimated that wages increased for 1.2 million workers when the National Minimum Wage was introduced, and of these two-thirds were women (Bellamy & Rake, 2005). The level of the National Minimum Wage is set by the Government on the basis of recommendations from the Low Pay Commission (an independent statutory public body). The rate has been increased annually since 1999 and in 2007–2008 was £5.52 per hour, which is about half of median hourly earnings for women in full-time work.

The second main element of the financial support for employment comes through the tax system, and in particular the introduction of "tax credits," which are income-tested transfers paid through the tax system to low-paid workers (the working tax credit) and to families with children (the child tax credit). In December 2008 there were 4.2 million working families receiving tax credits, including 1.7 million receiving the lowest basic family amount and 2.5 million receiving higher amounts according to income level. Almost all employed sole mothers receive tax credits (1.2 million in 2006), and most of these families are eligible for above the basic amount (HM Revenue and Customs, 2008).

In general, women have tended to gain from the tax and social security reforms introduced in recent years (Bennett, 2005). These have been targeted in particular on low-income families with children, as part of the measures to tackle child poverty. However, it is mainly in their role as mothers that women have benefited. Bellamy and Rake (2005, p. 15) suggest that there are three main policy approaches that governments can take to "alleviate the financial risk to women of being primarily responsible for household and care work." The first is to compensate for this work, by providing direct financial payment for care work. The second is to provide alternative provision for the caring work that would otherwise be done by women. The third is to seek to create a more equitable division of paid and unpaid work between women and men, so the costs of care work do not fall mainly upon women. As we can see from the above, there are some hints of all three in current policies, but the main focus has been on the second: enabling women to combine paid work and care work by the provision of child care and by the opportunity to work reduced hours or take breaks from paid work to focus on care work. Bellamy and Rake (2005, p. 56) conclude that

> These policies have not been guided by an over-arching aim of gender equality with the result that they have failed to narrow the economic gender gap for all women or to tackle the underlying gender inequalities which cause it. Labour's strong emphasis on paid employment as the key route to citizenship may actually reinforce the gender and motherhood gaps experienced by many women as the opportunity cost to unpaid care work increases. In addition, work-life balance policies and new maternity legislation have brought immediate benefit to many women, but in the long term may reinforce the notion that women are primarily responsible for caring work.

In the next two sections we focus specifically on the circumstances of sole mothers and lone, elderly women and on the nature and impact of policy measures targeted on these two groups of women.

## Sole Mothers

As we have seen, in the United Kingdom sole mothers have a high risk of poverty compared with other families with children, with almost half of all sole-parent families estimated to be living in poverty. Living in a sole-parent family is thus one of the key factors in child poverty. The child poverty figures (for 2007/8) show that there are approximately 4.0 million children living in poverty (in households with incomes below 60% of the median after paying for housing costs) in the United Kingdom (DWP, 2009). Of these poor children, 40% are in sole-parent families and 60% are in couple families (compared with 25% and 75% of all children). Children in sole-parent families are much more likely to be living in poverty (defined as above) if the sole parent is not working (75%) than if she is working part time (32%) or full time (22%). Employment is thus a key factor in understanding poverty among sole parents, but the situation is not simply that employment by itself provides a route out of poverty, or that employment usually protects people from becoming poor. For most employed sole parents, their own earnings would not alone be sufficient to ensure the family could keep out of poverty. Rather it is the total income package of earnings combined with direct state financial transfers, and sometimes with other sources of income such as child support, that enables some working sole mothers to stay out of poverty. In this section on sole mothers, we therefore focus on employment-related policies and the impact of these on poverty and living standards.

Extensive research on sole parents and employment in the United Kingdom has shown that sole-parent employment rates vary with factors such as the age and number of children, family type, level of education and training, receipt of child support payment, extent of work experience, housing tenure, health of parent and children, and age of mother at the birth of first child (Millar & Ridge, 2001). The sole mothers most likely to be employed are older women who are divorced, have school-age children, who worked before they became sole parents, who have some qualifications, are in good health, live in owner-occupied housing, and live outside London. By contrast, the sole mothers who are least likely to be employed are younger women, never-married, with young children of preschool age. Or they are older women, with poor health, or with children in poor health or with disabilities. In either case these are women who have low qualifications and limited employment experience, who may lack confidence in their abilities and have limited knowledge about how to go about finding work. In addition, the hardship imposed by many years of living on low incomes makes it more difficult to take positive steps to seek employment (Marsh, McKay, Smith, & Stephenson, 2001). In the United Kingdom, nonemployed sole mothers are eligible for a nationally available means-tested benefit (called "income support") which provides a weekly income (plus housing costs) to recipients. Sole parents can receive this support for as long as they have a youngest child aged under 12 (recently reduced from age 16). Income support thus provides long-term support and security. However, the level of support provided is low, and most recipients find it difficult to manage financially, with many falling into debt, especially long-term recipients.

Some sole mothers clearly find it easier to work than do others. Those who are in work are often in typically female-dominated service-sector occupations, and are therefore not highly paid. Part-time work (under 30 hours per week) is also quite common, especially among those with younger children, which again means lower incomes. Movements in and out of work are also quite common, more so than among women in general (Evans, Eyre, Sarre, & Millar, 2004) and sustaining regular employment can be problematic. Working can also be costly, in terms of the need to make provision for child care and other work costs, such as transport. As a group, sole mothers have become more work-oriented in recent years, with employment rates rising, as Table 5.5 shows, with employment rates up from 42% in 1994 to 56% in 2006 and full-time employment increasing from 21% to 30% over the same period. But there has been no further increase in employment rates and even some reduction in full-time employment rates in 2008. Surveys also show that most nonemployed sole mothers say that they would like to be employed, if they could find appropriate work that would fit in with caring for their children (Ridge & Millar, 2001). The fact that two-fifths of British sole mothers are not employed

TABLE 5.5 Employment Rates of Sole Parents, United Kingdom, 1994–2006

| | Full Time | Part Time | All |
|---|---|---|---|
| 1994 | 21 | 21 | 42 |
| 1996 | 22 | 22 | 44 |
| 1998 | 22 | 24 | 46 |
| 2000 | 25 | 26 | 51 |
| 2002 | 26 | 27 | 53 |
| 2004 | 28 | 26 | 54 |
| 2006 | 30 | 27 | 56 |
| 2008 | 27 | 28 | 56 |

*Source*: ONS, 2006b, Figure 4.7 and ONS, 2009b.

highlights the difficulties that many face. There are still 0.7 million sole mothers receiving Income Support, including 300,000 who have been in receipt for over 5 years (DWP, 2007a).

In 2000 the government set what was widely seen as an ambitious target: that 70% of sole parents should be employed by 2010. To achieve this would mean adding at least an extra 300,000 sole parents into work. A number of policy measures have been introduced in support of meeting this target. As noted earlier, there has been an expansion of child-care provision and various improvements in the rights of working parents. More specifically for sole parents, the "New Deal for Lone Parents" is a labor market program which provides individual advice and assistance to sole parents receiving Income Support. Participation is voluntary, and those who choose to take part are assigned to a "Personal Adviser" who can provide help with job search, with working out the financial implications of working, with claiming in-work tax credits and benefits, with finding child care, and with financial support to meet the costs of making the transition into work. There is some, but fairly limited, opportunity for education and training, but the main focus is on getting sole parents into employment (Millar, 2005).

By May 2007, approximately 740,000 sole parents had been through the New Deal for Lone Parents, and 365,000 had moved into full-time employment and 74,000 into part-time employment (DWP, 2007b). The evaluation of the New Deal shows that it has been effective in increasing employment rates for participants and that it has generally been popular with those sole parents who have taken part (Evans et al., 2003). However, many potentially eligible sole parents have not chosen to take part in the program, so the overall impact on employment rates has been relatively modest. As discussed previously, the government has also increased the financial support offered to working families through the tax credit system, and there are over a million employed sole parents receiving tax credits. These various policy measures have contributed to the increased employment rates. Gregg, Harkness, and MacMillan (2006) estimate that about half of the increase in sole-parent employment since 1999 has been due to the impact of policy, with the rest being a consequence of changes in the characteristics of sole parents and the generally buoyant labor market conditions in the United Kingdom. With the possible exception of London, this has been a period when there has been a high level of jobs available, including in the part time and service sectors.

The financial support available to working sole parents is a key factor in reducing poverty among those who are employed. Gardiner and Millar (2006) calculate that only 6% of sole parents working in low-paid jobs (earning less than two-thirds of the median) for 16 or more hours per week (the point at which eligibility for tax credit starts) were able to keep their families out of poverty by means of their wages alone. But adding tax credits and other in-work benefits to earnings did take 40% of these families out of poverty. Private transfers—maintenance and child support—from former partners play a relatively small role in sole-parent family income. Despite the attempts since the late 1980s to enforce a stricter regime for the assessment and collection of child support payments, the proportion in receipt of these has remained more or less constant at about one-third of sole parents (House of Commons Work and Pensions Select Committee, 2007). Those most likely to receive payments are divorced and separated women (rather than never-married mothers), and payment tends to be associated with contact between the father and the children. Child support payments rarely make up a substantial proportion of income although they can be important as part of the income package for employed sole mothers. Skinner and Meyer (2006) estimate that about one-quarter of low-income sole mothers receives some child support, and for about half of these families the child support helps to take the family income over the poverty line. There are ongoing attempts to reform child support (Henshaw, 2006), but the proposed changes will move the system toward a more voluntary compliance regime that (on past evidence) is not likely to deliver very much in terms of cash transfers to sole mothers.

The main policy attention thus continues to place strong emphasis on the importance and value of paid employment for sole mothers. Alongside the national programs discussed earlier there are several pilot and demonstration projects currently in operation. These include an in-work credit pilot (which pays £40 per week for the first 12 months in work) and the in-work emergency fund pilot (which provides discretionary financial support for specific needs in the first 60 days in work). Sole parents are also part of the target groups in the "Cities Strategy" that sets up public/private partnerships for the delivery of employment services and programs in selected city areas. There is also the Employment Retention and Advancement Demonstration Project that is testing the impact of the provision of financial incentives and job coaching on employment retention and which includes sole parents among the target groups (Dorsett et al., 2007; Hoggart, Campbell-Barr, Ray, & Vegeris, 2006).

However, the government will not reach the employment target of 70% by 2010. The government recently commissioned two external reviews of the direction and nature of welfare reform (Freud, 2007; Gregg, 2008). Freud (2007) proposes a more strongly work-focused regime for sole parents, to increase employment rates. This is justified by two main arguments. The first relates to the well-being of sole parents and their children ("having a job makes families materially better off ... work also improves the quality of life and well-being of parents and their children," p. 46). The second reason is that the government support offered through the tax credit and child-care provisions are now, or soon will be, at sufficient levels to make it reasonable to require sole parents to work. The Freud review also proposes similar extensions of employment conditionality to disabled people receiving income support and a much larger role for the private sector in the delivery of employment services. The government has broadly accepted these arguments, and from October 2008 lone parents with a child aged 12 and over are no longer entitled to income support. Instead nonemployed sole parents are entitled to Jobseeker's Allowance subject to the same availability for work requirements as unemployed claimants. From 2010 this age will be reduced to 7 (DWP, 2007c). This reform places more conditionality in the form of compulsory work requirements at the heart of future policy development. This is also the approach proposed by Gregg (2008), who recommends that benefit claimants no longer be classified by category (sole parent, disabled, unemployed) but according to an assessment of readiness to work. These proposals have been welcomed by the government (DWP, 2008a).

These work requirements for lone parents may seem rather light in comparison with the much stricter work tests that apply in some other countries, including the United States. Nevertheless, they have raised some concerns in the U.K. context. Targeting sole mothers with children aged 12 and above as the group for whom stronger work requirements would be introduced immediately is not the most obvious way to increase employment rates since this group already has employment rates of 68%—almost at the target—and those who are not working among these mothers are often women with multiple problems and difficulties, including high levels of poor health (Haux, 2007). The extent to which the support for employment is actually in place and working effectively is also open to question. The tax credits are an important source of income for sole parents, but the delivery of these has been a major source of problems. The annual assessment based on the previous year's taxable income means that many families are required to repay credits that they have received. Not only are these repayments difficult, but they also undermine the security and stability of income that is very important for low-income families. Of the 1 million working sole parents receiving tax credits, 257,000 were underpaid in 2007/8 and 150,000 were overpaid (HM Revenue and Customs, 2009). (This is a substantial fall in the level of overpayments since the scheme started, reflecting more generous income-testing rules.)

Similarly, although there has been a significant expansion in the level and income-tested subsidy of child-care services, child care is still costly, and provision is very variable across the country.

There are other options for encouraging employment among sole parents. For example, Gregg, Harkness, and MacMillan (2006) argue that this could be achieved by further investment in the New Deal for Lone Parents, by introducing specific measures to tackle the low employment rates for sole parents in London, and by stronger measures to improve job retention rates. Yeo (2007) similarly argues that employment retention policies are required in four main areas: financial incentives and support, case management, skills development, and employer-based measures. If the future for sole parents in the United Kingdom is to be a working future then these sorts of investments will be required not just to help sole parents get and stay in work, but also to ensure that they escape poverty by doing so. Moreover, even if a 70% employment target is reached there will still be up to half a million nonemployed sole parents with income almost entirely determined by the level of state benefits. The needs of these families must also be addressed in any anti-poverty strategy.

## Lone Elderly Women

As shown in Table 5.4, 23% of lone elderly women are estimated to be living in poverty, and these women make up over a third of poor elderly people and 6% of the total income poor population. These women would rarely be able to escape poverty, as they are unlikely to be able to draw on any new sources of income which would improve their situation. Thus for single elderly women it is the extent to which governments are willing and able to increase pensioner benefit levels which is the main determinant of poverty and living standards.

The current age of eligibility for state pension age for women is 60, but between 2010 and 2020, there will be a phased increase to 65, the same as men. However, people can, and do, go on working past the age when they are eligible for state pensions. Since 2007, they have the right to request continuing in work beyond the default retirement age of 65, and employers have a duty to consider this. Approximately 68% of women aged between 50 and 60 are employed, as are 11% of women over 60 (ONS, 2006a). Most are in part-time, rather than full-time employment. In 2006, the average age at which workers over 50 retired was 61.8 for women and 64.2 for men.

Table 5.6 shows the composition of gross income for single pensioners. Women have lower incomes than men, and benefit income makes up a larger proportion of the total (61% compared with 55% for men). Benefit income is particularly important for the very elderly, making up 68% of the total for single women pensioners aged over 75 (and 57% for men of that age). Burholt and Wiles (2006), in their study of material resources

TABLE 5.6 The Composition of Gross Income, Single Pensioners, 2006–2007

| | Women % | Men % |
|---|---|---|
| Benefit income | 61 | 55 |
| Occupational pension | 20 | 26 |
| Personal private pension | 2 | 3 |
| Investment income | 9 | 9 |
| Earnings | 7 | 5 |
| Other income | 2 | 1 |
| Gross weekly income | £240 | £267 |
| Median net weekly income after housing costs | £146 | £156 |

*Source*: DWP, 2008b, table 2.6.

of elderly people, found that women had lower resources (employment, property, savings) than men. They also found that older respondents (those over 75, many of whom were women) had the lowest material resources but tended to be more satisfied with their financial situation, perhaps because of reduced expectations.

Entitlement to the State Basic Pension is based on contributions or credits through working life, with 39 years of contributions required for women to receive the full basic amount (44 years for men as they retire later). However, only about half of elderly women get a full basic pension, and only 17% get a full basic pension on the basis of their own contributions (House of Commons Work and Pensions Select Committee, 2005). Of women aged from 65 to 69 receiving basic state pensions, 69% receive less than the full amount compared with 15% of men. There are several reasons why so many women do not have a full entitlement to the state pension.

First, the basic scheme introduced in the 1940s excluded most married women from full entitlement to pensions (Glendinning & Millar, 1987). It was assumed that married women would give up paid employment when married and certainly when they had children, and therefore their pension entitlement was derived through their husbands' contributions, as spouses or as widows. Those married women who did stay in work could pay a reduced rate of national insurance contributions ("the married women's stamp") that, in turn, entitled her to a more limited range of benefits and to a lower pension (60% of the pension that a married woman would receive on the basis of her husband's contributions). This option was abolished in the late 1970s, when there were 3.5 million women paying this reduced rate of contribution. These women could choose to continue with these reduced contributions, and there are thus still some women who are retiring with lower pensions as a result.

Second, the employment patterns associated with motherhood and other caring responsibilities mean that many women do not have the full

39 years of contributions required. This is partially recognized through the "Home Responsibilities Protection" that was introduced in the late 1970s. This is available to a person caring for a dependent child, or for a dependent adult receiving disability benefits, and also foster carers. The number of years of Home Responsibilities Protection is deducted from the number of qualifying years in working out entitlement to the basic state pension. Approximately 15% of women are building up some state pension entitlements through Home Responsibilities Protection.

Third, part-time working excludes some women from making contributions if they have earnings that fall below the "lower earnings limit" that is the entry point for the national insurance scheme. In 2007 this is set at £87 per week, and it is estimated that about 1.4 million women and about half a million men are paid under the lower earnings limit, and are therefore not accruing rights to most contributory benefits (Millar, Ridge, & Bennett, 2006).

This combination of factors thus means that current elderly women are less likely than men to have full basic state pension entitlements and are also less likely to have pension entitlements above this basic state pension. Moreover, the level of Basic Pension is low (in 2008 approximately £90 per week for the full amount) and those with only this source of income would have incomes below the poverty line. The Pension Credit, introduced in 2003, has therefore been very important in raising the income of women pensioners and in reducing poverty rates. Between 2000–2001 and 2005–2006 income poverty (as measured by income below 60% of the median after housing costs) among single women pensioners fell by about a third. The Pension Credit is made up of a basic amount (which effectively creates a minimum income to which all pensioners are entitled; in 2008 this was set at £124 per week for single people and £189 for couples) and a "savings credit" (which pays extra money to people who have an income that is higher than the basic State Retirement Pension or who have modest savings—this is intended to provide some incentives for people to save). The Pension Credit has been central to improving women's incomes in old age, but it does mean that large numbers of women are dependent on this income-tested support. In 2006 there were 1.7 million women receiving Pension Credit as claimants and another 0.5 million women who were the spouses or partners of men receiving Pension Credit.

It is also important to consider whether women currently of working age will be protected against future poverty in old age by their pension entitlements. Overall, it is estimated that there are 2.2 million women of working age who are not building up any rights to the basic state pension (DWP, 2005b) because of gaps in their employment records and part-time working. Younger women are just as likely to be contributing as younger men, but there is an increasing divergence for those in their thirties and forties, which implies that there will be a significant gap between women and men for many years to some. Women who do contribute on average pay less than men. Women working part time are least likely to contribute, in part because their employers do not have a scheme (40% of those without membership of a pension scheme) or because they are not eligible to join (approximately 10%). Women from ethnic minority groups are particularly unlikely to be contributing to private or occupational pension schemes. Ginn (2003) shows that it is the gendered patterns of employment associated with motherhood, especially reduced hours of work and lower earnings that are the key factors that handicap women in building up a private pension entitlement. She concludes:

> Policymakers need to consider the implications of pension privatization for mothers' ability to obtain an adequate, independent retirement income. Despite expectations among young women of gender equality and financial independence, current British policies mean that the pension prospects of young women who raise children may be little or no better than for their mothers and grandmothers (p. 508).

The Pensions Commission (2004) also makes the point that women may be catching up with men in terms of income and poverty risk in old age, but this is not only because the situation of women is getting better but also because the situation of men is getting worse. Both men and women are more at risk of unstable employment with gaps in their contribution records, and many people find it difficult to maintain high levels of savings for pensions. There may be a narrowing of the gender gap in pensioner incomes, but "this does not mean that the position of future women pensioners will be adequate, since the male position to which women are converging is itself getting worse" (p. 308).

Social care services are an important element in the quality of life for elderly people, especially those who live alone. Approximately a third of people aged over 65 report that they need help with daily living (domestic tasks, self care, and mobility), and women are more likely to report that they need such help than men, especially among the older age groups. They are also less likely to have a partner to provide such care (Yeandle & Stiell, 2007). Counsel and Care (2008) estimates that 80% of care needs are unmet, with 1.9 million disabled people aged 65 and above not receiving any public services but relying on informal, usually family, care.

Knapp and colleagues (2004) provide a review of the evidence on social care provision. In the United Kingdom the responsibility for social care for the elderly falls to local government, with a strong focus on community rather than institutional care, and with a "'mixed economy" of public, private, and voluntary provision. In 2003–2004, there were just over 400,000 care homes, and there has been a rapid growth in private sector homes in recent years. However, there is substantial variation in provision across the country, and some areas face severe shortages in provision. Community services have increased, but still fall short of needs. For example, DWP (2007d) estimates that in 2005/6 there were 12.2 households per 1000 population aged 65 and over receiving intensive home care services (an increase from 7.8 per 1000 in 1988–1999) and that 81 people per 1000 people aged 65 and above were receiving at least one community-based service. Unlike health care, personal social care is not provided as a free service in England (Scotland, by contrast, under devolved powers, does continue to provide free personal care). Costs of both care home and community care services have risen, and local authorities usually assess charges on a means-tested basis. This can reduce take-up, especially among some of the poorest elderly people. Family care remains an important source of care, and it is estimated that there are 4 million unpaid carers, including 1 million people providing more than 50 hours care per week (this includes those caring for nonelderly). The vast majority of elderly people with dependency needs receive some informal care alongside formal care. The workforce in the formal care sector is largely provided by women. As Manthorpe (2008, p. 86) puts it, "This is a world of women, in terms of staffing and recipients of care, most of whom are very old women." This work can be very demanding physically; it often requires shift work or unsocial hours. It is one of the lowest-paid sectors of employment. Wistow (2005, p. iv), in a paper for the Social Care Institute for Excellence, argues that "Adult social care has become increasingly focused on social services for people with high-intensity needs, at the expense of preventing exclusion and promoting well-being" and that the system needs to be rebalanced to meet the needs of "the many and the few." The government stresses the need for a wide range of flexible care services, prioritizing prevention and seeking to promote choice and independence, and proposals for reform of social care systems are promised soon (Churchill, 2008).

## Conclusions

What are the overall conclusions about the feminization of poverty in the United Kingdom? There is something of a mixed picture. Poverty rates have been falling, but poverty is still a major problem, affecting millions of people, sometimes over a period of many years. There are also many people who are on the margins of poverty, with little security in the short or longer term. Women are more at risk of poverty than men, especially women who live alone or who are solely responsible for dependent children. However, the poverty gap between women and men has narrowed substantially since the mid-1990s (Palmer, MacInnes, & Kenway, 2007). This reflects the fall in poverty rates for sole mothers and single elderly women. Women have increased opportunities for financial independence through their own employment, but having children still leads women to have lower employment participation rates and opportunities than men. The issue of part-time work is crucial here. Many British women do work part time, and part-time jobs are occupationally segregated, often low paid, and with limited chances for advancement. There is a significant long-term impact for women in terms of pension entitlements. Part-time work is an individualized solution that enables mothers to combine paid work and care, but it perpetuates gender differences in patterns of work and care over the lifecourse.

As we have seen sole mothers have a very high risk of poverty, and becoming a sole mother usually means a fall in income and for many a fall into poverty. The situation of British sole mothers has, however, improved in recent years. This is largely because of increases in employment rates and substantial financial subsidies for employment, including part-time work. Promoting employment is now the clear direction of policy. Sole mothers are increasingly expected—and soon more will be required—to take up paid work. This employment model will, however, require ongoing state support for services such as child care and for financial subsidies, which are currently provided through the tax credit system. Tax credits have been heavily criticized for poor administration. For example, a recent House of Commons Committee of Public Accounts report (2007) noted that £47 billion was paid in tax credits in the 3 years from 2003 to 2006 and that almost £2 billion has been lost to debts (where people have not paid back overpayments they received). There were also errors in payments of between £1.06 billion and £1.28 billion. The committee noted that the "cost in terms of the unforeseen level of overpayments and the scale of error and fraud continues to be significant." If these problems continue it may lead to a significant undermining of support for the system, and a change of government would almost certainly mean revisiting this policy approach, both in administration and also in respect of willingness to continue to commit such high levels of public expenditure to employed people. Employers will also have to be more willing than they are now to be flexible in recognizing the needs of employees with family responsibilities. The "work-life balance" agenda still has some way to go in terms of employer commitment and action. Moreover the strong reliance on employment as a route out of poverty looks increasingly fragile, in the context of economic downturn and rising unemployment.

There has also been improvement in the poverty rates for lone elderly women. As employment rates for women have risen, so more women are retiring with some pension entitlement. The government has also introduced measures to ensure a minimum income for current pensioners. Many elderly women receive this income-tested support, which keeps them above the poverty line but provides only a restricted standard of living. Nor does the future look particularly optimistic. The strong policy focus on individual provision for pensions in the private market will mean many women—especially women who have had breaks in employment or reduced employment because of family responsibilities—will continue to be at risk of poverty in old age.

Issues of women's poverty are not at the forefront of current policy. Many of the current family and employment policies are directly targeted on women, or have an important impact on women's lives, but it is women in their role as mothers who hold the policy attention, not least because of the focus on child poverty (Lister, 2003; Williams, 2005). Thus, as the Organisation for Economic Cooperation and Development (OECD) (2005, p. 20) concludes, in the United Kingdom "policy objectives such as promoting female employment and gender equity" are not pursued in their own right but because "they are seen as instrumental to achieving the goal of tackling child poverty." The Women's Budget Group (2005) has argued that it is impossible to separate issues of women's poverty and child poverty and that without an explicit recognition of the specific needs of women the child poverty target cannot be achieved. There is a danger that the focus on child poverty will make it more difficult to press claims for gender equality and the needs of women as women, and not only as mothers. There is thus a risk that the child poverty focus will reinforce, rather than challenge, gender divisions in work and care.

The United Kingdom has, like many other countries, moved away from a male-breadwinner model as the foundation for social policy and increasingly toward a more individualized "adult-worker" model that assumes that all adults are, or should be, independent workers in the labor market (Lewis, 2001). The male-breadwinner model disadvantaged women because it meant that they were treated as dependents of men and not therefore in need of either equality in the labor market or independent entitlement to benefits and pensions. But the adult-worker model also disadvantages women because it fails to recognize the extent and impact of caring responsibilities. Gendered differences in caring have a significant impact on women's employment and thus on their current and future incomes. The adult-worker assumption "over-estimates women's economic independence and capacity for self-provision" (Lewis, 2001, p. 168). Women will thus continue to be particularly vulnerable to the risk of poverty, particularly sole mothers and elderly women.

## Notes

1 The United Kingdom includes England, Wales, Scotland, and Northern Ireland. Some statistics cover all four countries, others cover just Great Britain (England, Wales, and Scotland). Where this is the case it is indicated in tables and text. The data here come from ONS (2007) *Social Trends 37*, which is fully available online at http://www.statistics.gov.uk/downloads/theme_social/Social_Trends37/Social_Trends_37.pdf. Accessed August 17, 2009. There is some political autonomy across the four U.K. countries, to differing degrees. Here we mainly focus on the national U.K. situation.

## References

Bellamy, K., & Rake, K. (2005). *Money, money, money, is it still a rich man's world? An audit of women's economic welfare in Britain today*. London: The Fawcett Society.

Bennett, F. (2005). *Gender and benefits*. Working Paper Number 30. Manchester: Equal Opportunities Commission.

Bradshaw, J., Finch, N., Kemp, P. A., Mayhew, E., & Williams, J. (2003). *Gender and poverty in Britain*. Working Paper Number 6. Manchester: Equal Opportunities Commission.

Bryan, M., & Taylor, M. (2004). *An analysis of the household characteristics of minimum wage recipients*. London: Low Pay Commission. http://www.lowpay.gov.uk/lowpay/research/pdf/t0IEZEJ7.pdf. Accessed July 30, 2009.

Burholt, V., & Wiles, R. (2006). *The material resources and well-being of older people*. York: Joseph Rowntree Foundation.

Callender, C., Millward, N., Lissenburgh, S., & Forth, J. (1997). *Maternity rights and benefits in Britain 1996*. Department of Social Security Research Report No. 67. London: The Stationery Office.

Churchill, N. (Ed.) (2008). *Advancing opportunity: Older people and social care*. London: The Smith Institute, 2008.

Counsel and Care. (2008). *A charter for change: Reforming care and support for older people, their families and carers*. London: Cousel and Care. http://www.counselandcare.org.uk/assets/library/documents/A_Charter_for_Change_03.01.08.pdf. Accessed July 30, 2009.

Daly, M., & Rake, K. (2003). *Gender and the welfare state*. Oxford: Polity Press.

Daycare Trust. (2009). *Childcare costs survey 2009*. London: The Daycare Trust. http://www.daycaretrust.org.uk/data/files/Policy/costs_survey_2009.pdf. Accessed August 10, 2009.

Department for Work and Pensions (DWP). (2004). *Low income dynamics 1991–2002*. Leeds: Corporate Document Services.

Department for Work and Pensions (DWP). (2005a). *Opportunity for all: Seventh annual report*. London: The Stationery Office.

Department for Work and Pensions (DWP). (2005b). *Women and pensions: The evidence*. London: The Stationery Office.

Department for Work and Pensions (DWP). (2007a). First release 2007DWP quarterly statistical summary. http://research.dwp.gov.uk/asd/asd1/stats_summary/Stats_Summary_Nov_2007.pdf and http://statistics.dwp.gov.uk/asd/tabtool.asp. Accessed August 10, 2009.

Department for Work and Pensions. (2007b). New deal for lone parents—leavers (individuals). http://83.244.183.180/new_deals/ndlp/live/tabtool.html. Accessed July 30, 2009.

Department for Work and Pensions (DWP). (2007c). *In work, better off: Next steps to full employment*. Cm 7130. London: The Stationery Office.

Department of Work and Pensions (DWP). (2007d). *Opportunity for all: Indicators update 2007*. London: The Stationery Office.

Department for Work and Pensions (DWP). (2008a). *Raising expectations and increasing support: Reforming welfare for the future*. London: The Stationery Office.

Department for Work and Pensions (DWP). (2008b). *The pensioners' incomes series, 2006/7*. London: The Stationery Office.

Department of Work and Pensions (DWP). (2009). *Households below average income 2007/8*. Leeds: Corporate Document Services.

Dex, S. (Ed.) (1999). *Families and the labour market: Trends, pressures and policies*. London: Family Policy Studies Centre.

Dorsett, R., Campbell-Barr, V., Hamilton, G., Hoggart, L., Marsh, A., Miller, C., et al. (2007). *Implementation and first year impacts of the UK Employment Retention and Advancement (ERA) demonstration*. Department for Work and Pensions Research Report No 412. Leeds: Corporate Document Services.

Equal Opportunities Commission. (2006). *Facts about men and women in Great Britain 2006*. Manchester: Equal Opportunities Commission.

Evans, M., Eyre J., Sarre S., & Millar J. (2003). *New deal for lone parents: Second synthesis report of the national evaluation*. Department for Work and Pensions Research Report Number 163. Leeds: Corporate Document Services.

Freud, D. (2007). *Reducing dependency, increasing opportunity: Options for the future of welfare to work*. London: Department for Work and Pensions.

Gardiner, K., & Millar J. (2006). How low-paid employees avoid poverty: An analysis by family type and household structure. *Journal of Social Policy, 35*, 3, 351–369.

Ghate, D., & Hazel, N. (2002). *Parenting in poor environments*. London: Jessica Kingsley.

Ginn, J. (2003). Parenthood, partnership status and pensions: Cohort differences among women. *Sociology, 37*, 3, 495–512.

Glendinning, C., & Millar J. (1987). *Women and poverty in Britain*. Brighton: Wheatsheaf Books.

Gregg, P. (2008). *Realising potential: A vision for personalized conditionality and support*. London: The Stationery Office.

Gregg, P., Harkness, S., & MacMillan, L. (2006). *Welfare to work and child poverty*. York: Joseph Rowntree Foundation.

Haux, T. (2007). *Lone parents with older children and welfare reform*. University of Bath, Centre for the Analysis of Social Policy. http://www.bath.ac.uk/casp/assets/LoneParentst.pdf. Accessed July 30, 2009.

Henshaw, D. (2006). *Recovering child support: Routes to responsibility. Cm 6894*. London: Department for Work and Pensions.

Hills, J. (2004). *Inequality and the state*. Oxford: Oxford University Press.

HM Revenue and Customs. (2008). *Child and working tax credits statistics*. London: HM Revenue and Customs. http://www.hmrc.gov.uk/stats/personal-tax-credits/cwtc-dec08.pdf. Accessed July 30, 2009.

HM Revenue and Customs. (2009). *Child and working tax credits statistics, finalised awards 2007–08, supplement on payments in 2007–08*. London: HM Revenue and Customs. http://www.hmrc.gov.uk/stats/personal-tax-credits/ctcw-tax-credit-final-may09-sup.pdf. Accessed July 30, 2009.

HM Treasury. (2004). *Choice for parents, the best start for children: A ten-year strategy for childcare*. London: HM Treasury.

HM Treasury. (2007). *Prosperity for all in the world economy: World-class skills*. London: The Stationery Office.

Hoggart, L., Campbell-Barr, V., Ray, K., & Vegeris, S. (2006). *Staying in work and moving up: Evidence from the UK Employment Retention and Advancement (ERA) demonstration*. DWP Research Report No. 381. Leeds: Corporate Document Services.

House of Commons Work and Pensions Select Committee. (2005). *Pension credit third report of session 2004–05*. Volume I, HC 43 – I. London: The Stationery Office.

House of Commons Work and Pensions Select Committee. (2007). *Child support reform: Fourth report of session 2006–07*. HC 219-I. London: The Stationery Office.

House of Commons Committee of Public Accounts. (2007). *Tax credits, twenty-second report of session 2006–07*. HC 487. London: The Stationery Office.

Hudson, M., Lissenburgh, S., & Sahin-Dikmen, M. (2004). *Maternity and paternity rights in Britain 2002: Survey of parents*. DWP In-house Report 131. London: Department for Work and Pensions.

Jarvis, S., & Jenkins, S. (1998) Marital dissolution and income change: Evidence for Britain. In R. Ford & J. Millar (Eds.), *Private lives and public responses* (pp. 104–117). London: Policy Studies Institute.

Jenkins, S. (2008). *Marital splits and income changes over the longer term.* University of Essex, Institute for Social and Economic Research. http://www.iser.essex.ac.uk/pubs/workpaps/pdf/2008–07.pdf. Accessed August 10, 2009.

Jenkins, S., & Rigg, J. (2001). *The dynamics of poverty in Britain.* Department of Work and Pensions Research Report 157. Leeds: Corporate Document Services

Knapp, M., Fernandez, J., Kendall, J., Beecham, J., Northey, S., & Richardson, A. (2004). *Developing social care: The current position.* London: PSSRU, London School of Economics and Political Science.

Lewis, J. (2001). Orientations to work and the issue of care. In J. Millar & K. Rowlingson (Eds.), *Lone parents, employment and social policy* (pp. 153–168). Bristol: Policy Press.

Lister, R. (2003). Investing in the citizen-workers of the future: Transformations in citizenship and the state under new labour. *Social Policy & Administration, 37,* 5, 427–443.

Lupton, R. (2003). *Poverty street: The dynamics of neighbourhood decline and renewal.* Bristol: Policy Press.

Manning, A., & Petrongolo, B. (2005). *The part-time pay penalty.* London: Women and Equality Unit, Department of Trade and Industry.

Manthorpe, J. (2008). Workforce reform. In N. Churchill (Ed.), *Advancing opportunity: Older people and social care* (pp. 82–91). London: The Smith Institute.

Marsh, A., McKay, S., Smith, A., & Stephenson, A. (2001). *Low-income families in Britain: Work, welfare and social security in 1999.* Department of Social Security Research Report No. 138. Leeds: Corporate Document Services.

Marsh, A., & Perry, J. (2003). *Family change 1999 to 2000.* Department for Work and Pensions Research Report No. 180. Leeds: Corporate Document Services.

Middleton, S., Ashworth, K., & Braithwaite, I. (1997). *Small fortunes: Spending on children, childhood poverty and parental sacrifice.* York: Joseph Rowntree Foundation.

Millar, J. (2003). Gender, poverty and social exclusion. *Social Policy and Society, 2,* 3, 181–188.

Millar, J. (2005). Work as welfare? Lone mothers, social security and employment. In P. Saunders (Ed.), *Welfare to work in practice: Social security and participation in economic and social life* (pp. 23–42). Aldershot: Ashgate.

Millar, J., & Ridge T. (2001). *Families, poverty, work and care: A review of the literature.* Department for Work and Pensions Research Report number 153. Leeds: Corporate Document Services.

Millar, J., Ridge T., & Bennett, F. (2006). *Part-time work and social security: Increasing the options.* Department for Work and Pensions, Research Report No 351. Leeds: Corporate Document Services.

Office for National Statistics (ONS). (2006a). *Pension trends.* London: The Stationery Office.

Office for National Statistics (ONS). (2006b). *Social trends 36.* London: The Stationery Office.

Office for National Statistics (ONS). (2007). *Social trends 37.* London: The Stationery Office.

Office for National Statistics (ONS). (2008). *Annual survey of hours and earnings.* London: Office for National Statistics. http://www.statistics.gov.uk/pdfdir/ashe1108.pdf. Accessed July 30, 2009.

Office for National Statistics (ONS). (2009a). *Social trends 39.* London: The Stationery Office.

Office for National Statistics (ONS). (2009b). *Focus on Gender*. London: Office for National Statistics. http://www.statistics.gov.uk/focuson/gender/default.asp. Accessed July 29, 2009.

Organisation for Economic Cooperation and Development. (2005). *Babies and bosses: Reconciling work and family life*. 4. Paris: OECD.

Palmer, G., & Kenway, P. (2007). *Poverty among ethnic groups: How and why does it differ?* York: Joseph Rowntree Foundation.

Palmer, G., MacInnes, T., & Kenway, P. (2007). *Monitoring poverty and social exclusion 2007*. York: Joseph Rowntree Foundation. http://www.jrf.org.uk/bookshop/eBooks/2152-poverty-social-exclusion.pdf. Accessed July 30, 2009.

Pantazis, C., & Ruspini, E. (2006). Gender, poverty and social exclusion. In C. Pantazis, D. Gordon, & R. Levitas (Eds.), *Poverty and social exclusion in Britain: The millennium survey* (pp. 357–404). Bristol: Policy Press.

Pensions Commission. (2004). *Pensions: Challenges and choices*. London: The Stationery Office.

Platt, L. (2007). Child poverty, employment and ethnicity in the UK: The role and limitations of policy. *European Societies, 9*, 2, 175–199.

Rake, K. (2000). *Women's incomes over the lifetime*. London: The Stationery Office.

Skinner, C., & Meyer, D. (2006). After all the policy reform, is child support actually helping low-income mothers? Benefits, *41*, 3, 209–222.

Stevens, J., Brown, J., & Lee, C. (2004). *The second work-life balance study: Results from the employees' survey*. Research Report number 27. London: Department of Trade and Industry.

Williams, F. (2005). New labour's family policy. In N. Powell, L. Bauld, & K. Clarke (Eds.), *Social policy review*, 17 (pp. 289–302). Bristol: Policy Press.

Wistow, G. (2005). *Developing social care: The past, the present and the future. Social Care Institute for Excellence*. Bristol: Policy Press.

Women & Equality Unit. (2006). *Delivering on gender equality: A progress report*. London: Department of Trade and Industry.

Women's Budget Group. (2005). *Women's and children's poverty: Making the links*. London: Women's Budget Group. http://www.wbg.org.uk/documents/WBGWomensandchildrenspoverty_Largeprint.pdf. Accessed July 30, 2009.

Yeandle, S., & Stiell, B. (2007). Issues in the development of Direct Payments Schemes for older people in England. In C. Ungerson & S. Yeandle (Eds.), *Cash for care in developed welfare states* (pp. 104–136). Basingstoke: Palgrave Macmillan.

Yeandle, S., Escott, K., Grant, L., & Batty, E. (2003). *Women and men talk about poverty*. Working Paper Number 7. Manchester: Equal Opportunities Commission.

Yeo, A. (2007). *Experience of work and job retention among lone parents: An evidence review*. Department for Work and Pensions Working Paper No 37. Leeds: Corporate Document Services.

# 6

# WOMEN'S POVERTY IN CANADA: CROSS-CURRENTS IN AN EBBING TIDE

*Patricia Evans*

## Introduction

Canada, a country of 32 million people, is frequently characterized as embracing a kinder and gentler version of the liberal welfare regime than the United States. By comparison, Canada's social safety net, although frayed, captures a broader section of the population, covers a more comprehensive set of risks, delivers higher benefits, and achieves lower poverty rates. It also fares well on a number of gender equality indicators. Canadian women have high rates of employment and, although the gender–wage gap remains wide, Canada is regarded as a leader in pay equity legislation (Pay Equity Task Force, 2004) and in policies dealing with violence against women (Weldon, 2002).[1]

The record of supporting mothers in employment, however, is distinctly mixed. Canada's paid maternity/parental leave of 50 weeks is considerably more generous than in other predominantly English-speaking countries (Evans, 2007a). However, regulated child care, with the exception of Québec, is available for less than 20% of children from birth to 6 years. This is a much lower percentage, for example, than in Sweden, France, and the United Kingdom (Organisation for Economic Co-operation and Development (OECD, 2004) and is not improving despite expanding federal finances.

Following the downturn of the 1970s and 1980s and beginning in the mid-1990s, Canada's economic and fiscal performance improved dramatically, resulting in employment growth and surplus budgets that lasted until the recent downturn in 2008. In times of economic growth, however, the globalizing economy produces not only high-paid jobs in the "knowledge" sector but also precarious forms of employment. Meanwhile, Canadian social policy increasingly emphasizes labor market participation, providing less protection for those who are expected to be, but are not, in paid work. As a rich body of feminist scholarship has established, gender is a critical nexus in the relations among families, states, and markets. How women's paid and unpaid work is valued in the marketplace, within families, and by the state is central to women's ability adequately to sustain households without the traditional "breadwinner" (O'Connor, Orloff, & Shaver, 1999).

How are lone mothers and elderly women faring in this environment? Is poverty becoming de-gendered, or does gender, especially as it intersects with class and race, become even more important as economic, political, and social processes transform the landscape of Canadian social policy? While the complexities of Canada's poverty measures are discussed later in this chapter, it is important to note at the outset that poverty rates have declined significantly over the past decade and, in the case of older women, gender appears to be less important. In 2007, the poverty rates for elderly women and elderly men living on their own were very comparable (14% vs. 13%) but considerably higher than elderly couples (1%). In contrast, in the same year, almost one in four (24%) lone-mother families live in poverty, almost five times the rate of two-parent families (5%) and more than double the rate for lone fathers (11%) (Statistics Canada, 2009). The gendered contours of low income remain stubbornly outlined in the case of sole-support mothers.

To probe beneath the surface, to understand these dimensions of low incomes in Canada, and to assess the extent to which poverty is feminized, this chapter begins with a discussion of the key factors that influence the changing profile of Canadian inequality and marginalization. The key factors I identify are the growth in precarious employment, the discourse and direction of government spending, including the income-based policies that are particularly important to lone mothers and elderly women, and the level of commitment shown to gender equity. The next two sections explore, in turn, the economic well-being of lone mothers and elderly women, the factors that underlie Canada's declining poverty rates, and the current challenges posed by precarious employment. The chapter concludes by assessing the degree to which poverty in Canada is feminized.

## Markets, States, and Families

Over the last 16 years and up until the 2008 recession, the Canadian economy expanded and the budgets of the federal government shifted from large deficits to sizable surpluses. In the early 1990s, the rate of growth in gross domestic product (GDP) placed Canada at the bottom of G7 rankings, but it ranked first every year from 2000 to 2004. Unemployment rates continue to be high relative to the United States, the United Kingdom, and Japan, but have declined considerably from a 32-year high of 12% in 1983 to 6% in 2007 (Statistics Canada, 2006a).[2] Economic expansion and an aggressive (some might say brutal) attack on the deficit and debt have enabled successive federal governments to head the only G7 country to post budget surpluses in every year, 1998–2008 (Department of Finance Canada, 2008, 2006, table 1).

This rosy state of federal government finances has been expensive. More of the costs of social programs have been downloaded to the provinces and municipalities which have had to pick up greater responsibilities with fewer resources, and to individuals and families, in the form of reduced services and benefits (for discussion, see Evans, 2002). During the 1990s, the rates and conditions of provincial social assistance benefits deteriorated, and cuts to the unemployment insurance system sharply reduced the proportion of the unemployed who were eligible for benefits, with particular impacts on women (Canadian Labour Congress, 2003; Sceviour & Finnie, 2004). These cuts resulted in increased poverty during 1993–1996 as the steep declines in social transfers eclipsed the rising earnings of low-income workers (Picot, Morissette, & Myles, 2003).

While transfers to individuals and families have increased in a number of areas, a shift in the direction of social policy has also taken place, a trend in evidence elsewhere. Instead of a social "welfare" state concerned with income inequality, protection, and redistribution, Canadian policy is shifting to what some term the social "investment" state, one that is primarily focused on improving people's capacities and productivities in the labor market (Banting, 2005; Jenson & Saint-Martin, 2003). In this environment, the most vulnerable, those regarded as the least "investment-worthy," are left behind as governments behave more like businesses with eyes on the margin of profit. Income-tested child benefits, for example, are targeted to employed low-income parents, and far less is provided to many lone mothers and other parents who are not in paid work. This shift has particular implications for women's poverty, which, many argue, has disappeared from public view, displaced by an emphasis on child poverty (Dobrowolsky & Jenson, 2004; McKeen, 2004).

A well-developed network of federal and provincially supported agencies whose goal has been to further women's equality is fast being dismantled. Many of these organizations were established in the wake of the landmark report by the Royal Commission on the Status of Women that was tabled in 1970. The Canadian Advisory Council on the Status of Women was abolished by the Liberal government in 1995. The National Action Committee for the Status of Women (NAC), an umbrella organization representing over 700 member groups, once a significant and vibrant voice on equality issues, lost all of its operational funding in 1998. It now struggles along on membership fees and donations, and its voice has been effectively muted. The first budget of the Conservative minority government in September, 2006 cut the federal Status of Women Canada funding by 40% and also eliminated a program that funded legal challenges to equality rights for women and other groups. Funding for women's issues was rolled back during a time when Canada was never better positioned to afford them.

In the globalizing economy, the liberalization of trade and deregulation of labor markets have left their mark in Canada, as elsewhere, by contributing to wage and earnings inequalities and expanding precarious forms of employment (Jenson, 2004). These processes have further embedded the gender, race, and class inequities in the Canadian labor market (Stanford & Vosko, 2004). Until the financial crisis of 2008, the economy was expanding and unemployment rates were falling; however, workers also experienced, repeated periods of unemployment and permanent layoffs in sectors such as manufacturing where international competition has been the fiercest (OECD, 2005). The jobs that are available to some Canadians appear increasingly fragile in the pay and security they offer—more are part-time and temporary, and low-paid work is increasing among women (Garlarneau, 2005a; Jackson, 2003; Saunders, 2005). As Pat Armstrong (1996) suggested a decade ago, improvements to women's wages and participation rates must be placed in the context of economic restructuring that creates more women's work in the labor market while men's jobs "harmonize" down as the labor market becomes more feminized. Wages have grown faster for women than for men since 2001 and unemployment has fallen for women while it has increased for men (Statistics Canada, 2006a). The proportion of low-wage jobs (less than $10.00 an hour) has not decreased despite increases in workers' education and job experience (Morissette & Picot, 2005).

What are the implications of a labor market that offers more jobs, but not necessarily good ones, and a social welfare "investment" strategy for lone mothers, our first group of special interest? This question is addressed, following a brief discussion of poverty measurement in Canada and the changing demographic profile of Canadian sole-support mothers.

## Poverty Measurement in Canada

Although Statistics Canada denies that its Low Income Cut-offs (LICOs) are poverty lines, they are commonly used and accepted as such. In use since 1967, the LICOs identify an income level at which households are likely to have to spend considerably more than the average household on food, shelter, and clothing and are therefore said to be in "straitened circumstances." The current LICOs are based on a 1992 survey (updated annually through the Consumer Price Index) which found that, on average, Canadian families spent 43% of after-tax income on food, clothing, and shelter. Statistics Canada adds (somewhat arbitrarily) a further 20%

so that the incomes with which families and individuals typically spend more than 63% of income for food, clothing, and shelters, become the LICO thresholds (Statistics Canada, 2006c). They are set for seven categories of household size and five population-based community sizes, resulting in 35 different lines. LICOs are derived for both before- and after-tax incomes. Unless otherwise indicated, I use the after-tax measures.[3]

Statistics Canada also produces a Low-Income Measure (LIM), calculated as 50% of median income, adjusted for family size and composition that differ slightly from the OECD equivalence scales. A comparison of the results achieved through the LICOs and the LIMs, however, suggests only slight differences: in 2000, the LICOs produced a poverty rate of 34% for lone-mother families in comparison to a LIM rate of 36% (Canadian Association of Social Workers, 2004).

Poverty lines are, of course, simply indicators that are most useful in documenting trends. However, they may tell us very little about whether a decline in a nation's poverty rate actually signals an improvement in living standards. For example, improving income through employment for a lone mother may place her above the poverty line, but take no account of the expenses (such as child care) holding a job entails, expenses that may actually reduce her disposable income below the poverty line. Because poverty rates are set in relation to average expenditure they are not especially sensitive to changes in other areas of policy which may be particularly important to low-income individuals and families. If in-kind supports are cut back or constrained in areas such as subsidized housing, child care, and home care, declines in poverty rates may occur at the same time that overall economic (and social) well-being may be eroding. The following discussion incorporates these dimensions.

## Lone Mothers

### Demography and Diversity

As elsewhere, the demographic profile of lone mothers in Canada is changing dramatically. Their share of families with children doubled from one in ten in 1971 to one in five by 2001. Children of lone mothers are disproportionately poor. In 2001, 43% of all poor children lived in mother-led families, although they account for only 13% of all children under 18 (Statistics Canada, 2006d).

Lone mothers are now much less likely to be widows and more likely never to have been married (Statistics Canada, 2006d). The gap in education between lone and married mothers has widened over time. In 1981, lone mothers were slightly more likely to hold a university degree than married mothers (4.1% vs. 3.7%). By 2001, they were three times as likely to receive the degree compared to their earlier cohorts, but married mothers were five times as likely (Garlarneau, 2005b).

During the last decade, lone mothers like Canadian society as a whole, have become increasingly diverse. The number of new immigrants has nearly doubled over the last 25 years.[4] In addition, source countries have shifted from Europe to countries of the South: in 2001, almost half (49%) of the women who came to Canada as immigrants were visible minorities. While immigrant women are only slightly more likely to be lone mothers than nonimmigrant women (9% vs. 8%), the rate is considerably higher (14%) for those who have arrived in the last 5 years (Statistics Canada, 2006d). Although they are a small proportion of immigrant families (4% in 2001), lone parents who come as immigrants (almost all mothers) are overwhelmingly poor: 74% in 2000 (Picot & Hou, 2003), compared to 32% of all one-parent families (Statistics Canada, 2009). They share, with other minority women and men, the enduring impacts of discrimination and of the economic restructuring processes that have particularly disadvantaged them in the labor market and increased their dependence on precarious forms of employment (Galabuzi, 2004).

But nowhere is the impact of systemic discrimination, coupled with colonialism, more apparent than in the situation of Canada's Aboriginal population, most (63%) who identify as Indian.[5] They are younger, less well educated, less likely to be employed, and twice as likely as other women to be poor (Townson, 2005). While Aboriginal women make up a very small proportion (3%) of all women in Canada, their numbers are growing at a much faster rate (Statistics Canada, 2006d). Their overall poverty rates are extremely high: 42% of Aboriginal women who identify as Indian were poor in 2000 in comparison to roughly 18% of non-Aboriginal women (Statistics Canada, 2006d). In 2001, they are also more than twice as likely to be lone mothers as non-Aboriginal women.[6]

## Less Poverty, More Paid Work: Good News and Bad News

Lone-mother families are less likely to be poor than was the case in 1986, when Goldberg reported poverty rates in the earlier volume (1990).[7] During the 1980s and up until 1997, approximately half of all lone mothers experienced low incomes. In 1998, the rate fell to 43% and to 29% in 2005. By 2007, the likelihood of poverty among lone mothers was at 24%, an all-time low and a drop of nearly one-half in 9 years (Statistics Canada, 2009). Nonetheless, as noted earlier, lone mothers are nearly five times as likely to be poor as families with two parents (5%) and more than twice as likely as father-led lone-parent families (11%). The poverty of lone mothers is also more likely to be persistent. While 8% of Canadians under the age of 60 were poor in every year from 1996 to 2001, this was true for 22% of lone parents (Hatfield, 2004).

Even before the current economic crisis, there were worrying indicators that the overall economic situation of lone mothers might be deteriorating. Although overall income inequality decreased among two-parent families between 2004 and 2007, it increased for lone-mother (and lone-father) families. In addition, while fewer lone mothers are poor, the depth of their poverty is deeper. In 2007, an average of $7500 was needed to bring their incomes above the poverty line, $800 (constant dollars) more than was the case in 2001 (Statistics Canada, 2009).

Earnings from increased labor force participation were an important factor in the decline in low-income rates of lone mothers in the mid- to late 1990s (Picot & Myles, 2005). Although they appeared to be more adversely affected by the 1990s' recession than their married counterparts, by 2004, sole-support mothers were almost as likely to be in the labor market as married mothers (68% vs. 73%), a considerable reduction in the gap that had existed in 1995 (50% vs. 68%). The employment gap, however, remains very wide when mothers are caring for children under 3 years (46% for lone mothers vs. 67% for married mothers in 2004) (Statistics Canada, 2006d, Chart 5).

Paid work does not necessarily provide an exit from low income, but it helps. While three-quarters (75%) of lone-mother families without paid work were poor in 2007, this was the case for less than one-fifth (17%) who reported earned income (Statistics Canada, 2009). However, a closer look suggests that, in comparison to earlier periods or relative to other families, the situation of lone mothers in paid work may be deteriorating:

- The poverty gap—the amount of income necessary to place them above the poverty line—was larger in 2007 than in any of the previous 9 years for one-earner, lone-mother families (Statistics Canada, 2009, table 13–3).
- Lone parents (mostly mothers) who earned low wages were more likely to be poor in 2004 (32%) than in 2003 (23%) or in 2002 (27%). In contrast, 19% of low-wage married men who were major income earners were poor in 2004 (Statistics Canada, 2006c, table 8).
- Between 1998 and 2007, inequality in earned income for families with one earner declined in two-parent families but increased in lone-mother families (Statistics Canada, 2009).[8]

Earnings are also more effective in decreasing poverty among two-parent families, primarily because of the increasing presence of a second earner. The latest Canadian statistics indicate a surprising shift in the poverty risk of families with children when only one parent is in the labor market. In 2007, for the first time, lone mother households with one earner had a lower poverty rate (17%) than one-earner two-parent households. However, the presence of a second earner (only an occasional possibility for lone-mother households), now the prevailing pattern in the majority of two-parent households, reduces their poverty rates to 2% (Statistics Canada, 2009).

The labor market disadvantage is stubbornly persistent as the gender gap in earnings indicates. The narrowest gap between full-time and full-year workers occurred in 1995 when women earned 72.4 cents for every dollar that men earned. By 2003, the gap had widened and women earned 70.5 cents to men's dollar. The gendered gap in the wages of workers who are not full-time, full-year, is much smaller, but it has also increased slightly, from its smallest in 1997 when women earned 81.2 cents compared to 2003 when they earned 80.6 cents on a man's dollar (Statistics Canada, 2006d).

While the data do not allow definitive interpretation, the problem of precarious employment is consistent with the worrying indicators that accompany the increasing prevalence of paid work among lone mothers. Precarious forms of employment—part-time, temporary, and low-wage—are on the rise and are both gendered and racialized (Cranford, Vosko, & Zukewich, 2003; Jackson, 2003). Some forms are particularly problematic for lone mothers. For example, Canadian lone mothers are twice as likely as married mothers to report that they work part-time because they cannot find full-time employment (Stephenson & Emery, 2003). But a full-time job can also be problematic for time-stretched and cash-strapped lone mothers in a labor market where jobs are increasingly temporary rather than permanent and often accompanied by few benefits and low pay. Women continue to be twice as likely to work in low-paid, full-time jobs as men (10% vs. 2%) (Statistics Canada, 2006d).

Low pay and part-time work are not the only features of precarious employment that are likely to pose particular problems for lone mothers. Most women (70%) who work shifts, work them on a rotating or irregular basis; for the overwhelming majority, it is not a matter of choice (calculated from Shields, 2002). The Canadian labor market is expanding in the sectors where hours are variable and wages are usually low, such as tourism and related services, telemarketing, and retail (Caragata, 2003). Irregular shifts are especially challenging for lone mothers who are usually without the additional child-care support that another parent may provide.

In their examination of the factors that account for the increasing employment rates and historically low poverty levels that lone mothers achieved over the 1980–2000 period, Myles and colleagues identify demographic changes as paramount (Myles, Hu, Picot, & Myers, 2006). Almost all of the gains made in employment and all of the earnings increases since 1980 were driven by changes in the age and education profile of lone mothers. The "baby boomer" generation of lone mothers, born in the 1950s and early 1960s, tended to be older, better educated, and with fewer children than their earlier counterparts. During the 1990s, lone-parent "boomers" were in their forties, a period when earnings and employment tend to be higher; as well, the baby boomer effect meant that these lone mothers were also increasing as a proportion of all lone mothers. In contrast, younger lone mothers showed only modest increases in employment and hardly any change in earnings over two decades. The authors conclude on a pessimistic note (2005, p. 6):

> The aging of the baby boomers was a one-time event that will only be faintly 'echoed' as their children enter their child-bearing years... in the absence of other policy or behavioural change, future earnings gains and the associated decline in single mothers' low-income rates are likely to be modest.

The labor market is one source of income for lone mothers. As this section suggests, while increased employment has helped to lessen the vulnerability of Canadian lone mothers to poverty, there are also indications that the paid work available to many lone mothers may be becoming less certain and more difficult to combine with caring for children. What role do cash benefits, housing, and child care play in protecting low-income mothers from poverty?

## Cash and In-Kind Benefits: Transfers, Housing, Child Care, and Child Support

While the economy was improving, other changes taking place in the 1990s also played a role in boosting the employment rates of lone mothers, although the effects are difficult to untangle (Myles et al., 2006). In the arena of transfers, changes to social assistance constituted the "stick" to make welfare an extremely unpalatable alternative to a job, while changes in child benefits provided the "carrot."

### *Social Assistance and Unemployment Insurance*

Not surprisingly, as the employment rates of lone mothers increased, their likelihood of receiving social assistance declined. Between 1995 and 2000, the percentage of sole-support mothers on social assistance fell from 50% to 34%. The expanding economy played a role in helping lone mothers leave or avoid welfare entirely. However, during the 1990s, almost all provinces cut welfare benefits, restricted eligibility, and increased the requirements for maintaining eligibility (Sceviour & Finnie, 2004). In 1995, changes in federal funding for social assistance opened the gateway to workfare, and provincial practice increasingly redefined lone mothers on social assistance as "employable" (for discussion of Ontario, see Evans, 2007b).

The National Council of Welfare (2006b) reports that the welfare incomes of lone mothers with one child fell across Canada, between 1989 and 2005. The declines ranged from a low of 6% in the small and poor provinces of Newfoundland and Labrador, to a high of 19% in Ontario, a large and wealthy province. These cuts made it much more difficult for mothers on social assistance to care adequately for their children and themselves, and it also made it more difficult for women to leave abusive relationships (Mosher, Evans, & Little, 2004). At the same time, levels of unemployment benefits were reduced and eligibility restricted, reflecting the federal government's concern to tighten ties to the labor market. These changes hit women the hardest: between 1994 and 2001, the proportion of unemployed women who were eligible to receive unemployment benefits decreased from 49% to 33% while men's eligibility fell from 45% to 44%.[9]

### *Canada Child Tax Benefit*

As eligibility and the value of social assistance and unemployment insurance benefits eroded, income-tested child benefits improved. The universal Family Allowance was eliminated in 1993 and replaced by the Canada Child Tax Benefit (CCTB). Reaching approximately eight out of ten families (Freiler, Rothman, & Barata, 2004), the basic portion of the 2007 CCTB is worth a maximum of $1271 a year for a family with one child. Beginning in 1998, the National Child Benefit Supplement (NCBS) provides an additional benefit to low-income families. Showing a distinct preference for a work incentive over an anti-poverty objective, the federal government expected provinces to deduct the value of the NCBS from welfare benefits and to reinvest the savings into programs that benefit working poor families with children. The NCBS was a more important factor in lowering poverty rates than increases in market income (Hatfield, 2004), but the primacy attached to work incentives prevented it from helping many of Canada's poorest families, those without employment.

The National Council of Welfare estimates that in 2005, 62% of Canada's poorest families, those receiving social assistance, lost all or part of their NCBS benefit because their welfare checks were reduced (calculated from National Council of Welfare, 2006b, p. 55). In 2007, a family with one child, eligible for the maximum, received an NCBS benefit of $1,972 a year. It is a significant benefit to lose, and represents, for example, 16% of the income in that year that a lone mother with one child received from Ontario social assistance.[10] The United Nations Committee on Economic, Social and Cultural Rights (2006) has criticized the NCBS' "clawback" for its discriminatory impact on Canada's poorest families, particularly lone mothers. Changes to Ontario's child benefits suggests that these criticisms were taken seriously: the clawback of the NCBS is to be phased out, and supplementary benefits to children in low-income families will be provided regardless of whether the source of parental income is earnings, social assistance, or some combination of both.

### *Housing*

Access to low-cost housing is important to low-income families and critical to lone mothers. Compared to lone fathers and two-parent families, lone mothers are more likely to live in rental housing and to pay higher proportions of their income on rent. As a result, they are also more likely to meet the criteria for social housing which gears rent to income (Canadian Feminist Alliance for International Action [CFAIA], 2005). And yet, while Canada's supply of lower-end rental housing on the private market is declining (TD Bank Financial Group, 2003), the creation of social housing units has plummeted, from approximately 24,000 in 1980 to less than 1000 in 2000. The availability of social housing in Canada lags behind every country considered in this volume, except the United States (Falvo, 2003).

A 2003 report estimated a $4000 "shelter gap" for Torontonians who fell into the lowest income quintile (TD Bank Financial Group, 2003). In Ontario, de-regulating rental housing resulted in increased rents. In some areas of Toronto, the gap between average rents and the rental component of the welfare check multiplied by as much as six between 1994 and 2002 (Oliphant & Slosser, 2003). Increasing the reliance of lone mothers on the private rental market not only reduces the value of their low incomes even further but also expands the gateway to discrimination on the grounds of their status as lone mothers, and on grounds of race and low income (CFAIA, 2005).

### *Child Care*

Over the last 30 years, reforming Canada's child-care policies has been on the agendas of federal and provincial governments, policy think tanks, and advocacy organizations. With the exception of Québec, which has implemented a $7 a day child-care program, Canada fares very badly in the international context. Canada's provision for the regulated care for children, 0 to 6 years old, stands at approximately one-quarter of the provision made in Denmark, one-third of that available in the United Kingdom, and half of that available in Portugal (OECD, 2004).

A Conservative minority federal government, elected in January 2006, cancelled a comprehensive child-care program the previous Liberal government was about to implement. It was replaced by a monthly $100 "child-care" allowance paid on behalf of every child under the age of 6, whether or not nonparental child care is used. Because the benefit is taxable to the parent with the lower income, nonemployed mothers in two-parent families keep a larger share of the benefit than many lone mothers who pay taxes on their low wages (Battle, Torjman, & Mendelson, 2006). The delivery of child care through the mailbox does nothing to address the lack of any significant expansion (apart from Québec) in child-care spaces over the last decade (OECD, 2004). However, the government of Ontario recently announced that, despite the economic climate, it will make available to all 4- and 5-year-old children a full-day program that integrates learning and care by 2010.

In 2007, 24% of all lone mothers were poor. While this represents a significant decrease in their incidence of low income over time, the discussion in this section suggests that their poverty rates are unlikely to decline further in the absence of positive policy interventions. Precarious forms of employment make it more difficult for lone mothers to earn their way out of poverty. As neither social housing nor child care is expanding, their ability to support themselves, and their children, already inadequate, may be further compromised in ways that current poverty rates do not necessarily capture.

### *Child Support*

Child-support payments are a potentially important source of income for lone mothers, particularly when countries take action to guarantee payments when parents (typically but not always, fathers) default. Canadian child-support policies limit their role to reinforcing the private responsibility of parents. In 1997, the federal government introduced child-support guidelines and provided funding to the provinces for their implementation and enforcement (Wiegers, 2002). While improvements have been made, the latest data suggest that only one-third of those who register child-support awards pay each month (Martin & Robinson, 2008).

The private responsibility model of Canadian child support continues into postseparation the economic divisions that divided poor and affluent women preseparation, and poor women formerly partnered to poor men are least likely to benefit. The poorest of lone mothers, those who must depend upon social assistance income, are usually required to pursue child support, but the amount of these payments is generally deducted, dollar for dollar, from their social assistance checks (Wiegers, 2002).

## Lone Elderly Women

### Demography, Diversity, and Supports for Seniors

Elderly women are a particularly heterogeneous group. They range from those still active in employment to those whose health and autonomy is severely compromised, a range that is associated with age, but not defined by it. In Canada, women over the age of 65 are a rapidly growing part of the population. Over the last 20 years, they have increased at twice the rate of younger women and now account for 15% of the population in comparison to 9% in 1971. In addition, the oldest of the old are growing at the fastest rate, and in 2004, women constituted 69% of all people 85 and older, although they account for only 57% of the overall population of older Canadians (Statistics Canada, 2006d).

Senior women are more than twice as likely to live on their own as are older men (38% vs. 17%). As well, the older women are, the more likely they are to live on their own. In 2001, 29% of women aged 65–74 lived alone, increasing to 47% of those aged 75–84, and climbing to 59% of people over the age of 85. Whether living on their own or not, elderly women are slightly more likely than elderly men to experience a handicap or long-term disability, the chance of which, of course, increases with age. Nearly three out of four (73%) women over the age of 85 report a handicap or disability (Statistics Canada, 2006d).

Social housing and home care are important forms of supports for elderly women, particularly those who are poor and/or have a disability or handicap. As noted earlier, Canada's supply of social housing has declined while expansion in the private sector has taken place at the higher, rather than the lower end of the rental market. Against this background, it is not surprising to find growing problems in housing affordability for Canada's elderly. Despite larger incomes, more than half (52%) of the seniors in the lowest income quintile lived in housing that was regarded as unaffordable (costing 30% or more of their before-tax income), compared to 45% and 44% of elderly people in 1981 and 1991, respectively. Those who were most likely to live in unaffordable housing had the following, and frequently overlapping, characteristics: living alone, renting, women, living in large cities, over age 85, recent immigrants, and members of visible minorities (Clark, 2005).

As with child care, home-care provision is minimally developed in Canada and varies widely across the provinces. A major review of Canadian health care recommended that selected home-care services should be placed under the Medicare umbrella, but this has not happened. Spending on home care has increased at twice the rate of other health-care spending (Romanow, 2002), but since the mid-1990s, funding has increasingly been targeted to posthospital services. As a result, other types of home care are harder to access, such as ongoing support for the frail elderly (Cohen et al., 2006; Neysmith, 2006).

### Less Poverty

The drop in poverty rates for elderly women has been identified as "one of the great success stories of social policy in Canada in recent decades" (Statistics Canada, 2006d, p. 280). The largest decline has occurred in the group of older women who live on their own: in 1980, 57% lived in poverty, while in 1995, the incidence had fallen to 27%, and by 2007, it was down to an all-time low of 14% (Statistics Canada, 2009). Over the last 30 years, Canadian poverty rates among the elderly have shifted from one of the worst in OECD rankings to one of the best, in spite of the fact that Canadian expenditures are relatively modest and projected to peak at levels well below most other nations. This success is largely attributed to targeted income transfers, the maturation of earnings-related public pensions, and the comparatively younger profile of Canadian seniors (Myles, 2000; Osberg, 2001). However, such success brings little comfort to the nearly one in five elderly women who live alone in poverty.

While poverty among Canada's elderly has fallen considerably, the risk of poverty remains much higher (14%) for lone older women than for elderly couples (1%), and slightly higher than that of lone older men

(13%). Elderly women make up 73% of all poor Canadian seniors who live alone (Statistics Canada, 2009, calculated from table 13–2). The salience of marital status is underlined by the fact that separated and divorced older women are most likely to experience low income, while widows and never-married women are least likely (McDonald & Robb, 2004). Widows have greater access to spousal benefits than do those who are no longer married, while women who never marry have fewer care giving responsibilities that cause them to interrupt their paid work and receive higher benefits in their own right.

An important part of the reason for Canada's success in lowering poverty rates for elderly women is the fact that Canadian social policy has targeted far more generous benefits to the elderly than to people who are expected to earn their income. As a result, the average amount of income needed to bring a lone elderly woman without earnings above the poverty line in 2007 was $2300 while a nonearning lone mother required $8100 (Statistics Canada, 2009).

## Role of Elderly Benefits

Unlike the cuts made to Employment Insurance and social assistance, proposals to reduce elderly benefits in the mid-1990s were rejected (Prince, 1997; Towson, 2000), and so the incomes of the elderly have remained relatively protected. Canadian retirement benefits consist of three major tiers: (1) noncontributory benefits; (2) social insurance pension and survivors' benefits; and (3) private pension plans and savings.

### *Noncontributory benefits*

This tier consists of two benefits: (1) the nearly universal Old Age Security (OAS), claimed by approximately 95% of Canadians at the age of 65 and (2) the Guaranteed Income Supplement (GIS), targeted to low-income seniors. In July 2008, the maximum OAS benefit payable to a single person was $502 per month; benefits are reduced when net annual income is above $66,335 and eliminated entirely at $107,692. Almost four out of ten (38 %) seniors who receive OAS are also eligible for the GIS, a nontaxable benefit with a maximum monthly value of $634. Both benefits are updated quarterly to take account of inflation. The GIS is particularly beneficial to women: in June 2008, women accounted for 63% of GIS beneficiaries (Social Development Canada, 2008).

To test the strength of Canada's safety net for older people living on their own, income from the noncontributory tier can be assessed against the most recent (2007) LICOs. In 2007, the OAS and GIS produce an annual, pretax income of $13,465. In addition, most low-income elderly are entitled to assorted federal and provincial tax credits and provincial income supplements, which I value at $1000.[11] These combined sources produce an income that falls, for almost all seniors, well below the poverty line. With the exception of older people living in rural areas and small communities, the Canadian social safety net, on its own, does not prevent poverty among seniors living on their own. The largest gap occurs for elderly individuals who live in large cities whose income falls nearly 25% ($3500) below the poverty line (calculated from Statistics Canada, 2009, table 14–1). Some seniors, especially relatively recent immigrants, cannot access OAS and GIS because they do not meet the 10-year residence requirement, while others, including the very elderly and those living in remote areas, are eligible but do not apply (Poon, 2005). While the safety net for elderly Canadian women is considerably stronger than for lone mothers, there are important gaps.

*Contributory benefits*

Most poor seniors, however, also report income from the second tier of Canadian retirement benefits, the Canada/Québec Pension Plans (C/QPP), established in 1966. The CPP, and its slightly different version in Québec, are earnings-related social insurance programs that provide retirement, disability, and survivors' benefits that are funded through employee and employer contributions.[12] In 2008, the maximum monthly benefit was $885 per month, although the average benefit paid is not much more than half of that amount.[13]

Even with income from both layers of Canadian income security programs, however, many elderly women (and men) live in poverty. In 2003, 86% of poor older women living on their own reported income from C/QPP, identical to the percentage of poor couples, only somewhat lower than the 90% reported by lone older men (National Council of Welfare, 2006a). C/QPP is of growing importance to elderly women, and, paralleling increases in women's labor force participation, the profile of women as contributors has increased. In 1981, women represented 33% of those who received retirement benefits but by 2006 it had increased to 47% (Social Development Canada, 2008). Earnings-related benefits reflect the gender inequities of paid and unpaid work. Thus, newly retired women, in June 2005, received an average monthly pension of $334 while their male counterparts received $527 (Townson, 2005). Survivors' benefits provide 60% of the spousal retirement pension. If a survivor is entitled to her own pension, her total pension income cannot exceed the value of the maximum retirement pension for a single person.

*Private pensions and savings*

Private pensions and savings constitute the third tier of Canadian retirement benefits. In keeping with a liberal welfare regime, this tier was expected to grow in importance, and serious consideration was given to replacing the C/QPP with private savings accounts (Townson, 2001). As occurred elsewhere, concerns about a brewing demographic "crisis" with the growth of an aging population raised questions about the long-term sustainability of the C/QPP. These fears were eventually allayed by a series of actions, including raising contribution rates to fund investments, which put the Plans on more secure footing (Myles & Pierson, 2001).

Canada's elderly benefit from private occupational pensions, including poor older women living on their own. The National Council of Welfare (2006a) estimated that in 2003, 29% of low-income older women living on their own received private pension income. However, participation rates in private plans are declining, albeit more steeply for men who had further to fall than women. Women's participation peaked in 1995 when 41% contributed to employer-sponsored pensions, but by 2002, it had fallen slightly to 39%. In contrast, men's participation peaked in 1984 when 55% contributed but fell to 40% by 2002 (Statistics Canada, 2006d). The decline in private plan membership, in part, results from the growth in precarious employment. The precipitous drop in men's membership may be an example of the "harmonizing down" that occurs when the conditions of men's employment deteriorate as paid work in the new economy increasingly resembles "women's work" (Armstrong, 1996).

Nevertheless, gender remains a factor of disadvantage in women's access to private pensions even if the gender gap is closing in participation rates. In 2003, the average income that older women received from private pensions amounted to $7000 less than men received, and it constituted 26% of older women's income, in comparison to 41% of the incomes of senior men (Statistics Canada, 2006d). But gender is not the only factor: private pension income accounted for only 13% of the total income of immigrants (National Advisory Council on Aging, 2006).

There is also a gender discrepancy, albeit smaller, in the contribution made by Canada's future elderly to tax-sheltered Registered Retirement Savings Plans (RRSPs). In 2002, 24% of women who filed tax returns contributed to RRSPs, in comparison to 29% of men and women's savings amounted to 71% of men's (calculations from Statistics Canada, 2006d, p. 138). The discrimination faced in the labor market by members of visible minorities means that they are less likely to contribute to private pensions, while those who do, tend to reap less because of their lower employment earnings (Morissette, 2002; Statistics Canada, 2006d). Declining participation rates in private plans suggest poor elderly women, and their nonpoor counterparts, will be even less likely in the future to count on income from this source.

## Are Elderly Poverty Rates Likely to Decline Further?

Between 1980 and 1996, poverty rates fell substantially for all elderly people, including older women living alone. The poverty gap also declined. In a comprehensive study of this period, John Myles (2000) suggests that the fall in poverty was the result of an increase in the percentage of seniors whose incomes were 50% above the poverty line, a magnitude too large to attribute to improvements in the GIS. An important part of the falling incidence of low-income, rising incomes, and decreases in income inequality for seniors over this period lies in the maturation of both public and private pension plans. During a period when the share of OAS and GIS income was not rising, income from public and private pensions increased from 21% in 1980 to 45% in 1995. More seniors were qualifying for C/QPP, including the increasing number of women who had been in paid work; in addition, more were significant contributors and so received larger shares of the available benefits. These better positioned C/QPP cohorts increasingly replaced the earlier and less advantaged ones. The position of lower-income seniors saw particular improvement.

While it is tempting to think that Canada's elderly will continue to benefit from increasing Q/CPP payments, Myles also suggests that the equalizing effect of the maturing of C/QPP is likely a one-time event. Given that private pensions and personal savings are concentrated among high-earners, income inequality among the elderly may increase. Noting that high earners are typically men, Lynn McDonald and Leslie Robb (2004) suggest that poverty rates are unlikely to continue to decline. Even with increasing rates of employment, women's ability to save for retirement will continue to be compromised if patterns of paid and unpaid work remain unchanged. And this seems to be the current situation. Morissette and Ostrovsky (2006) found that families at the bottom of the income quintiles, including those led by lone parents who are overwhelmingly mothers, are no better prepared for retirement than in the past. Meanwhile, families in the upper quintiles are better prepared and so have added a further edge to their advantage.

While poverty rates have fallen to historically low levels for Canada's elderly, there is little reason to expect further declines; indeed, rates may well increase, whatever the length of the current recession. The obstacles posed by precarious employment for current workers project into the future and jeopardize the adequacy of their income in retirement.

## Is Canadian Poverty Feminized?

In an earlier study, Gertrude Schaffner Goldberg suggested that Canada was bordering on the feminization of poverty and concluded (1990, p. 81): "If Canada fails to take steps to improve both the economic and social wage for women, it leaves itself prey to the demographic forces that could increase both the prevalence of poverty and its feminization." Only the United States met the necessary conditions of having sufficiently high rates of single motherhood coupled with a much higher incidence of poverty than other families with children (see chapter 1, this volume). Since then, poverty rates in Canada are at historically low levels, benefiting those with traditionally high poverty rates—lone mothers and elderly women living on their own. However, as this chapter suggests, there are important cross-currents that are visible as the rates decline

First, while overall poverty rates are lower, lone mothers and elderly women living on their own continue to experience a greater likelihood of low incomes than do two-parent families, lone-father families, and elderly men on their own. In 1998, elderly women accounted for 78% of the elderly poor, not very different from 2007 (73%). In 1998, lone-mother families accounted for 48% of all poor families with children, and in 2007, they accounted for 45%, Statistics Canada, 2009, calculated from table 13–2). While poverty rates are decreasing, their division by gender remains stubbornly persistent.

Second, the growth of precarious employment in the "new" economy affects the ability of lone mothers to earn their way out of poverty, a route made more difficult by the lack of affordable housing and child care. It also contributes to declining membership in private pension plans, at a time when individual savings for retirement are becoming more unequal.

Finally, the growth in immigration, visible minorities, and the Aboriginal population suggests that women subject to discrimination in paid work and elsewhere are likely increasingly to be represented in the ranks of low-income lone mothers and those who will be poor in their retirement. However, gender and its intersection with race receive diminishing attention as women's issues fall off the agenda of Canadian governments, and the emphasis on child poverty may serve to obscure further the challenges that the mothers of poor children face. Research that begins to examine the connections between women's poverty and precarious employment, especially as it relates to lone mothers and elderly women who confront particular forms of discrimination—Aboriginal people, members of visible minorities, and immigrants to Canada—will be critical if we are properly to understand and adequately to respond to what is likely to be their increasing profile among Canada's poor.

The buoyant economy and improvements in income benefits helped to reduce the risk of poverty for many Canadians. But, as this chapter has described, there are unsettling cross-currents that include growing income inequality, deepening poverty for those who are poor, and precarious employment. When the economic and fiscal picture was rosy, improvements in the social wage in terms of housing, child care, and home care were not clearly visible on the horizon. These critical supports are especially important for low-income lone mothers, whose social wage is very low and who will form the next generation of elderly women. The economic crisis has prompted a rethinking about the necessary role for government in promoting the well-being of all its citizens, a role largely rejected in neo-liberal thinking. It is not possible to predict whether the Canadian social safety net will ultimately emerge strengthened or more fragile from the current political and economic shifts, but it is certainly at a critical juncture.

## Notes

1 In 2005, Canada ranked sixth of the 30 OECD countries in the percentage of women employed (68%). Of the countries considered in this book, Canada fell behind Sweden (72%) and slightly above the United States and the United Kingdom. However, the age gap is larger in Canada than in other countries in this volume, with the exception of Japan and Germany; information was not available for Italy (OECD, 2007, Tables SSI.3 and EQ3.3).

2 There is considerable provincial variation, with the highest rate (September 2006) found in Newfoundland and Labrador (14%) and the lowest in Alberta (3%) (Statistics Canada, 2006e).
3 Anti-poverty groups, such as the National Council of Welfare, endorse the use of the LICO before-tax measures with the rationale that after-tax measures encompass only income tax, leaving the impact of indirect taxes unexamined.
4 In the 1990s, immigration entries averaged 225,000 per year compared to an average of 126,000 in the 1980s (Statistics Canada, 2006d).
5 The other groups are the Métis, mixed Indian and French ancestry (29%), and the Inuit (5%) (see Statistics Canada, 2006d).
6 Eighteen percent of Aboriginal women, 15 years and older were lone mothers in comparison to 8% of non-Aboriginal women (Statistics Canada, 2006d). These figures are based on all women aged 15 and over and so differ from figures cited earlier in the text that are based on women with children, aged 18 and younger.
7 The rates cited by Goldberg in the earlier volume are not directly comparable to those included in this chapter because she used before-tax LICOs calculated on the 1978 base.
8 The Ginicoefficient declined from 0.484 to 0.463 in two-parent families and increased from 0.455 to 0.474 for lone-mother families.
9 This does not take into account all the earlier cuts that had reduced the proportion of unemployed who were covered from 87% in 1990 to 48% in 2005 (Canadian Labour Congress, 2005).
10 On the basis of Ontario Works rates for October–December 2007 of $1029 per month.
11 In 2003, the National Council of Welfare (2006a) found that the overwhelming majority of low-income seniors living on their own received these benefits and valued them at $811; to err on the side of caution, I have provided a generous updating of this amount.
12 In 2006, the total contribution was 9.9% of maximum pensionable earnings, compared to 3.8% in 1987 (Social Development Canada, 2005).
13 In 2007–2008, the average monthly retirement benefit was $482.

## References

Armstrong, P. (1996). The feminization of the labour force: Harmonizing down in a global economy. In I. Bakker (Ed.), *Rethinking restructuring: Gender and change in Canada* (pp. 29–54). Toronto: University of Toronto Press.

Banting, K. (2005). Do we know where we are going? The new social policy in Canada. *Canadian Public Policy, 31*, 4, 421–429.

Battle, K., Torjman, S., & Mendelson, M. (2006). *More than a name change: The universal child care benefit*. Ottawa: Caledon Institute. www.caledoninst.org/Publications?PDF/589ENG.pdf. Accessed July 29, 2009.

Canadian Association of Social Workers. (2004). *Gendering the poverty line*. Ottawa: Author.

Canadian Feminist Alliance for International Action. (2005). *A decade of going backwards: Canada in the post-Beijing era*. Response to UN Questionnaire on Implementation of the Beijing Platform for Action (1995) and the Outcome of the Twenty-Third Special Session of the General Assembly (2000). www.fafia-afia.org/images/pdfB10_0105.pdf. Accessed July 29, 2009.

Canadian Labour Congress. (2003). *Falling Unemployment* Insurance *protection of Canada's unemployed.* Ottawa: Canadian Labour Congress.

Canadian Labour Congress. (2005). *A good program in bad times: The dismantling of Unemployment Insurance.* Ottawa: Author. http://canadianlabour.ca/index.php/Unemployment_Insuran/557. Accessed July 29, 2009.

Caragata, L. (2003). Neoconservative realities: The social and economic marginalization of Canadian women. *International Sociology, 18,* 3, 559–580.

Clark, W. (2005). What do seniors spend on housing? *Canadian Social Trends,* Statistics Canada cat no. 11-008, 78, pp. 2–6.

Cohen, M., McLaren, A., Sharman, Z., Murray, S., Hughes, M., & Ostry, A. (2006). *From support to isolation: The high cost of BC's declining home support services.* BC Office: Canadian Centre for Policy Alternatives.

Cranford, C., Vosko L, & Zukewich, N. (2003). Precarious employment in the Canadian labour market: A statistical portrait. *Just Labour: A Canadian Journal of Work and Society, 3,* 6–22

Department of Finance Canada. (2006). Canada's financial performance in an international context, Annex 1, Budget Plan 2006. http://www.fin.gc.ca/budget06/bp/bpa1e.htm. Accessed July 29, 2009.

Department of Finance Canada. (2008). Responsible leadership: Budget plan 2008. http://www.budget.gc.ca/2008/home-accueil-eng.asp. Accessed July 29, 2009.

Dobrowolsky, A., & Jenson, J. (2004). Shifting representations of citizenship: Canadian politics of "women" and "children." *Social Politics, 11,* 2, 154–180.

Evans, P. (2002). Downloading the welfare state, Canadian style. In G. S. Goldberg & M. G. Rosenthal (Eds.), *Diminishing welfare: A cross-national study of social provision* (pp. 75–102). Westport, CT: Auburn House.

Evans, P. (2007a). Comparative perspectives on changes to Canada's parental benefits: Implications for class and gender. *International Journal of Social Welfare. 16,* 2, 29–49.

Evans, P. (2007b). (Not) taking account of precarious employment: Workfare policies for lone mothers in Ontario and the UK. *Social Policy and Administration, 41,* 1, 29–49.

Falvo, N. (2003). *Gimme shelter! Homelessness and Canada's social housing crisis.* Toronto: CSJ Foundation for Research and Education.

Freiler, C., Rothman, L., & Barata, P. (2004). *Pathways to progress: Structural solutions to address child poverty.* Toronto: Campaign 2000.

Galabuzi, G. (2004). Racializing the division of labour: Neoliberal restructuring and the economic segregation of Canada's racialized groups. In J. Stanford & L. Vosko (Eds.), *Challenging the market: The struggle to regulate work and Income* (pp. 175–204). Montreal and Kingston: McGill-Queen's University Press.

Garlarneau, D. (2005a). Earnings of temporary versus permanent employees. *Perspectives, 6,* 1, 3–17.

Garlarneau, D. (2005b). Education and income of lone parents. *Perspectives, 6,* 12, 5–16.

Goldberg, G. S. (1990). Canada: Bordering on the feminization of poverty. In G. S. Goldberg & E. Kremen (Eds.), *The feminization of poverty: Only in America?* (pp. 59–81). New York: Praeger.

Hatfield, M. (2004). Vulnerability to persistent low income. *Horizons, 7.* 2. Ottawa: Policy Research. http://policyresearch.gc.ca/page.asp?pagenm=v7n2_art>04. Accessed July 29, 2009.

Human Resources and Social Development Canada. (2008). *CPP & OAS Statsbook 2008*. http://www.hrsdc.gc.ca/eng/isp/statistics/pdf/statbook.pdf. Accessed July 30, 2009.

Jackson, A. (2003). *Is work working for women?* Research Paper No. 22. Ottawa: Canadian Labour Congress.

Jenson, J. (2004). *Canada's new social risks: Directions for a new social architecture*. Research Report F/43. Ottawa: Canadian Policy Research Networks. http://www.cprn.com/en/doc.cfm?doc=1095. Accessed July 29, 2009.

Jenson, J., & Saint-Martin, D. (2003). New routes to social cohesion? Citizenship and the social investment state. *Canadian Journal of Sociology, 28*, 1, 77–99.

Martin, C., &. Robinson, P. (2008). *Child and spousal support: Maintenance enforcement survey statistics, 2006/2007*. Canadian Center for Justice Statistics. Ottawa: Minister of Industry. Cat. 85–228-XIE.

McDonald, L., & Robb, A. (2004). The economic legacy of divorce and separation for women in old age. *Canadian Journal of Aging, 23*, Suppl. S83-S97.

McKeen, W. (2004). *Money in their own name: Feminism and the shaping of Canadian social policy, 1960s to 1990s*. Toronto: University of Toronto Press.

Morissette, R. (2002). Pensions: Immigrants and visible minorities. *Perspectives, 6*, 3, 13–18.

Morissette, R., & Ostrovsky, U. (2006). *Pension coverage and retirement savings of Canadian families, 1986 to 2003*. Ottawa: Statistics Canada, Business and Labour Market Analysis Division, 11F0019, No. 286.

Morissette, R., & Picot, G. (2005). *Low-paid work and economically vulnerable families over the last two decades*. Ottawa: Statistics Canada, Business and Labour Market Analysis Division, cat no: 11F0019MIE-No. 248.

Mosher, J., P., Evans, P., & Little, M. (2004). *Walking on eggshells: Abused women's experiences of Ontario's welfare system: Final report of research findings from the woman and abuse welfare project*. www.yorku.ca/yorkweb/special/Welfare_Report_walking_on_Eggshells_final_report.pdf. Accessed July 30, 2009.

Myles, J. (2000). The maturation of Canada's retirement income system: Income levels, income inequality and low-income among the elderly. Statistics Canada and Florida State University. http://www.statcan.gc.ca/bsolc/olc-cel/olc-cel?catno=11F0019M2000147&=eng. Accessed August 10, 2009.

Myles, J., & Pierson, P. (2001). The political economy of pension reform. In P. Pierson (Ed.), *New politics of the welfare state* (pp.305–333). Oxford: Oxford University Press.

Myles, J., Hou, F., Picot, G., &, Myers, K. (2006). *Why did employment and earnings rise among lone mothers during the 1980s and 1990s?* Ottawa: Minister of Industry, Analytical Studies Branch Research Paper Series, Cat. No. 11F0019MIE-No. 282.

National Advisory Council on Aging. (2006). *Seniors in Canada: 2006 Report Card*. Ottawa: Author. www.naca-ccnta.ca/rc2006/pdf/rc2006_E.pdf. Accessed July 29, 2009.

National Council of Welfare. (2006a). *Poverty profile 2002 and 2003*. Ottawa: NCW, Summer.

National Council of Welfare. (2006b). *Welfare incomes 2005*. Ottawa: Author, October.

Neysmith, S. (2006). Caring and aging: Exposing the policy issues. In A. Westhues (Ed.), *Canadian social policy: Issues and perspectives* (4th ed.) (pp. 397–412). Waterloo, ON: Wilfrid Laurier University Press.

O'Connor, J., Orloff, A. S., & Shaver, S. (1999). *States, markets, families*. Oxford: Oxford University Press.

OECD. (2004). *Early childhood education and care policy: Canada, country note*. Paris: OECD Directorate for Education.

OECD. (2005). How does Canada compare? Briefing notes *Employment Outlook 2005*. Paris: Author. http://www.oecd.org/dataoecd/31/16/35050478.pdf. Accessed July 30, 2009.

OECD. (2007). *Society at a glance: OECD social indicators, 2006 Edition*. Paris: Author.

Oliphant, M., & Slosser, C. (2003). *Targeting the most vulnerable: A decade of desperation for Ontario's welfare recipients*. Ontario Alternative Budget Technical Paper #6. Ottawa: Canadian Centre for Policy Alternatives.

Osberg, L. (2001). Poverty among senior citizens: A Canadian success story. In Pay Equity Task Force. (2004). *Pay equity: A new approach to a fundamental right*. Ottawa: Department of Justice Canada.

Picot, G., & Hou, F. (2003). *The rise in low-income rates among immigrants in Canada*. Statistics Canada. Analytical Studies Branch research paper series No. 198.

Picot, G., Morissette, R., & Myles, J. (2003). *Low-income intensity during the 1990s: The role of economic growth, employment earnings, and social transfers*. Ottawa: Statistics Canada, Business and Labour Market Analysis Division, cat no: 11F0019MIE-No. 172.

Picot, G., &. Myles, J. (2005). *Income inequality and low income in Canada: An international perspective*. Ottawa: Statistics Canada, cat. no. 11F0019MIE, No. 240.

Poon, P. (2005). Who's missing out on the GIS? *Perspectives, 6*, 10, 5–14.

Prince, M. (1997). Lowering the boom on the boomers: Replacing old age security with a new seniors benefit and reforming the Canada Pension Plan. In G. Swimmer (Ed.), *How Ottawa spends, 1997–98: Seeing red: A Liberal report card* (pp. 211–234). Ottawa: Carleton University Press.

Romanow, R. (2002). *Building on values: The future of health care in Canada*. Ottawa: Commission on Health Care in Canada, Final Report.

Saunders, R. (2005). *Does a rising tide lift all boats? Low-paid workers in Canada*. Ottawa: Canadian Policy Research Networks, Inc. Vulnerable Workers Series—4. www.cprn.com/documents/36570_En.pdf. Accessed July 30, 2009.

Sceviour, R., & Finnie, R. (2004). Social assistance use: Trends in incidence, entry, and exit rates. *Canadian Economic Observer*, Statistics Canada, cat. no. 11–010.

Shields, M. (2002). Shift work and health. *Health Reports, 13*, 11–33. Statistics Canada cat. 82–003.

Social Development Canada. (2005). *The CPP & OAS Statsbook 2005*, Fall. www.hrsdc.gc.ca/en/isp/statistics/pdf/statbook.pdf. Accessed July 30, 2009.

Stanford, J., & Vosko, L. (Eds.). (2004). *Challenging the market: The struggle to regulate work and income*. Montreal and Kingston: McGill-Queen's University Press.

Statistics Canada. (2006a). *Canadian labour market at a glance* 2004, cat. 71–222-XIE. Ottawa: Minister of Industry.

Statistics Canada. (2006b). *Low income cut-offs for 2005 and low income measures for 2004*. Income Research Paper Series, cat. no 75F0002MIE, Vol. 4. Ottawa: Minister of Industry.

Statistics Canada. (2006c). *Low wage and low income*. Income Research Paper Series, cat. no 75–202-XIE, Ottawa: Minister of Industry.

Statistics Canada. (2006d). *Women in Canada: A gender-based statistical report* (5th ed.). Ottawa: Minister of Industry, cat. no. 89–503-XIE. 9.

Statistics Canada (2006e). *Labour force information*. Cat. no. 71-001-XIE, November 3. www.statcan.gc.ca/pub/71-001-x/71-001-x2006010-eng.pdf. Accessed August 17, 2009.

Statistics Canada. (2009). *Income in Canada 2007*, cat. 75–202-X. Ottawa: Ministry of Industry.

Stephenson, M., & Emery, R. (2003). *Living beyond the edge: The impact of trends in non-standard work on single/lone-parent mothers*. Ottawa: Status of Women Canada.

TD Bank Financial Group. (2003). *Affordable housing in Canada: In search of a new paradigm*. TD Economics Special Report. Toronto: Author. www.td.com/economics/special/house03.pdf. Accessed July 30, 2009.

Townson, M. (2000). *Reducing poverty among older women: The potential of retirement incomes policies*. Ottawa: Status of Women Canada. www.swc-cfc.gc.ca/pubs/pubspr/0662659271/200008_0662659271_E.pdf. Accessed July 29, 2008.

Townson, M. (2001). *Pensions under attack: What's behind the push to privatize public pensions*. Ottawa and Toronto: Canadian Centre for Policy Alternatives and James Lorimer & Company.

Townson, M. (2005). *Poverty issues for Canadian women*. Background paper prepared for the Status of Women Canada. www.swc-cfc.gc.ca/resources/consultations/ges09–2005/poverty-e.html. Accessed July 29, 2008.

United Nations Committee on Economic, Social and Cultural Rights. (2006). *Concluding observations of the Committee on Economic, Social and Cultural Rights, Canada*. E/C.12/CAN/CO/5, 19 May. http://www.unog.ch/80256EDD006B9C2E/(httpNewsByYear_En)/C712A902B8453645C125717300508E2D?OpenDocument. Accessed July 29, 2009.

Weldon, S. (2002). *Protest, policy, and the problem of violence against women: A cross-national comparison*. Pittsburgh: University of Pittsburgh Press.

Wiegers, W. (2002). *The framing of poverty as "child poverty" and its implications for women*. Ottawa: Status of Women Canada.

# 7

# THE ITALIAN CASE

*Enrica Morlicchio and Elena Spinelli*

## Introduction: Italian Poverty

In Europe, women's poverty has mainly been associated with sociodemographic characteristics such as lone motherhood and old age or with individual characteristics that interfere with economic self-sufficiency such as emotional instability or bad health. These types of poverty, however, have less weight in Italy than other types of poverty. This does not mean that single mothers or lone elderly women—the two groups that are emphasized in this volume—are not at risk of poverty. It means only that in Italy their risk is less than that of large families in which both parents are present. In Italy, in 2006, 1.8 million or 17% of all minors under 18 years were living in poor families, and just under 7% of them lived with one parent, mainly the mother (Freguja, 2008).

According to Andrea Brandolini and Giovanni D'Alessio (forthcoming), the economic situation for large families has worsened since the end of the 1970s, while it has improved for lone persons aged 65 and more. In particular, these authors stress that there has been a clear improvement, in relative terms, in the condition of older people who lived alone: in 1977; lone, older women had incomes 55% of the average, compared to 71% for their male counterparts. Nearly 20 years later, the figures had risen to 71% and 82%, respectively. Conversely, the situation of large households has gradually worsened; their incomes have declined from close to the average in the early 1980s to about one-tenth below average in the 1990s.

* We would like to thank Enrico Pugliese for his helpful comments.

An additional aspect of the Italian case is the high concentration of poverty in Southern Italy, both historically and currently. Residing in the South in 2006 was about one-third of both Italian families and the Italian population (32.2% and 35.4%, respectively), but around two-thirds of poor families and poor persons (65.3% and 69.0%, respectively) and 70% of poor minors lived in that region of Italy (Istat, 2007b). Further, the intensity of poverty or how far on average the poor are from the poverty line is higher in the South.[1] The high proportion of Southern families among the poor has led some scholars to conclude that Southern poverty has its own "specific characteristics" (Mingione, 2000a, p.100). The difference between North and South—and between what characterizes poverty in the North and South—stems from the dual character of the Italian economic system in which there is a more developed North and a poorer South with a high rate of unemployment and low rate of women's employment. Families living in the less industrialized and poorer South have less economic and employment opportunities, less and lower quality social services, and, consequently, more poverty.

Because Italian statistics on poverty are based mainly on family types and rarely take gender into consideration, it is not easy, on the basis of the official data, to estimate the size of the several groups of poor women in which we are interested. We know, for instance, how many one-parent families are headed by a woman but not how many *poor*, one-parent families are headed by a woman. Moreover, estimates are often extracted from secondary analyses of surveys of family income and/or consumption and are not calculated on an individual basis. As with most such statistics, we do not know how income is distributed within families. In this chapter, we will therefore try to integrate available national data with more detailed information coming from studies and research that address the problem of women's poverty only indirectly. Finally, the definition of the household head reflects a statistical convention that can vary according to the different sources. In the Bank of Italy's Survey of Households' Income and Wealth, for example, the head is the person who declares herself or himself to be "responsible for the economic and financial choices of the household" (Brandolini & D'Alessio, forthcoming), while according to the Italian Central Statistical Office the head is the "nominee [person named] on the household certificate in the registry office of the municipality of residence" (Istat, 1998).

As concerned the gender of the head of the household in Italy in the mid-1990s, the poverty rates of female-headed families were higher than that of male-headed families (more than a percentage point) (Figure 7.1, p. 176). In the ensuing decade, the rates converged because women's rates declined and men's rates, though fluctuating, remained about the same at the end of the interval. In the graph as elsewhere in this chapter, the poverty standard is less than 50% of mean expenditure income unless otherwise noted.

Moving onto the poverty rates of different household types (Table 7.1, p. 177), we find that poverty is less widespread among single-parent

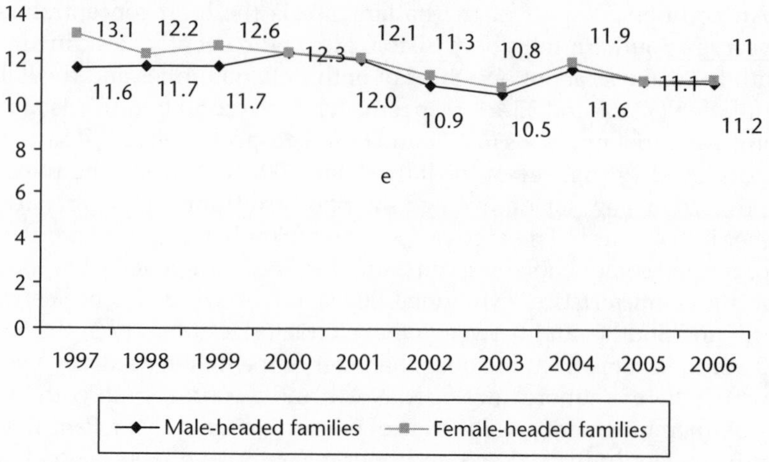


**Figure 7.1.** Poverty rates of male-headed and female-headed families, Italy, 1997–2006.

families (mostly single mothers) than among couples with three or more children. These large, two-parent families have nearly twice the poverty rate of single-parent families: 25.6% compared to 13.8% in 2006, and their poverty level is close to that of two-parent families with two children. The poverty rate of families designated as "other typologies" in Table 7.1 (which include relatives other than children, or unrelated persons) was also higher than that of single parents (17.8%). High rates for both of these types of families are largely a result of their very high rates in the South. It is worth recalling that in Italy, "the presence of more than one minor child within the family is associated with increased economic hardship when the children are minors" (Istat, 2007b, p. 4).

In Italy as a whole, the rates of the lone elderly are not markedly different from those of elderly couples and are, in fact, lower in Central and Southern Italy. In the North and Central regions where overall poverty rates are low, older couples have higher rates than for all families, and that is the case for elderly couples but not the lone elderly in Central Italy. In the South, the elderly groups share a high risk of poverty with other family types and are close to the rate for all families. For Italy as a whole, the poverty rates of both elderly groups fell between 1997 and 2006 (by 15.4% for lone older persons and 23.3% for elderly couples). In the same interval, the poverty rates of families with two or more children, one-parent families, and cohabiting families have risen. It should be noted, however, that the failure of Italian statistics to consider gender in relation to poverty tends to mask the economic disadvantage of women, for, according to the Luxembourg Income Study, the poverty rate in Italy of lone elderly women was about twice that of lone older men in 2000 (see Chapter 10, Table 10.4).

David Benassi and Sara Colombini (2007) provide documentary evidence of geographical differences in poverty rates by gender in 2006,

TABLE 7.1 Relative Poverty Rates[a] by Main Family Types, 1997 and 2006

| | Northern Italy[b] | | Central Italy[c] | | Southern Italy[d] | | All Italy | |
|---|---|---|---|---|---|---|---|---|
| | 1997 | 2006 | 1997 | 2006 | 1997 | 2006 | 1997 | 2006 |
| Couples with one child | 5.1 | 3.2 | 4.3 | 6.0 | 20.1 | 19.4 | 9.1 | 8.6 |
| Couples with two children | 6.2 | 6.2 | 4.9 | 7.0 | 23.3 | 25.5 | 12.8 | 14.5 |
| Couples with three or more children | n.s[e] | 8.3 | 13.5 | n.s[e] | 32.5 | 38.0 | 23.5 | 25.6 |
| One-parent families | 7.2 | 8.1 | 5.7 | 7.7 | 23.6 | 25.0 | 12.1 | 13.8 |
| Lone person aged 65 and over | 11.6 | 8.2 | n.s[e] | 6.9 | 28.8 | 22.9 | 14.9 | 12.6 |
| Couple with at least one spouse aged 65 and over | 9.1 | 7.0 | 8.5 | 8.7 | 30.7 | 24.5 | 16.3 | 12.5 |
| Other typologies (more than one family cohabiting) | 8.1 | 9.1 | 12.0 | 16.5 | 29.2 | 29.9 | 14.9 | 17.8 |
| All families | 6.0 | 5.8 | 6.0 | 7.9 | 24.2 | 23.9 | 12.0 | 11.7 |

[a] Poverty is defined as less than 50% of mean expenditures.
[b] Northern Italy: Piemonte, Valle d'Aosta, Lombardia, Trentino-Alto Adige, Veneto, Friuli-Venezia, Liguria, Emilia-Romagna.
[c] Central Italy: Toscana, Umbria, Marche, Lazio.
[d] Southern Italy: Abruzzo, Molise, Campania, Puglia, Basilicata, Calabria, Sicilia, Sardegna.
[e] Not significant due to the fact that the sample is too small.

*Source*: Istat, 2002, 2007a.

TABLE 7.2 Poverty Rates[a] by Gender in Italy and Some Northern Italian Cities, 2006

| Gender | Italy | Modena | Trento | Brescia | Milan |
|---|---|---|---|---|---|
| Male | 19.5 | 2.8 | 14.6 | 11.1 | 12.8 |
| Female | 20.7 | 3.8 | 18.6 | 14.3 | 19.2 |

[a] Poverty is defined as less than 60% of median income.
*Source*: Benassi & Colombini, 2007, p. 79.

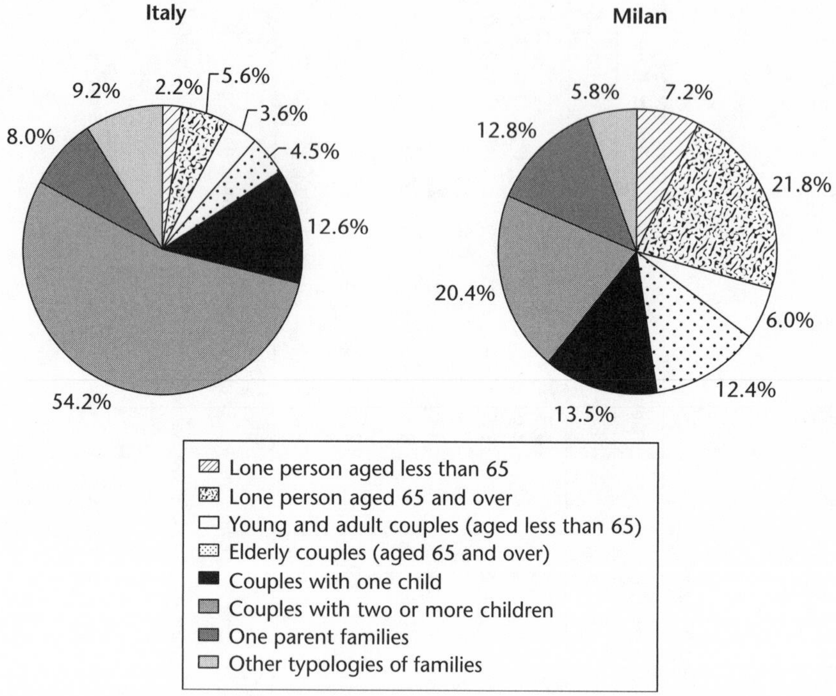


**Figure 7.2.** Poverty composition: Italy and Milan, 2006 (less than 60% of median income).

based on a threshold equivalent to less than 60% of the median income (Table 7.2). They found that the poverty rates of men and women are similar in the country as a whole but that women in some large Northern cities had higher rates than men. For example, in Milan there was a difference of 6.4 percentage points between the poverty rates of all men and all women, compared to only 1.2 percentage points in Italy as a whole (Benassi & Colombini, 2007).

Differences in composition of poverty were also found (Figure 7.2). For example, taking the country as a whole, more than half of the poor (54.2%) are couples with two or more children, while single-parent families and elderly people are much smaller proportions. However, the picture changes radically if we take into consideration a large Northern city such as Milan, where couples with two or more children are only 20.4% of the poor, more than 60% less than their proportion in the country as a whole. On the other hand, lone elderly people (mostly women) rise more than three-fold, from 5.6% of the poor to 21.8%, and single-parent families (mostly single mothers) increase from 8.0% to 12.8%, still remaining a small proportion of the poor, even though their share increases by 60%.

Although the poverty of lone mothers and lone elderly women is not as high as some other groups and does not loom large as a proportion of the poor in Italy, many partnered women are members of poor families and would be counted among the poor if they supported themselves. Indeed, the risk of poverty may be too great for them to be single. Their poverty is hidden in their families, and we will show that they carry a heavy burden as poor women in these families.

The chapter proceeds as follows. We first describe some of the structural conditions that contribute to the main risks of poverty for women, such as their exclusion from the labor market and the absence of policies to support the cost of children—costs in terms of both time and economic resources.We shall then review the conditions of different types of poor families and the social policies that contribute to, or alleviate, poverty. We shall take into consideration first lone-mother families and married couples with minor children where women play a fundamental role in managing budgets that are not sufficient to meet the needs of the family. We then examine the condition of older women, showing how, within a framework of a general capacity of the Italian welfare system to protect older people, they are at risk of poverty due to their past weakness in the labor market and to longevity that is often accompanied by a loss of self-sufficiency. We shall, in addition, examine immigrant women, distinguishing between lone mothers living with their children in Italy and "long distance" lone mothers who provide for the subsistence of their children and other members of their family through remittances.[2] We shall finally give brief consideration to other situations of marginality, such as the homeless persons who live in the streets or in occasional lodgings.

## The Labor Market, Social Welfare System, and Italian Poverty

A number of factors help to explain the nature of Italian poverty, particularly that of Italian women. The first one concerns the tendency to exclude women from the labor market or to confine them to the more precarious or low-wage jobs—what Enrico Pugliese has defined as the "patriarchal character" of Italian labor relations (1993). Consequently, many women are unable to contribute enough money as second earners to keep their families out of poverty or to attempt independence as single mothers.

The second factor—in part connected with the first—is the nature of the Italian social security system which up to now has been effective in protecting the elderly (as ex-workers or widows of ex-workers) but does little to reduce poverty among families with children. Whereas old-age benefits (retirement and survivors' pensions) accounted for 14.6% of Gross Internal Product (GIP), the proportion devoted to families and children was less than 1% (Pizzuti, 2007, p. 322). Finally, as mentioned, historically, Italy has been characterized by a high concentration of poverty in the South.

## Labor Market Patriarchy and Welfare State Familism

Italy is one of the developed countries with the lowest female activity rate: 50.8% (see Table 7.3). As stressed by Paola Villa, among others, the low level of women's participation in the labor force is likely to be due to a "discouragement effect": women disappear from labor market official statistics because they give up searching actively for work. They are part of the "hidden unemployment" and are willing to work if an opportunity arises. This is confirmed by the fact that "even the small increase in employment opportunity that occurred in Southern Italy in the last 10 years led to an increase in women's employment rates. In other words, a modest growth of job opportunity is sufficient to see women's labor force participation increase" (Villa, 2004, p. 18).

Even if women's employment rate has increased substantially in the last decades, the gap between male and female employment is still very high (more than 20 percentage points) (Table 7.3). There are also very strong regional differences: in the South of Italy; only one of three women aged 15–64 is employed while in Central and Northern Italy, it is one out of two. In both cases, female employment rates are still below the EU average and quite far from the Lisbon target.[3] This paucity of employment for women is an important factor in the poverty of Italian families. Compared to families with both parents in paid employment, those in which only one parent has paid work are almost three times more likely to be poor if they have one or two children and four times more likely if they have three or more (Saraceno, 2005). Further, the "meritocratic-occupational" character of the Italian welfare system—that links eligibility for benefits to the status of workers and their contributions to social insurance funds—makes women's employment very important in preventing family poverty (Morlicchio, Pugliese, & Spinelli, 2002).

The burden of domestic work seems to have had a strong effect on women's participation in the labor market, especially for those with low levels of education. A comparative study shows that, in all European countries, education encourages participation in the labor market, even when motherhood and age are taken into account (Bettio & Villa, 1998). However, in Italy (and Greece) the impact is significantly higher. Southern Italian women with very little education have the lowest activity rates

TABLE 7.3 Activity, Employment, and Unemployment Rates by Gender, 2006

| | Activity (Male) | Activity (Female) | Employment (Male) | Employment (Female) | Unemployment (Male) | Unemployment (Female) |
|---|---|---|---|---|---|---|
| Northern Italy | 78.1 | 59.5 | 75.9 | 56.4 | 2.8 | 5.1 |
| Central Italy | 76.3 | 56.0 | 72.9 | 51.3 | 4.5 | 8.2 |
| Southern Italy | 69.3 | 37.3 | 62.3 | 31.1 | 9.9 | 16.5 |
| All Italy | 74.6 | 50.8 | 70.5 | 46.3 | 5.4 | 8.8 |

*Source*: Istat, 2007c.

in Italy: 14.6% in 2006, which means that among women aged 15–64 who are without compulsory education (less than 8 years), only about one in seven had a regular job or were looking actively for it. (In the Central and Northern regions, their activity rate is 10 percentage points higher, 23.4%, but still low.) Marginality in the labor market has often made it difficult for women with little education to perceive their real occupational situation. A Neapolitan lone mother in her thirties who is registered with the employment office, reads job advertisements in the newspaper and has had odd jobs in a bag factory, puts it this way: "The work I've always done and that I still do isn't regular.... I don't know if it means that I'm unemployed. I've never worked, so I've always been unemployed. I've just been a housewife" (Morlicchio, 2002, p. 73). She considers herself a housewife although she has always worked in the "hidden" economy—in jobs that are very low paid and occasional. The disadvantage of Southern women, compared to those living in Central or Northern Italy, tends to be reduced with education. The activity rate of highly educated Southern women (with a B.A. or Ph.D. degree) was 75.0%, compared to 80.8% for women of comparable education in the Northern and Central regions (Istat, 2006).

It should also be noted that the lower activity levels of poorly educated women are not attributable, in this case, to the effects of the so-called poverty trap. As Esping-Andersen (1996) has shown, the deterrent effects of subsidies and other tax relief on women's employment in Italy are rather limited. Given the limited rights to child benefits or unemployment subsidies, the loss of income due to the employment of a second spouse is quite insignificant (while it is very high, for example, in the United Kingdom, Finland, and Belgium).

Owing to the lack of adequate social services and to precarious and often demanding working conditions, there is an inverse relationship between women's number of children and their employment rates. The latest data from the National Italian Labour Force Survey show that among partnered women between 35 and 44 years of age, 75.4% of those without children were employed, compared to 56.9% with at least one child and 40.5% for those with three or more children (Istat, 2007c, p.15). Moreover, almost one woman in five leaves or loses work when her child is born. Over three-fifths (63%) of children, of 1–2 years of age with a working mother are looked after by relatives or friends (mostly grandparents), 9.2% by babysitters, 13.5% by public nurseries, and 14.3% by private nurseries (Istat, 2007c, p. 17).

## Cash Benefits and Paucity of Services

The lack of social services and cash benefits for families, working conditions that do not mesh well with child rearing and limited employment opportunities are some reasons why Italy, along with Eastern Europe and Greece, has one of the lowest fertility rates in Europe—1.35 children per women of child-rearing age in 2006. By contrast, the rates of France, Sweden, and Norway—all countries with more generous cash benefits and services and, in the case of Sweden and Norway, much more employment opportunity for women—are nearly two children per woman.

Another aspect of the Italian welfare system that has significance for our analysis is the dominance of cash over in-kind benefits or services and the consequent, heavy burden of care work for Italian women. In 2003, cash transfers amounted to 82% of the total social welfare budget, compared to 17.2% of the total for social services (Ministry of Welfare, 2004).

In recent decades some specific benefits to facilitate elder care have been added to the usual social security provisions for older, retired workers: the cash attendance allowance to pay for an attendant or caregiver (*indennità di accompagnamento*) and the cash carer's allowance (and assegno di cura). The first one indennitá di accompagnamento is intended for nonself-sufficient and seriously disabled people (of any age); it is not a means-tested provision and not related to household composition; it amounts to €436 a month. The case carer's second allowance, the assegno di cura, is a means-tested provision intended for the elderly, but, in contrast to the indennità di accompagnamento, cash attendance allowance the sum varies greatly among localities and is usually lower.

Despite these additional benefits, Italy is still quite deficient in provision of home-care assistance and availability of places in public old age homes—even though in some cities, like Rome or Bologna, services for old people are more developed. In Italy the rate of institutionalization of the elderly population is only 2%, but once again the national average obscures the strong differences between North and Central Italy and the Southern regions and, in this case, between men and women. In the former, 1.8% of men but 4.2% of women older than 65 live in public old age homes, while in the South the rates for both men and women are very low (respectively 0.6 % and 1%). The number of elderly persons living in public old age homes is 225,000, 73% of whom are concentrated in the North and Central Italy. According to the last Census, women are three-fourths of the population living in public old age homes. The number of older women in nursing homes is 106,000, an increase of 12% since 1991, while the number of men is more or less the same (30,000) (Istat, 2004, p. 395).

The number of nursing homes is small in relation to the total population of elderly people. The common alternative solutions for the care of older persons are basically two: to entrust family members (i.e., daughters and daughters-in-law) with caregiving responsibilities or to hire carers in the market, mainly among immigrant women. It is useful to note how turning to either one solution or the other (and sometimes to a combination) occurs differently in the different Italian regions. In the South, the care of the elderly falls more heavily on families. By contrast, families in the North and Central Italy tend to turn more often to immigrant women or to public services (Bettio, Simonazzi, & Villa, 2006).

## Tilt toward the Elderly

Italian social policy, as noted, is relatively generous with income transfers to the elderly but not toward families with children (neither couples nor one-parent families). Indeed, Italy and Greece are the only European countries not to have intervened with a national minimum of income support for people of working age and their families who are unable to meet basic needs. The public contribution to the cost of children is sustained almost exclusively through a modest, means-tested transfer—*assegni al nucleo familiare*—that goes only to regularly employed or retired workers.[4] This family allowance provided €111.55 monthly in 2004 to a family with two children, 4 and 2 years of age, and a gross annual income of €23,000 (Sabatinelli, 2007, p. 6). In 1999, a means-tested benefit for households with at least three minor children was also introduced, but nonnational families (including refugees) could not apply for it.[5]

After the devolution—following the Constitutional Reform of 2001 that limits the legislative power of the national State in favor of the regions—the local governments have become the main jurisdictions responsible for the support of families with children in economic straits. Welfare provisions have been organized mainly on a local basis, with strong differences among the regions or municipalities in both the type and level of services. For example, in Emilia-Romagna in the North, 2220 children out of 10,000 (22%) under 2 years of age benefit from municipal public nurseries while in Campania and Calabria in the South they are, respectively, 105 and 139 out of 10,000 or less than 1% (Istat, 2007b, p. 288).

Not only the availability but also the cost of public and private childcare services varies considerably between the Central-Northern and the Southern regions and from one municipality to another.[6] Ranci Ortigosa, Da Roit, and Sabatinelli have estimated the cost of the different solutions to which families can have recourse: a medium-income household, living in a municipality in Central or Northern Italy, can pay €350–400 a month in a public nursery, €600–650 in a private nursery, and €800–1000 for a personal baby-sitter. "That means," they write, "households with a second wage earner spend almost all the second salary for [child] care in order to maintain a job that will become profitable only when the children are three years old" (2007, pp. 100–101). Thus, the cost of these services is not affordable for most families in the South and even less for immigrant families. The latter also have less access to an informal network of support.

## The High Poverty Risk of Married Mothers in Southern Italy

Before furthering the analysis of lone mothers—both immigrant and native—and older women, it is important to return to the case of Southern married women, who live in large two-parent families (five or more members) and who are either housewives or precariously employed.[7] In this specific case, the risk of becoming poor is not linked to the difficulty of supporting children in the absence of a spouse. Nor is it in facing old age without an adequate pension and in contexts producing social exclusion (as in large cities or depopulated mountain villages). This specific group of poor women is not socially excluded or marginal, but, on the contrary, maintains informal exchanges within a close neighbor and kin network.[8]

Therefore, one must refrain from applying the category of social exclusion to these women. In fact, as Daly and Saraceno write, "it appears particularly out of focus." These women, in fact, "are excluded because of an 'excess' of integration within their family network and an 'excess' of activity in caring and domestic work" (Daly & Saraceno, 2002, p. 99).

Some scholars have focused on the distribution of income within families and on women who "have lived as poor in families that were not poor at all" (Mingione, 2000b, p. 5; see also Millar, 2003; Pantazis & Ruspini, 2006). The case we are considering, however, concerns women who are poor within families that *are* poor. These women, living in low income households with job opportunities scarce for all their members, are further disadvantaged because of their low levels of education, premature marriages, and the need to provide for home and children without adequate services. Consequently, they end up renouncing completely the search for a job and assume the whole burden of family reproduction, including management of a several-generation household, a situation made necessary by the scarcity of resources and the lack of social services. It is important to keep in mind that the poverty of these women does not necessarily mean the absence of control over family resources. On the contrary, research has documented how the responsibility weighs heavily on the poor Southern housewife who has to decide "what to eat, and when to buy shoes for one or the other, which payment of bills can be delayed and which debts must be paid" (Saraceno, 2005, p. 14). She also maximizes and uses the resources of the informal network and of charitable institutions. This decision-making power, however, is rarely a source of real autonomy. It is rather an expression of an overload of responsibilities that we have elsewhere defined as "forced familism" (Gambardella & Morlicchio, 2005).

This pattern has little to do with the persistence of traditional family models and forms of patriarchal oppression, that is, with the persistence of an archaic and rural South. Such traditional models have been strongly attenuated by mass education, by widespread images from the media, and, more generally, by processes of modernization in the South of Italy (which often causes conflicts with the husbands). It is rather a survival strategy pursued in a coherent way that allows these households to make ends meet, to avoid social exclusion, and, above all, deviant behavior. Nonetheless, they are not able to break the intergenerational transmission of poverty that is one of the most important aspects of Southern Italian poverty.

## Poor Lone Parents

As we have already noted, the poverty rates of one-parent families do not exceed that of other family types. This is surprising and can be explained by analyzing their sociodemographic characteristics.[9] In Italy, there are 2.113 million one-parent families (8.6% of all families), but only about one-third (32%) of them are families with minor children. As in other countries, one-parent families are almost entirely (83.9%) headed by a women because, after a separation or a divorce, women usually have the custody of the children. Furthermore, children of unmarried parents are mostly acknowledged and cared for by the mother.

What distinguishes Italy from most other countries is that half of lone mothers are aged 55 and over, mostly widows whose adult children live with them. As Sabbadini points out:

> If the civil status of one-parent households with children up to 26 years of age and the others [all other one-parent households] are compared, two completely different worlds will be discovered: in the first case 62.9% of lone mothers are separated or divorced and 24.5% are widows; in the second case 12.4% are separated or divorced and 85.9% are widows (2005 p. 28).

Therefore, we can single out two main types of lone mothers: on the one hand, separated or divorced women less than age 55 with minor children (less than 18) and/or young, unemployed children; on the other hand are older women, widowed and with nondependent children cohabiting. There are few lone, adolescent mothers because out-of-wedlock births, though slowly increasing, are still very low. Furthermore, teen pregnancy is followed, in more traditional contexts, by an early wedding, while in more modern families, the adolescent mother can continue to live with her parents, enjoying her family's protection and economic support.

It should also be noted that poor, lone mothers usually do not appear in the statistics, for they are part of multigeneration families that in Southern Italy, as pointed out, have poverty rates that are above the national average and above all other family types except couples with three or more children. The poverty of these lone mothers is then absorbed in the poverty of multigeneration families. As the Commission of Inquiry into Social Exclusion wrote in its 2001 Report: "It could be even supposed that living with other relatives, mostly one's own parents, is the more or less unavoidable choice of lone parents who do not have access to an income of their own" (Commissione di Indagine sulla esclusione sociale, 2002, p. 143). In other words, such lone mother poverty is invisible because these women lack the resources to live independently. For several reasons, including this invisibility and the greater poverty of other family types, lone mother poverty is not perceived as a relevant political question, and little scholarly attention has been paid to them.

According to Chiara Saraceno the Italian anomaly—compared to most European countries—that one-parent households (mostly lone mother) do not have a higher than average incidence of poverty may be explained with the following factors:

> First, in Italy almost all these families come from a previous marriage. Thus they involve mostly adult women, well integrated in their kin network and with expectation of receiving some support from the non-cohabitant father, either through a pension, if they are widows, or through child support payments if they are separated or divorced. Second, marital instability is higher in the Centre-North, where women's employment rates are also higher, than in the South. Third, marital instability tends to involve to a much higher degree dual worker couples than male breadwinner ones (2006, p. 98).

Moreover, up to the mid-1990s divorce and marital instability rates had been higher among upper class and well-educated women who can support themselves after their marriages than among middle- and lower-class and less-educated women with few or no resources of their own. Only in the last years has a sort of "democratization" of conjugal instability occurred (Saraceno, 2006). Finally, it should be noted that single-parent families are on average small: 68.2% of them have only one child, compared to 45.1% of two-parent families (Sabbadini, 2006, p. 39).

The lone mother living in cities of Southern Italy (such as Naples) can rely on important informal resources as a result of family solidarity, which is often not present elsewhere, particularly in Northern Italian cities such as Milan. For example, a lone mother in Naples often visits and eats with her mother who gives her small amounts of money: "The main thing is that there I come back to be a daughter, and I do not think of my problems" (Morlicchio, 2002, p. 30). By contrast, a lone mother in Milan complains, "nobody has helped me; it's me that everyday I went to the municipal office to make such a row to have a house. And then my brother didn't maintain me. I kept on with working, and I paid him what was needed for the shopping, the bills" (Andreotti, 2003, p. 30).

## Lone Elderly Women

In Italy, due to the joint effect of the low birth rate and increase in life expectancy, the number of people aged 65 and over exceeds that of the population age 15 and below. Such demographic changes have affected women more than men.

Several local surveys also document the existence of a gap between women's and men's pensions. A survey carried out some years ago in the Northern Italian Region, Piemonte, pointed out that women's pensions were remarkably lower than men's, and only women who can rely on two pensions—their own and that as survivors—can equal the level of men's pensions and thus avoid the risk of poverty (Peruzio, 1994).

If widows have no other income, they are eligible for a survivors' pension equal to their deceased husband's pension. If they have their own pension and/or another source of income, the survivors' pension can be added to their pensions in amounts ranging from a minimum of 25% to a maximum of 50% of the deceased husband's pension.

Women receive about 80% of the survivors' pensions. Women over 65 years old, with no income or with an income below poverty, can apply for a minimum social security pension or for a "social check" that was €389.36 a month in 2007. The number of women 65 years old and over receiving the social checks is more than double the number of men, about 221,000 men compared to about 549,000 women (Istat, 2007d). Moreover, women are about two-thirds of retired people receiving the minimum social security pension (approximately €500 per month: (Pizzuti, 2007, p. 253).

The more vulnerable older women are those who never married or are separated or divorced and thus never had spousal support or have not had it for any length of time. This is linked to the fact that the reversibility pensions—those derived from spouses—are generally higher than the minimum social security pension or the "social check." Moreover, as one gets older, disabilities increase and self-reliance decreases, health tends to deteriorate, and self-sufficiency is harder. The situation of poor, lone, older women can become unbearable due to a number of factors that undermine the quality of life. For example, a study of poverty carried out in the Veneto region has shown that 9% of the houses of older women, most of them part owned or held in life tenancy, were in poor condition, as opposed to 6.5% of other houses; 17.4% did not have a telephone, and 32% were without heating (Facchini, 2000b).

The most common form of social aid for lone, older women with low incomes is economic assistance from municipalities. Relief payments to supplement income, usually scant amounts, can consist of occasional cash payments and contributions to rent and utilities.

Even if the Italian social security system has been able until now to protect most elderly women, some of them do not receive enough money to escape poverty. In fact, as former workers they can often apply only for a minimum social security pension, and as widows they have access only to a survivors' pension or to a means-tested social check, both of which are lower than the mean social security pension received by male, retired workers with a more regular and longer contributory record.

## Immigrant Women

Besides the more traditional figure of poor, lone mothers, and poor women in large families in Southern Italy, a new type of poor woman, completely responsible for her children's maintenance, has appeared in Italy. This is the poor immigrant woman. In the following sections, we will distinguish between immigrant lone mothers with children in Italy and immigrant lone mothers with children abroad.

Italy, with 2,923,922 legal immigrants at the end of 2006, has become the European country with the fourth largest immigrant population—after Germany (7.3 million), Spain (3.4 million), and France (3.3 million) (Caritas, 2007). Eighty-eight percent of immigrants live in Northern and Central Italy, a quarter of them in Lombardy in the North. The largest groups of immigrant women in 2007 are from Eastern Europe (Ukraine, Romania, Moldova, and Albania), and after that from the Philippines, Poland, Ecuador, Peru, and Sri Lanka.[10] According to the latest Istat Report, "At the start of 2006 the relationship between the sexes [of immigrants] appears to be substantially balanced (102 males for 100 females) even though there still are substantial differences among the communities, and in some cases they are even more accentuated than in the past" (Istat, 2007b, p. 326).

The occupational sector in which the largest number of immigrant women are employed is domestic work and elderly and child care (Caritas, 2007). Some of this work is irregular and performed by immigrant women without a residence permit (1,134,000, of which 700,000 are regular). Recognizing the role of immigrant domestic workers in the Italian welfare regime, the right-wing government, in office from 2001 to 2005, provided amnesty for domestic and care workers as part of an otherwise repressive immigration bill in 2002. The high demand for immigrant, domestic workers occurred in Italy in the mid-1970s. At the time, growing numbers of middle-class women were entering the labor market and hiring immigrant women to care for their children because the welfare system, regarding families as principal caregivers, was not providing either child or elder care. Consequently, women workers turned to the market for this service.

Chell-Robinson (2000) claims there is some upward mobility from "domestic" to "care" work as the second requires more skill. To the contrary, almost 30 years in the labor market has not yet led to upward mobility for immigrant women, that is, from one sector to another or with the possibility of utilizing previous training and professional skills (de Filippo, 2000). However, as Antonella Spanò (2005) points out, it is not surprising that an immigrant woman who generally has the qualifications for a higher status job in her own country is willing to do domestic work in Italy at 10 times the salary in the country of origin.[11] Thus, she accepts a low-wage job by Italian standards with hard conditions of work that an Italian woman with only a high school diploma would be likely to refuse. Rachel Parreñas (2001) has defined this arrangement—immigrant women caring for middle-class Italian children—as an international transfer of caretaking.

Occupational segregation by gender is reinforced by the stereotype that women are naturally suited to caring work, and most migrant women are forced to accept jobs that are below their qualifications. However, the association of domestic work and caring has secured for immigrant women a protected area of employment, even if disadvantaged, and they are unlikely to be without a job. The domestic help sector, a significant gender specialization, is characterized by lower wages than in other sectors (construction, agriculture, industry) where immigrant men are employed.[12] The salaries in this sector are generally disproportionate to the services rendered and do not match the range of tasks required. Salaries can go from €500 to €1000 a month for a full-time job. As some researchers have pointed out, wages under the same working conditions in Northern and Southern Italy differ very much.[13] Bargaining with their employers can be very difficult for immigrant women, even if they are aware of the rights granted by the national labor contract.

Moreover, because domestic work is often irregular, the workers have no legally enforceable rights; more than half of foreign domestic workers live with their employers and are often underpaid and forced to work long hours. In fact, it is not infrequent that the job has been carried out irregularly for many years with employers failing to make social security contributions.[14] Consequences of this situation are becoming evident with the small number of lone, immigrant women over 60 years of age who arrived in the 1970s during the first wave of immigration.[15] Since their employers have not paid their social security contributions, they cannot have a pension, and generally they do not have any savings, having sent remittances home to their families. They always worked, but now nobody wants them because they are old. As a consequence of not working, they no longer have residence permits and therefore no right to social services. After 30–40 years in Italy, they do not want to go back to countries where they do not feel at home anymore, or sometimes they cannot go back due to war.

## Immigrant Lone Mothers with Children Abroad

As many scholars have noted, among the reasons that lead women to emigrate, besides those in common with migrant men (economic, cultural, or political), there are some that are typically women's: family reunification, a desire for emancipation, escape from the inferior conditions for women associated with the cultures and traditions of their countries and sometimes to break family ties. Women not infrequently decide to emigrate after divorce or separation, both because they have become a burden for their families, and, more often, they wish to improve the economic condition of their children. Their poverty is also the consequence of the difficulties of getting child support from their ex-husbands (Balsamo, 2003). Among migrant women there are also those who come as unmarried mothers, especially from South America.[16] One important consequence of working in the domestic sector is the difficulty of reconciling work with motherhood. The result is that children are often left behind in the home country with relatives. Not surprisingly, more than a third of female immigrants is in Italy without their children. In 2001, there were 167,603 immigrant women (both married and single mothers) with children, only 12.3% of the total immigrant population (1,362,630) (Caritas, 2003).

One of the problems in gathering statistical data on immigrant lone mothers who have left their children in the country of origin is their invisibility, for they do not appear as "immigrant lone mothers" in any official statistical survey. Moreover, they are often undocumented, so they would not be included in statistical data anyway. These women seek a good salary in order to send money home for the support of their children or to finance their children's studies; therefore, they work as many hours as they can, frequently having more than one job. Yet, there is little economic independence for these women as they remit most of their earnings to support their children and the relatives who are caring for them. Whether documented or undocumented, women migrants are key actors in their families' survival strategies.[17] The children and the relatives who take care of them may even be able to rise out of the poverty that has driven these women to migrate. By contrast, immigrant, lone mothers are able to save very little money out of their salaries for themselves and consequently are at risk of poverty, particularly when illness, accidents, or unemployment keep them out of work, their only source of income. However, unemployment is usually a temporary situation, and, generally, a new job puts a halt to their impoverishment. Compared to Italian families, immigrant lone mothers would be considered poor, but if their incomes are compared to their earnings in their countries of origin, where their children live, they would not be considered poor.

## Immigrant Lone Mothers with Children in Italy

Among foreign-born women with children in Italy, there were 183,500 mothers of whom 8500, 4.6%, were lone mothers (Caritas, 2003). Generally, after a number of years (three to five, even six or seven) lone mothers succeed in bringing their children to Italy, or they bear children in Italy. These latter ones are sometimes separated or divorced women with children in the country of origin whom they have maintained with regular remittances, and then, another child is born from a relationship that developed in Italy.

Others are women who left their country when they were young and find themselves alone and pregnant, often as illegal immigrants. The fertility rate of immigrant women is almost double that of Italian women: 2.45 compared to 1.24 for women of child-bearing age. However, this group of immigrant women find it more difficult to raise children, and as a consequence the voluntary abortion rate is nearly four times that of Italian women: 29.4 per thousand immigrant women, compared to 7.7 Italian women.

The conditions for family unification are restrictive, given the position of most non-EU migrants, particularly women (Spinelli, 2006). However, this has not prevented lone mothers who were unable to meet these conditions from reuniting with their children "illegally," without waiting for legal papers.[18] They are often unaware that if unification is not well prepared and thoroughly organized, immigrant women can find themselves and their minor children entangled in problems of poverty and homelessness. The cost of living is generally higher in Italy than in the native country, and traveling expenses are still another burden. Housing is one of the main problems.[19] For long periods they live with other people and/or groups of families they do not know, often from different countries in conditions such as overcrowding that make cohabitation difficult. The exorbitant prices in the private housing market and the existence of forms of discrimination in a context of general weakness of social housing make it very difficult for immigrants to settle adequately. Immigrants pay between 40% and 70% more than the Italians for the same property.

The precarious means of livelihood are present in the daily lives of migrant lone mothers, whether regular or irregular. They generally have difficulties in obtaining and keeping full-time work and in most cases have an irregular job.[20] Formally, only immigrant mothers with regular residence permits are entitled to a public nursery school or child care or to economic help from the municipality. Most requests for social services concern the possibility of finding low-cost housing and child care in order for mothers to be able to work. Moreover, the lack of infrastructure for child care makes it very hard to combine family and work for lone immigrant mothers as they do not have enough time off to look after their own children. The options are public residential-care institutions or foster care, if available from the welfare state.

The most excluded group is undocumented migrants, a group to which many immigrant lone mothers belong. There is no formal source of social support for those unlawfully present, but until now Italy has maintained a relative tolerance toward "undocumented" migrants through informal responses to their needs. The help of philanthropic and nonprofit organizations has made it possible to get around the constraints of the lack of a residence permit. But not having clear entitlement has meant insecurity and, for many lone immigrants, also a life in poverty.

Evidence of this comes basically from local social services, direct observation and a few data, usually based on empirical studies conducted at a territorial level. (Spinelli, 2003, 2005). A recent survey on immigrant families (Simoni & Zucca, 2008) shows that almost two-thirds of one-parent families (often with only one source of income) have experienced prolonged periods of economic difficulties: 50% of those interviewed declared having had often or at least sometimes difficulty in maintaining basic family consumption (purchase of food, paying of bills, rent, etc.) with consequent daily sacrifices. Owing to the difficulties of raising their children in Italy, some immigrants, particularly lone mothers, have sent their children back to their extended families and sent money to them in the countries of origin.

## Homeless Women

In Italy the phenomenon of homelessness among women is generally hard to quantify due to the high territorial mobility of this population and the absence of systematic registration among the myriad of voluntary organizations and religious bodies that offer temporary solutions to the problems that lead to homelessness (family break-up, domestic violence, and alcohol addiction). Antonio Tosi, for instance, argues that "While we can certainly speak of an increase, in recent years, of situations of vulnerability and of the risk of homelessness among women, it is more difficult to say whether the absolute number of homeless women is increasing" (2001, p. 163). There is also a latent risk of homelessness among older women which is more accentuated in metropolitan areas like Milan where, according to Francesca Zajczyk, there are twice as many women as men seeking rental units in social housing, and 70% of the women are elderly, compared to only 40% of the men (2006, p. 70).

At the national level there are not many data about women's homelessness, but we can take into account an estimate of the Commission of Inquiry into Social Exclusion that places the number of homeless people between 44,853 and 61,753 people, a third of whom are women (Commissione di Indagine sulla esclusione sociale, 2001). Among homeless women psychiatric problems are more widespread than alcohol and drug addiction, the problems that predominate among homeless men.

Homelessness manifests itself differently among immigrant women. They rarely live in the street, both because they can count on their community's solidarity for a place to stay on their arrival and because working as domestics or caring for the elderly, they generally sleep in their employers' homes. Furthermore, for immigrant women, the lack of adequate accommodations is usually a temporary situation at the time of arrival, an initial phase in the path of settlement. As Tosi points out:

> Women immigrants infrequently present socialization problems, and they rarely have the problem of drug addiction or substance abuse. They simply find themselves in a condition of extreme poverty, with a transitory problem of not having a place to sleep, at least in the first stages of immigration.... They are simply poor people without housing (2001, pp. 168, 170).

We can say that they do not have a visible "homeless" status, but at the same time, they suffer from lack of a home of their own.

Local authority provision of services for women at risk of marginalization and exclusion (emergency accommodation, temporary accommodation for women victims of domestic violence or for immigrant prostitutes who are victims of the racket) is quite different from other types of welfare provision and is often inadequate both in quantity and in the approach adopted. However, when these services are provided—not only by local administrations but more often by voluntary organizations and religious bodies—they temporarily alleviate situations of extreme hardship and homelessness.

In general, the very high percentage of home owning families in Italy (73.3% of families, according to the last Istat data [2007e, p. 21]) represents a strong protection against the risk of becoming homeless. The highest percentage of homeowners is among the elderly (87.2%). However, since spending for social housing is very limited in Italy, the main alternative for those who do not own homes is to rent a house. In large urban centers, rent can represent a significant part of total spending.

It is among people older than 65 (where, as we have seen, women prevail) that rent consumes a greater portion of spending: 25.8% compared to an average of 17.9% for all Italian families. A recurring solution for lone mothers and older lone women is to share the house with other relatives (parents or married adult children). Here, too, family solidarity manages to hide economic hardship.

## Concluding Remarks

In this chapter we have tried to highlight the condition of women at risk of poverty and social exclusion, drawing some inferences from our own and other scholars' research on poor, two-parent or multigeneration families, on immigrant women, lone mothers and single, elderly women. There is enough evidence to suggest that in Italy women's vulnerability to poverty is widespread and sometimes hidden because it is "embedded" in large families with children in which both parents are present.

As we have seen, poverty in Italy, besides being concentrated in Southern regions, is concentrated mainly in three types of families: large families (including both couples with three or more children and multigeneration families) with only one member earning a living (usually the father); families composed of a lone, older person (usually a woman); and one-parent families (Italian women who are divorced, separated and widowed, and immigrant women with children who are mainly responsible for family economic maintenance).

The difficulties of finding a job make it hard for women to achieve a level of economic self-sufficiency that would allow them to divorce if they wanted or needed to. Lone elderly women suffer the consequences of irregular working careers, interrupted by birth and care of children, or of not being protected by social security. Lone mothers who do not have any employment or child support often have to depend on their families of origin with a consequent loss of autonomy while immigrant women are more isolated from the kinship network and less able to take care of their children due to the characteristics of their jobs.[21]

One of our main conclusions is that for Italian women employment at a living wage is fundamental for escaping poverty, not only in case of divorce or widowhood but also when the problem is the imbalance between the number of consumers (mainly children) and number of earners—as it is in the case of large families with children where both parents are present. Because of the prevalence of low-paid and badly protected work, one worker in a family is not sufficient, and social welfare does not offset market deficiencies.

In the absence of a system of welfare services that is adequate both qualitatively and quantitatively, family and kinship resources are mobilized. This is especially the case in Southern Italy, where, as we have seen, poverty is concentrated. These networks still play a central role in the survival strategies of the economically weaker layers of the population. The family network is a fundamental dispenser of both monetary and nonmonetary help.

The general weakness of the local welfare system renders the situation of immigrant, lone mothers even more problematic than that of poor, native families. In fact, the specific services for this sector of the population are still very poor. On the other hand, the existing services are scarcely used by immigrants both because of a lack of information about the benefits for which they are eligible or their ineligibility for some of these services. With little support coming from the Italian welfare system, these families have greater difficulties than the Italian-born poor, because they lack network resources other than those of their ethnic groups. The main welfare agency for both Italians and immigrants turns out to be the family or the ethnic community.

To summarize, in Italy conditions of economic vulnerability occur when women are the only ones responsible for children's economic maintenance, and perhaps because of the high risk of poverty, there are relatively few single mother families. Poverty also affects Southern Italian married women who, along with their spouses, are precariously attached to the labor market and immigrant married mothers whose children are not living with them. All these are examples of the substantial risk of poverty of certain groups of women in Italy.

As Gesano and Heins point out, between 1991 and 2001, more than 2.1 million people over age 65 joined the retired population (an increase of 17.7%), and 55% of them were women (2004, p. 50). In the same period, the probability for old people to live in one-person families has not increased significantly: 53.5% of the elderly lived alone in 2001, compared to 52.3% in 1991. However due to the greater longevity of women and their tendency to live alone after the death of their husbands, 77% of older, single-person families are women. Some older women who do not live alone escape poverty by residing with their grown children and/or grandchildren.

While the relative poverty risk for lone elderly people has decreased in the last decade, women are still more vulnerable than men. As pointed out by Istat, men—though representing 46.8% of retired people—receive 55.5% of total pensions. In 2003, men's pensions were, on average, over 40% higher than those of women—€13,736 annually compared to €9688 (Istat, 2004, p. 375). According to a survey carried out in Milan in 2001, the average pension received by older women is 40% lower than men's (Zajczyk, 2005, p. 48).

Women can claim a pension when they reach 60 years of age and have contributed at least 20 years. According to Istat, men between the ages of 65 and 69 received an average, annual pension of about €15,400, while the average for women was about €8700 or 57% of men's average (2005). The disparities persist in the older age groups with the gender gap being greatest between the ages of 80 and 84 when women's pensions are only 49% of men's. Lower pensions for women are linked to the fact that the rate of employment of women is less than that of men, to interruptions of work due to family care and to lesser pay for various reasons, including reduced opportunities to obtain a higher education.

## Notes

1 The figures are 22.5% in the South, compared to 17.5% and 16.9% in the Northern and Central regions, respectively. These data are from the Italian Central Statistical Office (Istat) that conducts an annual large-scale survey of household consumption. Household consumption, as reported in the survey, is used to create relative-consumption poverty lines based on proportions of mean equivalent disposable household consumption. In 2006, the poverty threshold for one person was equal to €582.20 per month and €2328.82 for a family of seven or more (Istat, 2007a).

2 When we try to compare immigrants' poverty with that of the Italian population using the International Standard of Poverty Line, a number of methodological problems arise that we cannot take into consideration here.

3 According to the agenda for employment set by the European Union in 2000 the target for female employment is 60% for the year 2010.

4 In Italy it is very difficult to get general data concerning the proportion of families receiving means-tested benefits because of the variety, fragmentation, and heterogeneity in the form of delivery as well as in the public bodies responsible for administering benefits. This is particularly true in the case of minimum income benefits that are always locally provided (Saraceno, 2002).

5 A non-means-tested bonus of €1000 for the first born child was introduced in 2005 but only for that year and has been discontinued.

6 In Italy the funding for social services comes from the central government, supplemented by local taxes and charges for some services (like child-care centers). Social services may be delivered directly by the local authority and partners such as the public health system or education agencies, or they may be contracted to the voluntary sector or other agencies. There is almost no involvement of the market sector in provision of publicly funded social services.

7 In Italy large families (with three or more children) are 6.5% of all families, but in some regions such as Campania and Calabria in the South, they are more than 10% of all families.

8 This is one of the reasons that explains why there is no correspondence between subjective poverty indicators, based on family perceptions of their own conditions, and indicators based on current income or spending. It is in particular families living in Southern Italy who do not consider themselves poor, even though their income or spending is very low, while on the other hand almost half of the lone older people and more than one-third of mono-parental families consider themselves poor or very poor (Freguja & Pannuzi, 2007, p. 55).

9 In 2006, one-parent families were less than 10% of Italian families (8%), while couples with children are 39% of the total. One out of four households (26%) is a lone person, and 20% are couples without children. The remaining 2% are classified as "other type of families."

10 Since 2005/2006 Poland and Romania have entered the EU, and the legal status of immigrants from those countries has changed from extra-European to European.

11 Recent surveys of women coming from Eastern Europe reveal "that in their countries the monthly pay is equivalent to €25 for factory workers, cooks, and waitresses; to €50 for teachers, secretaries, and office workers; to €100 for gynecologists, pediatricians, engineers.... a tenth of what they earn as domestic workers in Italy" (Spanò, 2005, p. 3).

In the Philippines the average salary for jobs equivalent to the educational level of teachers, nurses, and social workers is 8–10 times lower than pay for domestic work in Italy (Chell-Robinson, 2000).

12 Generally, immigrants earn less than Italians, and even increases in earnings are always within a medium–low wage band. An average salary has been calculated in 2004 to be about €10,000 per year. Women earn about 58% of what men earn (Caritas, 2007).

13 The difference between north and south has an impact on immigrant as well as native families. The poorest immigrant families live in southern regions. The difference between northern and southern regions is not limited to working conditions but also to regional welfare systems, which are very inadequate in the South. Another difference is linked to the cost of housing in small and larger cities. In small cities, costs are more affordable. The choice to live in one place or another seems to produce notable differences in living conditions of immigrant families (Ascoli, 2001).

14 Essential health care is available for all people present in the territory regardless of residence status. Public health care facilities ensure outpatient emergency and essential or continuing health care services for illness and accidents as well as preventive medicine programs.

15 Only 2% of immigrant women in Italy are over age 60. Two-thirds (68.4 %) of foreign domestic workers are below 40 years of age with an average age of 31 (Caritas, 2006).

16 As a group, immigrant women in Italy have the following marital statuses: 56.4% married, 2.5% divorced, 4% separated, 2.9% widowed, and 34.2% single. Sixty-six percent of women have dependent children, including those left behind (Caritas, 2007).

17 The transnational family links and immigrants' major responsibility for providing for families left in the homelands are confirmed by remittance data. In 2006, the total amount of remittances sent abroad from Italy was more than 7 times (7.4) the amount sent in 2000.

18 On the basis of the 1989 UN Convention on the Rights of the Child, immigrant minors cannot be expelled from a country. Italy has constitutional guarantees that protect family life, including protection from deportation. The current Italian law on immigration states that immigrant minors residing in Italy must attend school, regardless of their legal status, and are entitled to medical care in the National Health Service and to some of the social services. In short, they may enjoy better living conditions than in some of their countries of origin.

19 One of the main features of Italian housing policy for immigrants is its temporary character. Immigrants often live in substandard housing that creates an obstacle to meeting the legal conditions for family reunion.

20 Under current law, the residence permit is contingent on the possession of a job with specific salaries and hours of work (minimum 25 hours per week), generally not compatible with a part-time job in domestic or care work. Thus, it becomes difficult for them to achieve and /or maintain legal immigrant status and to claim essential welfare services.

21 A recent survey of immigrant poverty shows that the risk of falling below the level of poverty is higher in the initial phase of immigration and during the phase of stabilization. In the first case, there is the impact of entering the new country; in the second there are additional family expenses connected with the arrival of children or other family members (Rovati, 2007).

## References


Andreotti, A. (2003). Strategie di selezione per la mobilitazione di capitale sociale. *Inchiesta, 23*, 139, 24–33.

Ascoli, U. (2001). Immigrazione nelle regioni adriatiche, accesso ai servizi e processi di integrazione. *InterMigra, 2*, 16–28.

Balsamo, F. (2003). *Famiglie di migranti: Trasformazione dei ruoli e mediazione culturale.* Roma: Carocci.

Benassi, D., & Colombini, S. (2007). Caratteristiche e distribuzione territoriale della povertà e della disuguaglianza sulla base dei dati dell'archivio disrel. In A. Brandolini & C. Saraceno (Eds.), *Povertà e benessere: Una geografia delle disuguaglianze in Italia* (pp. 61–88). Bologna: Il Mulino.

Bettio, F., & Villa, P. (1998). A Mediterranean perspective on the breakdown of the relationship between participation and fertility. *Cambridge Journal of Economics, 22*, 2, 137–171.

Bettio, F., Simonazzi, A. M., & Villa, P. (2006). Welfare mediterraneo per la cura degli anziani e immigrazione. In A. M. Simonazzi (Ed.), *Questioni di genere, questioni di politica. Trasformazioni economiche e sociali in una prospettiva di genere* (pp. 183–211). Roma: Carocci.

Brandolini, A., & D'Alessio, G. (forthcoming). *Household structure and income inequality*. In D. del Boca, & R. G. Repetto, (Eds.), *Women, work, family and social policy in Italy.*

Caritas. (2003). *Dossier Statistico immigrazione. XIII Rapporto Caritas/Migrantes.* Roma: Antares.

Caritas. (2006). *Dossier Statistico immigrazione. XVI Rapporto Caritas/Migrantes.* Roma: Antares.

Caritas. (2007). *Dossier Statistico immigrazione. XVII Rapporto Caritas/Migrantes.* Roma: Antares.

Chell-Robinson, V. (2000). Female migrants in Italy: Coping in a country of new migration. In F. Anthias & G. Lazaridis (Eds.), *Gender and migration in Southern Europe* (pp. 102–123). New York: Oxford University Press.

Commissione di Indagine sulla esclusione sociale. (2001). *Rapporto sulle politiche contro la povertà e l'esclusione sociale, 1997–2001.* C. Saraceno (Ed.). Roma: Carocci.

Commissione di Indagine sulla esclusione sociale. (2002). *Rapporto sulle politiche contro la povertà e l'esclusione sociale, Anno 2003.* Roma: Istituto Poligrafico dello Stato.

Daly, M., & Saraceno, C. (2002). Social exclusion and gender relations. In B. Hobson, J. Lewis, & B. Siim (Eds.), *Contested concepts in gender and social politics* (pp. 84–104) . Northampton: Elgar.

de Filippo, E. (2000). La componente femminile dell'immigrazione. In E. Pugliese (Ed.), *Rapporto immigrazione: Lavoro, sindacati e società* (pp. 47–63). Roma: EDIESSE.

Esping-Andersen, G. (1996). Welfare state without work: The impasse of labour shedding and familialism in continental European social policy. In G. Esping Andersen (Ed.), *The welfare state in transition* (pp. 66–87). London, Sage Publications.

Facchini, C. (2000a). Storia lavorativa, storia familiare e povertà nelle donne anziane. *Inchiesta, 20,* 128, 47–55.

Facchini, C. (2000b). Indagine sulla povertà nel Veneto associata alla condizione femminile. In Caritas Italiana & Fondazione Zancan, *Cittadini Invisibili Rapporto 2002 su esclusione sociale e diritti di cittadinanza* (pp. 54–63). Milano: Feltrinelli.

Freguja, C., & Pannuzi, N. (2007). La povertà in Italia: Che cosa sappiamo dalle varie fonti? In A. Brandolini & C. Saraceno (Eds.), *Povertà e benessere: Una geografia delle disuguaglianze in Italia* (pp. 23–59). Bologna, Il Mulino.

Freguja. C. (2008). Minori e anziani: povertà e deprivazione materiale, ppt presented at the workshop *La povertà dei minori e degli anziani,* Roma, CNEL (National Institute on Labor and Economic Issues), May 9.

Gambardella, D., & Morlicchio, E. (Eds.) (2005). *Familismo forzato. Scambi di risorse e coabitazione nelle famiglie povere a Napoli.* Roma: Carocci.

Gesano, G., & Heins, F. (2004). La popolazione italiana negli anni novanta. In E. Pugliese (Ed.), *Lo stato sociale in Italia: Un decennio di riforme. Rapporto IRPPS-CNR 2003* (pp. 27–75). Roma: Donzelli.

Istat. (1998), La distribuzione quantitativa del reddito in Italia nelle indagini sui bilanci di famiglia; Anno 1996. *Informazioni, No 62.*

Istat. (2002). La stima ufficiale della povertà in Italia, 1997–2000. *Argomenti, 24.* Roma: Istituto Poligrafico dello Stato.

Istat. (2004). *La situazione finanziaria delle famiglie e degli individui in Italia e in Europa.* Roma: Istituto Poligrafico dello Stato.

Istat. (2006). *Strutture familiari e opinioni su famiglia e figli: Indagine multiscopo sulle famiglie "Famiglia e soggetti sociali," Anno 2003.* Roma: Istituto Poligrafico dello Stato.

Istat. (2007a). La povertà relativa in Italia nel 2006, *Statistiche in breve.* October 4. Roma: Poligrafico dello Stato.

Istat. (2007b). *Rapporto annuale. La situazione del Paese nel 2006.* Roma: Istituto Poligrafico dello Stato.

Istat. (2007c). *La famiglia in Italia, dossier statistico.* Conferenza Nazionale della Famiglia, Firenze, May 24–26.

Istat. (2007d). *Rapporto sulla previdenza e assistenza nel 2005.* Roma: Istituto Poligrafico dello Stato.

Istat. (2007e). *L'accesso alla casa d'abitazione in Italia: proprietà, mutui, affitti e spesa delle famiglie.* Roma, July 17.

Millar, J. (2003). Gender, poverty and social exclusion. *Social Policy and Society, 2,* 3, 181–188.

Mingione, E. (2000a). Modello sud-europeo di welfare, forme di povertà e politiche contro l'esclusione sociale. *Sociologia e Politiche Sociali, 1,* 87–112.

Mingione, E. (2000b). La povertà delle donne in Italia: Dalla casalinga proletaria meridionale all'anziana sola. *Inchiesta, 30,* 128, 5–8.

Ministero del lavoro e delle politiche sociali. (Ministry of Welfare). (2004). *Rapporto di monitoraggio sulle politiche sociali.* Roma: Author.

Morlicchio, E. (Ed.). (2002). *The spatial dimensions of social exclusion and integration: The case of Naples.* Amsterdam: AME.

Morlicchio, E., Pugliese, E., & Spinelli, E. (2002). Diminishing welfare: The Italian case. In G. S. Goldberg & M. G. Rosenthal (Eds.), *Diminishing welfare: A cross-national study of social provision* (pp. 245–270). Westport, CT: Auburn House.

Pantazis, C., & Ruspini, E. (2006). Gender, poverty and social exclusion. In C. Pantazis, D. Gordon, & R. Levita (Eds.), *Poverty and social exclusion in Britain: The millennium survey* (pp. 375–472). Bristol: Policy Press.

Parreñas, R. (2001). *Servants of globalization: Woman, migration and domestic work.* Stanford: Stanford University Press.

Peruzio, G. (1994). Il welfare esploso: Analisi della distribuzione dei redditi da pensione Inps in Piemonte. *Quaderni di ricerca Ires, 2,* 16–21.

Pizzuti, F. R. (Ed.). (2007). *Rapporto sullo stato sociale 2007.* Torino: Utet.

Pugliese, E. (1993). *Sociologia della disoccupazione.* Bologna: Il Mulino.

Ranci Ortigosa, E., Da Roit, B., & Sabatinelli, B. (2007). Per una politica pubblica dei servizi per le famiglie con figli. In L. Guerzoni (Ed.), *Le politiche di sostegno alle famiglie con figli: Il contesto e le proposte* (pp. 73–108). Bologna: Il Mulino.

Rovati, G. (2007). Anziani: Migranti e giovani in povertà: Quali politiche? Paper presented at the conference on *Verso il Bilancio Sociale del Paese,* Roma, CNEL (National Institue on Labor and Economic Issues), April 18.

Sabatinelli, S. (2007). Local differences and social inequalities in access to childcare options: A comparison between and within Italy and France. *Cahier Europèen du Sciences,* PO numèro 01/07, Paris.

Sabbadini, L. L. (2006). Profili e tempi di vita nel quadro italiano. In F. Bimbi & R. Trafiletti (Eds.), *Madri sole: Sfide politiche e genitorialità alla prova* (pp. 27–44). Roma: Edizioni lavoro.

Saraceno, C. (Ed.). (2002). *Social assistance dynamics in Europe: National and local poverty regimes.* Bristol: Policy Press.

Saraceno, C. (2005). Prefazione: I rischi della solidarietà familiare obbligata. In D. Gambardella & E. Morlicchio (Eds.), *Familismo forzato: Scambi di risorse e coabitazione nelle famiglie povere a Napoli* (pp. 9–30). Roma: Carocci.

Saraceno, C. (2006). Poverty and poverty discourses in Italy in comparative perspective. In M. Petmesidou & C. Papatheodorou (Eds.), *Poverty and social deprivation in the Mediterranean* (pp. 95–115). London: Zed Books.

Simoni, M. & Zucca F. (2008). Lavoro domestico e immigrazione femminile: Nuovi modelli di mobilità. *Enaip Formazione e Lavoro, 3,* 201–217.

Spanò, A. (2005). L'esperienza migratoria: Progetti, significati, profili di donne immigrate. Paper presented at the conference *Migrazioni al femminile*. Roma.
Spinelli, E. (2003). Badanti donne come noi. *La Rivista di Servizio Sociale, 2,* 18–22.
Spinelli, E. (2005). *Immigrazione e servizio sociale.* Roma: Carocci.
Spinelli, E. (2006). *Limitations to the rights of immigrants in Italy.* Paper presented at the Conference organized by the Globalization Studies International Doctoral Network on "*Global migrants, global diasporas.*" Firenze, May 26–27.
Tosi, A. (2001). Just looking for a home: Immigrant women in Italy. In E. Bill & J. Doherty (Eds.), *Women and homelessness in Europe* (pp. 163–173). Bristol: The Policy Press.
Villa, P. (2004). La diffusione del modello di famiglia a doppia partecipazione nei paesi europei e in Italia. *Inchiesta, 24,* 146, 6–20.
Zajczyk, F. (2005). Emergenze, povertà e marginalità a Milano e in Lombardia. In F. Bimbi (Ed.), *Madri sole: Sfide politiche e genitorialità alla prova* (pp. 45–83). Roma: Edizioni Lavoro.

# 8

# FEMINIZATION OF POVERTY IN JAPAN: A SPECIAL CASE?

*Kimiko Kimoto and Kumiko Hagiwara*

## Introduction

In 1990, economist June Axinn concluded that the feminization of poverty had not occurred in Japan in the same way as in the United States. The situation of Japan was grasped as a special case. Marriages were stable, and there was intergenerational family unity. Many Japanese women were potentially poor, but few opted for independence because it risked their economic stability as dependents in their households. Women's prospects in the labor market were dim, and social policy did little to offset their disadvantages (Axinn, 1990).

The 1996 Japanese White Paper on the National Lifestyle, under the heading, "U.S. Feminization of Poverty Not Seen in Japan," equated the problem with the number of households "headed by women" who received public assistance:

> Nearly 60 percent of [U.S.] households in poverty are now headed by women. In Japan, there was a slight increase in the rate of female household heads that were granted public assistance between the late 1970s and the early 1980s. This figure, however, has since decreased, and men still account for 70 percent of household heads that were granted public assistance (Economic Planning Agency of Japan, 1996, pp. 74–75).

This confused perception on the part of the government—feminization of poverty is confined to the relatively small number of households on public assistance that are "headed by women"—is one of the reasons why the nature of women's poverty has been minimized and overlooked in Japanese society. Nonetheless, since the late 1990s, it has become unrealistic to categorize the poverty of women as a marginal issue in Japan.

Since the collapse of the bubble economy in 1993, Japan has been undergoing drastic economic and social changes. After the collapse of the bubble, neo-liberal, structural reforms were put forth, especially by Prime Minister Junichiro Koizumi whose 5-year administration began in 2001. With this period of reform over, Japan has now entered a new phase in the rediscovery of poverty. This trend was reflected in the Organisation for Economic Co-operation and Development (OECD) report, *Economic Surveys of Japan 2006*, that focused on the rising income inequality and poverty in Japan (OECD, 2006). Domestically, interest in "social disparities" has risen since the late 1990s. There are discussions of whether poverty is increasing and what causes such social and economic disparities (Hashimoto, 2003, 2006; Shirahase, 2005; Tachibanaki, 1998). More attention has also been given to the so-called working poor. Such arguments have been triggered by the increase in nonregular work and lack of employment opportunities for young people due to the prolonged economic recession. It is no longer possible to ignore either the unstable employment and poverty among youth or the poverty among single mothers and lone elderly women that has until now been latent.

This chapter will explore how and why the poverty of women has become apparent as an issue in contemporary Japan. In this chapter, we argue that the mechanisms that force women into poverty were already functioning in Japanese society, even at the time of the economic boom of the late 1980s. It is likely that these mechanisms were simply rendered invisible due to a number of factors. It is also conceivable that this phenomenon was already deeply rooted in the relationships among families, women, and the company society system that was built by large corporations after World War II.

The first part of this chapter will analyze the characteristics of the social welfare system during the establishment and consolidation of the company society system in order to consider how these are connected to current poverty among women. The second part will focus on single mothers and elderly women presenting a number of indicators of their poverty. Although Japan is not a member of the Luxembourg Income Study (LIS), the data we cite are based on less than 50% of median income, the principal LIS standard used in this book, and are thus comparable to the LIS data for the other seven countries presented in Chapter 10.

## The Company Society System, the Japanese-style Welfare State, and Women

The company society that began to be formed by large corporations after World War II was based on a system that incorporated both seniority-based wages for male breadwinners and dependency allowances for their full-time housewives and children. In addition to these direct wages, larger companies were able to institute more generous welfare systems than were required legally, including such voluntary benefits as company housing, dining services, dormitories, medical care, and discount sales of daily commodities. This, in turn, created a strong work incentive for the male breadwinners. Over time, this system developed into comprehensive coverage that was designed to meet all the various needs and demands at different stages of the employees' lives, such as financing for the purchase of their family homes, ensuring their children's high educational achievement, and providing for their retirement. At the same time, this system also resulted in a growing number of full-time housewives during the high economic growth period in the 1960s, and it contributed to shaping the Japanese family structure with a strict sexual division of labor. The housewife role became the norm for Japanese women, including working class women. This led to the so-called birth of housewives on a mass level in the working class as well as the middle class.

During the same period, the Japanese welfare state began to emerge with the introduction by the government of the National Medical Insurance System and the National Pension System. The company society system, however, created conditions for the government to maintain a low-level of expenditures in social welfare and to build the social welfare system primarily on the assumption that the insurees have stable employment status and a certain number of years of employment. Thus, the predominance of men in the labor market was built into the social welfare system. Various forms of preferential treatment were given to male employees with dependent, full-time housewives, and these were reinforced by the tax system and social security reforms. In the 1980s, the government established a series of measures favoring men with dependent housewives. Preferential treatment for housewives of employed husbands, introduced in the pension system in 1985 and discussed later in this chapter, was in accordance with this trend.

As advanced welfare states in the West faced financial difficulties during the oil shock years of the beginning of 1970s, the Japanese government reviewed its welfare policies and announced the "Proposal for a Japanese-Style Welfare Society" (1978). "Welfare Society" means that the intention is to limit public social security to a minimal level with the expectation of "innovation" and "initiative" in company welfare systems and the requirement of extra "self-help efforts" from each family unit (Harada, 1992; Jinno, 1992). The "Japanese-Style Welfare Society" views the family as the welfare service provider, and it assumes and expects that women will care for the aged parents and young children in their families (Nomura & Kimoto, 2002). During the oil shock crisis, companies firmly protected their existing staff and refused to dismiss employees. Companies coped with the crisis by reducing the recruitment of new staff and by reshuffling, transferring, and relocating their existing male employees. Individual companies managed to enhance their own company welfare systems as a reward to their employees for coping with these drastic changes. As a result of this process, male, regular employees increased their loyalty toward their companies, and Japan was able to reconstruct the foundation of its internationally recognized, Japanese-style management system in the 1980s (Kimoto, 2004a).

## Transformations in the 1990s: *Employment*

**Recession and the company response.** The 1990s ushered in a major period of transition that jolted the company society system. The response of the companies to economic globalization and recession following the collapse of the bubble economy was quite different from the way they acted during the oil shock years. This time, the crisis resulted in the personnel reduction of companies, numerous business failures, and bankruptcies among regional banks and securities companies, and widespread endorsement of a radical review of the seniority-based personnel system that had become characteristic of Japanese management practices. "Ruthless" layoffs of regular male employees by large corporations and a spate of bankruptcies of banks and securities companies flooded headlines, creating a social climate that began to reject the seniority-based system and instead began to emphasize individual responsibility.

**Effect on women's employment.** This climate also brought changes to the female labor market. Under the company society system, married women were seen primarily as housewives, and women were expected to resign from their jobs when they married. From the mid-1970s, there was a significant rise in the number of middle-aged and older married women engaged in part-time work, meaning that women worked outside of a system of long-term employment designed primarily for men. The majority of women who continued to work found that they were held back by low wages and poor working conditions.

Today, working women in Japan are still profoundly affected by this historical background and remain much lower in status than men. There is an exceedingly large gender disparity in wages, with full-time rank-and-file female workers earning 64% of what their male counterparts earn. Women are infrequently in management positions, accounting for only 10.8% of section heads, 5.8% of division heads, and 3.7% of department heads (Equal Employment, Children & Families Bureau of Ministry of Health, Labor and Welfare [MHLW], 2006). In comparison with other advanced industrial countries, Japan is far behind and ranks last with respect to the condition of women in the labor force (Kimoto, 2004b).

Until the 1980s, as long as the company society blocked women's paths to economic independence, it seemed necessary for the majority of women to be housewives in order to have economic security. For example, as discussed below, they were—and are—entitled to social security as dependent housewives.

Nevertheless, the number of working women continued to increase, and their years of continuous employment also rose as more women chose to marry later or remain single. There was also a strong trend for middle-aged and older married women to work, and in 1989, for the first time, among married women whose husbands were regular employees, the number of working wives exceeded the number of full-time housewives.

Along with those changes, however, the government implemented the deregulation of labor laws, with the result that the number of nonregular workers increased, particularly in the late 1990s. In taking this action, the government acceded to requests from employers' associations to make employment more flexible as a means of coping with the prolonged economic recession and globalization. The main types of these nonregular workers are part-time workers and *Haken,* that is, temporary workers dispatched to the companies from staffing agencies and contract workers with limited earnings and lower pay. Youth and women predominate in nonregular work. According to the Special Survey on Employment Trends, the proportion of women in nonregular work was already high in 1985 (32.1%) compared to men (7.4%). In the 1990s, nonregular work became increasingly common in the Japanese economy, and, by 2006, the rates reached 52.8% for women and 17.9% for men. Both male and female nonregular workers increased sharply, and more than half of female workers are now working as nonregular workers. The total number of female employees has increased every year (from 14.6 million in 1985 to 21.9 million in 2006). The increase in employed, married women in the 1990s was, in fact, concurrent with this increase in nonregular employment and the deeper feminization of low-paid, unstable, nonregular work.

## Transformations in the 1990s: *The Family*

Amid the changes in the labor market itself, transformation of the family structure has also become apparent. A prime example is the increase in young people's delaying or avoiding marriage due to the unstable employment conditions since the late 1990s. The rate of unmarried men between the ages of 30 and 34 increased from about one-third (32.6%) in 1990 to over two-fifths (42.9%) in 2000. The rate of unmarried women in that age group almost doubled, from 13.9% to 26.6% in the same period. This was caused not only by the unstable employment conditions but also by the change of sexual and marriage norms. These changes, in turn, created several phenomena other than the younger generation's unwillingness to marry. One is *dekichatta-kon,* a word newly coined to refer to a marriage resulting from pregnancy. Pregnancy before marriage was never common in Japan, but there has been a particularly rapid increase in *dekichatta-kon* among young couples in their late teens and early twenties, which potentially leads to divorce and single motherhood. Another change is the increase in divorces. In the 1990s, the relatively low divorce rate began to rise and continued to rise sharply until it reached its peak in 2002. In 2003, the divorce rate was 2.25 (per thousand of population) and was edging up to rates in other developed countries (e.g., Sweden: 2.4 [2001], United Kingdom: 2.6 [2000]) (Inoue & Ehara, 2005, p. 15). In light of these statistics, Japan can no longer be classified as a country with a low divorce rate.

These major changes in the family, in conjunction with deterioration in labor market conditions, have made poverty visible. In other words, the combination of the company society system and the "Japanese-Style Welfare Society" was somehow able to conceal the poverty of individuals by absorbing it into the family unit in the 1980s, but that system has reached its limits as more people either avoid forming families or are unable to do so.

The increased numbers of young people employed in nonregular work during the recession have difficulties finding opportunities to break away from this type of work. Increasing numbers of the young people who face unfavorable employment conditions are living with their parents, even after the latter become eligible for pension benefits, but because they live with their parents, the poverty of these young workers is not immediately apparent. The low wages of the large number of Japanese women who are nonregular workers make it very difficult for them to move out of the family home and to be economically independent. For married women employed as nonregular workers, their potential poverty as individuals is not considered an issue as long as there is a core income earner within the household. However, their individual poverty becomes visible in the event of a divorce or if their husbands are unemployed or become nonregular workers.

In the framework of the Japanese-Style Welfare Society, three-generation families were assumed and expected to be "welfare service providers" to their elders. However, there has been a dramatic decline in the proportion of three-generation families from over half (54.4%) of all family households in 1975 to just over one-fifth (21.3%) in 2005. Concurrently, elderly, single-person households increased rapidly, from 8.6% to 22.0%, as did couple-only elderly households (from 13.1% to 29.2%) (MHLW, 2005). As the latter became single-person households after the death of a spouse, the number of households consisting of a single, elderly person also increased.

Japanese society has now clearly entered an era in which poverty is being exposed. Formerly concealed by the company society system, the "Japanese-Style Welfare Society," and the adaptive behavior of families, poverty is now becoming visible.

## Single Mothers

**Poverty and employment status**. Single mothers in Japan have high employment rates but low income levels. Kilkey's cross-national study (2000) classified welfare regimes by employment status and poverty rates of single mothers. Japanese single mothers were in the group with relatively high poverty risk despite a high employment rate. Among this group of countries, Japanese single mothers have the highest employment rate (87%).

The high poverty rate of single-mother households, even at the height of the Japanese economic boom in the late 1980s, had already been pointed out by Japanese researchers. Masami Iwata analyzed this issue based upon the National Survey of Family Income and Expenditure that used approximately the same poverty standard as the OECD and found that the poverty rate for couples with children was 13.6%, compared to double (27.2%) that for employed single parents and almost triple for unemployed single parents (36.9%) in 1988 (Iwata, 1998). A subsequent analysis of a Household Economics Panel Survey from 1994 to 2002 by The Research Institute, called *Kakei Keizai Kenkyusho*, found that being a single mother, along with limited education and temporary employment, puts women at high risk of poverty (Iwata & Hamamoto, 2004). The poverty line for this panel study was 1.2 times the eligibility level for public assistance (roughly 2 million yen annually for a three-person household)[1] which was approximately equal to 60% of average expenditures. What they found was that 53.9% of single-mother households were continually under this poverty line during the period covered by the panel survey, and the rate came to 92.4% when those temporarily under the poverty line were included. The rate was extremely high compared to the average of 35% for all households, and most of these were temporarily under the poverty line (Iwata & Hamamoto, 2004).

The annual income of single-mother households was extremely low compared to other households (Table 8.1), and they have high rates of poverty (Table 8.2, p. 210). In fact, single mothers had the highest poverty rate and highest poverty gap ratio of any household type (Table 8.2, p. 210). In Japan, employed single mothers typify the working poor.

Even though many single mothers do not earn enough to escape poverty, the proportion of social income transfers in the household budgets of Japanese employed single mothers is only 6.7%, while that of nonemployed single parents is 74.7% (Murozumi, 2006). Estimates using the data in 1994 have shown that a single mother working as a part-time worker would need to work 59–68 hours a week to earn an income as much as public assistance provided to single-mother households (consisting of a mother and two children), and even a single mother working on a full-time basis would need to work 42 hours (Ogawa, 2000).

Even if public assistance and various allowances are kept at low levels, it seems that their very low wage rates, especially that of part-time employee, would give single mothers a strong incentive to rely on welfare rather than

TABLE 8.1 Income Distribution of Single-Mother Households,[a] Couple Households,[b] and All Households, 2004

| Annual Income (Millions of Yen) | Single-Mother Households, % | Couple Households, % | All Households, % |
|---|---|---|---|
| < 0.5 | 5.6 | 0.7 | 1.9 |
| 0.5 <1 | 15.7 | 1.3 | 4.7 |
| 1 < 1.5 | 13.5 | 1.9 | 6.0 |
| 1.5 < 2 | 15.7 | 2.2 | 6.0 |
| 2 < 2.5 | 19.1 | 3.7 | 6.1 |
| 2.5 < 3 | 10.1 | 3.2 | 5.8 |
| 3 < 3.5 | 7.9 | 4.9 | 6.7 |
| 3.5 < 4 | 1.1 | 4.1 | 5.6 |
| 4 < 4.5 | 1.1 | 5.3 | 5.5 |
| 4.5 < 5 | 1.1 | 7.3 | 5.5 |
| 5 < 6 | 1.1 | 10.1 | 8.0 |
| 6 < 7 | 2.2 | 9.6 | 6.7 |
| 7 and more | 5.6 | 45.7 | 31.6 |
| Average annual income | 2.33 million yen | 7.19 million yen | 5.80 million yen |
| Average annual income per capita | 0.83 million yen | 1.61 million yen | 2.03 million yen |
| Median income | 1.98 million yen | 6.45 million yen | 4.62 million yen |

[a]Single mothers only with children under age 20.
[b]Couples only with children under age 18.

*Source*: MHLW, 2005.

employment. Despite this, the employment rates for single mothers have remained steady at approximately 85% since the end of the World War II (Table 8.3). Since 1988, the proportion of these employed single mothers who work part time has almost tripled (2.75 times), and between 1998 and 2003, alone, has increased 40%.

According to the National Survey of Single-Mother Households, Equal Employment, Children and Families Bureau of MHLW, 2005, almost 60% of single mothers had an income less than 2 million yen, and a large proportion of those households are probably eligible for public assistance benefits. Yet, the proportion of single-mother households receiving public assistance benefits in the same year was 1 in 10 at most. How can we explain why these single mothers choose "independence," even though it means low-wage employment, poor working conditions, and a high poverty risk?

## History of Policies toward Single-Mother Families

Expressed numerically, despite the rise of divorce and single motherhood in recent years, Japan still has a relatively low rate of single motherhood.

TABLE 8.2 Poverty Rates[a] and Poverty Gap Ratios[b] of Households, 1995 and 2001

| | Number | | Poverty Rate | | Poverty Gap Ratio | |
|---|---|---|---|---|---|---|
| | 1995 | 2001 | 1995 | 2001 | 1995 | 2001 |
| All households | 8132 | 7621 | 15.2 | 17.0 | 5.3 | 5.9 |
| Couple households, with 3 or more children[c] | 412 | 303 | 12.9 | 8.9 | 2.9 | 2.7 |
| Couple households with 2 children[c] | 1453 | 1042 | 6.7 | 7.3 | 2.0 | 2.0 |
| Couple households with 1 child[c] | 1256 | 1124 | 10.4 | 8.5 | 3.0 | 2.8 |
| Couple households with no children | 1019 | 1012 | 10.0 | 10.3 | 3.3 | 3.8 |
| Single households under 65 | 765 | 971 | 20.0 | 26.9 | 6.4 | 9.6 |
| Elderly households[d] | 720 | 732 | 21.7 | 20.5 | 7.6 | 7.1 |
| Single households over 65 | 547 | 628 | 47.9 | 43.0 | 20.2 | 16.0 |
| Single-mother households[e] | 103 | 115 | 55.3 | 53.0 | 18.7 | 18.3 |
| Three generation households | 1063 | 860 | 8.5 | 8.4 | 2.9 | 2.7 |
| Other | 794 | 834 | 16.9 | 20.1 | 6.6 | 7.3 |

[a] Poverty line is set at 50% of median equivalent disposable income. In 1995, this was 1.42 million yen; in 2001, 1.31 million yen.

[b] The average difference between household income and the poverty threshold / the poverty threshold.

[c] Couples and their unmarried children only.

[d] Men over 65 and women over 60 with or without children under 18.

[e] Single mothers and children under 20, only.

*Source*: Tachibanaki and Urakawa (2006, p. 81). Analysis is based on data of the Income Distribution Survey (MHLW, 1996, 2001).

According to the Comprehensive Survey of the Living Conditions, Health and Welfare of the People (MHLW, 2007), single-parent households were only 1.7% of a total of 47.5 million households and a minority, 6.3% of 12.9 million households with children (unmarried under 18) (2006). These very small percentages are partly due to the statistical classification of households that excludes single parents living with their parents or relatives, and it is one of the reasons that single mothers have been viewed as a minor issue. This classification of "single-parent households" in the government statistics is often criticized by researchers for not reflecting the actual numbers of single-mother families, and also there is a big difference in numbers compared to another government source, the National Survey of Single Mother Households that has been conducted every 5 years by the MHLW[2] since 1952. According to this survey that includes

TABLE 8.3 Employment Rates of Single Mothers, Selected Years, 1952–2003

| | Total | Self-Employed | Full-Time | Part-Time and Other Temp. Employment | Others |
|---|---|---|---|---|---|
| 1952 | 89.8 | 44.5 | 23.4 | 31.2 (day worker, 19.4; home worker, 11.8) | 0.9 |
| 1956 | 91.9 | 36.5 (farming 23.9) | 28.1 | 22.2 (day worker, 14.6; home worker, 7.6) | 13.2 |
| 1961[a] | 85.6 | — | — | — | — |
| 1973 | 83.9 | 28.1 | 52.3 | 9.4 (day worker, 6.45; part-time, 2.95) | 10.6 |
| 1978 | 85.2 | 15.2 | 60.6 | 8.5 (day worker, 3.4; part-time, 5.1) | 15.7 |
| 1983 | 84.2 | 16.9 (farming 4.3) | 65.4 | 9.0 | 8.8 |
| 1988 | 86.8 | 12.2 | 55.5 | 19.4 | 12.9 |
| 1993 | 87.0 | 7.8 | 53.2 | 31.3 | 7.7 |
| 1998 | 84.9 | 5.7 | 50.7 | 38.3 | 5.3 |
| 2003 | 83.0 | 4.2 | 39.2 | 53.4 (*haken* or temporary workers, 4.4) | 3.2 |

[a] Only total employment rate available.

*Source*: Data for 1952–1998, Children and Families Bureau of MHW; for 2003, Equal Employment, Children and Families Bureau of MHLW, 2005.

single mothers living on their own as well as with parents or relatives, the estimated number of single-mother households is 1,225,400 in 2003 (Equal Employment, Children and Families Bureau of MHLW, 2005), and the increase since 1983 was 507,300. By contrast, the Comprehensive Survey of the Living Conditions, Health and Welfare of the People that counts only those single parents living on their own estimated the number of single-parent households at 788,000 in 2006, with an increase of just 188,000 in the 20 years since 1986 (MHLW, 2007). According to the survey that includes both those living with relatives and those living on their own, single-mother households are nearly 3% of total households and just under 10% of all families with children (based on the population shown in the Comprehensive Survey of the Living Conditions, Health and Welfare of the People in 2003). Therefore, to see the changes in single-mother families and the structural poverty abetted by government policy toward them, we use the data from the National Survey of Single Mother Households that also identifies both the marital statuses and employment statuses of the single mothers.

According to the first survey in 1952, 7 years after World War II, 85% of single-mother households had resulted from their husbands' deaths, and only 8% from divorce. Beginning in the 1970s, there was an increase in the number of single mothers who were unmarried, divorced, or separated from their husbands (Table 8.4). By 1978, these exceeded the number of widowed single mothers. Since 1983, divorced women have been

TABLE 8.4 Marital Status of Single Mothers,[a] Selected years, 1952–2006, Percentages.

| | Widowed | Divorced | Never Married | Other | Total Number |
|---|---|---|---|---|---|
| 1952 | 85.1 | 7.5 | 1.6 | 5.8 | 694,700 |
| 1956 | 77.9 | 14.5 | 1.9 | 5.6 | 115,000 |
| 1961 | 77.1 | 16.8 | 1.9 | 4.2 | 102,900 |
| 1967 | 68.1 | 23.7 | 1.8 | 6.4 | 515,300 |
| 1973 | 61.9 | 26.4 | 2.4 | 9.4 | 626,200 |
| 1978 | 49.9 | 37.9 | 4.8 | 7.4 | 633,700 |
| 1983 | 36.1 | 49.1 | 5.3 | 9.5 | 718,100 |
| 1988 | 29.7 | 62.3 | 3.6 | 4.4 | 849,200 |
| 1993 | 24.6 | 64.3 | 4.7 | 4.2 | 789,900 |
| 1998 | 18.7 | 68.4 | 7.3 | 4.2 | 954,900 |
| 2003 | 12.0 | 79.9 | 5.8 | 2.2 | 1,225,400 |

[a] Single mothers refer to all households with a single mother and unmarried children under 20. It includes other persons and is not confined to those with only a single mother and her children.

*Source*: Data for 1952–1998, Children and Families Bureau of MHW; for 2003 Equal Employment, Children and Families Bureau of MHLW, 2005.

the great majority of single mothers. In 2003, the proportion of divorced single-mother households reached 80% of the total, and the total number of single-mother households had increased 28% or hit the highest number recorded (1,225,400) since the survey begun. According to Kambara, an estimated 2.2 million children lived in single-parent households (Kambara, 2007).

It is interesting to note that, despite the increase and the changes in sources of single parenthood, employment rates for single mothers, including the self-employed, are consistently high and unaffected by fluctuations in employment rates for women in general (Fujiwara, 2005b). This raises the question of how the government policies affect the employment behavior of single mothers. In the immediate postwar period, the Japanese government commenced income support for war widows, beginning with public assistance for single-mother households. In 1946, single-mother households were included in the general provisions for the poor in the Public Assistance Law. Social allowances, such as the Child Rearing Allowance, were also enacted for single-mother households in 1961 and fully funded by the national treasury. Since then, the Child Rearing Allowance has been provided to all unmarried and divorced single-mother households with children under the age of 18, but later a means test and a strict income scale were introduced (see below).

Around the same period, soon after the end of World War II, the government also introduced extensive employment support programs for single mothers, including training and education and loans for launching small businesses. This was significantly earlier than in other developed countries. This has been identified as one of the reasons for the continuously high employment rate for single mothers. It was the war-widowed single mothers who played the central role in demanding these employment support policies. They saw the public assistance offered by the government as "humiliating" and preferred to support themselves with regular jobs without relying on government for their livelihoods. Thanks to their efforts, the Loans for Single-Mother Families Program was established in 1952, and the loans were granted to create self-reliant and independent small businesses, provide work skills training and assist with their children's schooling. This program was a clear reflection of war-widows' sense of "independence" (Fujiwara, 2005b). The government focused on creating employment opportunities for war widows for a different reason: given the financial constraints in the immediate post-war years, it was difficult to provide a level of public income security that would enable them to be full-time mothers.

There is another important element in addition to this historical background: that is, the obvious shift since the late 1970s to policies that put more emphasis on employment support than on income transfers. At that time, changes in the marital status of single mothers were occurring: that is, the numbers of divorced single mothers were exceeding widowed single mothers. It was also the time when the "Japanese-style Welfare Society" policy was established. In keeping with this trend, the government, at the beginning of the 1980s, launched a fiscal austerity program, the Ad Hoc Committee on Administrative Reform.

During the late 1970s and early 1980s, a new category called "parted single-mother households" appeared in the supervisory guidelines for households receiving public assistance. The MHW instructed its welfare officers to ask mothers in the category of "parted single-mother households" to confirm any arrangements made with former husbands regarding child-rearing expenses and to provide details of any other payments made to their families. Mothers in these families were subjected to psychological stress as a result of being required to contact their former husbands when applying for benefits. This discouraged single mothers from applying for public assistance. In 1981, the government also reinforced measures to prevent fraudulent receipt of benefits and strengthened its supervisory capacity with its third revision of the eligibility standards for public assistance. Subsequently, in 1982, single-mother households were classified as families "including persons of working age," and this resulted in stricter employment requirements for single mothers (Yuzawa, 2005).

The definition of households with "persons of working age" also posed another dilemma for single mothers because children are counted as persons of working age once they complete their compulsory education at the age of 15 and are expected to work. Thus, at the same time that high school enrollment rates rose sharply—from approximately 60% in 1960 to over 90% in 1975, single-mother households were forced to choose between educating their children and receiving public assistance (Fujiwara, 2003).

As to the Child Rearing Allowance, it has been means-tested since 1985, and the sliding scale became stricter in 2002. As a result of reforms, full benefits (42,000 yen monthly) are provided to single mothers with one child and with an annual income under 1.3 million yen instead of the former, higher income eligibility of 2 million yen. Partial benefits are provided to those with annual incomes between 1.3 million and 3.6 million yen. Interestingly, during the 1970s and 1980s, when these restrictions were being imposed on single-mother households, the budget for the loans program, established in 1953, had expanded approximately five-fold by 1978, and the budget relied greatly on redemption money or repayment of loans by single mothers (Tarukawa, 1982). Instead of ensuring a minimum standard of living through public assistance or the Child Rearing Allowance for single mothers, the government chose to go ahead with the loans program and have single mothers work to make repayments.

The policy toward single mothers focused on the maintenance and expansion of employment support. The goal was to limit the burden on public finances, rather than to support the caregiving role of mothers through income support, even though the expectation for married mothers was that reproductive work was primary. Before other developed countries made the transition from welfare to workfare in the 1990s, Japan had steadily established a "workfare system" (Uzuhashi, 1997). The poverty of single-mother households was considered the result of their deviation from the "normal" family model that had prevailed since the 1960s under the company society system. This led to the persisting failure to link single-mother poverty to women's labor market disadvantages. Similarly ignored was the fact that the poverty of married women was hidden within the household. Furthermore, still lacking understanding of the true roots of the problem, the government, in 2002, imposed a stricter "work only" system (Fukawa, 2004) to "promote" the independence of single mothers.

**Workfare policy and the 2002 reform.** In 2002, the MHLW presented its "Outline of the Policy of Self-reliance and Economic Independence Support Program for Single Mother Families" and revised the Child-Rearing Allowance Law. Despite the fact that the income threshold for child-rearing allowances had been lowered on two occasions, in 1985 and 1998, decreasing the income threshold of the child-rearing allowance was again made the vehicle for "encourag[ing] single mothers to work." The 2002 revision construed the child-rearing allowance as "intensive support during the period of upheaval after a divorce" but with gradual reduction of benefits or suspension of them after 5 years of benefit receipt.[3] This meant "excessive self-help requirements" and "punitive measures" for single mothers (Yuzawa, 2005). In fact, the MHLW estimated that 330,000 recipients, approximately half, would have their allowances reduced as a result of this revision (National Diet of Japan, 2002).

The Law on Special Employment Support Measures for Single Mothers was passed in 2003 (temporary legislation until March, 2008). On the basis of this law, MHLW instructed local governments to open "employment and independence support centers" for single mothers to offer free job placement, employment counseling, vocational training, and other services. By the end of February 2005, 80 centers had been established throughout Japan. However, only 7,944 out of 81,553 single mothers who had undergone counseling—less than 10%—got jobs between April 2003 and December 2005. Of these, 56% were part-time, 40% were full-time, and 4% other types of work (MHLW, 2006). Although the MHLW anticipates that the number of those centers will reach 99 by the end of 2008 and that the increase of centers will possibly provide more employment opportunities for single mothers, the outcomes are not sufficient so far to improve the current labor market situation of the many single mothers in temporary employment with limited benefits.

In sum, these reforms were intended to increase the employment and earning power of single mothers. These revisions, along with the increase in the divorce rate and the number of single-mother households, ironically, led to social awareness of unfair labor conditions for the growing numbers of nonregular workers and the social arrangements that were conducive to the high risk of poverty for Japanese women.[4]

## Child Care

Government policy is to "increase" the employment and earning power of single mothers, but has it improved the conditions of single mothers and decreased their poverty? Child care is one place to begin in answering this question.

The declining birthrate became one of the main policy issues in Japan in the 1990s, and the government responded with a series of child-care reforms, including work–family harmonization programs. The Angel Plan (1994), the Second Angel Plan (2000), and the third Angel Plan (2006) are programs to increase child-care centers and offer more flexible services compatible with parents' working hours. It is now estimated that 20%–30% of the population from birth to 2 years and 60%–85% of those from 3 to 5 years are covered by some sort of child-care services.

The centerpiece facilities are the licensed child-care centers (*ninka-hoikusho)* established by the Child Welfare Law (1947). The law established the fundamental child-care system in Japan for children lacking care due to their parents' employment or ill health and with the responsibility of the national and local governments. According to the summary of MHLW (2003–2008), there were 23,000 centers with 2.1 million slots in 2007, 2.0 million children (8 weeks to 5 years) enrolled, accounting for 8% of the population under 1 year of age, 27% of 1- to 2-year-olds, and 40% of 3- to 5-year-olds. These licensed centers are mainly run either by local governments or officially accredited foundations undertaking social welfare activities and must meet certain minimum national government standards.

Unlicensed child-care centers (*muninka-hoikusho*) also play an important role. According to the MHLW, there were 7178 unlicensed child-care centers serving approximately 180,000 children in 2006, but there are some more that are not registered with the local government offices. Generally without public subsidies, these include nonprofit parent groups, companies, and hospitals providing onsite child care for employees; small businesses running so-called baby hotels; and child-care business chains. Since the 1980s, baby hotels and child-care business chains have been growing in number in urban areas and serving children on waiting lists for licensed care centers or whose parents' working hours do not match those of licensed centers. Their quality and cost vary, regardless of the family income.

Kindergartens (*yochien*) have increasingly gained significance in child care since the mid-1990s. In 2007, there were 13,700 kindergartens with 1.7 million children enrolled, accounting for approximately 50% of the population aged 3–5. Administered by the Ministry of Education (MOE), their mission is early childhood education, but in response to the declining birth rate they began, in the early 1990s, to provide longer hours of care, and currently, over half of them provide longer hours of care, in some cases until 5:00–6:00 PM.

Lastly, new, licensed facilities for children called *Nintei-Kodomo-en* were set up in 2006 under coadministration of MOE and MHLW, with the aim of combining the systems of licensed child-care centers and kindergartens. In 2007, there were approximately 100 of these, and they were on the rise. Although licensed child-care centers basically accept the children of employed parents, these facilities accept all children.

Licensed child-care centers have a sliding scale. They also give priority to single parents and have a special scale for single mothers ranging from no charge for those with annual incomes less than 2 million yen to 15,500 yen per month for incomes between 2 and 3 million yen. These measures make child care affordable for most single parents.

As to the hours of service provided by licensed child-care centers, prefectural and local governments have, since the 1960s, been adding extra subsidies to open centers for longer hours, and the national government has done the same since the mid-1990s. In 2006, 87% of licensed child-care centers were open more than 10.5 hours, and nearly half of these, for more than 12 hours.

In sum, recent reforms extended the hours of licensed child-care centers and expanded services for children of the families who are not eligible to be enrolled under the current, licensed child-care system. The current child-care policy in general is not against or opposed to mothers' employment, especially that of single parents. However, there is also anxiety over the future of the licensed child-care centers. Governments at all levels are strongly committed to child care but are inclined to the idea that the child-care services are to be purchased privately on the market, and they began to retreat from the earlier policy that child-care services are a public responsibility. Thus, even with the expansionary reforms, the number of publicly funded licensed child-care centers has not increased dramatically since 1985. Consistent with the neo-liberal trend toward deregulation, the standards have been loosened. While the number of children on the waiting list for licensed care dropped from over 40,000 to 17,000 in the 10-year span from April 1997 to April 2007, this dramatic decline has been achieved partly by lowering standards in practice and ceasing to include children in unlicensed care on the waiting lists. The capacity is and will be the critical issue.

## Equal Opportunity Policies

In addition to child and elder care (the latter, see below) policies that promote gender equality have also been developed by the Government: the Law for Child Care Leave (1991, in effect in 1992); the revision of the Equal Employment Opportunity Law (1997); and the Basic Law for a Gender-Equal Society (1999). These legal measures are intended to achieve gender equality, especially in the field of employment. However, these policies have a limited effect because they have been undermined by the deregulatory labor market measures introduced during the prolonged economic downturn.

The revision of the Labor Standards Law abolished the regulation of overtime and late-night work of women in 1997. In 1999, the Law for Temporary Workers (*Haken*) permitted some formerly banned types of work, leaving temporary workers without adequate protective measures, and political measures to improve the disparities between regular full-time workers and nonregular part-time workers are still limited. In May, 2007, the Part-Time Worker Law was revised, banning discriminatory treatment in wage and other labor conditions but with narrow and limited application. Only an estimated 4%–5% of all part-time workers benefit from this law.

The Law for Child Care leave provides a year of job-protected leave, and Employment Insurance covers the payment of social insurance premiums and provides up to 50% income replacement (up from 40% in 2007) for parents taking care of infants. Although this was a progressive measure, it excluded nonregular workers until 2006. After the revision in 2006, employers often excluded them in practice from the compulsory programs established by law and also from voluntary workplace programs as well.

Considering the two trends—of nonregulatory and equal opportunity policies—there are some favorable effects for regular, full-time female workers; but not for the single mothers who work mainly as low-wage, part-timers; nor for the mothers who have limited reemployment opportunities for regular, full-time jobs. It is reasonable to say that deregulatory employment measures pushed forward by business are limiting the effect of gender equality policies in Japan.

## Elderly Women

The issue of poverty among lone, elderly women in Japan emerged as a result of both the rapid aging of the population (at a rate rarely seen in other countries) and the transformation of the family structure. The public pension that reflects the sexual disparities in the labor market, including both wages and years of employment, in itself creates a risk of poverty for women later in life. The poverty risk for older women remained hidden as long as women had male breadwinners to depend on.

Even in the postwar period, this issue did not receive much attention because a large proportion of elderly people in Japan lived with their children. Thus, the Japanese family functioned as a "hidden welfare asset" (Harada, 1992). When newspapers reported the solitary deaths of lone and elderly people, particularly those who had died alone in rented apartments, these cases were often treated as rare exceptions. However, as mentioned before, the number of three-generation family units has dropped significantly in recent years. In 2005, the most common households with elderly members over 65 were the elder, couple-only households (29.2%), followed by the single-person elderly households (22.0%). The number of three-generation households declined rapidly but ranked a close third (21.3%). The remainder of households consisted of elderly parents and unmarried children (16.2%) and other types of households (11.3%). Women already account for over three-fifths (63.2%) of the population over age 75 because the average life expectancy of women has been consistently longer than men (85.5 years, compared to 78.5 in 2005). Considering the difference in average life expectancies for men and women and the rapid increase of the elderly population with the changes in family structure, it is not surprising that three-fourths (75.2%) of elderly persons who live alone are women and the number of households consisting of a single, elderly woman is predicted to increase (Equal Employment, Children and Families Bureau of MHLW, 2005).

**Elder care policy.** With the rapid increase of the elderly population accompanied by the changes in family structure, discussion of reform of elder care began in the 1980s. Following the Policy Outline for the Longevity Society in 1986, a 10-year emergency plan for elder care or "Gold Plan" was introduced in 1989. It aimed to increase home care workers, day care service centers, and short- and long-term care institutions. However expansionary the reform was, the number of the elderly in need of care was estimated at 2.8 million, and it was clear that the plan would not catch up with the demand. As a result of the simmering debate over elder care in the 1990s, the national government decided to establish Long-Term Care Insurance (LTCI) modeled on the German Care Insurance scheme.

Under the LTCI system (in operation since 2000), insurance contributions are compulsory for people over age 40. Unlike the German Care

Insurance scheme, which is funded solely by insurance revenue, LTCI is funded half by general taxation and half by insurance revenue. The insurance covers care and support services for people over 65, and they receive benefits in-kind such as in-home care services and institutional care services, according to the level of the need for care. The level is judged basically without regard to whether their families can care for them, but based on what care would facilitate their independence. For this reason, LTCI has the potential to socialize or de-familialize care.

Although the LTCI is designed to socialize care, the families are still burdened in practice. One reason is that the elderly often lack adequate information and knowledge to determine the services that they need. Further, since local governments administer the LTCI, there are regional disparities depending on their budgets and the size of their elderly population. In addition, there is already a move to contain the cost of care. The number of individuals covered by the LTCI increased by 1.7 times, and the total amount of the benefit paid from the LTCI fund increased by 1.6 times from 2000 to 2005. Anxiety over the financial deterioration of the fund led the MHLW to require elderly people to bear part of the cost of their care. Especially for those in institutions, full payment for food and accommodation is required. According to the National Federation of Insurance Association (Zenkoku hoken dantai rengoukai), which surveyed 2,194 institutions in 19 prefectures, 3,200 older people left institutional care after payment was required. Those who left are to rely on the care by their families.

In 2006, further cost containment measures were taken: lowering the total amount of care services one can receive and omitting housekeeping assistance from the LTCI coverage. Partial payment and restriction of services make it harder for less well-off elderly people to receive sufficient care services, and thus their families, if themselves in straitened circumstances, have no choice other than taking care of their elderly relatives themselves. Nonetheless, as we mentioned above, the Japanese family as a "hidden welfare asset" is faltering.

**Low income and lone, elderly women.** A comparative study of low income elderly women living alone in Japan, the United States, the United Kingdom, Italy, Germany, Sweden, and Taiwan found that among these seven countries Taiwan had the highest proportion of low income, lone elderly women (62.6%), followed by the United States (45.5%) and Japan (43.7%) (Shirahase, 2006).[5] In the Shirahase study, the low income rate of single, elderly women (43.7%) was much higher than that of their male counterparts (24.7%) and a much larger disparity than the U.S. figures of 45.5% for women and 35.0% for men. Moreover, there is a much larger difference between woman-only and couple-only elderly households than between male and female single households. The ratio of the incomes of single, elderly women to that of elderly couples was lowest in Japan (58.2%), and the U.S. ratio was only slightly higher (59.5%). The low income rate of single, elderly Japanese women is somewhat lower than in the United States, but the differences between the single men and women and between single women and couples in Japan are more striking than in the United States. Overall, it is clear that Japan is in a similar position to the United States in regard to the poor economic conditions of lone elderly women.

Another nine-country comparative study (Canada, Finland, Germany, Italy, Japan, the Netherlands, Sweden, the United Kingdom, and the United States) has also been carried out based on LIS data. The method for calculating the Japanese data is similar to that used by LIS. The study found that the proportion of Japanese households consisting of single elderly women (over 75 years old) in the lowest income quintile was highest among those countries, for example, 79% for Japan, 56% for United States, and 38% for Sweden (Yamada & Casey, 2002).

These studies suggest a relation between low income among lone, elderly women and the Japanese public pension system. According to estimates of the National Survey of Family Income and Expenditure (1984–1999), single-person elderly households continue to have a high risk of low income. This is the case, even though improvement in the pension system decreased the risk of low income generally among elderly households (Komamura, 2003). Another study on income gaps in relation to earned income and household composition of the elderly found that (1) unemployed, elderly women who live alone have the highest rates of poverty among the elderly; (2) basic living expenses for such necessities as housing, utilities, and food take up a large part of the household budgets of lone elderly women, making it difficult for them to afford anything beyond these essentials if their only source of income is a public pension (Iwata, 1996).

The Tokyo Metropolitan Institute of Gerontology and the University of Michigan have jointly conducted a number of longitudinal surveys of elderly people, both men and women. Their initial survey (1987) revealed that over 30% of those surveyed had incomes below the poverty line or the public assistance threshold (an annual income of 1.2 million yen). The follow-up investigation (1990) found persisting poverty among elderly women and indicated a clear feminization of older poverty. In the period between the initial follow-up surveys, over one-fifth of those below the poverty line or the public assistance threshold in the initial survey had not been able to increase their annual incomes and that nearly four-fifths (78.9%) of those were elderly women. It should be noted that these surveys were done at the time when Japan's economy was at its peak. Second, the poverty risk for elderly women is strongly affected by their husbands' employment history, rather than their own employment and academic achievement. Third, the death of a spouse increases the risk of low income for women but not for men. These results led Harada and colleagues to conclude that "a phenomenon known as the feminization of poverty" had already been clearly identified between 1987 and 1990 (Harada, Sugisawa, Kobayashi, & Liang, 2001).

## Women and the Pension System

According to the Comprehensive Survey of the Living Conditions, Health and Welfare of the People (2007), pension benefits are the major source of income for elderly households, accounting for 70% of average income (approximately 3 million yen), compared to 18% from work. Over three-fifths of elderly households relied on the public pension as their only source of income in 2006.

The public pension system in Japan consists mainly of two parts, the National or Basic Pension and the Employees' Pension or earnings-related component. The Basic Pension is the fundamental public pension in which everyone enrolls regardless of employment history and marital status. On reaching age 65, everyone who pays fixed premiums receives pension benefits based on the number of years he/she has contributed. The amount of the full pension is approximately 792,000 yen annually or 66,000 yen monthly—below the public assistance threshold for a single, elderly household.

Under the 1985 reform of the pension system, persons insured under the Basic Pension are classified in three categories according to employment and marital status. Category 1 insured persons are mainly the self-employed, farmers, and the unemployed (22.17 million people, including 11.04 million women in 2004). Category 2 insured persons are employees (37.13 million people, including 12.56 million women in 2004). Category 2 insurees are also covered by the Employee's Pension or earnings-related component. Since the Employees' Pension covers regular and full-time employees in practice, most irregularly employed persons such as day workers, part-time and *Haken* workers are often excluded and are classified as Category 1 insured persons who get only the Basic Pension.

Category 3 (10.91 million women out of 10.99 million people in this category) was established by the 1985 reform to cover dependent spouses of Category 2 insured persons. As a result, dependent spouses or the full-time housewives of Category 2 employees are entitled to their own Basic Pension benefits. Before the reform, the enrollment in the basic pension system of those "dependent" housewives who did not have their own earnings was optional, and they had to pay their own premiums if they wanted to be covered by a basic pension. After the reform, Category 2 insurees bear the cost of dependent housewives' premiums. Although this reform was in the name of "the establishment of pension rights for women," the establishment of the Category 3 insurance system has been criticized from the perspective of gender equity by women in general and also by female Category 2 insured persons who share the cost of Category 3 premiums, along with male Category 2 insurees. This system treats housewives as "dependents" of their husbands (Tamiya, 2003), and policy makers continue to envisage that wives are mainly allocated indirect security in old age through their husbands (Murakami, 2000). Thus, the pension system not only reflects disparities in wages and years of employment but also—because of the preferential treatment for housewives—among women themselves.

As mentioned above, the benefits of the Basic Pension are very low. Women classified in Category 1 are poor unless they enroll in private pensions or have other income. If the husbands of women in Category 1 insurees are also in Category 1—such as self-employed in small businesses or irregularly employed who are often excluded from the Employees' Pension, they have to pay their own premiums, unlike dependent housewives whose spouses are in Category 2. Along with their husbands, they receive approximately 1.5 million yen annually or slightly above the public assistance threshold, but, as widows, they lose their husbands' pension benefits. If they are over age 65, they get neither a survivors' pension nor a widows' pension from the Basic Pension. They only receive their own Basic Pension that is below the public assistance threshold for a single elderly person.

However, things are different for women in Category 3, even if their own pension benefit is the same as women in Category 1. According to an estimate by MHLW (2003), for Category 2 households with women in Category 3 in which husbands work for 40 years, the benefits of these couples, including the Employees' Pension for which Category 2 employees are eligible, is 236,000 yen per month or nearly 3 million yen annually. When women over the age of 65 in Category 3 become widowed, they get a survivors' benefit of 75% of the pension benefit of their late husbands from the Employees' Pension and their own pension as Category 3.

As a widow over 65, the dependent wife of a Category 2 employee gets a survivors' benefit of 75% of the pension benefits of her late husband from the Employees' Pension, plus her own Basic Pension benefits as a Category 3 insuree.

Differences in women's and men's wages and years of employment create gender disparities among Category 2 pensioners. It is obvious, especially among Category 2 pensioners in the private sector. The average male pensioner had 35 years and 1 month of enrollment period for which he received an average earnings-related benefit and a basic pension benefit of 190,000 yen per month as of March 2007. The contrasting figures for women are 25 years and 1 month for an average benefit of 110,000 yen per month—a gender gap of 42.1%, and those disparities have not been reduced much in this decade. Thus, the average pension for Category 2 women is slightly above public assistance. As widows, Category 2 women have to choose either their own or the survivors' benefits that are equal to 75% of the benefits of their late husbands from the Employees' Pension in which their husbands are enrolled. The latter is usually higher, and the premiums these wives paid are nonrefundable.

What is observed in this preferential treatment for dependent spouses is the persistence of the male breadwinner model and, hence, the idea that the older woman living alone is a widow of a stably employed worker. In fact, their treatment as "dependents" was originally premised on the condition that they had no income. However, in 1977, the Social Insurance

Agency eased the definition of "dependents" and issued the notification that wives were to be considered "dependent" on their husbands as long as their incomes did not exceed a fixed amount. This was the policy the government chose to meet in the rapid increase in the number of married women engaged in part-time work in the 1970s. On this occasion, it would have been possible to establish women's pension rights by allowing married women who work part-time to enroll in the Employees' Pension scheme. Rather, the government chose to modify the definition of "dependent" to apply to married, female, part-time workers in order to hold down the increase in female insured person in Employees' Pension schemes (Tamiya, 2003). Thus, Category 3 resulted both in the current low level of individual pension benefits for elderly women and a high poverty risk for working women who are ineligible for employee pension schemes due to their status as nonregular employees.

The Category 3 enrollee system has also been strengthened by "dependent" status in the tax system. The inequity resulting from women's working and contributing more than the benefits they could get as dependents has been reduced by the spousal income tax deduction scheme with its income-tax-free threshold for "dependents."

An analysis of resampled data from the National Survey of Family Income and Expenditure (Nagase, 2003) has found that the higher a husband's income (a monthly income of 250,000 yen or more), the more women intentionally modify working hours to lower their wages to the level of the income-tax-free threshold (1.03 million yen) and the social insurance premium threshold (up to 1.3 million yen). This response by married women exerts downward pressure on part-time wage levels, including those of part-time and nonregular workers who are not subject to the incentives of this taxation and the pension provisions. The policy orientation in the pension scheme in conjunction with the spousal income tax deduction scheme has affected the working behaviors of married women and their access to the more advantageous Employees' Pension system.

It is also important to note the impact of the preferential treatment for housewives in pension and taxation on the demand side of the workforce, for employers do not treat nonregular workers as Category 2 enrollees, thereby excluding them from the Employees' Pension, even though their working hours and pay levels meet the legal requirements for enrollment (Osawa, 2007). The official report, "Recommendations Based on Administrative Evaluation and Supervision of Employee Pension Insurance Schemes" (Ministry of Internal Affairs and Communications, 2006) estimated that 2.67 million employees who meet legal requirements for enrollment are not covered by the Employees' Pension scheme. Thus, nonregular workers, about 70% of whom are women (2005), are mainly forced to depend on the low-benefit Basic Pension, and this leads to low income levels in old age.

The current public pension system influences the life course of women and leads them to behave as dependents of Category 2 husbands. The income of women, especially in their old age, depends upon whether they have taken the role of dependent wife. In fact, until 2006, divorced women lost all of the "privileges" of dependent wives of Category 2 insurees. A bright spot is the reform of 2004 (that took effect in 2007) that allows part of a household's pension benefits to be transferred to a divorced wife on the basis of premiums paid by the husband during their marriage. There is also some indication that the preferential treatment for housewives in pension and tax systems will be reconsidered—a result of criticisms raised by researchers and a large number of women's groups who have identified the public pension system as a major gender issue since the 1990s.

## Conclusion

From the late 1990s onward, "social disparities" and the issue of the working poor have become the great concern in Japanese society, and accordingly the increasing number of households receiving public assistance became apparent, especially those "headed" by women. The poverty of women—both of families with children and the lone elderly—is rising to the surface. Women predominate among the lone elderly and have much lower incomes than their male counterparts. The poverty rates of lone mothers are very high—indeed even higher than lone, elderly women. However severe their impoverishment becomes, in the strict sense of the term, it is interpreted as indicating that feminization of poverty does not occur in Japan since neither the single-mother households nor the households "headed" by women have become large enough to predominate among poor families. Is the poverty of Japanese women again "a special case" in which married women are potentially poor but stable in the households as long as they remain married and have access to their husbands' incomes and pensions?

As we argued in this chapter, the company society that was constructed on the basis of a woman's stable marriage to the regularly employed male breadwinner, with families as the welfare providers and pension systems based on the male breadwinner model, forced women into poverty—even when the company society was functioning well. Yet, at this time it has been losing ground, especially since the 1990s. Japanese working women have been more disadvantaged by the increase of nonregular work both in the labor market and in a pension system based on the persisting idea of the company society. Consequently, they are much less able than men to support themselves adequately. The narrow and the strictest definition of feminization of poverty do not capture the relations between women and poverty in the Japanese context. In the broader sense of the term, the feminization of poverty is clearly evident in Japan.

Which group—single mothers or single, elderly women—gets more attention from policy makers depends on several conditions. The rapid growth of the population over age 65, which is estimated to become 25% of the total population in 2025, could make elderly women the focal group in the short and medium term. Families themselves have changed due to the rise in the rate of divorce, the change in the marital behavior of youth, and an economy in which fewer families are now able to be "the welfare providers" they were formerly expected to be. The economic hardships resulting from these changes in the family could overshadow the poverty of elderly women. The low status of women in the labor market and the pension basically built on women's marital status and their spouses' employment status directly impact women later in life. Viewed in this light, the single-mother group would be the focal group either in the economic deterioration or in the long term because the conditions that put them at immediate risk of poverty are not only during the child-rearing years but also later in life.

What is really necessary in the long term is that political measures be taken to change the outmoded social system based on the idea of the company society. This system in which women are positioned as dependent wives in households with a sole male breadwinner keeps their status in the labor market at a low level. It is single mothers who suffer most from the repercussions of this system in which they are a minority but a growing one.

The directions that social and economic policy should take in order to break through this problem are clear: to promote and put gender equity policies into practice; to readjust the pension system to secure women livable benefits as individuals regardless of either their marital status or their husband's employment status; and to advance women's status in the labor market.

Such changes in policy have been hinted since the 1990s. However, this was a time of economic depression and greater emphasis on neo-liberal policies. Instead of taking the necessary, innovative measure to change the social framework based on the company society, the major result was an increase in the number of temporary workers with unstable working conditions and in the poverty risk among women.

Under this circumstance, it is needless to say that a living wage for all should be achieved with secure working conditions. Furthermore, the urgent priority of policies at present is to secure some form of cash benefits and public care services for poor elderly women until the readjustment of the pension system is completed. At the same time, an urgent need is to secure cash benefits for single mothers as well as to provide them more effective job training opportunities that offer the prospect of income security.[6]

## Postscript

When this paper was submitted in April 2008, it did not refer to the financial crisis of September 2008. The influence of the meltdown is striking, and poverty and a widening economic gap have been of concern in Japan. Yet, it is clear that the basic framework of contemporary Japan that we presented here—that puts women at high risk of poverty—has not changed.

## Notes

1 Monthly subsistence costs applied to public assistance vary regionally and according to the types of family. In 2003, the monthly subsistence cost for a standard family (couple and a child) was approximately between 138,000 and 180,000 yen, that for single elderly household was between 70,000 and 93,000 yen, that for a single mother household (a mother and two children) was between 160,000 and 200,000 yen. Public assistance is applicable to those with income under the level of the subsistence cost, taking into consideration their savings and other assets.

2 MHLW is the Ministry of Health, Labor and Welfare which was created by the merger of the former Ministry of Labor and the former Ministry of Health and Welfare (MHW) in 2001. The National Survey of Single Mother Households, formerly conducted by the Ministry of Health and Welfare, has been taken over by MHLW.

3 Implementation of the reduction and suspension of the child-care allowance for single mothers after five years was tentatively held off in 2008 because of the strong opposition by the grass-root campaign of single mothers and women's groups.

4 A study investigating the status of single-mother households in recent years identified the potential for "generational reproduction of poverty," particularly in single-mother households receiving public assistance due to a combination of social and economic disadvantages (Sumioka, 2006; Kushiro Public University Research Center for Regional Economics, 2006; Nakazono, 2006). As another survey shows the relation between the poverty and academic background of single mothers (Japan Institute of Labor, 2002), it is necessary to focus on this as "a structural issue involving multiple layers of disadvantage that have accumulated over a long period of time" (Fujiwara, 2005a, p. 172).

5 This study of Shirahase uses LIS data from 2000 (1999 data for the United Kingdom) and the Comprehensive Survey of the Living Conditions, Health and Welfare of the People from 2001 for Japan since Japan is not included in the LIS data set. The data for low income of persons aged 60 and over for Japan for this study is adjusted as less than half of the median disposable incomes which is comparable to the most commonly used poverty standard in this book.

## References

Axinn, J. (1990). Japan: a special case. In G. S. Goldberg & E. Kremen (Eds.), *The feminization of poverty: only in America?* (pp. 91–106). New York: Praeger.

Cabinet Office, Government of Japan. (2006). *White paper on the aging society.* Tokyo: Gyosei.

Children and Families Bureau of MHW. (each year). *Zenkoku Boshi Setai tou Chousa* [*The National Survey of Single-Mother Households*]. Tokyo: Author.

Economic Planning Agency of Japan. (1996). *White paper on the national lifestyle.* Tokyo: Okura Shou Insatsu Kyoku.

Equal Employment, Children and Families Bureau of MHLW. (2005). *Zenkoku boshi setai tou chousa [The National Survey of Single-Mother Households].* Tokyo: Author.

Equal Employment, Children and Families Bureau of MHLW. (2006). *Josei rodo no bunseki [Analysis of women's work, 2006].* Tokyo: 21 Seiki Shokugyo Zaidan.

Fujiwara, C. (2003). Josei no shotoku hosho to koteki fujo [Women's income security and public assistance]. In M. Osawa (Ed.), *Fukushi kokka to jendaa [Welfare State and Gender]* (pp. 199–232). Tokyo: Akashi Shoten.

Fujiwara, C. (2005a). Hitori-oya no shugyo to kaisosei [Single parenthood, paid work, and social class in Contemporary Japan]. *The Journal of Social Policy and Labor Studies, 13*, 161–175.

Fujiwara, C. (2005b). Fukushi to josei rodo kyokyu no kankei-shi – Haha no shugyo to boshi fukushi [History of women's labor supply and welfare]. In K. Saguchi & K. Nakagawa (Eds.), *Fukushi shakai no rekishi – dento to henyo [History of social welfare]* (pp. 109–132). Kyoto: Minerva Press.

Fukawa, H. (2004). Doitsu ni okeru waakufea no tenkai [Workfare in Germany]. *The Review of Comparative Social Security Research, 147*, Summer, 39–61.

Harada, S. (1992). Nihonngata hukushi to Kazoku seisaku [Japanese Welfare and the Family]. In C. Ueno, S. Tsurumi, H. Naka, T. Nakamura, N. Miyata, & T. Yamada (Eds.), *Kazoku ni shinnyuu suru shakai [Families penetrated by society]* (pp. 39–61). Tokyo: Iwanami Shoten.

Harada, K., Sugisawa, H., Kobayashi, E., & Liang, J. (2001). Koreisha no shotoku hendo ni kanren suru yoin: Judan chosa ni yoru hinkon no dainamikkusu kenkyu [Factors related to income change among the elderly: Dynamics of poverty based on a longitudinal survey]. *Japanese Sociological Review, 52*(30), 328–397.

Hashimoto, K. (2003). *Class structure in contemporary Japan*. Melbourne: Trans Pacific Press.

Hashimoto, K. (2006). *Kaikyu-Shakai* [*Class Society*]. Tokyo:Kodansha.

Inoue, T., & Ehara, Y. (2005). *Josei no Data Book Ver.5* [*Data book on women in Japan 5th ed*]. Tokyo: Yuhikaku.

Iwata, M. (1996). Koreisha no "Jiritsu" to hinkon – Fubyodo no kakudai [Poverty and inequality among the elderly]. *Journal of Ohara Institute for Social Research, 447*, 15–25.

Iwata, M. (1998). Shakaiteki futan to kakei no tachiba [Social burden and household economics]. *Japanese Journal of Research on Household Economics, 38*, 19–26.

Iwata, M., & Hamamoto, C. (2004). Defure jokyoka no hinkon keiken [Experiences of poverty during deflation]. In Y. Higuchi, K. Ohta, & Kakei Keizai Kenkyusho (Eds.), *Joseitachi no Heisei fukyo [The Heisei recession for women]* (pp. 203–234). Tokyo: Nihon Keizai Shimbun-sha.

Japan Institute of Labor. (2002). *Boshi setai no haha he no shugyou shien ni kansuru chosa [Survey of employment support for single mothers]*. Tokyo: Japan Institute of Labor.

Jinno, N. (1992). Nihongata fukushi kokka zaisei no tokushitu [Characteristics of national budget in Japanse style welfare]. In K. Hayasshi & E. Kato (Eds.), *Fukushi kokkazaisei no kokusai hikaku [international comparative study of national welfare budget]* (pp. 217–238) Tokyo: Tokyo Daigaku Shuppannkai.

Kambara, F. (2007, July 22). *Boshikatei no genjo* [Present situation of single mothers]. *Tokyo Shimbun*, Sunday Edition.

Kilkey, M. (2000). *Lone mothers between paid work and care: The policy regime in twenty countries*. Aldershot: Ashgate.

Kimoto, K. (2004a). Kazoku to kigyo shakai: Rekishiteki hendo katei [Families and the company society: A historical transformation]. In O. Watanabe (Ed.), *Henbo suru "kigyo shakai" Nihon [Transformation of the Japanese "company society"]* (pp. 299–340). Tokyo: Junposha.

Kimoto, K. (2004b). Labor conditions for women in contemporary Japan: Where do the problems lie? (pp. 227–228). Paper presented at the conference, *Social Policy as if People Matter: A Cross-National Dialogue*, at Adelphi University, Garden City, New York, November 11, 12. http://www.adelphi.edu/peoplematter/pdfs/Kimoto.pdf. Accessed May 31, 2009.

Komamura, K. (2003). Teishotoku setai no suikei to seikatsu hogo seido [Estimates of low-income households and the public assistance system]. *Mita Business Review, 46*, 3, 107–126.

Kushiro Public University Research Center for Regional Economics. (2006). *Seikatsu hogo jukyu boshi setai no jiritsu shien ni kansuru kiso kenkyu [Basic research into supporting the independence of single mother households receiving public assistance]*. Kushiro: Author.

Ministry of Health, Labor and Welfare (MHLW). (2003–2008, each year) Hoikusho-no-Jyokyo [The condition of child care centers]. Tokyo: Unpublished.

Ministry of Health, Labor and Welfare (MHLW). (2003). The Report for the 19th Pension Section of the Social Security Council of the MHLW. Tokyo: Unpublished.

Ministry of Health, Labor and Welfare (MHLW). (2005, 2007). *Kokumin seikatu kiso chosa [Comprehensive survey of the living conditions, health and welfare of the people]*. Tokyo: Kosei Tokei Kyokai.

Ministry of Health, Labor and Welfare (MHLW). (2006). *Boshi katei no haha no shugyo shien ni kan-suru shisaku no jokyo hokoku [White paper on the status of implementation of employment support policies for single mothers]*. Tokyo: Author.

Murakami, K. (2000). Nenkin kyufu ni miru haigusha gainen to josei no nenkin-ken jiritsu [The concept of the spouse in relation to pension benefits and independent pension rights for women]. In Y. Soeda & N. Tarukawa (Eds.), *Gendai kazoku to kazoku seisaku [The modern family and family policies]* (pp. 195–215). Kyoto: Minerva Press.

Murozumi, M. (2006). *Nihon no hinkon* [*Poverty in Japan*]. Kyoto: Horitsu Bunka-sha.

Nagase, N. (2003). Josei no nenkin-ken no mondai [Women's pension rights]. *Quarterly of Social Security Research, 39*, 1, 83–96.

Nakazono, K. (2006). Seikatsu hogo jukyu boshi setai to "jiritsu" shien [Single mother households receiving public assistance and support for "independence"]. *Chingin to Shakai Hosho, 1426*, 11–33.

National Diet of Japan. (2002). Minutes of 115th House of Councilors, Committee on Health, Labor and Welfare, 19 November. http://kokkai.ndl.go.jp/. Accessed May 31, 2009.

Nomura, M., & Kimoto, K. (2002). Is the Japanese-style welfare society sustainable? In G. S. Goldberg & M. G. Rosenthal (Eds.), *Diminishing welfare: A cross-national study of social provision* (pp. 295–320). Westport: Auburn House.

OECD. (2006). *OECD Economic Surveys of Japan, Vol. 2006 Issue 13*. Paris: Author.

Ogawa, H. (2000). Hinkon setai no genjo: Nichi-Ei hikaku [The current status of poverty: Comparative study of Japan and United Kingdom]. *Economic Review, 51*, 3, 220–231.

Osawa, M. (2007). Report for the 22nd Ochanomizu University Evening Seminar (unpublished), Tokyo.

Shirahase, S. (2005). *Shoshi Koreika Sahakai no Mienai Kakusa [Invisible gaps in the aging society with low birth-rate]*. Tokyo: Tokyo Daigaku shuppankai.

Shirahase, S. (2006). *Widowhood later in life in Japan: Considering Social Security System in aging societies.* Luxembourg Income Study Working Paper, No., 444.

Luxembourg: Luxembourg Income Study. http://www.lisproject.org/publications/liswps/444.pdf. Accessed May 31, 2009.

Single Mothers' Forum. (2001). *Shinguru mazaa no nenkin kanyu jokyo hokokusho [Report of the enrollment of single mothers in pension schemes].* Tokyo: Author.

Sumioka, T. (2006). Kosodate bunka: Hinkon no sedaiteki sai-seisan [Childrearing culture: the generational reproduction of poverty]. In Kushiro Public University Research Center for Regional Economics, *Seikatsu hogo jukyu boshi setai no jiritsu shien ni kansuru kiso kenkyu [Basic research into supporting the independence of single mother households receiving public assistance]* (pp. 55–73). Kushiro: Kushiro Public University Research Center for Regional Economics.

Tachibanaki, T. (1998). *Nihon no keizai kakusa [Economic disparities in Japan].* Tokyo: Iwanami Shinsho.

Tachibanaki, T., & Urakawa, K. (2006). *Nihon no hinkon kenkyu [Poverty study in Japan].* Tokyo: Tokyo Daigaku Shuppankai.

Tamiya, Y. (2003). Koteki nenkin seido no hensen: Jendaa shiten kara no saiko [Reconsidering the history of the public pension system from a gender perspective]. *Journal of the National Women's Education Center of Japan, 7,* 55–68.

Tarukawa, N. (1982). Boshi fukushi shikin kashi-tsuke no rekishi [The history of welfare loans for single mother families]. *Boshi Kenkyu, 5,* 5–27.

Uzuhashi, T. (1997). *Gendai fukushi kokka no kokusai hikaku [Comparative study of the modern welfare states].* Tokyo: Nippon Hyoron-sha.

Yamada, A. & Casey, B. (2002). *Getting older, getting poorer? A study of the earnings, pensions, assets and living arrangements of older people in nine countries,* Working Paper, No. 314. Luxembourg: Luxembourg Income Study. http://www.lisproject.org/publications/liswps/314.pdf. Accessed May 31, 2009.

Yuzawa, N. (2005). Hitori-oya kazoku seisaku to waakufea [Single-parent families and workfare]. *The Journal of Social Policy and Labor Studies, 13,* 92–109.

# 9

# FEMINIZATION OF POVERTY IN THE UNITED STATES: ANY SURPRISES?

*Gertrude Schaffner Goldberg*

## Introduction: Economic and Political Trends in Historical Perspective

Between 1980 and 2005 U.S. national output per person increased 40%. This substantial gain could have lifted all incomes, including those of thee women who are the subjects of this study. Instead, income *trickled up*. The share of the top fifth of the income distribution increased to over 50% of total income while the lower four quintiles all lost ground. Wealth is even more top heavy. Arguably, this great economic inequality and consequent concentration of political power, combined with anti-government ideology, contributed substantially to the economic crisis that began in 2008 (MacEwan, 2009). After briefly recounting relevant developments in social and economic policy since the 1960s, the chapter turns first to a description of the U.S. model for family/workplace responsibilities and then to a discussion of the condition of lone women, particularly and women, generally, in the United States.

**The 1960s to the present**. The United States was dubbed a "reluctant welfare state" in the 1960s, even in a time when social programs were expanding (Wilensky, 1965). In the ensuing years, it became "more than reluctant" (Goldberg, 2002). Conservatives were never in favor of federal responsibility for social welfare.[1] However, they were temporarily stilled by the progressive social movements that gained ground during the economic crisis of the 1930s and again during the social revolutions of the 1960s.

In the 1970s, reactionary forces became more aggressive politically and greatly expanded their lobbying activities and the scope and influence of right-wing think tanks (Goldberg & Collins, 2001). They mounted a propaganda blitz that exacerbated a white backlash against African American gains of the 1960s. The new phenomenon of stagflation—the combination of high unemployment and inflation—was used to discredit postwar Keynesian economic policies and to promote, instead, freer markets and reduced government regulation.

The New Deal in the 1930s and the Great Society in the 1960s proved that government could be a positive force in the lives of ordinary people. Reactionaries' success in discrediting this idea is famously epitomized in President Ronald Reagan's slogan, "government is not the solution to our problem; government is the problem." Particularly pertinent to women who need government support is the class strategy begun by Reagan (1981–1989) and carried forward by George W. Bush (2001–2009): huge income tax cuts to the wealthy and a military build-up. Together these resulted in massive budget deficits that served as a rationale to shrink or restrain spending for social programs. Fighting two wars since 2003 and spending hundreds of billions to bailout financial institutions later in the decade could further crowd out social spending.

The administration of Democrat Bill Clinton (1993–2001) was centrist in ideology and indicative of distancing from the party's New Deal policies. The Clinton years included cutbacks and restructuring in social welfare, a failed effort led by First Lady Hillary Clinton to achieve national health insurance, and continued deregulation and trade treaties that lacked sufficient protection of labor or the environment. On the other hand, the Clinton years brought deficit reduction, in fact, a budget surplus, and much lower unemployment. Under Clinton, an attack on welfare or public assistance for single mothers that began in the late 1960s culminated in "welfare reform": repeal of Aid to Families with Dependent Children (AFDC), the entitlement to welfare of poor women and children, and its replacement with Temporary Assistance to Needy Families (TANF). Old Age, Survivors' and Disability Insurance (OASDI), known popularly as Social Security, has been under siege since the early 1980s. Privatization is the goal of the attackers, but so far Social Security remains a largely unscathed, defined benefit. The huge decline in the stock market in 2008 that could have wiped out the privatized Social Security of older Americans should keep Social Security public and out of the hands of Wall Street.

In the late 1990s, during the Clinton administration, unemployment was the lowest in 30 years. Average wages rose but not to the level of the 1970s.[2] The recession that began in 2001, early in the administration of President George W. Bush, was very short, but a "jobless recovery persisted almost four years, taking more than twice as long as in past recessions to regain a prior employment peak" (Mishel, Bernstein, & Allegretto, 2007).

In the midst of a recession that began in December 2007 and that threatened to become the first depression since the 1930s, the rate of unemployment had climbed to 6.7% (November 2008), the highest since 1991, and had reached 7.6% in January 2009, when President Barack Obama took the oath of office. It had climbed to 9.4% by May of that year.. In the first year of the recession, mass layoffs (involving 50 or more persons from a single employer) amounted to 2.1 million initial claims for unemployment insurance (U.S. Bureau of Labor Statistics, 2008).

**Lone women**. Inspired by the African American freedom movement, the "second wave" of women's liberation took significant strides toward gender equality. Nonetheless, as the predecessor to this study observed: "The relatively brief span of years from 1960 to the mid-1970s witnessed not only the resurgence of American feminism but the feminization of American poverty" (Goldberg & Kremen, 1990, p. 1). Two factors account for this seeming paradox:

- Demographic change—a near tripling of the number of single-mother families; and
- A rate of single-mother poverty that, although lower than in 1960, was nonetheless much higher than that of other families.

This was the situation before welfare "reform." What about after?

The picture for single mothers has been mixed since welfare reform. Their employment rate increased in the years immediately following the imposition of work requirements in public assistance. This was the "push" of welfare reform, but there was also the "pull," in the closing years of the century, of the lowest rate of unemployment in 30 years. Earlier research found that U.S. single mothers suffered high poverty rates, even when they worked (Kilkey & Bradshaw, 1999). This chapter explores whether that is still the case.

Harder to quantify but no less important is the psychological and social impact of being a single mother in the United States. The Congressional rationale for repealing AFDC referred to single parenthood as "the crisis in our Nation"—blaming it for a host of social ills—violent crime, juvenile delinquency, school failure, and public dependency (U.S. Congress, 1996, sec. 101).

Do women who are alone in old age fare better than younger lone women? Popular opinion in the United States is that the elderly are a well-off, perhaps even pampered, group that claims resources for itself to the detriment of the nation's children. The poverty of the elderly fell steeply in the last half century According to the official U.S. poverty standard, persons over 65 are less likely to be poor than children. However, these thresholds are lower than for single individuals under age 65, implying that the elderly don't need as much money as younger people and ignoring their higher health costs.

If poverty is measured instead by less than half the median income, elderly poverty is more than 50% above the overall rate for the population and, surprisingly, higher than that of the nation's children (Luxembourg Income Study [LIS], 2007). Even by the minimal U.S. poverty standard, lone elderly women have high rates of poverty, especially those of minority race and ethnicity. Following a description of the U.S. approach to family/workplace responsibilities, this chapter discusses the labor market, social welfare, and demographic factors relevant to the poverty of women generally and to the two groups of lone women on whom the study focuses.

## Family/Workplace Responsibilities: The U.S. Model

Most U.S. mothers are breadwinners and providers of care but with little state support for this dual role. This has been called an "earner strategy" (Misra, Moller, & Budig, 2007).[3] Well-off families pay for child care privately, sometimes hiring immigrant nannies who leave their own children in the mother country. Many mothers stretch to pay high child-care costs, choose jobs that fit family rather than career needs, or settle for less-than-ideal child care. Further, parental leave is without pay except in a few of the 50 states or when granted at employers' volition (Palley, 2008).[4] Women also minister to elder kin at a loss of employment and earnings as well as physical and psychological strain.

Public assistance and social insurance policies send mixed messages. Enacted during the 1930s, both favored caring over paid employment for women. Soon after its passage, Old Age Insurance (Social Security) began to cover women and children as survivors and dependents of deceased or retired workers. A male breadwinner/female carer model made more sense when fewer women went out to work, and it is still necessary for older women who were stay-at-home wives or sporadic and low-wage workers. However, the section on Social Security will show how this system is unfair to employed, low-wage spouses.

While social insurance continues the male breadwinner model, public assistance has moved in the opposite direction. An initial intent of AFDC was to free single mothers from the breadwinning role so that they could be nurturers, a policy also dictated by the Depression-era effort to remove women from the labor market in a time of very high unemployment. "Welfare reform" cast poor single mothers as breadwinners. They must work while they are on assistance, and the federal government sets a 5-year lifetime limit on TANF benefits.[5] Mandatory work requirements are imposed even though neither living-wage jobs nor affordable child care are assured.

## Women and the Labor Market

**Gender gap in employment**. Despite women's greatly increased participation in the labor force, a gender gap in employment remains. Just about three-fifths of U.S. women aged 16 and over were in the labor force in 2005, compared to almost three-fourths of men (U.S. Bureau of Labor Statistics [USBLS], 2007a, table 4). Education has a large impact on the employment

TABLE 9.1 Rates of Labor Force Participation, Full- and Part-Time Employment, and Unemployment by Sex and Age of Children, 2005

| | Labor Force Participation | Full-Time Employment[a] | Part-Time Employment[b] | Unemployment |
|---|---|---|---|---|
| With children under 18 | | | | |
| Women | 70.5 | 74.7 | 25.3 | 5.3 |
| Men | 94.1 | 96.6 | 3.4 | 3.1 |
| With children 6–17 | | | | |
| Women | 76.5 | 77.0 | 23.0 | 4.4 |
| Men | 93.0 | 96.6 | 3.3 | 3.2 |
| With children under 6 | | | | |
| Women | 62.8 | 70.9 | 29.1 | 6.7 |
| Men | 95.4 | 96.4 | 3.6 | 3.2 |
| With children under 3 | | | | |
| Women | 58.4 | 69.0 | 31.0 | 7.2 |
| Men | 95.5 | 96.2 | 3.8 | 3.1 |

[a] Percent of those employed who work full time.
[b] Percent of those employed who work part time.
*Source*: Calculated from U.S. Bureau of Labor Statistics, n.d.

gender gap. In the prime working years (25–64), there is a gap of 27 percentage points for those lacking a high school diploma but only seven points for those with doctoral degrees (USBLS, 2006, table 2.8). Part-time employment is quite gendered; women's rate is more than double that of men (OECD, 2007, table E). Women predominate in other types of nonstandard work such as temporary employment that often pays low wages and lacks retirement and health insurance (Mishel et al., 2007).

Motherhood looms large in the gender gap. Whereas the age of their children has virtually no impact on fathers' labor force participation, the effect is dramatic for mothers (Table 9.1). Mothers with a child under 3 are almost one-fourth less likely to be in the labor market than those with school-age children. Women's part-time employment exceeds men's regardless of children's ages but is higher for mothers of children in the youngest two groups. Discontinuity and nonstandard work lower current and retirement income.

**More single mothers at work**. The "push" of welfare reform, the "pull" of improved market conditions, or a combination of the two are reasons why single mothers were more likely to be in the labor market and employed in 2000 than in 1995, whereas married mothers were equally likely to be active at these two times (Table 9.2). In the less favorable labor market of the early years of this century single mothers suffered more loss in activity and employment rates than married mothers. Nonetheless, the rate for single mothers was 10% higher than a decade earlier. Many single mothers remained in the labor market despite losing their jobs.

TABLE 9.2 Labor Market Status of Mothers with Children Under 18 by Marital Status, 1995–2005, Percentages

| | Single Mothers | | | Married Mothers | | | All Mothers | | |
|---|---|---|---|---|---|---|---|---|---|
| | Labor Force[a] | Empl./ Pop.[b] | Unem- ployed[c] | Labor Force | Empl./ Pop. | Unem- ployed | Labor Force | Empl./ Pop. | Unem- ployed |
| 1995 | 69.4 | 61.7 | 11.0 | 70.0 | 66.9 | 4.4 | 69.8 | 65.5 | 6.2 |
| 2000 | 78.9 | 73.0 | 7.5 | 69.8 | 67.8 | 2.9 | 72.3 | 69.2 | 4.3 |
| 2005 | 76.1 | 69.1 | 9.2 | 68.2 | 65.8 | 3.6 | 70.5 | 66.7 | 5.3 |

[a] Percent of the population either employed or unemployed and looking for work.
[b] Percent of the population employed.
[c] Percent unemployed and looking for work.
*Source*: Calculated from U.S. Bureau of Labor Statistics, n.d.

TABLE 9.3 Single Mothers' Labor Force Participation Rates by Educational Level, 1995–2005

| | 1995 | 2000 | 2005 | 1995–2000 | 1995–2005 | 2000–2005 |
|---|---|---|---|---|---|---|
| College grad. | 90.7 | 90.9 | 89.2 | 0.2 | –1.5 | –1.7 |
| Some college or assoc. degree | 79.4 | 85.3 | 81.9 | 5.9 | 2.5 | –3.4 |
| High school graduation, no college | 71.5 | 79.5 | 76.4 | 8.0 | 4.9 | –3.1 |
| Less than high school diploma | 44.6 | 61.2 | 56.1 | 16.6 | 11.5 | –5.1 |

*Source*: Mosisa & Steven, 2006, Table 11.

Among single mothers, divorced mothers are most likely to be in the labor market, and never-married and widowed mothers least likely (84%, compared to 72% and 65% respectively, in 2005). Participation increased for all of these single mothers between 1995 and 2000, with the greatest gain—25%—among never-married mothers (U.S. Bureau of Labor Statistics, n.d.).

Social class, as reflected in educational attainment, affects labor force participation. Thus single mothers' rates rise with education (Table 9.3). Although differences narrowed between 1995 and 2005 (and especially between 1995 and 2000 when overall unemployment fell), single mothers who graduated from college were still about 60% more likely to be in the labor force than those with less than a high school diploma. The greatest gains in the boom years of exceptionally low unemployment were for single mothers with less than high school education. They also experienced the greatest losses after the recession that began in 2001.

Race and ethnicity are also related to labor market status. Black or African-American and Asian single mothers were more likely than their Latina counterparts to be in the labor market in 2005. Although black single mothers are almost as likely to be in the labor market as whites, their unemployment rates are nearly twice as high (U.S. Bureau of Labor Statistics, n.d.).

**Low-wage labor market**. Labor market participation is considered liberating for women, but for many low-wage workers, employment is fraught with economic and social indignities. The social critic, Barbara Ehrenreich worked at low-wage jobs and bore witness to some of these assaults (2002, p. 208): "What surprised and offended me most about the low-wage workplace ... was the extent to which one is required to surrender one's basic civil rights and—what boils down to the same thing—self-respect."

As precarious, exploitative, and impoverishing as low-wage work often is, some studies show that most women prefer work to welfare and that their self-esteem is enhanced by employment (Altman & Goldberg, 2007; Edin & Lein, 1997; Newman, 2006). Yet, preference for work may also speak to the stigma of welfare. "To demean and punish those who do not work is to exalt by contrast even the meanest labor at the meanest wage" (Piven & Cloward, 1993, pp. 3–4).

The low-wage workplace hardly guarantees women an escape from poverty. In 2005, nearly 30% of women who worked year-round, full-time earned less than the poverty level for a family of four ($15,577), compared to about one-fifth of men. Poverty-level earners were even more prevalent among minority women: over a third of black women and nearly half of Latinas (Mishel et al., 2007, pp. 128–131). The annual income of women who earned the median weekly wage was about three-fourths of a more realistic, higher poverty standard developed by the respected Economic Policy Institute (EPI), and those of black women and Latinas were even further below (Allegretto, 2005). Only women with a college education had median incomes above the EPI budget. Thus, market income does not enable millions of U.S. women to be economically independent. With work expenses like transportation and child and health care, families, even with incomes above the poverty line, could be worse off than on welfare (Pearce, 2004).

The wage gap persists. Among year-round, full-time workers, women's median incomes are slightly more than three-fourths those of men. In the 1990s, the wage gap decreased at a much slower rate than in the previous decade. Between 2000 and 2005, the ratio of women's to men's earnings remained virtually the same—from 74% to 75% (DeNavas-Walt, Proctor, & Lee, 2006, table A-2).

The full-time, year-round wage gap underestimates women's inequality in two ways. First, if it were to include part-time employment, women's earnings would be only two-thirds of men's. Further, there is a continuity gap. Over a 15-year period (1983–1998), women's total earnings were only 38% of men's (Hartmann, Rose, & Lovell, 2006).

**The motherhood penalty**. Contributing to the employment and wage gaps is the motherhood penalty. Perhaps as a result of employers' perception that their major responsibility for child care red productivity, mothers are much less likely to be with comparable credentials, and they are also m starting salaries (Correll & Bernard, 2007; Waldfog cially the case for single mothers who now have resp proportion of child-rearing than stay-at-home wives in 2006). Benefits available in other countries—parental l child care—would mitigate some of the burden.

## Government Policies to Increase Employment and Earn

**Targeting gender**. Sixty percent of women still work in female-dominated occupations. Segregation declined from 1960 through the 1980s, but since 1990, has increased or leveled off among those with high school education or less while declining slightly among those with some college and more so among college graduates (England, 2006). For the three-fifths of women workers who are employed in female-dominated jobs, earnings are low, even in "good jobs" such as supervisors in food service and retail work (Hartmann et al., 2006). On the basis of data from a large, nationally representative sample, economists Francine Blau and Lawrence Kahn (2006) concluded that occupational and industry categories explained nearly half the wage difference between full-time men and women workers.

Persisting segregation in jobs that pay less than male occupations implies the need for affirmative action and pay equity. But both equalization measures have fallen on hard times. Affirmative action has suffered setbacks in the courts and on the ballots of a number of states (Anderson, 2004; Kellough, 2006; Messer-Davidow, 2002). Initially, pay equity achieved some important gains in unionized employment, but the movement never really gained momentum in the private sector, and progress was limited in public jurisdictions as well (Figart & Hartmann, 2000).

**Class strategies**. There are some good reasons to target class rather than gender: setbacks in equalization policies and the stagnation in male wages that make parity with men less desirable (Madrick & Papanikolaou, 2008, on male wages). Women are nearly three-fifths of minimum wage workers and thus stood to gain disproportionately in 2007, when, for the first time in a decade, the national minimum was raised (Mishel et al., 2007).

Unionization is another class strategy that benefits women. Union women have median weekly earnings about 30% more than nonunion women (2006), and the gains are greater for minorities, particularly Latinas (USBLS, 2007c, table 2). However, not quite 11% of women wage and salary workers are unionized, and overall union density is only slightly higher (USBLS, 2007c, table 1). For a number of reasons U.S. unions lost ground from the early 1950s when about one-third of the American work force was unionized. Anti-Communist purges early in the Cold War removed ve union leaders and left in their stead those who virtually ceased ganize the unorganized (Schrecker, 2000; Yates, 1997).[6] More recently, government policy, through tax advantages for off-shoring, trade agreements that fail to protect workers' rights, and anti-labor appointments to the National Labor Relations Board, have contributed to the decline of a movement that raises workers' wages and helps to close the wage gap.[7]

Women are aided by low levels of unemployment. In the low unemployment years of the late 1990s, wages of women in the bottom two deciles of the wage distribution grew at an average rate more than four times that of the preceding 6 years (Bernstein & Baker, 2003, p. 43).[8] Sustained, low levels of unemployment—especially full employment—would be a boon to women, but as historian Frank Stricker (2007) observes, periods of high growth never run long enough to cure unemployment and job-related poverty.

**Reducing the mother penalty.** Although child care is usually seen as social welfare or an income transfer, it is also an equalization policy that can reduce the motherhood penalty. Moreover, affordable, quality child care can alleviate mothers' financial, emotional, and physical strains.

Increased when work requirements for welfare recipients were tightened, child-care subsidies in the late 1990s were still available for only 12%–14% of income-eligible families (Helburn & Bergmann, 2003). A survey of child care in all 50 states in 2006 found that "still far too many low income families who are unable to qualify for child-care assistance remain trapped on waiting lists, strain to pay their co-payments even if they are receiving assistance, or cannot find good care for their children because state reimbursement rates are too low" (Schulman & Blank, 2006, p. 6).[9] In most states, families with earnings of $18,000 or less who do not get subsidies would have to spend 30% or more of their annual income for child care for an infant, and in five states—New York, Connecticut, Minnesota, Massachusetts, and New Jersey—the average cost of child care for two children is more than $18,000 per year (Nation's Network of Child Care Resources & Referral Agencies, 2006). While there is concern and some policy response to the need for care of pre-school children of working parents, Jody Heymann's cross-national research has led her to conclude that the dialogue about the needs of school-age children in the United States is "at a mere whisper" (2006, p. 46).

## Income Support for Families

**Cash benefits**. The United States and other countries classified as liberal welfare regimes are said to emphasize means-tested over universal programs (Esping-Andersen, 1990). Actually, the largest U.S. social program, Old Age, Survivors,' and Disability Insurance or Social Security, is not means-tested, but is primarily for the elderly, the disabled, and their dependents rather than families with children.[10]

Altogether, non-means-tested income transfers reduced single mothers' poverty by about10% in 2005, and cash, means-tested benefits by another 6% for a total of 16% (U.S. Census Bureau, 2006a, table RD-REV POV01). Thus the problem is more the inadequacy of income support than liberal-regime emphasis on means-tested benefits. It should be noted, however, that the Census Bureau does not count the Earned Income Tax Credit (EITC) as an income transfer, even though it is essentially means-tested public assistance—that is, a refundable tax credit for working-poor families with children, most of whom do not pay a federal income tax. If it were counted, the poverty of single mothers would have been reduced an additional 14%, bringing the total reduction to 30%, still small compared to European welfare states.[11]

For some families with earnings within the range of the federal poverty standard, the EITC could increase their incomes by 40% and even more in the 20 states that also have an EITC, but it pays substantially less to families with lower earnings and nothing to the unemployed. Its rise, moreover, has been concurrent with a fall in the value of the minimum wage. The combined value of the EITC and the minimum wage for year-round, full-time workers is less than the inflation adjusted value of the minimum wage alone in the late 1960s.[12]

Although it was an entitlement, the former AFDC program had very meager benefits—combined benefits of AFDC and food stamps fell below the official U.S. poverty level for a family of three in every state (Goldberg & Collins, 2001). Benefits for poor families have continued to decline under TANF, falling an average of 13% in real terms from 1994 to 2003 (calculated from U.S. House of Representatives, 2004, Table 7-10).

Much has been written about the decline in the welfare caseloads following "welfare reform" but less about the fact that one million poor mothers in an average month are without work or welfare. Nor is there much publicity about the precipitous decline in the participation rate of income-eligible families. Approximately four-fifths of those poor enough to qualify for AFDC were enrolled in the early 1990s, compared to just under one-half for its successor TANF in 2002 (latest data available). The drop in participation among eligible families accounts for more than half of the decline in TANF caseloads since 1996 (Parrott & Sherman, 2006).

In addition to leaving some of the poorest families unaided, TANF, with its emphasis on "work first," reduced access to education and training for welfare recipients. Further, programs leading to a baccalaureate degree—a clear employment advantage—cannot be counted toward the work participation requirements that the federal government imposes on the states (Lower-Basch, 2007).

Whereas some countries in this study assure child support to single parents, the U.S. government attempts to collect this private income transfer from noncustodial parents. Despite stepped-up efforts to enforce child support in recent years, only a little over three-fifths of custodial mothers were awarded child support, two-fifths got at least one payment, and only one-fourth got the full amount awarded (2001) (U.S. House of Representatives, 2004, Table 8-6).

**Benefits-in-kind**. The United States provides some important benefits-in-kind for poor families, but, like child-care subsidies, these fall short in various respects. Housing assistance, like child care, is not an entitlement. According to the Urban Institute (2006), "Only about one in every three eligible families gets assistance.... 6.1 million low-income renters still face severe housing hardship—paying more than half their monthly income for housing or living in seriously run-down or overcrowded housing." Much higher amounts of government assistance are provided to middle- and upper-income home owners in the form of tax expenditures (Abramovitz, 2001). These, moreover, are entitlements. Lack of affordable housing is a cause of homelessness that afflicts an estimated 2.3–3.5 million people, between one-third and one-half of them homeless families, mostly single mothers and their children (Burt, Aron, & Lee with Valente, 2001; National Alliance to End Homelessness, 2007a, 2007b).

In contrast to other countries in this study, health care in the United States is not a universal public responsibility. Medicare, part of the social insurance program, pays for part of the health care costs of the elderly and disabled but not for nondisabled, working-age adults and their families. Medicaid and its program for poor children, State Child Health Insurance Program (SCHIP), pay for the medical bills of children in families with incomes up to two to three times the poverty level, but in most states, parents in families with incomes above the poverty level are ineligible for Medicaid. Over 8 million children had no health insurance in 2005 (DeNavas-Walt, Proctor, & Lee, 2006, table C-2; Ross, Cox, & Marks, 2007), but legislation signed by President Barack Obama in the early days of his presidency will extend coverage to millions more children and will allow SCHIP and Medicaid to provide coverage to legal immigrants. Another in-kind benefit, Food Stamps (Supplemental Nutritional Assistance Program [SNAP] since 2008) stretches family income, yet in 2006, only about 67% of eligible persons received benefits (57% of the working poor) (U.S. Department of Agriculture, 2007).

## Prevalence of Single Motherhood

Our earlier cross-national study found that the growth of single motherhood was one reason why poverty had become feminized in the United States. In 2005, single mothers were just about one-fourth of all families with children—a larger proportion than at the time of our earlier study of the feminization of poverty. The proportion almost doubled from 1965 to 1985, continued to increase but more slowly in the next decade, and grew only scantily since the mid-1990s. Over the life course, more than half of all women in the 1965 and 1970 birth cohorts will be single mothers.

TABLE 9.4 Single Mothers by Marital Status, Race, and Ethnicity, 2005, Percentages

| | Never Married | Divorced | Separated | Widowed |
|---|---|---|---|---|
| All races/ethnicities | 40.0 | 35.5 | 16.9 | 7.6 |
| White, non-Hispanic | 31.1 | 43.5 | 17.3 | 8.1 |
| Black | 57.2 | 20.8 | 15.7 | 6.4 |
| Hispanic | 42.3 | 27.1 | 23.7 | 6.9 |

*Source*: U.S. Census Bureau, 2006a.

The estimated, average length of a "spell" of single motherhood is just over 5 years, and the total number of years spent as single mothers for those who have at least one spell is 9 (Moffitt & Rendall, 1995).[13] Thus, single motherhood is a significant part of the life course for many women, especially black women, four-fifths of whom will experience it (Moffitt & Rendall, 1995). Slightly over half of all single mother families are nonwhites or minorities (U.S. Census Bureau, 2006c, table 4).

Over the years, the marital status of single mothers has changed. Widows were almost one-third of a much smaller group of single mothers in 1960 (U.S. Census Bureau, 1961) but are currently a tiny minority (Table 9.4). The great increase is in never-married mothers who were under 5% of single mothers in 1960 but are now two-fifths. Together, divorced and separated mothers are still the most numerous—though a smaller majority than in 1960. However, although they are conventionally combined, the latter are a much poorer group confirming the epithet, "poor man's divorce." As Table 9.4 shows, the marital status of single mothers varies by race and ethnicity, with nonmarriage being more frequent among minorities, especially blacks, and divorce the mode among whites.

## Poverty of Single Mothers

The poverty rates reported in this chapter are based on the official poverty standard of the U.S. government. It is important to bear in mind that U.S. poverty rates are much higher when measured by the middle of three European relative standards (less than 50% of the median disposable income). According to that lower European standard, the poverty rate of U.S. single mothers was 44.0% in 2000, compared to the U.S. official rate of 33.0% (Tables 10.1 and 9.7).

As Table 9.5 shows, race/ethnicity and marital status are both related to the poverty of families with children. Single mothers have twice the poverty rate of single fathers and five to six times that of married couple families. Here we observe effects of both gender and single parenthood—of a woman's wage and a single wage. The poverty rate of Hispanic couples is much higher than that of white and black couples—owing partly to the low labor force participation rates of married, Hispanic women and to low

TABLE 9.5 Official Poverty Rates of Families with Children by Family Type, Race, and Ethnicity, 2005, Percentages

| | Married Couple | Single Fathers | Single Mothers | All Families |
|---|---|---|---|---|
| All races/ethnicities | 6.5 | 17.6 | 36.2 | 14.5 |
| White, non-Hispanic | 3.6 | 13.1 | 29.2 | 8.2 |
| Black | 9.3 | 29.2 | 42.0 | 28.4 |
| Hispanic, all races | 16.9 | 20.6 | 45.2 | 24.4 |

*Source*: U.S. Census Bureaus, 2006b, Table POV04.

TABLE 9.6 Poverty Rates of Single-Mother Families by Proportions of the Official Poverty Standard, Race, and Ethnicity, 2005

| | 100% | 125% | 150% | 175% | 200% |
|---|---|---|---|---|---|
| All races/ethnicities | 36.2 | 44.5 | 52.2 | 59.2 | 65.2 |
| White, non-Hispanic | 29.2 | 35.6 | 43.1 | 49.7 | 55.3 |
| Black | 42.0 | 51.8 | 59.9 | 67.1 | 73.4 |
| Hispanic, all races | 45.2 | 55.0 | 62.0 | 69.6 | 76.5 |

*Source*: U.S. Census Bureau, 2006b, Table POV04.

wages when they do work. Nevertheless, the poverty rate of Hispanic couples is much below all groups of single mothers. Native American women are the poorest among single mothers, nearly half of whom live in poverty (U.S. Census Bureau, 2006a).

Employment does not provide an escape from poverty for single mothers, but it helps. Single mothers who were employed still had a poverty rate of about one in four (26%) in 2005, but the risk for those who did not work at all was nearly three times higher. Those working full-time, year-round had a poverty rate of 12%, less than half that of those who worked some time during the year (U.S. Census Bureau, 2006a).

The U.S. Census Bureau computes poverty rates for various multiples of the official standard. As Table 9.6 shows, the poverty rate of single mothers in 2005 ranged from over a third at the 100% standard to nearly two-thirds at the 200% level, a standard recommended by the moderately progressive Urban Institute. Poverty rates of black and Hispanic single mothers range from over two-fifths at the meager 100% standard to about three-fourths at the 200% level.

**Decline in single-mother poverty?** According to the official U.S. standard, poverty among single mothers has declined in recent years, particularly between 1995 and 2000, the years of low unemployment and increased labor market participation of single mothers (Table 9.7). Indeed, in 2000, the poverty rate of single mothers was the lowest in 20 years, but better times were short lived. Recession led to a rise in poverty but not

TABLE 9.7 Trends in Single-Mother Poverty by Race and Ethnicity, Percentages

| | All Races/Ethnicities | White | Black | Hispanic |
|---|---|---|---|---|
| 1990 | 44.5 | 33.5 | 48.1 | 58.2 |
| 1995 | 41.5 | 29.7 | 45.1 | 57.3 |
| 2000 | 33.0 | 24.6 | 34.3 | 42.9 |
| 2005 | 36.2 | 29.2 | 42.0 | 45.2 |

*Source*: U.S. Census Bureau, 2006d, table 4.

TABLE 9.8 Poverty Rates of Single-Mother Families by Marital Status, Race, and Ethnicity, 2005

| | Divorced | Separated | Never Married | Widowed | All Marital Statuses |
|---|---|---|---|---|---|
| All races/ethnicities | 22.3 | 43.4 | 47.5 | 26.6 | 36.2 |
| White | 19.6 | 38.3 | 44.0 | 19.3 | 29.1 |
| Black | 23.9 | 45.9 | 47.8 | 35.6 | 41.9 |
| Hispanic | 31.2 | 47.8 | 54.0 | 37.8 | 45.2 |

*Source*: U.S. Census Bureau, 2006a.

up to the level of the mid-1990s. However, especially for whites and to a lesser extent, blacks, poverty in 2005 was not substantially below the 1995 rate, particularly considering that the poverty threshold does not reflect changes in the standard of living. In fact, according to a relative poverty standard (less than 50% of median disposable income), there was hardly any change from the mid-1990s to 2004: 45.4% in 1994, 44.0% in 2000, and 43.7% in 2004 (Christopher, 2001; table 10.11).

**Feminized poverty?** The United States continues to have the two requisites for feminized poverty: prevalence of single motherhood and high rates of single-mother poverty in relation to other families with children. Consistently, about three-fifths of poor families with children (100% poverty standard) are single-mother families (calculated from U.S. Census Bureau, 2006d, table 4). On the basis of this, we refer to U. S. family poverty as feminized.

Minority status also plays an important part in family poverty. In 2005, three-fifths of poor single mothers were minority women (blacks, Asians, and Hispanics). Interestingly, as the poverty standard becomes higher, single-mother families become less dominant, and at levels of 175% and 200% of the standard, they are just under half (49.2% and 46.6%, respectively). Even at these higher levels, minority families, single or partnered, are over 55% of the total (U.S. Census Bureau, 2006b, table POV04). In the United States, poverty is both feminized and, perhaps to a greater extent, "minoritized."

**Differences among single mothers.** Marital status and race/ethnicity are sources of difference among single-mother families (Table 9.8). Divorced single mothers have the lowest poverty risk and widowed, the next lowest. Never-married mothers, with more than twice the poverty rate of their divorced counterparts, are most prone to poverty, followed closely by the small group of separated mothers. Indeed, although white, single mothers have the lowest poverty rate in all marital statuses, nonmarriage carries a higher poverty risk for whites than for black and Hispanic divorced or widowed mothers.

What are some factors that account for differences in poverty among the marital statuses? A class factor, educational attainment, is one. Divorced single mothers have the lowest poverty rates and are the best educated, with nearly three-fifths having some college or more. On the other hand, widows are the least well-educated—most likely to have less than a high school diploma, and least likely to have some college or more; yet their poverty rates are lower than all but divorced single mothers. One reason is that they and their children are likely to be eligible for Survivors' Insurance. Never-married mothers have the highest poverty rate but are not markedly less well educated than the others. Their poverty is related to their younger age and lesser likelihood of child support. Thirty percent are under age 25, compared to less than 5% of those in the other marital statuses (U.S. Census Bureau, 2006d). Thus, they are likely to have younger children and to face more limitations in employment.

## Immigrants

Because the large foreign-born population of the United States is heterogeneous, one should be cautious in drawing general conclusions about the conditions of these new Americans. Nearly half of the foreign born is of Hispanic origin, just under one-fourth is from Asia, one-fifth is white, non-Hispanic, largely of European origin, and the remainder, less than 10%, black.

**Education and employment**. The educational attainment of the foreign born is bi-modal (Table 9.9). On the one hand, they are much less likely

TABLE 9.9 Educational Attainment of Foreign and Native-Born Women, Ages 25–64, by Marital Status, 2005, Percentages

| | All Women | | Married Mothers | | Single Mothers | |
|---|---|---|---|---|---|---|
| | Native | Immigrant | Native | Immigrant | Native | Immigrant |
| < High school | 8.1 | 28.6 | 6.0 | 31.2 | 15.1 | 39.9 |
| High school diploma | 30.5 | 25.0 | 28.1 | 24.4 | 36.8 | 26.6 |
| Some college | 31.4 | 17.3 | 30.1 | 16.3 | 33.1 | 18.3 |
| B.A.+ | 30.1 | 29.2 | 35.9 | 28.2 | 15.0 | 15.1 |

*Source*: U.S. Census Bureau, 2006a.

than natives to have finished high school, and this, of course, hampers them severely in the labor market.

Possession of a bachelor's degree or more is, however, about the same for both native and immigrant women as a group. Among single mothers, however, native women are more likely to be college graduates. Single mothers, whether native or immigrant, are less likely to have a college degree than married mothers, but the absence of a high school education is particularly marked for immigrant single mothers, about two-fifths of whom are in this educational category, one that puts them at high risk of poverty. The same is true for married immigrant mothers, nearly one-third of whom have not finished high school.

Not surprisingly, immigrant women are concentrated in low-skill, low-wage work. In 2004, slightly over half earned less than twice the minimum wage, compared to two-fifths of native women (Capps, Fortuny, & Fox, 2007). Among native and immigrant men and women, the median income of immigrant women was the lowest: $21,000, compared to $25,000 for native women and immigrant men and $38,000 for native men (Capps et al., 2007).

**Missing benefits.** Cash benefits and services are deficient for all groups but especially for immigrants, thereby making it very unlikely that transfers would offset their labor market disadvantages. Noncitizen immigrants were three times as likely as native-born citizens to lack medical insurance (Ku, 2006). The changes in welfare law in 1996 made noncitizens ineligible for Food Stamps and reduced benefits for households containing mixtures of citizens and noncitizens.

**Poverty.** Disadvantaged in education, employment, and government benefits, immigrants, not surprisingly, are over a third more likely to be poor than natives (Table 9.10). Among single mothers, immigrants are only somewhat more likely to be poor than natives (40% vs. 36%) and are less at risk than black and Hispanic single mothers as a group (U.S. Census Bureau, 2006b and Table 9.5). Immigrants are nearly half of poor, Hispanic lone mothers and have a higher poverty rate than their native counterparts (13%). The poverty rate of immigrant families, both single and married-couple, is high and not as disparate as that of natives. Thus, immigrant family poverty is not feminized.

TABLE 9.10 Poverty Rates of Families with Children by Family Composition and Nativity, 2005

| | Married Couple | Single Mother | Total |
|---|---|---|---|
| Foreign born | 11.9 | 40.1 | 19.7 |
| Native | 4.4 | 35.7 | 13.4 |
| All families | 6.5 | 36.2 | 14.5 |

*Source*: U.S. Census Bureau, 2006a.

The proportion of all poor single mothers who are immigrants is just above the proportion of immigrants in the U.S. population: 14.3% versus 12.4%. Thus, the poverty rate of single mothers is minimally influenced by immigrant women. However, an undetermined number of immigrant women who have left their children behind are not counted as single mothers. They send much of their usually low salaries back home, stinting on themselves and suffering from the separation from their children (Ehrenreich & Hochschild, 2002; Parreñas, 2001). Not to mention the effect on offspring who are left behind while their parents care for the children of upper-income Americans. Nonpayment of social security payroll taxes for immigrant servants—revealed when a high-profile employer was considered for high public office—suggests that such women may be without pensions and at substantial risk of poverty in old age.

## Older Women

Comparative research spanning more than a decade has found that older women in the United States, particularly those who live alone, have higher poverty rates than those in other wealthy, developed nations (Smeeding & Sandström, 2005; Smeeding, Torrey, & Rainwater, 1993; Wu, 2005). Why is old age in a rich nation often anything but golden?

**Income.** The incomes of older people are derived from current employment, savings, private pensions, social insurance, and public assistance (Gornick, Munzi, Sierminska, & Smeeding, 2006; see also He, Sengupta, Velkoff, & DeBarros, 2005). Except for current employment and public assistance, their incomes are dependent on previous earnings and marital status. Those who have worked little, earned low wages, whose spouses had low wages, who were single mothers or young widows, or are minorities are unlikely to derive sufficient income from savings and private or public pensions. Nor is public assistance a real safety net. It is not at a level of minimum adequacy and is denied to most immigrants. Minority race and ethnicity are disadvantages with respect to all of these factors save public assistance; consequently older African-American and Hispanic women are at high risk of poverty.

Women married to lower-wage men are more likely than partners of higher-income men to become widows at an early age and are thus forced to stretch meager resources over a longer period (Sevak, Weir, & Willis, 2003/2004). Sevak and colleagues conclude that although widowhood increases the incidence of poverty among previously nonpoor women, "the substantial number of widows in poverty reflects poor economic status that continued from marriage into widowhood" (p. 31).

**Employment.** The gender gap in labor force participation persists in old age even though women tend to live longer and are more likely than men to need income from employment. In 2005, about 12% of women age 65 and older were in the labor force, compared to 19.0% of older men. For those age 70 and older, the figures for both were lower but the gender gap was even wider (U.S. Bureau of Labor Statistics, 2006, table 1). Employment after age 65 is often a way of supplementing inadequate retirement income. Indeed, some Social Security beneficiaries who work after receiving benefits become poor or near-poor when they stop working (Shaw & Yi, 1997).

Although they are likely to need the income more, older women with little education are less likely than better educated women to be in the labor force. One reason is the greater physical demands of their jobs. Of those older women with less than a high school diploma, approximately 6% are in the labor force, compared to more than twice that proportion with a college degree and nearly six times that rate with professional degrees or doctorates (U.S. Census Bureau, 2006a).

For a number of reasons, labor force participation of older workers has risen in the last decade: earnings of beneficiaries 65 years and older no longer lead to reductions in Social Security benefits; the retirement age for receipt of full Social Security benefits is rising; the number of individuals covered by defined-benefit private pensions has declined; and the number with defined-contribution plans increased.[14] And lower-income workers have suffered the steepest declines in employer pension coverage (Ghilalrducci, 2008). Employer coverage of retiree health benefits has declined; and out-of-pocket health costs have increased (Mosisa & Hippie, 2006). Social Security, though decreasing less than private pensions, has fallen as a result of lower replacement rates of former earnings and deductions from benefits for health insurance.

"Older people," writes pension expert, Teresa Ghilarducci, "are working more hours, postponing retirement, and going back to work after being retired, mainly because of the collapse of the pension system" (2008, p. 41). Retirement can mean the loss of a social role and of contacts in the workplace (Moen, Fields, Quick, & Hofmeister, 2000), and for some older people voluntary employment can have both economic and social benefits. Being forced to work in old age, however, is another thing.

One of the outstanding trends in the second half of the twentieth century was the exit of older workers from the labor market (Mosisa & Hippie, 2006). The wherewithal to *have* a retirement is one of the benefits made possible by Social Security (Aaron & Reichauser, 1998). Involuntary employment for people in the retirement years can be viewed as a form of recommodification, the loss of the right to opt out of the labor market in old age.

**Assets.** Even though the majority of the elderly receive some income from assets, the median amounts are only $1,330 for women and $1,650 for men (Shaw & Lee, 2005). According to the Luxembourg Wealth Study (LWS), nearly two-fifths of American older women lack financial assets equivalent to half the poverty threshold, meaning they do not have sufficient financial assets to live at the poverty line, even for 6 months (Gornick et al., 2006).

**Public income transfers.** Because most of the elderly have little or no income from employment, pensions, or assets, public income transfers—overwhelmingly Social Security—are the mainstay for many. Social Security supplies at least half of the income for 54% of elderly couples, and for almost three-fourths of nonmarried beneficiaries. Over two-fifths of nonmarried recipients rely on Social Security for 90% of their income (U.S. Social Security Administration, 2006, p. 7).

Social Security benefits are financed by equal payroll taxes on employers and employees. Full retirement benefits are based on earnings in the 35 highest-earning years out of the required 40 years in covered employment. Although women are disadvantaged by low earnings and interrupted employment, Social Security, to some extent, offsets these deficits. Especially important to women who tend to live longer than men are lifetime, inflation-protected benefits that, unlike defined contributions and assets, cannot run out. The progressive benefit formula of Social Security—providing a higher replacement rate for lower-wage workers, is some compensation for older women who had low and interrupted earnings. Further, spouses and former spouses (married 10 or more years) are eligible for retirement benefits equal to half their spouses' pensions and to survivors' benefits equal to those of their deceased spouse, if these benefits exceed those based on their own earnings. However, as Teresa Ghilarducci (2008) points out, when a main worker dies, the Social Security income of the surviving spouse drops by one-third, but, owing to fixed costs like housing, her household consumption is only 20% less.

With declining marriage rates fewer women in each successive cohort are likely to be eligible for spousal or widows' benefit, and while more will have longer and higher earnings, their own benefits are likely to remain lower than those of men (Harrington-Meyer, Wolf, & Hines, 2005). This is particularly true for black older women who are less likely to have been married than women of other races or ethnic groups.

One consequence of Social Security's male breadwinner model is a disadvantage for low-wage employed wives. If the benefit based on her own earnings is no more than half her spouse's benefit, she gets the same retirement benefit as the nonemployed wife whose husband's benefits and former earnings are the same as her husband's. Moreover, her income from Social Security is exceeded by that of a nonemployed wife whose husband earned more than hers.

There is no minimum benefit in Social Security that would serve as insurance against poverty. The average benefit for a retired female worker was just 11% above the poverty level ($10,408) and that of a widow, 24% above ($11,621), leaving many older women with benefits below those very meager thresholds (U.S. Social Security Administration, undated). The benefits of retired women reflect the low level and limited duration of earnings of this generation of older women and the higher benefits of widows than of women workers, the male breadwinner premise of Social Security. Although Social Security benefits have fallen less than employer pensions, its benefits have declined owing to an increase in premiums for health insurance that are deducted from Social Security payments, an increase in the retirement age and lower replacement rates.

Instead of working toward better safeguards against poverty, advocates have had to protect Social Security from privatization proposals that would reduce benefits and undermine the program's financial stability. Using unduly pessimistic projections about the future of the U.S. economy (DuBoff, 1997; Wray, 2005–2006),[15] proponents of privatization have undermined confidence in the program. Even though privatization is temporarily off the agenda, benefit cutbacks and predictions that Social Security will run out of money have reduced political support for the program among younger groups.

The poor elderly have recourse to public assistance—Supplemental Security Income (SSI). The SSI benefit was about three-fourths of the poverty level for an aged individual in 2002; half the states supplement the federal allowance, but even with the extra amount only a few exceed the paltry official poverty standard for individuals. Considered a means of "assisting recipients in escaping extreme poverty" (Davies et al., 2001–2002, p. 32), SSI benefits less than three-fifths of income-eligible elderly persons (U.S. House of Representatives, 2004, pp. 3–51). One reason for this is its very strict assets levels. In 1996, legal immigrants were denied SSI benefits, and despite subsequent easing of the restrictions, most still remain ineligible.

Although the elderly have better health coverage than younger people, out-of-pocket expenses cost women aged 65 and older nearly $2,400 in 2002. The Luxembourg Wealth Study calls attention to the relationship between the high rates of income and asset poverty of older American women and the burden of their health costs (Gornick et al., 2006). In 2003, Congress enacted limited coverage of prescription drugs in legislation that contained costly privatization options and limitations on federal general revenue funding that could burden beneficiaries of the Medicare program (Hacker & Marmor, 2003).

Medicaid, the federal-state health-care program for the poor that pays out-of-pocket costs of Medicare or the whole price for those who are uninsured, varies widely from state to state. According to one survey by the Public Citizen Health Resource Group, no state got high marks on an evaluation of eligibility, scope of services, quality of care, and reimbursement of providers, and "Almost all state programs ...[were] doing poorly in meeting all the[se] basic objectives" (Arellano & Wolfe, 2007, p. 35).

**Social isolation**. Poor, older persons who live alone—the majority of whom are women—"are more likely than seniors who live with others to be depressed, isolated, impoverished, fearful of crime, and removed from proximate sources of support than the elderly who live with others" (Klinenberg, 2002, pp. 44–45; see also, Pillemer & Glasgow, 2000). Today, there are an estimated 15,000 senior centers across the country serving about 10 million older persons and providing a wide range of social and recreational services that help mitigate social isolation (U.S. Administration on Aging, 2004). Yet, in relatively service-rich New York City, there is just one senior center for every 3638 seniors and only one for every 465 of the elderly poor (Gotbaum, 2002).

**Elder care**. For persons who need help with activities of daily living, community care is largely the responsibility of family members, especially women over the age of 55 (Eaton, 2005). In fact, 85% of elder care is provided free of charge by family and friends (U.S. Administration on Aging, 2002, cited by Eaton, 2005). Problems created by several converging social trends are highlighted in a study by Brenda Spillman and Liliana Pezzin (2000, p. 347): "Trends toward delayed childbearing and increased female labor-force participation ... suggest a growing 'sandwich generation,' especially of women who are caught between the demands of child rearing and elder care while attempting to play a more demanding role in the work force." Lone mothers would, of course, feel an even greater strain. Under these conditions, the elderly could stand to lose informal care or to experience the guilt that comes with dependence on adult children who have other demanding family and occupational responsibilities. There is a clear need for more publicly-funded formal care for the elderly.

Writing on the gendered dimension of elder care, Smith (2004) cites several studies that found approximately 70% of the unpaid care givers of the elderly are women who carry the responsibility of care irrespective of employment status. Medicaid is the main source of public funding for long-term care, the overwhelming amount of which is for institutional care even though most elderly persons who need assistance with daily living reside in the community (Smith, 2004).

Lacking economic and often social resources as well, many frail elderly women are only able to obtain the care they need in nursing homes which, owing to low reimbursement rates (Eaton, 2005) and deficient government standards (Bates, 1999), often provide inadequate care to the 4% of the elderly population who are institutionalized. With longer life expectancies and typically married to older men, women often care for their husbands but, as widows, lack care givers for themselves. Women are 70% of the lone elderly and the same proportion of the institutionalized elderly. There is a clear need for more publicly-funded formal care in the community.

**Income and poverty of lone older women**. Economic disadvantages early and later in life, demographic factors such as their greater longevity and likelihood of living alone, and inadequate private and public provision conspire to produce low incomes and high poverty rates for lone older women. Among those 65 years and older, the median incomes of elderly couples are between two and three times (2.6) that of lone elderly women.

TABLE 9.11 Poverty Rates of Elderly Persons, 65+, by Living Arrangem
Race, and Ethnicity, 2005

| | Female | | | | Male | | | |
|---|---|---|---|---|---|---|---|---|
| | White | Black | Hispanic | All | White | Black | Hispanic | All |
| Alone | 17.7 | 36.7 | 41.2 | 20.8 | 11.0 | 34.2 | 31.7 | 14.7 |
| Married | 2.8 | 9.8 | 10.7 | 4.0 | 3.1 | 12.0 | 12.1 | 4.5 |
| All | 10.0 | 25.3 | 22.0 | 12.3 | 5.1 | 20.1 | 17.0 | 7.3 |

*Source*: U.S. Census Bureau, 2006b, Tables POV01, POV02.

Although they are worse off than married couples, lone elderly men have median incomes approximately 40% higher than lone elderly women (U.S. Census Bureau, 2007, table HINC-02). The median income of lone elderly women is less than 200% of the U.S. poverty level, a threshold recommended by several experts.

Lone elderly women have a poverty risk 40% greater than their male counterparts (Table 9.11). Minority status and much higher poverty rates go together among the elderly. Foreign-born elderly persons have higher poverty rates than the native population (14.4% vs. 9.6%) but are less at risk than the Black and Hispanic populations as a whole (U.S. Census Bureau, 2006b). As with median incomes, there is a deep divide between the poverty of elderly married couples and those who live alone (Table 9.11). Indeed, elderly women who live alone have five times the poverty risk of their married counterparts.

Although lone elderly women are more likely to be poor than their male counterparts, the difference between the sexes is less than the gulf between living alone and being married. Elderly women, however, are much more likely to be alone and, in fact, are over 70% of that population. Here, too, minority status is an additional risk factor. Among older women living alone, whites are much less likely to be poor than Blacks or Hispanics. Older white males who live alone are not only much less at risk of poverty than their female counterparts but slightly less likely to be poor than married black and Hispanic men.

The marital status of elderly women, like that of lone mothers, carries different risks of poverty. The great divide, here, too, is first, between those women who have a partner and those who do not (Table 9.11). Among those who are alone, widows (the longer partnered) have the lowest risk of poverty but still almost five times that of their married counterparts, and about one in four of the divorced and never married are poor, compared to one in three separated older women (U.S. Census Bureau, 2006a). Whereas never-married lone mothers are the lone mothers most vulnerable to poverty, this is not the case for never-married older women, some of whom are childless and thus not subject to the motherhood penalty.

The poverty rate of lone elderly women fell nearly 13% between 1995 and 2005 whereas men's remained about the same (U.S. Census Bureau, 1996,

01). Women's gains could be a reflection of longer nger elderly. The decrease in poverty notwithstand- derly women were poor (2005). If the poverty of lone, sured by the relative standard of less than half the te was almost two-fifths (2004) (Table 10.4).

s, elderly poverty is even more feminized than fam- are almost four-fifths of the elderly poor who live bout the same whether the standard is 100%, 125%, e poverty level. Women predominate among the lone elderly but ore so among those who are poor (U.S. Census Bureau, 2006b, table POV01).

## Political Resources

The findings of this study imply that many women in the United States lack the political resources to overcome actual and potential poverty. The decline of organized labor is a loss to women. Powerful, popular movements advocating economic justice are nearly nonexistent. According to Theda Skocpol (2004), popular mass membership organizations have been eclipsed by professionally managed groups responsive to big donors and the interests of the highly educated and the wealthy. The result is a loss of opportunities for active civic participation by ordinary women and men Citizen groups abound, but, emphasizing quality-of-life issues that appeal to the more affluent, "they empower only part of the population" (Berry, 2004, p. 391).

**Women's movements and poor women**. The "second wave" of the U.S. women's movement made impressive gains in education, employment, cultural norms, and "body rights" (abortion, freedom from domestic violence, and sexual harassment at work) (for the last three, see, O'Connor, Orlof, & Shaver, 1999). According to one scholar of social movements (Epstein, 2002), feminism has become a "culture current" rather than a mass movement for social change. From the perspective of power, it is important to point out that two women's movements emerged in the last 40 years. One championed equal rights. The other, led by women associated with conservatism and the religious Right, defeated the Equal Rights Amendment, even though it was passed by both Houses of Congress and signed by the President (Mansbridge, 1986). The combined power of social and fiscal conservatives, the former often opposed to the feminist agenda on religious grounds and the latter to direct federal spending, has successfully defeated such policies as paid parental leave and direct child care subsidies for the nonpoor (although there are very modest tax expenditures for dependent child care) (Morgan, 2006).

The equal rights women's movement has been forced by the conservative women's movement and its allies to expend its energy and resources to protect the right to abortion. Whether she is pro-choice is the major criterion for supporting women candidates by EMILY'S List, the organization that has done much to promote the election of women to public office.

Many more women are in Congress than even a few years ago. A woman is Speaker of the House of Representatives—third in line for the presidency, a woman is secretary of state in the present and two past administrations, and in 2008, a woman narrowly lost the Democratic nomination for president, and another was the vice presidential nominee of the Republican party. Still, the United States ranks low in the proportion of women in Congress (18% of the Senate, 22% of the House of Representatives, 2008), and where will the women in government stand when it comes to issues other than abortion that are important to women of modest means? A movement less bogged down by a fight to maintain abortion rights and perhaps oriented toward other issues that affect poor and minority women—as it was in earlier decades—might be equally *pro-choice* and *pro-child-care*.[16]

The welfare rights movement of the 1960s has been regarded as a "movement of poor women" (West, 1981). Its leaders clearly recognized the connections among race, class, and gender (Nadasen, 2002) that this chapter highlights and that must inform a genuine anti-poverty movement in the United States. But the National Welfare Rights Organization (NWRO) did not even live to see the entitlement to welfare die. Since NWRO's demise, groups of low-income women focused on welfare have mobilized locally, independently, and often successfully (Davis, 1996).

Of possible potential for uniting the concerns of single mothers with the much larger group of partnered mothers is a newly formed organization, MomsRising. Its Motherhood Manifesto calls for policies still missing in the United States: paid family leave, affordable, accessible child care, and "realistic and fair wages." That single mothers are especially disadvantaged in the workplace is also emphasized as is the pressure and time bind that so many employed mothers suffer.[17]

What about resources for the elderly? The powerful American Association for Retired People (AARP) claimed a membership of 38 million people in 2007, but is not representative of the poor elderly. AARP sells health insurance and prescription drugs and supported the deeply flawed prescription drug legislation, Medicare Part D. Some more progressive, but very much less powerful organizations—the Older Women's League (OWL) and the Gray Panthers—advocate for elderly women.

**Potential resources.** Women need the state to overcome their inequality in the market and the family and have made gains everywhere, including the United States, when government has intervened on behalf of women's political, civil, and social rights. The assault on government *for* the people that gained ground with the administration of President Ronald Reagan and subsequent Republican administrations is a political setback for women.

Some hope lies in the fact that the American people, according to public opinion surveys, are less conservative than the media, economic elites, and most politicians (Cook & Barrett, 1992; Perlstein, 2007; Pew Research Center, 2007). This may be so, but these Americans are not organized or mobilized. U.S. history tells us that moderate Democrats like Franklin Roosevelt, John F. Kennedy, and Lyndon B. Johnson do not move on issues like unemployment, poverty, or civil rights unless pressured by mass movements and civil unrest. That will probably be true of Democrat Barack Obama who took office in January 2009. It is not clear whether or when such mobilization will again arise although economic crisis has been a critical catalyst in the past.

## Conclusion

There *are* no surprises, and despite the view that the elderly are the social policy winners, extending the study of women's poverty further along the life course offers no ground for optimism. Poverty remains feminized in the United States despite reduction in official poverty levels of both single mothers and lone elderly women since the mid-1990s. Yet, the poverty rates of both groups remain high, whether based on the very low, static, and unrealistic threshold of the United States or more realistic relative or absolute standards that register higher rates. Minority status stands along with gender in both risk and prevalence of poverty. And the less educated, as well, are more prone to poverty. Consequently, there is a need for anti-poverty strategies that target inequalities of gender, race, and class.

There were some grounds for optimism before the financial crisis. More single mothers were working, and with an increase in the minimum wage—after being frozen for 10 years—their incomes could have improved The Earned Income Tax Credit is a big boost to the incomes of those who are employed and earning incomes around the poverty level, but it does less for those with lower earnings and is no help to the unemployed. Still, there was and is no minimally adequate cash benefit for families with children or for the elderly. And in-kind benefits that pay for necessities such as housing, child, elder, and health care are insufficient.

**Reliance on the market**. The U.S. welfare regime relies more on the market than on the family or social welfare, but the market alone leaves millions of people poor and fails women and minorities disproportionately. Market failure is chronic in the United States, albeit less than in some other rich countries. Nevertheless, market or pre-transfer poverty is lower in some countries that do much more than the United States to reduce it, and is not significantly higher in countries that also do much more.[18] In the United States, in contrast to the other countries, disposable income must pay for all or part of health care of employable adults, except for very poor parents. Health care for the great majority of employable, nonelderly adults is financed through employment or privately, and under this system, almost 46 million Americans are uninsured (2007) and millions more inadequately served. Since most health care is employer-provided, rising unemployment means rising numbers of uninsured people.

If the preference is for market rather than social provision, then much more could be done to prevent market poverty. The United States is formally committed to minimum wage, anti-discrimination, and collective bargaining laws. The minimum wage could be a living wage, and the latter two could be more strictly enforced. Support for equalization policies has waned, but they remain justified because even the strictest compliance with anti-discrimination laws would fail to overcome the disadvantage of widespread and long-standing occupational segregation and outright racism and sexism in hiring and promotion. Research by the Institute for Women's Policy Research (Hartmann, Allen, & Owen, 1999) found that if women were paid the same as men for comparable work, even if only for the hours women currently work, poverty rates would fall by half for both single mothers and married women.

**Education**. Analysis of labor market conditions for women showed a deep divide along educational lines, particularly between those with and without a college education. The United States once ranked high in the percentage of its population who were college graduates but has been falling behind in that respect since the early 1990s. A particularly formidable barrier is the high cost of higher education, even in the public universities, and it is increasingly beyond the reach of many middle- and lower-income persons. The students from such families who do go on to higher education find themselves saddled with substantial debt as they begin their careers (Callan, 2006).

Higher education is a good strategy for individuals but is not a societal solution or panacea. According to the U.S. Bureau of Labor Statistics (2005), the principal post-secondary education or training for 12 of the 20 occupations with the greatest projected increases between 2004 and 2014—such as physical therapist aides, home health aides, medical assistants, dental assistants, retail salespersons—is on-the-job training. These jobs will continue to exist, and the workers who hold them perform vital services in the economy. These jobs should provide living wages and other rights *at* work. A tighter labor market would, as the experience of the late 1990s showed, help disadvantaged workers, especially low-wage women and minorities, to earn higher wages.

**Job creation and public investment**. A strategy to create living-wage jobs that would reduce chronic unemployment and at the same time rebuild or expand the nation's physical and social infrastructure was important before the economic crisis of 2008 (Ginsburg & Goldberg, 2007). Such an approach would simultaneously address the country's double deficits: its chronic unemployment and underemployment, on the one hand, and on the other, its unsafe bridges, weak dams and levees, deep deficiencies in public transportation and affordable housing, and serious undersupply of child and elder care. For a nation facing its deepest recession, perhaps even depression, since the 1930s, such a program is an urgently needed economic stimulus. Crises can be opportunities, not only for recovery but for permanent reform. As Harry Hopkins, the administrator of federal relief programs in the Great Depression and a close advisor to President Franklin Roosevelt expressed it: "Recovery connotes ... a policy of reconstruction in which the social order will be amended to include the right of people to work and an assurance of benefits for the workers that ... are grounded in the fabric of social justice" (1933/1966, p. 158).

An increase in living-wage jobs would, of course, benefit women, particularly those who support themselves. However, improved labor market conditions will not be enough. These will not pay child support (except indirectly if some men earn more *and* meet their obligations). And what about the single intervention that would do most to reduce women's discontinuity in the labor market: affordable child care that supports children and families and also creates jobs for women. And what about paid parental leave that would enable parents to nurture their newborn children with less financial loss?

Older women would, in the future, benefit from the reforms that reduce poverty during the working years and from enforcement of antiageist laws that offer the opportunity to remain at work if they chose to do so. These expanded employment opportunities, along with child care, would also increase their lifetime earnings, hence Social Security benefits in their own right. Present dependent and survivor policies support a model that is no longer the norm, but in the interest of choice should be continued along with adoption of those that give greater recognition to the career interruptions that motherhood continues to entail. An adequate, minimum Social Security benefit could do much to reduce elderly poverty.

For women of all ages, races, ethnic, and national origins, increased political resources are the basis for reforms that offer more choice, more autonomy, and the opportunity to invent policies that may well meet their needs, perhaps more effectively than those envisaged here. With political will, there is always a way, particularly in a country with still abundant—if currently so unequally distributed—resources.

## Notes

1 Business elites, of course, continued to welcome corporate welfare. For documentation of corporate welfare, see Abramovitz (2001).

2 A major contributor to the low unemployment rates was the stock market bubble that burst in 2001, ushering in a recession. For an analysis of the economic policies of President Bill Clinton (1993–2001), see Robert Pollin's *Contours of Descent* (2003, esp. pp. 221–248). Pollin refers to Clinton's "hollow boom."

3 The authors identify three other strategies: the "carer strategy" that is close to the male breadwinner-female caregiver approach; the "choice strategy" in which women are valued and rewarded for providing care but also encouraged

to engage in employment; and the "earner-carer strategy" in which both women and men balance informal carework and employment.

4 A few states have temporary disability insurance that covers pregnancy. For example, New York State covers pregnancy under its Disability Benefits program for a maximum of 26 weeks or half a year.

5 The federal government shared responsibility with the states for financing Aid to Families with Dependent Children and does so for TANF. The lifetime limit is on support from the federal government. States may place stricter limits—and some do, or, like New York, may finance benefits beyond the 5-year limit with their own funds.

6 The Taft-Hartley Act of 1947 also made it more difficult to organize in states where unionization was low. It allowed union shop agreements but permitted states to pass laws outlawing them. Approximately 20 states have enacted so-called "right-to-work" laws that outlaw union shops.

7 Democrat Bill Clinton made more friendly appointments to the National Labor Relations Board but supported trade treaties that failed to protect workers' rights and did not vigorously advocate legislation protecting strikers (Galenson, 1996).

8 The U.S. unemployment rate was considerably below the continental European countries in this study, but if all of the jobless, the underemployed, and working poor are counted, it still has a loose labor market. In January 2007, when the official unemployment rate was 4.4% or 6.7 million persons, an additional 4.3 million were involuntary part timers, and 4.5 million wanted jobs but weren't counted because they were not looking for work, making this "hidden employment" greater than official unemployment. Seventeen million people or 16.2% of the workforce were employed year-round for less than the four-person poverty standard (National Jobs for All Coalition, 2007, using figures from the U.S. Department of Labor and the U.S. Bureau of the Census).

9 There is some fiscal welfare to offset costs of care for both children and other family members. For families with $15,000 adjusted gross income or less, the Child Care and Dependent Tax Credit is worth up to $1050 a year for one child and $2100 for two or more children, depending on care expenses. Since 2001 the credit has been refundable.

10 However, some single mothers and their children get Survivors' Insurance or non-means-tested unemployment insurance.

11 The Luxembourg Income Study (LIS) includes the EITC in calculating relative poverty standards and the poverty-reduction effects of income transfers. Using a higher poverty standard than the US measure (less than 50% of median disposable income) LIS reported a poverty reduction rate for US lone mothers half the average for the other countries in this study (excluding Japan which is not in the LIS database) (Table 10.10). Using U.S. Census Bureau data, the Center on Budget and Policy Priorities estimated that the EITC lifted 4.4 million people out of poverty in 2003 (Greenstein, 2005). For a summary of research on the EITC, see Hotz & Scholz (2003).

12 For a full-time, year-round worker, the value of the minimum wage alone was 120% of the official poverty standard for a family of three in 1968. The 2006 value of the minimum wage, plus the Earned Income Tax Credit for a family of three with two children was 94% of the poverty standard. Even with the rise in the minimum wage in 2007, the combined value of the minimum wage and the EITC will be well below the real value of the minimum wage alone in 1968.

However, some states have EITCs in addition to the federal benefit, and these raise the combined minimum wage and EITC supplements to a higher level.

13 Moffitt and Rendall's estimates are from the national Panel Study of Income Dynamics (PSID). Whereas the U.S. Census Bureau data that are used for most of this analysis pertain to female householders with no spouse present living with children under 18 years of age, the PSID data include both household heads and subfamily heads.

14 A defined benefit plan generally provides pensions based on a percentage of the retiree's final pay, according to years of service in one's place of employment, and is typically paid as an annuity. In defined-contribution plans a specific payment out of each pay check is placed in an employee-specific account to which an employee often adds a partially or fully matched contribution (Campbell & Munnell, 2002). As Campbell and Munnell point out the defined contribution plans provide more flexibility and portability for employees and less cost and risk for employers. As the name connotes, employees are not assured any specific benefit upon retirement.

15 For example, the Trustees of Social Security funds based their predictions of a shortfall in 2042 on a real GDP growth rate of only 1.8% for most of the next 75 years, whereas the U.S. economy has grown by an amount equal to 3.4% over the past 75 years.

16 For an interesting discussion of the relationship between NOW and the National Welfare Rights Organization, see Martha Davis (1996), who emphasizes the commitment to welfare rights of NOW's leadership, if not its largely white, middle-class general membership. She also identifies some conflicts arising partly out of NOW's emphasis on mothers' right not to work and NOW's primary concern for women's rights at work. Davis concludes that "A closer working relationship between welfare rights activists and women's rights activists would have required both groups to confront and reconcile their differences around the issues of work, motherhood, and child care, perhaps developing a nuanced view that accounted for class and race differences, and even ceding some of their principles (at least for the time being) in order to move beyond the impasse that inhibited true collaboration" (p. 162).

17 Rowe-Finkbeiner (2004, p. 32) calls attention to the "persistent wage gap between women and men and an even larger wage gap between mothers and nonmothers, with single mothers taking the largest wage hit of them all." In their Motherhood Manifesto, Blades and Rowe-Finkbeiner (2006) draw on the work already cited here of Correll & Bernard (2007) and Waldfogel (1998) regarding labor market discrimination against mothers and, especially, single mothers. However, the Manifesto falls short of health care for all (calling only for "Healthcare for All Kids"), and its call for "Realistic and Fair Wages" that would make it possible for two full-time working parents to earn enough to support a family could leave the single earner, single parent without enough. There is also *The Motherhood Manifesto* DVD Video, October 18, 2006, the cover of which pictures a working woman, Rosie the Riveter (the symbol of Second World War working women) holding a baby. Kim Gandy, President of NOW, takes part in the video and makes the case for universal child care, perhaps suggesting more emphasis on this policy by the major organization in the U.S. women's movement, even though this is not one of the main issues listed on NOW's website (visited May 1, 2008).

18
Pre- and Post-transfer Poverty Rates[a] and Percent Poverty Reduction, c. 2000

| | Pre-transfer | Post-transfer | % Reduction |
|---|---|---|---|
| Finland | 18.1 | 5.4 | 70.2 |
| Netherlands | 21.6 | 8.9 | 58.8 |
| U.S. | 23.7 | 17.0 | 28.3 |
| Canada | 24.8 | 11.9 | 52.0 |
| Germany | 28.6 | 8.2 | 71.3 |
| Sweden | 29.2 | 6.4 | 78.1 |
| U.K. | 31.8 | 12.3 | 61.3 |

[a]Less than 50% MDI.
*Source*: Smeeding, 2005, figure 2.

## References

Aaron, H. J., & Reischauer, R. D. (1998). *Countdown to reform: The great Social Security debate.* New York: The Century Foundation Press.

Abramovitz, M. (2001). Everyone is still on welfare: The role of redistribution in social policy. *Social Work, 46,* 297–308.

Altman, J. C., & Goldberg, G. S. (2007). The quality of life paradox: A study of fomer public assistance recipients. *Journal of Poverty, 11,* 4, 71–90.

Allegretto, S. (2005). *Basic family budgets.* Briefing Paper # 165. Washington, DC: Economic Policy Institute. http://www.epi.org/content.cfm/bp165. Accessed July 29, 2009.

Anderson, T. H. (2004). *The pursuit of fairness: A history of affirmative action.* New York: Oxford University Press.

Arellano, A. B. de, & Wolfe, S. M. (2007). *Unsettling scores: Ranking of state Medicaid programs.* Washington, DC: Public Citizen Health Resource Group. http://www2.citizen.org/hrg/medicaid/assets/reports/2007UnsettlingScores.pdf. Accessed July 30, 2009.

Bates, E. (1999). The shame of our nursing homes. *The Nation,* March 29, 11–19.

Bernstein, J., & Baker, D. (2003). *The benefits of full employment: When markets work for people.* Washington, DC: Economic Policy Institute.

Berry, J. M. (1999). The rise of citizen groups. In T. Skocpol & M. F. Fiorina (Eds.), *Civid engagement in American democracy* (pp. 367–394). Washington, DC: Brookings Institution Press.

Blades, J., & Rowe-Finkbeiner, K. (2006). The motherhood manifesto. *The Nation,* May 22, 11–16.

Blau, F. D., & Kahn, L. M. (2006). The gender pay gap: Going, going … but not gone. In Francine D. Blau, M. C. Brinton, & David B. Grusky (Eds.), *The declining significance of gender?* (pp. 37–66). New York: Russell Sage.

Burt, M., Aron, L. Y., Lee, E., & Valente, J. (2001). *Helping America's homeless: Emergency shelters or affordable housing?* Washington, DC: Urban Institute Press.

Callan, P. M. (2006). College affordability: Colleges, states increase financial burden on students and families. *In National report card on higher education* (pp. 19–22). San Jose, CA: National Center on Public Policy and Higher Education. http://measuringup.highereducation.org/_docs/2006/NationalReport_2006.pdf. Accessed July 30, 2009.

Campbell, S., & Munnell, A. H. (2002). *Sex and 401(k) plans: Just the facts on retirement issues.* May, No. 4. Boston: Center for Retirement Research at Boston College.
Capps, R., Fortuny, K., & Fox, M. (2007). *Trends in the low-wage immigrant labor force, 2000–2005.* Washington, DC: Urban Institute. http://www.urban.org/UploadedPDF/411426_Low-Wage_Immigrant_Labor.pdf. Accessed July 30, 2008.
Christopher, K. (2001). *Welfare state regimes and mothers' poverty.* Luxembourg Income Study Working Paper No. 286. Luxemborg: Luxembourg Income Study. www.lisproject.org/publications/liswps/286.pdf. Accessed July 30, 2009.
Cook, F. L., &. Barrett, E. J. (1992). *Support for the American welfare state: The views of Congress and the public.* New York: Columbia University Press.
Correll, S. J., & Bernard, S. (2007). Getting a job: Is there a motherhood penalty? *American Journal of Sociology, 112,* 5, 1297–1338.
Davies, P. S., Huynh, M., Newcomb, C., O'Leary, P., Rupp, K., & Sears, J. (2001–2002). Modeling SSI financial eligibility and simulating the effects of policy options. *Social Security Bulletin, 64,* 2, 15–44.
Davis, M. F. (1996). Welfare rights and women's rights in the 1960s. *Journal of Policy History, 8,* 1, 144–165.
DeNavas-Walt, C., Proctor, B. D., & Lee, C. H. (2006). *Income, poverty, and health insurance coverage in the United States: 2005.* Current Population Reports, P60–231. Washington, DC: U.S. Government Printing Office. http://www.census.gov/prod/2006pubs/p60–231.pdf. Accessed July 30, 2009.
DuBoff, R. B. (1997) The welfare state, benefits, privatization: The case of Social Security in the United States. *International Journal of Health Services, 1,* 1, 1–23.
Eaton, S. C. (2005). Eldercare in the United States: Inadequate, inequitable, but not a lost cause. *Feminist Economics, 11,* 2, 37–51.
Edin, K., & Lein, L. (1997). *Making ends meet: How single mothers survive welfare and low-wage work.* New York: Russell Sage Foundation.
Ehrenreich, B. (2002). *Nickled and dimed. On (not) getting by in America.* New York: Henry Holt.
Ehrenreich, B., & Hochschild, A. R. (Eds.). (2002). *Global woman: Nannies, maids and sex workers in the new economy.* New York: Metropolitan/Owl Books.
England, P. (2006). Toward gender equality: Progress and bottlenecks. In F. D. Blau, M. C. Brinton, & D. B. Grusky (Eds.), *The declining significance of gender?* (pp. 245–264). New York: Russell Sage.
Epstein, B. (2002). Feminist consciousness: After the women's movement. *Monthly Review, 54,* 4, 31–37.
Esping-Andersen, G. (1990). *The three worlds of welfare capitalism.* Princeton, NJ: Princeton University Press.
Figart, D. M., & Hartmann, H. I. (2000). Broadening the concept of pay equity. In R. Baiman, H. Boushey, & D. Saunders (Eds.), *Political economy and contemporary capitalism: Radical perspectives on economic theory and policy* (pp. 1285–1293). Armonk, NY: M. E. Sharpe.
Galenson, W. (1996). *The American labor movement: 1914–1995.* Westport, CT: Greenwood Press.
Ghilarducci, T. (2008). *When I'm sixty-four: The plot against pensions and the plan to save them.* Princeton, NJ: Princeton University Press.
Ginsburg, H. L, & Goldberg, G. S. (2007). The drive for decent work: A big step toward shared prosperity. *New labor forum, 16,* 3 , 123–133.

Goldberg, G. S. (2002). The United States of America: More than reluctant. In G. S. Goldberg & M. G. Rosenthal (Eds.), *Diminishing welfare: A cross-national study of social provision* (pp. 33–74). Westport, CT: Auburn House.

Goldberg, G. S., & Collins, S. D. (2001). *Washington's new poor law: Welfare "reform" and the roads not taken, 1935 to the present*. New York: Apex Press.

Goldberg, G. S., & Kremen, E. (1990). The feminization of poverty: Discovered in America. In G. S. Goldberg & E. Kremen (Eds.), *The feminization of poverty: Only in America?* (pp. 1–15). New York: Praeger.

Gornick, J. C., Munzi, T., Sierminska, E., & Smeeding, T. (2006). Older women's income and wealth packages: The five-legged stool in cross-national perspective. Working Paper No. 3, Luxembourg: Luxembourg Wealth Studies. http://www.lisproject.org/publications/lwswps/lws3.pdf. Accessed July 30, 2009.

Gotbaum, B. (2002). *Just getting by: New York City nutrition services for seniors*. New York: Public Advocate for the City of New York. http://pubadvocate.nyc.gov/policy/pdfs/Senior_hunger.pdf. Accessed July 30, 2009.

Greenstein, R. (2005). *The Earned Income Tax Credit: Boosting employment, aiding the working poor*. Washington, DC: Center on Budget and Policy Priorities. http://www.cbpp.org/7–19–05eic.htm. Accessed July 29, 2009.

Hacker, J. S., & Marmor, T. R. (2003). *Medicare reform: Fact, fiction and foolishness. Public policy and aging report*. Washington, DC: National Academy on an Aging Society.

Harrington-Meyer, M., Wolf, D. A., & Himes, C. L. (2005). Linking benefits to marital status: Race and Social Security in the US. *Feminist Economics, 11*, 2, 145–162.

Hartmann, H., Allen, K., & Owens, C. (1999). *Equal pay for working families*. IWPR Publication #344. Washington, DC: Institute for Women's Policy Research.

Hartmann, H., Rose, S. J., & Lovell, V. (2006). How much progress in closing the long-term earnings gap? In F. D. Blau, M. C. Brinton, & D. B. Grusky (Eds.), *The declining significance of gender?* (pp. 125–155). New York: Russell Sage.

He, W., Sengupta, M., Velkoff, V. A., & DeBarros, K. A. (2005). *65+ in the United States: 2005*. Current Population Reports, P23–209. Washington, DC: U.S. Government Printing Office.

Helburn, S. W., & Bergmann, B. (2003). *America's child care problem: The way out*. New York: Palgrave Macmillan.

Heymann, J. (2006). *Forgotten families: Ending the growing crisis confronting children and working parents in the global economy*. Oxford: Oxford University Press.

Hopkins, H. (1933/1966). The war on distress. *Today, 1* (December 16, 1933), 8–9, 23. Excerpted in H. Zinn (Ed.), *New deal thought* (pp. 151–158). Indianapolis: Bobbs-Merrill

Hotz, V. J., & Scholz, J. K. (2003). The earned income tax credit. In R. A. Moffitt (Ed.), *Means-tested transfer programs in the United States* (pp. 141–197). Chicago: University of Chicago Press.

Kellough, J. E. (2006). *Understanding affirmative action: Politics, discrimination, and the search for justice*. Washington, DC: Georgetown University Press.

Kilkey, M., & Bradshaw, J. (1999). Lone mothers, economic well-being, and policies. In D. Sainsbury (Ed.), *Gender and welfare state regimes* (pp. 147–184). London: Oxford University Press.

Klinenberg, E. (2002). *Heat wave: A social autopsy of disaster in Chicago*. Chicago: University of Chicago Press.

Ku, L. (2006). *Why immigrants lack adequate access to health care and health insurance.* Washington, DC: Center for Budget and Policy Priorities. http://www.migrationinformation.org/Feature/display.cfm?id=417. Accessed July 29, 2009.

Lower-Basch, E. (2007). *Improving access to education and training for TANF participants.* Washington, DC: Center on Law and Social Policy. http://www.clasp.org/publications/tanf_Ed_2pgr.pdf. Accessed July 30, 2009.

Luxembourg Income Study (LIS). (2007). *Key Figures as of 21 June 07.* Luxembourg: Author. http://www.lisproject.org/keyfigures/full_kf.xls. Accessed July 30, 2009.

Luxembourg Income Study (LIS). (2008). United States—6th Wave. Calculation by Ann Morissens.

MacEwan, A. (2009). Inequality, power, and ideology: Getting it right about the causes of the economic crisis. *Dollars & Sense, 281,* March/April, 23–31.

Madrick, J., & Papanikolaou, N. (2008). *The stagnation of male wages. Policynote.* New York: Schwartz Center for Economic Policy Analysis, The New School.

Mansbridge, J. J. (1986). *Why we lost the ERA.* Chicago: University of Chicago Press.

Messer-Davidow, E. (2002). *Disciplining feminism: From social activism to academic discourse.* Durham, NC: Duke University Press.

Mishel, L., Bernstein, J., & Allegretto, S. (2007). *The state of working America 2006/2007.* Ithaca, NY: ILR Press.

Misra, J., Moller, S., & Budic, M. J. (2007). Work-family policies and poverty for partnered and single women in Europe and North America. *Gender & Society, 21,* 6, 804–827.

Moen, P., Fields, V., Quick, H. E., & Hofmeister, H. (2000). A life-course approach to retirement and social integration. In K. A. Pillemer, P. Moen, E. Wethington, & N. Glasgow (Eds.), *Social integration in the second half of life* (pp. 75–107). Baltimore: Johns Hopkins Press.

Moffitt, R. A., & Rendall, M. S. (1995). Cohort trends in the lifetime distribution of female family headship in the United States, 1968–1985. *Demography, 32,* 3, 407–424.

Morgan, K. J. (2006).*Working mothers and the welfare state: Religion and the politics of work-family policies in Western Europe and the United States.* Stanford: Stanford University Press.

Mosisa, A., & Hippie, S. (2006). Trends in labor force participation in the United States. *Monthly Labor Review, 129,* 10, 35–57.

Nadasen, P. (2002). Expanding the boundaries of the women's movement: Black feminism and the struggle for women's rights. *Feminist Studies, 28,* 2, 271–301.

National Alliance to End Homelessness. (2007a). *Fact checker: Homeless families & poverty.* Washington, DC: Author. http://www.endhomelessness.org/content/article/detail/1525. Accessed July 29, 2009.

National Alliance to End Homelessness. (2007b). *Explainer: Why is homelessness an important issue?* Washington, DC: Author. http://www.endhomelessness.org/content/article/detail/1074. Accessed July 29, 2009.

National Organization for Women. Website. Washington, DC: Author. http://www.now.org/. Accessed July 29, 2009.

Nation's Network of Child Care Resources & Referral Agencies . (2006). *Breaking the piggy-bank: Parents and the high price of child care.* Arlington, VA: Author. http://www.naccrra.org/docs/policy/breaking_the_piggy_bank.pdf. Accessed July 30, 2009.

Newman, K. S. (2006). *Chutes and ladders: Navigating the low-wage labor market.* New York: Russell Sage.

O'Connor, J. S., Orloff, A. S., & Shaver, S. (1999). *States, markets, families: Gender, liberalism and social policy in Australia, Canada, Great Britain and the United States.* Cambridge: Cambridge University Press.

Organisation for Economic Co-operation and Development (OECD). (2007). *OECD in figures, 2006–2007.* Paris: Author. http://www.oecd.org/document/43/0,3343,en_2649_34489_37806443_1_1_1_1,00.html. Accessed July 29, 2009.

Palley, E. (2008). Who cares for children? Why are we where we are with American child care policy? Paper presented at the Law and Society Annual Conference, Montreal, May 30, 2005.

Parreñas, R. S. (2002). *Servants of globalization: Women, migration and domestic work.* Stanford, CA: Stanford University Press.

Parrott, S., & Sherman, A. (2006). *TANF at 10: Program results are more mixed than often understood.* Washington, DC: Center on Budget and Policy Priorities. http://www.cbpp.org/8–17–06tanf.htm. Accessed July 29, 2009.

Pearce, D. (2004). *How work supports impact family budgets: An analysis of the interaction of public policies and wages.* Washington, DC: Wider Opportunities for Women. http://wowonline.org/docs/dynamic-CTTA-45.pdf. Accessed July 6, 2007.

Perlstein, R. (2007). Will the progressive majority emerge? *The Nation,* July 9, 11–16.

Pew Research Center for the People and the Press. (2007). *Political landscape more favorable to Democrats: Trends in political values and core attitudes: 1997–2007.* Washington, DC: Author.

Pillemer, K. A., & Glasgow, N. (2000). Social integration and aging: Background and trends. In K. A. Pillemer, P. Moen, E. Wethington, & N. Glasgow (Eds.), *Social integration in the second half of life* (pp. 19–47). Baltimore: Johns Hopkins Press.

Piven, F. F., & Cloward, R. A. (1993). *Regulating the poor: The functions of public welfare,* updated ed. New York: Vintage Books.

Pollin, R. (Ed.). (2003). *Contours of descent: U.S. economic fractures and the landscape of global austerity.* London: Verso.

Ross, D. C., Cox, L., & Marks, C. (2007). *Resuming the path to health coverage for children and parents: A 50 state update on eligibility rules, enrollment and renewal procedures in Medicaid and SCHIP in 2006.* Washington, DC: Kaiser Commission on Medicaid and the Uninsured. http://www.kff.org/medicaid/upload/7608.pdf. Accessed July 30, 2009.

Rowe-Finkbeiner, K. (2004). *The F word: Feminism in jeopardy: Women, politics and the future.* Emeryville, CA: Seal Press.

Schrecker, E. (2000). McCarthyism and organized labor: Fifty years of lost opportunities. *WorkingUSA,* January-February, 93–101.

Schulman, K., & Blank, H. (2006). *State child care assistance policy 2006: Gaps remain, with new challenges ahead.* Washington, DC: National Women's Law Center. http://www.nwlc.org/pdf/StateChildCareAssistancePoliciesReport2006.pdf. Accessed July 30, 2009.

Sevak, P., Weir, D. R., & Willis, R. J. (2003/2004). The economic consequences of a husband's death: Evidence from the HRS and AHEAD. *Social Security Bulletin, 65,* 3, 3–44.

Shaw, L. B., & Lee, S. (2005). Growing old in the U.S.: Gender and income adequacy. *Feminist Economics, 11,* 2, 174–185.

Shaw, L. B., & Yi, H. (1997). How elderly women become poor: Findings from the new beneficiary data system. *Social Security Bulletin, 60,* 4, 46–50.

Skocpol, T. (2004). The narrowing of civic life. *American Prospect, 15*, 6, A5–7.

Smeeding, T. M. (2005). *Government programs and social outcomes: The United States in comparative perspective*. Luxembourg Income Study Working Paper No. 426. Luxembourg: Luxembourg Income Study. http://www.lisproject.org/publications/liswps/426.pdf. Accessed July 30, 2009.

Smeeding, T. M., & Sandstrom, S. (2005). Poverty and income maintenance in old age: A cross-national view of low-income older women. *Feminist Economics, 11*, 2, 163–186.

Smeeding, T. M., Torrey, B. B., & Rainwater, C. (1993). International perspectives on the economic status of the United States aged. Luxembourg Income Study Working Paper No. 87. Luxembourg: Luxembourg Income Study. http://www.lisproject.org/publications/liswps/87.pdf. Accessed July 30, 2009.

Smith, P. R. (2004). Elder care, work and gender: The work-family issue of the 21st century. *Berkeley Journal of Employment and Labor Law, 25*, 2, 351–399.

Spillman, B. C., & Pezzin, L. E. (2000). Potential and active family caregivers: Changing networks and the "sandwich generation." *Milbank Quarterly, 78*, 3, 347–374.

Stricker, F. (2007). *Why America lost the war on poverty—and how to win it*. Chapel Hill: University of North Carolina Press.

Urban Institute. (2006). *Housing America's low-income families*. Washington, DC: Author. http://www.urban.org/toolkit/issues/housing.cfm#findings. Accessed July 29, 2009.

U.S. Administration on Aging. (2004). *Senior centers*. Washington, DC: Author. http://www.aoa.gov/prof/notes/Docs/Senior_Centers.pdf. Accessed August 4, 2007.

U.S. Bureau of Labor Statistics. (n.d.). Unpublished data from the Current Population Survey. Washington, DC: Author.

U.S. Bureau of Labor Statistics (USBLS). (2005). *Women in the labor force: A databook, 2005 edition*. Washington, DC: Author. http://www.bls.gov/cps/wlf-databook-2005.pdf. Accessed July 29, 2009.

U.S. Bureau of Labor Statistics (USBLS). (2006). *Women in the labor force: A databook, 2006 edition*. Washington, DC: Author. http://www.bls.gov/cps/wlf-databook2006.htm. Accessed July 29, 2009.

U.S. Bureau of Labor Statistics (USBLS). (2007a). *Civilian labor force participation rates approximating U.S. concepts by sex, 1960–2006*. Washington, DC: Author. http://www.bls.gov/fls/flscomparelf.htm. Accessed July 29, 2009.

U.S. Bureau of Labor Statistics (USBLS). (2007b). *Comparative real gross domestic product per capita and per employed person: Fifteen countries, 1960–2006*. Washington, DC: Author. http://www.bls.gov/fls/flsgdp.pdf. Accessed July 29, 2009.

U.S. Bureau of Labor Statistics (USBLS). (2007c). *Union members in 2006. News, BLS*. Washington, DC: Author. http://www.bls.gov/news.release/union2.nr0.htm. Accessed July 29, 2009.

U.S. Bureau of Labor Statistics (USBLS). (2008). *Mass layoffs in November 2008. USDL 08–1829*. Washington, DC: Author. http://www.bls.gov/news.release/mmls.nr0.htm. Accessed July 29, 2009.

U.S. Census Bureau. (1961). *Household and family characteristics: March 1960*. Current Population Reports, Series P-20, No. 106. Washington, DC: U.S. Government Printing Office.

U.S. Census Bureau. (1996). *Detailed poverty tabulations from the Current Population Survey*. Washington, DC: Author. http://www.census.gov/hhes/www/poverty/detailedpovtabs.html. Accessed July 29, 2009.

U.S. Census Bureau. (2006a). *Current Population Survey, Annual Social and Economic Supplement, 2006*. Washington, DC: Author. http://www.census.gov/hhes/www/cpstc/cps_table_creator.html. Accessed July 29 2009.

U.S. Census Bureau. (2006b). *Detailed poverty tabulations from the Current Population Survey*. Washington, DC: Author. http://www.census.gov/hhes/www/poverty/detailedpovtabs.html. Accessed July 29, 2009.

U.S. Census Bureau. (2006c). *Historical income tables*. Washington, DC: Author. http://www.census.gov/hhes/www/income/histinc/inchhtoc.html. Accessed July 29, 2009.

U.S. Census Bureau. (2006d). *Historical poverty tables*. Washington, DC: Author. http://www.census.gov/hhes/www/poverty/histpov/histpovtb.html. Accessed July 29, 2009.

U.S. Census Bureau. (2007). *Current Population Survey, Annual Social and Economic Supplement, 2007*. Washington, DC: Author. http://pubdb3.census.gov/macro/032007/hhinc/new02_000.htm. Accessed July 29, 2009.

U.S. Congress. (1996). *Public Law 104–193. Personal Responsibility and Work Opportunity Reconciliation Act of 1996*. Washington, DC: Author.

U.S. Department of Agriculture, Food and Nutrition Service. (2008). *Food Stamp participation rates: 2006*. Washington, DC: Author. http://www.fns.usda.gov/ora/MENU/published/SNAP/SNAPPartState.htm. Accessed August 10, 2009.

U.S. House of Representatives, Committee on Ways and Means. (2004). *2004 Green Book: Background material and data on the programs within the jurisdiction of the Committee on Ways and Means*. Washington, DC: Author. http://www.gpoaccess.gov/wmprints/green/2004.html. Accessed July 29, 2009.

U.S. Social Security Administration. (undated). *Social Security on-line: Beneficiary data*. Washington, DC: Author. http://ssa.gov/OACT/ProgData/icp.html. Accessed July 29, 2009.

U.S. Social Security Administration. (2006). *Fast facts & figures about Social Security, 2006*. Washington, DC: Author. http://www.socialsecurity.gov/policy/docs/chartbooks/fast_facts/2006/fast_facts06.pdf. Accessed July 30, 2009.

Waldfogel, J. (1998). Understanding the "family gap" in pay for women with children. *Journal of Economic Perspectives, 12*, 1, 137–156.

West, G. (1981). *The National Welfare Rights Movement: The social protest of poor women*. New York: Praeger.

Wilensky, H. L. (1965). The problems and prospects of the welfare state. In H. L. Wilensky & C. N. Lebeaux (Eds.), *Industrial society and social welfare: The impact of industrialization on the supply and organization of social welfare services in the United States* (pp. v–lii). New York: Free Press.

Wray, L. R. (2005/6). *Social Security's 70th anniversary: Surviving 20 years of reform*. Annandale-on-Hudson, NY: Levy Economics Institute of Bard College. http://www.levy.org/pubs/pn_6_05.pdf. Accessed July 30, 2009.

Wu, K. (2005). *How Social Security keeps older persons out of poverty across developed countries*. Working Paper No. 410. Luxembourg City: Luxembourg Income Study. http://www.lisproject.org/publications/liswps/410.pdf. Accessed July 29, 2009.

Yates, M. D. (1997). Does the U.S. labor movement have a future? *Monthly Review, 48*, 9, 1–18.

# 10

# SUMMARY, SYNTHESIS, AND CONCLUSIONS, PART I: THE POVERTY OF LONE WOMEN, THEIR DIVERSITY, AND INCOME SOURCES

*Gertrude Schaffner Goldberg*

In the past half century, new movements for women's liberation have risen the world over, and in some respects—education, government, and the professions—women have "come a long way." Focusing on lone mothers and lone elderly women in eight wealthy countries, the preceding chapters explored liberation from the perspective of women's actual or potential ability to achieve an adequate standard of living or an escape from poverty free of family relationships. Judged by this criterion of de-familialization, how far have women come?

In addition to comparing the poverty of lone mothers in the eight study countries and viewing it in relation to that of the general population and partnered mothers, this chapter examines a question posed by earlier research: "whether the countries with policies that allow solo mothers to form an autonomous household with little risk of poverty crystallize into a cluster corresponding to a particular welfare state regime" (Sainsbury, 1999, pp. 247–248).[1] In this study, the question was extended to older lone women. A subsequent section deals with the heterogeneity of both groups of lone women and its relationship to their poverty. The text then turns to the labor market, providing data on the gender gaps in employment and wages, generally, and, specifically, on lone mothers. Finally, the poverty of the two groups of lone women is analyzed from the perspective of two sources of income—the market and government transfers.

The preceding chapters depended primarily on data published by the governments of the separate countries. In this chapter, several international data sets are used to compare the poverty of both groups of lone women, the sources of their income, and their labor market characteristics in the eight study countries. These data sets both facilitate and complicate comparability. Scholars who use only international databases or who confine themselves to statistics from one or more countries are unlikely to face the discrepancies between national and cross-national data that are encountered by a study like this one that uses both. A brief Appendix to this chapter identifies some of these difficulties.

## Poverty of Lone Mothers

"Due to the difficulties they face," write Sainsbury and Morissens, "solo mothers provide a rigorous test in terms of justice and social citizenship" (Chapter 2). Are the wealthy countries in this study passing that test? A relative poverty standard of less than 50% of median disposable income (MDI) is the basic benchmark for exploring this question. However, the discussion sometimes turns to the lowest standard, less than 40% of MDI, the threshold closest to the official U.S. poverty standard.[2] Some attention is also paid to the highest standard, less than 60% of MDI. This standard is used in chapters on Britain and Germany and, in fact, is becoming the norm in Europe.

An important reason for using all three standards is that different thresholds can lead to different impressions. Some countries may have relatively low or relatively high poverty rates at all three levels, but others may succeed only at the lowest or lowest two levels.

According to the 50% standard, an average of one in three lone mothers was poor at the turn of the century (Table 10.1).[3] The range was from a low of 12% in Sweden to 3.5 times that much in the United States. Even at the lowest standard, the country average was 17%, with the U.S. rate nearing one in three, almost twice the average. At the highest standard, the average was almost 50%.

Classified as a social democratic regime, Sweden predictably comes closest to achieving an escape from poverty or de-familialization for lone mothers. At all three poverty standards, Sweden had the lowest rate of lone-mother poverty, with runner-up France being much higher, in fact, at the middle standard, 80% higher. France is categorized as conservative in the typology of Esping-Andersen (1990, 1999), but its strong emphasis on family policy has led some scholars to distinguish it from the Bismarckian or conservative regime (Martin, Chapter 5; Kesselman, 2002) or to assert that it defies categorization (Levy, 1998). France's lone-mother poverty rates are between those of Sweden and Germany, respectively the exemplars of the social democratic and conservative regimes. Lone-mother poverty rates in Germany were above average at all three levels whereas those of France were consistently below.

The poverty rates of the liberal countries, except for Britain at the lowest standard, were above average. Canada's rates, however, were closer to Germany than to the United Kingdom or the United States.

TABLE 10.1 Poverty Rates of Lone Mothers and Lone Parents, 2000 and Mid-decade[a]

| | Lone Mothers, 2000, LIS | | | Lone Parents,[b] 2000 | Lone Parents,[b] 2005 | Lone Mothers, 2004 LIS | | |
|---|---|---|---|---|---|---|---|---|
| | | | | Eurostat, ECHP[c] | Eurostat EU-SLIC[c] | | | |
| | <40% MDI | <50% MDI | <60% MDI | <60% MDI | <60% MDI | <40% MDI | <50% MDI | <60% MDI |
| Canada | 22.8 | 37.5 | 49.9 | – | – | – | – | – |
| France | 8.5 | 27.5 | 41.3 | 31 | 26 | – | – | – |
| Germany | 24.8 | 34.9 | 52.6 | 44 | 30 | – | – | – |
| Italy | (17.7) | (18.23) | (22.8) | (28) | (35) | – | – | – |
| Sweden | 4.5 | 12.4 | 23.0 | 13 | 18 | 4.0 | 9.7 | 27.7 |
| U.K.[d] | 12.3 | 41.5 | 58.6 | 57 | 37 | 9.9 | 30.5 | 48.7 |
| U.S. | 31.0 | 44.0 | 55.0 | – | – | 33.0 | 43.7 | 55.1 |
| Average[e] | 17.3 | 33.0 | 46.7 | 36[f] | 28 | | | |

[a] LIS figures for mid-decade were only available for three study countries, United Kingdom and United States (2004) and Sweden (2005).

[b] Eurostat (ECHP and EU-SLIC) does not provide lone parent poverty rates by gender. Single mothers are 70% or more of single parents in all the countries.

[c] The European Community Household Panel (ECHP) is the source from which Eurostat data were derived in 2000, and the European Survey of Living and Income Conditions. (EU-SLIC) was the source for 2005. See Appendix to Chapter 10 for differences between the two surveys.

[d] 1999 for LIS 2000.

[e] Averages are not weighted by population and they omit Italy.

[f] For the four European countries (omitting Italy) the LIS average for <60% MDI was 43.9% compared to the Eurostat average of 36.3% for the four countries in 2000.

*Sources*: LIS for 2008 and 2009. Calculations by Ann Morissens.
Eurostat, n.d.

Sainsbury (1999) observed that the United Kingdom, once apart from the other Anglo-Saxon countries, drew closer to them under the neo-liberal policies of Prime Minister Margaret Thatcher (1979–1990). By mid-decade, as a result of policies of the New Labour regime of Tony Blair (1997–2007), the United Kingdom appeared to be pulling away from the United States and becoming more progressive (Table 10.1).

Italy is classified as conservative in Esping-Andersen's three-world scheme—along with three other countries in this study, France, Germany, and Japan. According to the LIS, Italian lone mothers have relatively low poverty rates. However, the LIS sample for Italian lone mothers is small and probably unreliable—so small a difference between the 40% and 50% rates is very unlikely. For this reason, Italy is omitted from the unweighted country averages.

As discussed in Chapter 7, Italian lone mothers who form their own family units are not as disadvantaged as in some other countries because potentially more deprived lone mothers usually do not live independently.[4] Further, about half of those women counted as lone mothers by Italian sources—although not by LIS—are age 55 and older, mostly widows whose adult children live with them. In general, Italian women have very low rates of employment (Chapter 7 and Table 10.8). By contrast, Italian single mothers are predominantly paid employees (Bimbi, 1997) and thus better able to live independently than many other Italian women. Because of their poor prospects in the labor market and limited support from social policy, some mothers without partners live as members of cohabiting families with their poverty as single mothers uncounted (Chapter 7). Bimbi has described lone mothers as "a hidden and embarrassing issue in Italy's familist welfare regime" (1997). Notwithstanding the labor market advantages of some Italian lone mothers, Eurostat data for 2005 (Table 10.1) show a poverty rate comparable to the European study countries that have relatively high poverty rates.

Japan is not included in the LIS. A study using data from the Japanese Ministry of Health, Labour and Welfare and a poverty standard of less than 50% MDI found that in 2001, the poverty rate for lone mothers was 53.0% (Table 8.2). That suggests that the rate for Japanese lone mothers may be higher than the United States rate of 44% the preceding year (Table 10.1). However, as discussed in the appendix to this chapter, rates based on the same proportion of median income can differ considerably. This poverty rate is for the small but increasing numbers of Japanese lone mothers who form separate households with their children under 20 years of age. We can assume that Japanese single mothers who live as part of other families may do so because they, like their Italian counterparts, would be highly vulnerable to poverty if they were on their own.

**Country vs. international data.** It should be noted that LIS poverty rates for 2000 tend to be higher than the official data from France, Germany, Italy, and Sweden (Table 10.1 and Appendix Table 10.1).[5] That was also the case

TABLE 10.2 Comparison of Poverty Rates[a] of Lone Mothers and Total Population, 2000

| | 1 | 2 | 3 |
|---|---|---|---|
| | Lone Mothers | Total Pop. | ½ |
| Canada | 37.5 | 12.3 | 3.0 |
| France | 27.5 | 7.3 | 3.8 |
| Germany | 34.9 | 8.3 | 4.2 |
| Italy | (18.2) | (12.7) | (1.4) |
| Sweden | 12.4 | 6.6 | 1.9 |
| U.K[b] | 41.5 | 13.7 | 3.0 |
| U.S. | 44.0 | 17.0 | 2.6 |
| Average[c] | 33.0 | 10.9 | 3.0[d] |

[a] The poverty standard is <50% of Median Disposable Income (MDI).
[b] 1999
[c] Averages not weighted by population and do not include Italy.
[d] Dividing the averages of columns 1 and 2 = 3.0. The average of column 3 = 3.1.

*Source*: LIS data for 2000. Calculations by Ann Morissens.

for Eurostat 2000 for France, Germany, and Sweden. Some reasons for this are discussed in the appendix to this chapter. Nonetheless, the LIS data on which the major comparisons of poverty are based offer an important advantage: the income concepts and household definitions are harmonized. Moreover, despite the differences in actual rates, the rankings on LIS and country data are similar, with Sweden having the lowest rate, France second lowest, and the United States or United Kingdom the highest (in 2000).

**Lone-mother poverty compared to other populations.** Lone mothers have much higher poverty rates than the general populations of their countries, on average three times as high (Table 10.2). The rates range from over four times that of the general population in Germany to less than twice that in Sweden. Lone mother poverty is low in Sweden as is that of the population, generally, so the difference is small. The poverty gap between U.S. single mothers and the general population is relatively low but for the opposite reason: both have high rates of poverty. Germany stands out as a country with high single-mother poverty and relatively low total poverty, hence a large gap between solo mothers and the total population. Country data for Japan (Table 8.2) show that single mothers in that country have the highest poverty rate of any household type and are just over three times as likely to be poor as the general population, thus comparable to the average for six other countries in the study. Like the United States, Japan's poverty rate for both the total population and lone mothers is high.

The escape from poverty is much more likely for women who have partners (Table 10.3). On average, lone mothers are more than four times as likely to be poor as partnered mothers. The gap between women who

TABLE 10.3 Comparison of Poverty Rates[a] of Lone and Partnered Mothers, 2000 and Mid-decade[b]

| | 1 | 2 | 3 | 4 | 5 | 6 |
|---|---|---|---|---|---|---|
| | Lone Mothers | Partnered Mothers | 1/2 | Lone Mothers | Partnered Mothers | 4/5 |
| | 2000 | | | Mid-decade | | |
| Canada | 37.5 | 10.2 | 3.7 | – | – | – |
| France | 27.5 | 4.9 | 5.6 | – | – | – |
| Germany | 34.9 | 4.2 | 8.3 | – | – | – |
| Italy | (18.2) | (14.8) | (1.2) | – | – | – |
| Sweden | 12.4 | 2.2 | 5.6 | 9.7 | 3.2 | 3.0 |
| U.K.[c] | 41.5 | 10.2 | 4.1 | 30.5 | 7.7 | 4.0 |
| U.S. | 44.0 | 13.1 | 3.4 | 43.7 | 12.2 | 3.6 |
| Average[d] | 33.0 | 7.5 | 4.4[e] | | | |

[a] The poverty standard is <50% of Median Disposable Income (MDI).
[b] 2004 for U.K. and U.S.; 2005 for Sweden.
[c] 1999 for LIS 2000.
[d] Averages are not weighted by population and do not include Italy.
[e] Dividing the averages of columns 1 and 2 = 4.4. The average of column 3 = 5.1.

*Source*: LIS data for 2000 and 2004/2005. Calculations by Ann Morissens.

have male support and single mothers is greater than that between single mothers and the total population. Belonging to a much poorer group than either the nation as a whole or other families can be alienating and stigmatizing, even if a person is herself not poor.

The difference between lone and partnered mothers is especially marked in Germany where lone mothers were more than eight times as likely to be poor as partnered mothers. German women who deviate from a diminishing male breadwinner norm still suffer stiff penalties (Klammer, Chapter 4). The difference between Japanese single and partnered mothers is also very high. It is closest to Germany in this respect.[6] After Germany, France and Sweden have the largest differences between the poverty of lone and partnered mothers. However, these differences are to some extent mitigated because the rates of both single and partnered mothers are well below average, particularly in Sweden. By 2005, moreover, the difference in Sweden was less than for all countries in 2000 (except Italy). Differences between lone and partnered mothers are relatively low in the countries classified as liberal where both have poverty rates well above average. Even so, the poverty rates of lone and partnered mothers differ substantially.

These lone/partner gaps not only reflect the disadvantage of a single-earner but of women's lower wages and, in most countries, a failure of social policy to compensate for these handicaps. According to Canadian government data, employed single mothers had poverty rates of 22%, compared to 16% for single-earner partnered families and only 4% for two-earner, partnered families (Chapter 6). In the United States the differences are even greater (U.S. Census Bureau, 2007, table POV07). We turn now to the poverty of our second focal group, lone elderly women.

## Poverty of Lone Elderly Women

In most countries of this study and on average, lone elderly women have lower poverty rates than lone mothers (Tables 10.4 and 10.1). Sweden, perhaps reflecting its emphasis on family policy, is an exception. The average differences between the two groups of lone women narrow considerably as the poverty standards increase, but even at the highest, the average LIS rate for lone mothers was over one-fourth higher than for lone elderly women.[7] Although lone elderly women are less likely to be poor than lone mothers, their average poverty rate at the 50% standard was more than one in five.

Of particular interest is Canada, which, according to LIS figures, did much better in preventing the poverty of lone elderly women than the other two countries classified as liberal. It was, in fact, a leader at the two lower poverty standards. However, country data, as discussed below, tell a different story.

As with lone mothers, France's poverty rates are among the lowest at all three levels. Sweden's poverty rates are well below average at the two lower levels but are above—indeed the second highest—at the 60% level. Sainsbury and Morissens observe that

> Swedish policies have generally warded off poverty if it is defined as less than 50% of the median disposable income, but many solo mothers and elderly women have a disposable income between 50% and 70% of the average. They are at risk if a more ambitious measure of financial well-being like that of the current EU poverty line is used (Chapter 2, p. 57).

That was not the case for Swedish lone mothers, but it does apply to older lone women. Although Germany, Italy, and France are categorized as conservative regimes, the poverty rates of Germany and Italy were well above the French rates at all three levels.

A Japanese study that used LIS methods for calculating income found that at less than 50% MDI more than two out of five (43.7%) lone elderly women were poor in 2001 (Shirahase, 2006). Japan's poverty rate was closest to the United States rather than to the other study countries classified as conservative.

Mid-decade LIS figures show the United Kingdom making progress against the poverty of lone elderly women (Table 10.4), again giving some evidence of its pulling away from the United States, the prototypical liberal regime. Sweden reduced its rates at the two lower standards but remained high at the 60% standard, and the very high rates of the United States continued.

TABLE 10.4 Poverty Rates of Lone Elderly Persons, 2000 and Mid-decade[a]

| | Lone Elderly Persons, LIS, 2000 | | | | | | One Adult over 65, Eurostat, 2000[b] | One Adult over 65, Eurostat, 2005[b] | Lone, Elderly Women, LIS, 2004 | | |
|---|---|---|---|---|---|---|---|---|---|---|---|
| | <40% MDI | | <50% MDI | | <60 MDI% | | <60% MDI | <60% MDI | <40% MDI | <50% MDI | 60% MDI |
| | F | M | F | M | F | M | | | | | |
| Canada | 3.2 | 1.7 | 13.5 | 9.8 | 35.5 | 24.2 | – | – | – | – | – |
| France | 5.3 | 4.7 | 12.1 | 11.4 | 22.1 | 18.9 | 25 | 21 | – | – | – |
| Germany | 7.1 | 5.6 | 18.7 | 8.7 | 31.4 | 16.9 | 20 | 25 | – | – | – |
| Italy | 8.9 | 2.4 | 22.6 | 10.7 | 33.0 | 23.1 | 24 | 34 | – | – | – |
| Sweden | 4.3 | 4.2 | 17.4 | 10.6 | 43.7 | 27.3 | 27 | 19 | 3.7 | 14.7 | 45.4 |
| U.K.[c] | 13.7 | 7.8 | 25.6 | 17.8 | 42.6 | 35.3 | 37 | 22 | 13.7 | 24.3 | 36.8 |
| U.S. | 25.0 | 20.0 | 38.0 | 29.6 | 48.7 | 36.8 | – | – | 24.7 | 39.2 | 52.0 |
| Average[d] | 9.6 | 6.6 | 21.1 | 14.1 | 36.7 | 26.1 | 26.6[e] | 24.4 | | | |

[a] 2004 for U.K. and U.S; 2005 for Sweden.

[b] Pertains to One Adult over 65, Eurostat, 2000 and One Adult over 65, Eurostat, 2005.

[c] 1999 for LIS 2000.

[d] Averages are not weighted by population. LIS averages for lone elderly women without Italy are somewhat different from those including Italy: 9.8% (<40% MDI); 20.9% (<50% MDI); and 37.3% (<60% MDI).

[e] The LIS averages for the five European countries are 34.6% for lone elderly women and 24.3% for lone elderly men, compared with the Eurostat figure for lone adults of both genders of 26.6%.

*Sources*: LIS data for 2000 and 2004/2005. Calculations by Ann Morissens.
Eurostat, n.d.

Country data on the poverty of lone elderly women conflict with LIS figures (Appendix Table 10.2). LIS rates are much higher than those provided by the governments of Sweden, France, Germany, and Italy.[8] According to country data, France, Sweden, and perhaps Germany were approaching de-familialization of lone elderly women.

The exception to the general pattern of LIS rates exceeding those of the individual countries is Canada. Whereas LIS shows Canada to be a leader in poverty prevention, its government figures exceed those of France, Germany, Italy, and Sweden and by mid-decade, the United Kingdom. The latest data from Canada show a 30% decline in the poverty of lone, elderly women between 2005 and 2007, bringing the rate down to 14% but probably still higher than these other countries (Appendix Table 10.2).

**Gender differences.** Among the lone elderly, women have higher poverty rates than men (Table 10.4). (The reasons for the differences are discussed in Chapter 11.) For example, at the middle level, the average poverty rate for women was 50% more than their male counterparts. France is exceptional, not only in having low poverty rates for lone elderly women but also in its small gender gap. Wide disparities between Italian men and women at the lowest and middle standards and German men and women at the two higher levels reflect the greater persistence of patriarchy in these societies. In this regard, too, France differs from Italy and Germany, two countries with which it is categorized in the Esping-Andersen scheme. Not surprising is the very wide gender gap—larger than any other study country—between single elderly persons in Japan where women's rates were over 75% higher than those of men (Shirahase, 2006).

While single older women are more prone to poverty than their male counterparts, this gender divide is smaller than the gap between the single and partnered elderly (Tables 10.4 and 10.5). Whereas single elderly women are 1.5 times as likely to be poor as single older men, they are nearly three times more likely to be poor than the partnered elderly (50% standard).

Gender, however, is a big determinant of who is alone in old age because of women's longer life expectancies and their tendency to marry older men.[9] In the United Kingdom, for example, both younger and older, elderly women (65–74 and 75 and above) are about twice as likely to live alone as men (Millar, Chapter 5); the same is true in Canada (Evans, Chapter 6). As Claude Martin writes, "Many more women than men are getting older alone" (Chapter 3, p. 77).

## Women's Poverty and Welfare Regimes: A Summary

Do those countries in which lone women achieve an acceptable standard of living cluster according to regime types? Based on Kilkey and Bradshaw's cross-national research on lone mothers, Sainsbury (1999) answered this question in the negative. This research was conducted a decade later and addressed the question from two stages of the life course.

TABLE 10.5 Poverty Rates[a] of Lone and Partnered Elderly, 2000

| | 1 | 2 | 3 |
|---|---|---|---|
| | Lone Elderly Women | Partnered Elderly Women[b] | 1/2 |
| Canada | 13.5 | 2.3 | 5.9 |
| France | 12.1 | 6.2 | 2.0 |
| Germany | 18.7 | 5.2 | 3.6 |
| Italy | 22.6 | 10.1 | 2.2 |
| Sweden | 17.4 | 1.5 | 11.6 |
| U.K.[c] | 25.6 | 12.4 | 2.1 |
| U.S. | 38.0 | 15.7 | 2.4 |
| Average[d] | 21.1 | 7.6 | 2.8[e] |

[a] The poverty standard is <50% of Median Disposable Income (MDI).
[b] Couples with at least one person 65 or older.
[c] 1999.
[d] Averages are not weighted by population.
[e] Dividing the averages of columns 1 and 2 = 2.8. The average of column 3 = 4.3.

*Source*: LIS data for 2000. Calculations by Ann Morissens.

**Lone mothers.** Kilkey and Bradshaw categorized countries according to whether their poverty rates were above or below average. In the present study that could have meant poverty rates as high as 28% for lone mothers and 17%–18% for older lone women. This research was concerned with whether most lone women achieved an "acceptable standard of living," defined as at least half of MDI. According to LIS data, none of the wealthy countries in this study permitted an autonomous escape from poverty for nearly all lone women, say rates no higher than 5%–10%.

On the dimension of lone mother poverty, Sweden, the social democratic regime, behaves as predicted—with a poverty rate much lower than the other countries but still over 10%. At the 50% standard, the three liberal countries have high rates of poverty, also as predicted by regime types, but they are joined by conservative Japan whose small lone-mother population has a very high risk of poverty. Moreover, there are substantial differences within the liberal regime. Canada, with the lowest rate of the three, is closer to Germany than to its liberal partners.

Although the LIS data for Italy are unreliable, those from the Italian government and Eurostat 2000 post relatively low poverty rates for the small population of lone mothers. That distinguishes Italy from the other regimes classified as conservative and, as labor market data will show, it should probably be categorized as Mediterranean or Latin rim. Its very scant de-commodification of the nonelderly also supports this conclusion.

Given its emphasis on family policy, one would expect France to have relatively low poverty rates for lone mothers. Although it ranks next to Sweden on this variable, it is closer to Germany. Nonetheless, the conservative regimes did not form a distinct cluster.

Before the effects of Sweden's lapse from full employment and cutbacks in benefits, it came closer to achieving the standard set here: in 1992, its lone mother poverty rate was below 5% (Christopher, 2001, using LIS data). A study included in our earlier work found that the Swedish poverty rate for all groups was so low that it made no sense to speak of the feminization of poverty (Rosenthal, 1990). Although it showed considerable improvement in the first 5 years of the century, Sweden's lone mother poverty rate was still higher than in 1992 when it had achieved de-familialization.

**Lone elderly women.** Gender cuts across and fragments regime types differently when the criterion is the poverty of lone elderly women. According to LIS, the nations in which lone elderly women have the lowest poverty rates at the 50% standard include all three regime types: conservative France, liberal Canada, and social democratic Sweden. Germany, the prototypic conservative regime was next, but its rate is over 50% higher than France (Table 10.4).

According to LIS, Canada was closer to France, Sweden, and Germany than to the other two liberal countries on the two lower standards and to Germany and France at the highest.[10] Whereas the LIS data suggest that Canada stands apart from the liberal countries and add weight to the view that gender cuts across regime typologies, the country data show the poverty rate of Canadian lone elderly women to be higher than the continental European countries in this study, despite very impressive gains in the first years of this century and a 75% drop since 1980 (Chapter 6 and Appendix Table 10.2). Careful analysis of the differences in how the Canadian government and the LIS calculate poverty rates at the same fraction of median income would be necessary to resolve these contradictory findings.

The United States, the prototypic liberal regime, has a higher poverty rate at all three levels than the European countries and Canada, and at the two lower levels, it stands far apart from Britain, the next highest. Moreover, the mid-decade data show that at the highest standard, the United States and United Kingdom had moved in opposite directions.

Whereas the social democratic regime performed as expected in relation to lone mother poverty, that is not the case for the older group of lone women. Sweden has a below-average poverty rate at the two lower standards although it is not the frontrunner in either, but, surprisingly, at the highest level, it is among the study countries with the highest poverty rates. Mid-decade data register improvements at the lower two levels but not at the highest. Had there been more social democratic regimes in this study differences among them might have emerged.[11] It is possible that the other countries so classified might have achieved lower poverty rates for lone elderly women than Sweden, thus behaving more predictably in relation to regime type.

As with lone mothers, the conservative regime type breaks apart. Japan probably has at least as high a poverty rate as the United States. France, also classified as conservative, has one of the lowest at all three levels. Given the emphasis on the elderly among the conservative countries, one might have expected low rates of poverty for lone elderly German women

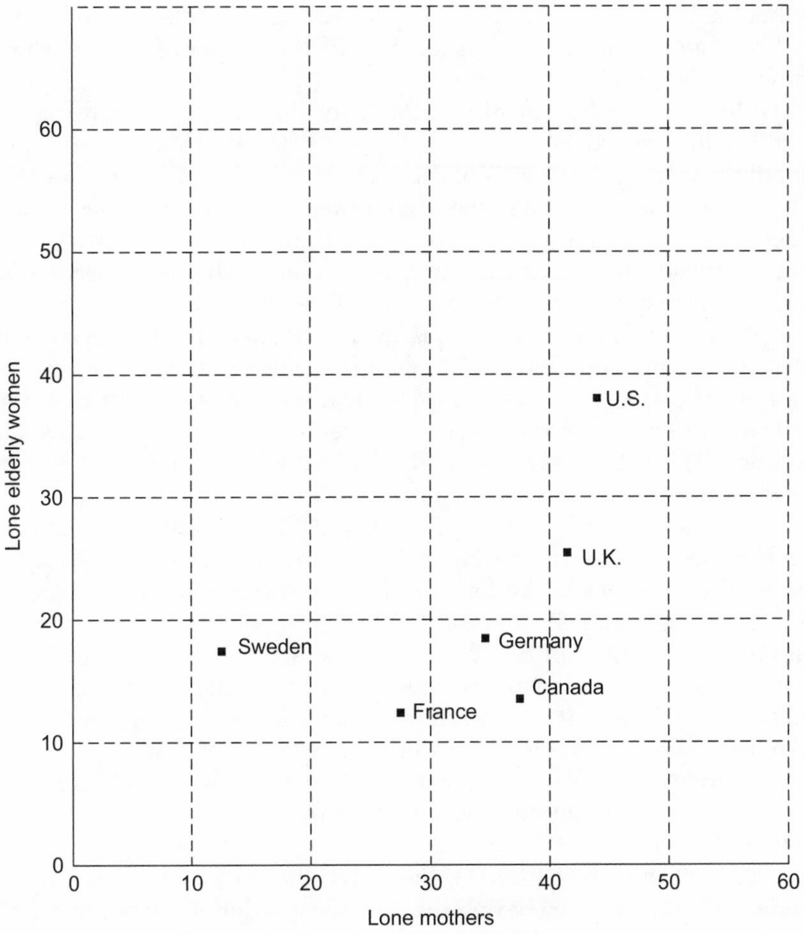


**Figure 10.1.** Poverty rates (<50% MDI) of lone mothers and lone elderly women, 2000[a], percent.
[a] U.K., 1999.
*Source*: LIS data for 2000. Calculations by Ann Morissens.

as well. Elderly couples have relatively low rates in both Germany and France, indeed somewhat lower in the former (Table 10.5). Clearly, gender is at play here with the French rate for lone elderly women more than a third lower than the German.

What does combining the data on the two groups of lone women reveal about the clustering of regime types? Figure 10.1 summarizes the poverty rates for lone mothers and lone elderly women. On the basis of the LIS data, a lone mother might wish to be in Sweden in 2000, and if conditions remained the same and she continued to be single, to spend her old age in Canada or France. The latter would be a distant second choice for lone mothers but a relatively good one for older women. What is most certain is that the United States is no country for younger or older single women, and the same could be said of Japan, which as explained below, is not shown in Figure 10.1.

It is important to bear in mind that relationships among welfare regimes might be different, depending on the poverty standard and the year. If the standard were less than 60% of MDI rather than 50%, Sweden would be among the countries with higher rather than lower poverty rates for lone elderly women, and at mid-decade, the U.K. rate for lone elderly women would probably be among the lower rather than the higher poverty countries. Country data would also present a different picture.

Japan has been omitted from Figure 10.1 because the data, even when based on LIS methods and the 50% standard, are not strictly comparable.[12] Despite this, Japan is probably close to the United States on both measures and closer to it than to the conservative regimes with which it is usually grouped. This is more evidence of the fragmentation of the countries classified as conservative.

When Esping-Andersen (1999) added de-familialization to de-commodification as a means of classifying welfare regimes types, he maintained the earlier classification based on de-commodification alone. As noted in Chapter 1, Daly and Rake hold that typologization "underplays differences among countries ... [and] is ill-suited to deal with the context-rich and complex information necessary for a gender-focused analysis" (2003, p. 167). Clearly, the classification scheme is not a reliable predictor of all outcomes related to the poverty of lone women, and that is particularly the case for those categorized as conservative. The United States conforms to the liberal model, but the other countries in this study that are classified as liberal are less true to type.

Arts and Gelissen (2002, p. 137) surveyed the debate regarding Esping-Andersen's typology, including the feminist critique. They point out that "real welfare states are hardly ever pure types and are usually hybrid cases" and that "the issue of ideal-typical welfare states cannot be satisfactorily answered given the lack of formal theorizing and the still inconclusive outcomes of comparative research" (p. 137). This study lends some support to those conclusions. Chapter 11 calls attention to the omission of employment rights as a criterion for distinguishing among welfare regimes in the three-world typology—despite Esping-Andersen's recognition that prior to the 1990s, the social democratic regime was as fully committed to full employment as to generous income support (1990).

## Feminized Poverty

Feminized poverty is a problem of both lone and partnered women. While married women are at lower risk of poverty than single mothers, many are potentially poor because they do not have control of a fair share of family income. In the mid-1990s, around one-fourth or more (24%–29%)

of married French, British, U.S., and German women had less than a tenth of total family resources in their own names, and that was the case for half of Italian married women (Daly & Rake, 2003). At the turn of the century, German women with a male partner and two children contributed only 11% of the family's income. "This has dramatic effects on their ability to support themselves in case of divorce or widowhood" (Klammer, Chapter 4, p. 100). Not surprisingly, a German woman's poverty risk doubles 1 year after she divorces.

In addition to the economic measures of poverty emphasized in this book, a likely, nonmaterial deprivation should be included. If poverty were regarded as paucity of free time—resulting from the combination of paid employment and work in the home, it would be feminized. In Sweden, the United States, Germany, the United Kingdom, and Italy, full-time women workers spend from 1.7 to 3.6 as much time on household chores as their partners (Esping-Andersen, 2002, using OECD figures). Needless to say the quality of life suffers when there is little time for leisure and recreation. The time bind is undoubtedly greater for lone mothers.

**Measuring feminized poverty: Lone elderly women.** Feminized poverty in the narrow sense is the predominance of lone women among certain groups of the poor such as poor families or the poor elderly. For the lone elderly, feminized poverty is the unequivocal reality in all the countries in this study (Table 10.6); it is an international phenomenon.

There is no question that the great majority of those who are poor, older, and alone are women. At all three poverty levels they are, on average, about four-fifths of that group and at least about three-fourths. Women predominate among the lone elderly but to a greater extent among those

TABLE 10.6 Poor Elderly Women as Proportion of All Poor Lone Elderly Persons, 2000 and Mid-decade[a]

| | 2000 | | | Mid-decade | | |
|---|---|---|---|---|---|---|
| | <40% MDI | <50% MDI | <60% MDI | <40% MDI | <50% MDI | <60% MDI |
| Canada | 77.6 | 81.6 | 80.8 | – | – | – |
| France | 80.5 | 78.5 | 80.3 | – | – | – |
| Germany | 86.4 | 91.9 | 90.1 | – | – | – |
| Italy | 86.2 | 86.0 | 82.1 | – | – | – |
| Sweden | 72.9 | 81.7 | 81.4 | 81.4 | 79.0 | 81.6 |
| U.K.[b] | 84.1 | 77.3 | 75.3 | 78.9 | 75.5 | 72.2 |
| U.S. | 79.0 | 79.7 | 80.2 | 79.5 | 78.3 | 78.1 |
| Average[c] | 81.0 | 82.4 | 81.5 | | | |

[a] 2004 for the U.K. and U.S.; 2005 for Sweden.

[b] 1999 for 2000.

[c] Averages are not weighted by population.

*Source*: LIS data for 2000 and 2004/2005. Calculations by Ann Morissens.

TABLE 10.7 Poor, Lone Mothers as Percent of All Poor Families with Children, 2000 and Mid-decade[a]

| | 2000 | | | Mid-decade | | |
|---|---|---|---|---|---|---|
| | <40% MDI | <50% MDI | <60% MDI | <40% MDI | <50% MDI | <60% MDI |
| Canada | 51.1 | 44.3 | 37.6 | – | – | – |
| France | 44.9 | 46.6 | 37.4 | – | – | – |
| Germany | 65.6 | 55.4 | 51.9 | – | – | – |
| Italy | (10.6) | (7.3) | (6.7) | – | – | – |
| Sweden | 34.4 | 41.1 | 35.0 | 27.9 | 27.7 | 36.6 |
| U.K.[b] | 44.8 | 57.2 | 54.0 | 49.2 | 60.4 | 56.2 |
| U.S. | 51.9 | 46.1 | 42.0 | 57.8 | 51.8 | 46.3 |
| Average[c] | 48.8 | 48.5 | 43.0 | | | |

[a] 2004 for U.K. and U.S.; 2005 for Sweden.
[b] 1999 for 2000.
[c] Averages are not weighted by population. Italy is excluded from lone mother averages.
*Source*: LIS data for 2000 and 2004/2005. Calculations by Ann Morissens.

who are poor in old age. This would also seem to be the case in Japan where lone elderly women not only have much higher poverty rates than their male counterparts (Shirahase, 2006). Further among the study countries, Japan has the second highest gap in male and female life expectancy (OECD, 2006, pp. 10–11).

**Measuring feminized poverty: Lone mothers.** Whether single-mother families dominate among poor families depends on their poverty rate in relation to that of other families with children and a demographic factor as well, the proportion of all families that are single-mother families. Despite the increase of lone-mother families in recent decades, they remain a minority of families with children in all countries, at most about one-fourth. For this reason, their poverty is less likely to be feminized than that of elderly single women, even though their rates of poverty are nearly always higher. Nonetheless, on average, lone-mother families are close to the majority of poor families at the two lower poverty standards. At the highest standard, they are over two-fifths (Table 10.7).

In Sweden and France, lone mother poverty rates are relatively low, and in these two countries, they do not predominate among poor families at any of the three poverty standards. However, at the two lower standards, French lone-mother families are nearing the majority of poor families with children.

What about the countries with higher poverty rates? In Germany, where single mothers are much more likely to be poor than partnered mothers, poverty is feminized at all three levels although the proportions fall as the standards rise. The trend is the same for Canada and the United States, but in those countries, it is only at the 40% standard that single-mother families predominate. By contrast, U.K. family poverty is feminized at the top two levels but not at the lowest. Whether lone mother poverty is feminized depends partly on the poverty standard.

In view of the prevalence and high poverty rates of lone mothers in the United States, it is surprising that in 2000, according to LIS, U.S. family poverty was only feminized at the lowest standard. By contrast, calculations based on U.S. Census Bureau data found that single-mother families ranged from nearly three-fifths of all poor families at the official rate (close to the 40% standard) to about one-half at 150% of the standard (U.S. Census Bureau, 2001a). Feminized poverty depends partly on the difference between the poverty rates of lone mothers and married couple families. Whereas the lone mother poverty rate was 4.5 times as high as that of married mothers, according to the LIS 40% standard, they were 5.4 times as likely to be poor, according to the roughly comparable U.S. poverty standard. This could explain why calculations based on the U.S. poverty standard found poverty to be more feminized than those based on the 40% LIS standard. In 2004, however, calculations based on the LIS standards found poverty to be feminized at the two lower levels but less so than those based on the U.S. standard.[13]

Lone mothers are minorities of poor families in Japan, but this is not a cause for optimism. At the time of our earlier study (Axinn, 1990), Japanese lone mothers, like those today, had very high poverty rates. Japanese women are more likely to divorce than they were two decades ago, but the numbers of those who live independently are not sufficient to predominate among poor families. If divorce continues its steep rise and poverty rates remain high, family poverty could become feminized in Japan.

## Differences in Race, Ethnicity, Nativity, and Marital Status

As most of the country chapters attest, neither group of lone women is homogeneous. They differ in marital status which, in turn, can be associated with different risks of poverty at each of the two life stages on which this study focuses. Heterogeneity of race, ethnicity and nativity is also related to differences in the rate of poverty among both groups of lone women.

**Marital status: Lone mothers.** In general, unmarried mothers seem to be at greater risk of poverty than either divorced or widowed mothers. Indeed, one reason for the very high poverty rate of US lone mothers is that unmarried mothers are the most numerous marital status. They are usually younger, in some countries less well educated or qualified, have younger children, and are more likely to lack child support when it is not guaranteed by government. In the U.S. these factors are compounded by the minority status of a large proportion of never-married mothers. In the U.K., younger women, never-married women, and those with young children of pre-school age are among the sole mothers least likely to be employed, hence at higher risk of poverty. In the 1990s, Swedish never-married mothers had a poverty rate much higher than those who were divorced and widowed. In the United States, too, divorced and widowed mothers had much lower rates than those of never-married mothers[14].

**Marital status: Lone elderly women.** Marital status impacts poverty differently for the younger and older groups of lone women. Widows have advantages because in most countries they can claim pension benefits as surviving spouses, and never-married women include those without children who are more likely than mothers to have had uninterrupted working lives. Thus, in Canada, separated and divorced older women are most likely to experience low income, while widows and never-married women are less likely (McDonald & Robb, 2004, cited by Evans). By contrast, in Germany, differences in income among the three groups are not large.[15]

**Minority race or ethnicity.** Because most of the countries in this study do not collect data on racial and ethnic minorities, this section pertains only to the three that do: Canada, the United Kingdom and the United States. Immigrants are of different ethnicity from native populations and often of different race as well. Consequently, the section on nativity is of relevance to minority status in some of the countries that do not collect data on minorities.

Often suffering discrimination in employment, minorities of color have higher risks of poverty than native whites. This is especially the case in the United States where Black and Hispanic single mothers have poverty rates much higher than their white counterparts. Higher minority than white rates hold for all four marital statuses. With high rates of single motherhood and high poverty rates, minorities of color predominate among poor lone mothers in the United States, exposed not only to the disadvantages of gender but those of race/ethnicity and class as well as marital status. Nearly three-fifths of African American and over two-fifths of Hispanic lone mothers are unmarried. There are even greater race-ethnic disparities among lone elderly women. African Americans and Hispanics have poverty rates more than twice as high as their white, non-Hispanic counterparts.

In the U.K., women of color have much higher poverty rates than white women, and this is the case among all family types. High rates of single parenthood are associated with the high poverty rates of black Caribbean and black African populations.

The chapter on Canada emphasizes the discrimination faced by "visible minorities" and some of its consequences. For example, as a result of labor market discrimination they are less likely to contribute to private pensions, and because of low earnings, their benefits are lower when they do contribute (Evans, citing Morissette, 2002) Visible minorities are also among those most likely to live in unaffordable housing. In both Canada and the United States, aboriginal or Native Americans are the single mothers with the highest poverty rates

**Nativity.** Most of the country studies document the effect of immigration on the poverty of women, both partnered and single. Although immigrants are not homogeneous, in general they face discrimination in labor markets, sometimes compounded by minority racial and ethnic status, and they have lower levels of education and skill. In some cases, however, immigrant women are over-qualified for their jobs, employed as domestic or care workers when they have higher skills.

Some countries deny immigrants social benefits for which native populations are eligible, but even where they enjoy rights comparable to the native population, as in Sweden, they have substantially higher poverty rates, often because of higher rates of unemployment and various forms of precarious work. The poverty rate of immigrants in Germany is almost twice that of German citizens. Here, too, they are at higher risk of unemployment and underemployment. Moreover, limited access to social security and different household structures (e.g., more children) contribute to this situation.

Undetermined numbers of lone mothers have migrated alone to richer countries and might well swell the ranks of poor, lone mothers if their children were with them. The chapter on Italy records the economic and social hardships endured by women who are separated from their children, who immigrate with them or unite with them later. In Italy and some other countries as well, immigrant women are employed as domestic or care workers, live with their employers and are often underpaid and obliged to work long hours. Caring for other people's children, these mothers find it very difficult to maintain their own children. Such immigrant women often lack pension coverage, and having sent money to relatives in their countries of origin, find themselves with little or no savings. Consequently, they are likely to have scant retirement income.

Poverty is particularly intense for immigrant solo mothers but also a high risk for the larger numbers who are partnered. In the United States, foreign born married mothers have a much higher poverty rate than their native counterparts. Immigrant women as a group are at the bottom of the income scale.

What Klammer (Chapter 4) has to say about pension claims of immigrant women in Germany applies to other countries as well. Their relatively low level and continuity of labor market activity and low wages lead to low pension claims on their own behalf. For those whose spouses migrated relatively recently, survivors' or derived benefits are likely to be low, not to mention those who have no such claims as dependents.

In some countries, immigrant poverty, related to gender but also to class, race, and nativity, is likely eclipsing as well as compounding the poverty of women. Indeed, Sainsbury and Morissens conclude that in

Sweden the "ethnicization of poverty"—the poverty of immigrant groups who are different in ethnicity from native Swedes—is a more imminent prospect than the feminization of poverty. In Germany, one of two big shifts in poverty during recent decades has been from the native German population to immigrants.[16]

## Labor Market Conditions

**Activity, employment, and unemployment rates.** A gender gap in the labor market exists in all eight countries, but there are sizable national differences (Table 10.8). With a difference in women's and men's participation of only 6%–7%, Social Democratic Sweden is nearest to closing the gender gap, and, among the eight study countries, it also has the highest activity and employment rates for women. Canada is the distant runner-up in both categories. France, the United States, the United Kingdom, and Germany have similar activity gaps, all around three times that of Sweden. Japan's activity gap is twice as large as these countries, and reflecting its "patriarchal labor market," Italy's is even wider.

Motherhood still exacts a heavy employment penalty. British men and women without children have the same employment rates, whereas mothers' and fathers' rates differ widely (Chapter 5). While the labor force participation of U.S. fathers is very high and hardly varies with the age of children, mothers' rates differ widely and are much lower (Mosisa & Hippie, 2006). In West Germany, mothers of teen-agers are more than twice as likely to be employed as those with very young children (Chapter 4, Table 4.3).

**Part-time employment.** Part-time work—not only less pay but often at lower rates—is highly gendered. Women's predominance in part-time work reflects the difficulty of combining full-time employment and motherhood. "One of the main ways that British mothers manage employment and family is by moving into part-time employment when they have children" (Chapter 5, p. 125). In general, part-time work is highly concentrated in the service sector, and the jobs tend to be poor in quality with less opportunity for skill development (Gallie, 2002). Indeed, occupational mobility is another part-time casualty. Comparing full- and part-time wages for women workers, a study of six OECD countries (all but France and Japan in this study) found a part-time wage penalty except in Sweden (Bardasi & Gornick, 2007).

Part-time employment rates often modify the impression given by activity rates. The employment and activity rates of British and U.S. women are about the same, but part-time employment is more than twice as high in the United Kingdom. However, for the low wages they earn, many full-time U.S. workers should be working part-time. German activity and employment rates are higher than those of France, but about two-fifths of German women workers are part-timers, compared to under one-fourth

TABLE 10.8 Employment/Population, Labor Force Participation, and Unemployment Rates by Gender, Ages 15–64, 2006

| | Employment/Population | | | Labor Force Participation | | | Unemployment | | |
|---|---|---|---|---|---|---|---|---|---|
| | Women | Men | % Diff.[a] | Women | Men | % Diff.[a] | Women | Men | % Diff.[b] |
| Canada | 69.0 | 76.8 | 11.3 | 73.5 | 82.2 | 11.8 | 6.1 | 6.6 | 8.2 |
| France | 57.1 | 67.5 | 18.2 | 63.9 | 74.2 | 16.1 | 10.7 | 9.1 | 17.6[b] |
| Germany | 61.5 | 72.9 | 18.5 | 68.5 | 81.4 | 18.8 | 10.3 | 10.4 | 1.0 |
| Italy | 46.3 | 70.5 | 52.3 | 50.8 | 74.6 | 46.9 | 8.8 | 5.5 | 60.0[b] |
| Japan | 58.8 | 81.0 | 37.8 | 61.3 | 84.8 | 38.3 | 4.1 | 4.4 | 7.3 |
| Sweden | 72.1 | 76.8 | 6.5 | 77.7 | 82.6 | 6.3 | 7.2 | 7.0 | 2.9[b] |
| U.K. | 66.8 | 78.4 | 17.4 | 70.3 | 83.2 | 18.3 | 5.0 | 5.8 | 16.0 |
| U.S. | 66.1 | 78.1 | 18.2 | 69.3 | 81.9 | 18.2 | 4.7 | 4.7 | 0 |
| Average[c] | 62.2 | 75.3 | 21.0[d] | 66.9 | 80.6 | 20.5[d] | 7.1 | 6.7 | – |

[a] Percent by which men's rate exceeds women's.

[b] Percent by which women's rate exceeds men's.

[c] Averages are not weighted by population. The average percent differences are women's average employment/population and labor force participation rates divided by men's.

[d] The averages of the percent difference columns for employment and labor force participation are 22.5% and 21.8%, respectively.

*Source*: OECD, 2007, table B.

TABLE 10.9 Incidence of Low Pay,[a] 1995 and 2005

| | 1995 | 2005 |
|---|---|---|
| Canada | 22.0 | 22.2 |
| France | – | – |
| Germany | 11.1 | 15.8 |
| Italy | – | – |
| Japan | 15.4 | 16.1 |
| Sweden | 5.7 | 6.4 |
| U.K. | 20.0 | 20.7 |
| U.S. | 25.2 | 24.0 |
| Average[b] | 16.6 | 17.5 |

[a] Share of workers earning less than 2/3 of median earnings

[b] Averages are not weighted by population.

*Source*: OECD, 2007, table H.

in France. The high activity rate of Swedish women is not qualified by part-time employment (OECD, 2007, Table E).

**Wage gap.** The wage gap persists, but according to the OECD, between 1995 and, 2005, it narrowed on average in the seven countries for which data are available.[17] The average ratio of women's to men's full-time wages was just over three-fourths in 1995 and four-fifths a decade later (OECD, 2007, Table H).[18] In both years France had the narrowest wage gap, followed by Sweden, and Japan's was the highest.

Annual wage gaps understate the difference between the earnings of women and men whereas longitudinal data register the effects of the discontinuity in women's employment (Hartmann, Rose, & Lovell, 2006). Further, basing the gap on full-time work overlooks women's much higher rates of part-time employment. Although the wage gap may be narrowing, equaling the stagnating wages of males has become a less desirable goal.

**Low wages.** Among six of the countries in this study for which there are comparable data, only Sweden had a very low incidence of low pay (Table 10.9). This is a likely consequence of its high rate of unionization and solidarity wage policy. The next lowest were Germany and Japan, both much more likely to have low pay than Sweden. With still higher incidence of low pay were the three countries classified as liberal: the United Kingdom, Canada, and the United States; in the latter, nearly one-fourth of the work force had low wages. The low-wage burden, moreover, is not equally borne by women and men. U.S. women, for example, are 50% more likely than men to earn poverty-level wages (Chapter 9).

**Occupational segregation.** Women's low wages owe much to occupational segregation. Labor markets in all of the countries are heavily segregated, with women concentrated in low paying occupations. German women are still concentrated in a very limited range of "female" jobs with low salaries. Occupational segregation is high in the Swedish labor market, but owing to solidarity wage policies, the gender wage gap is low. Although occupational segregation is not as great in the United States as in other countries, its cost nonetheless is great Economists Blau and Kahn (2006) found that nearly half the wage difference between full-time men and women workers is explained by occupational and industry categories. Even when women increase their education, they may still be in segregated, low-wage occupations.

There is some skepticism about the effect of educational upgrading on wages. Despite increases in workers' education and job experience, the proportion of low-wage jobs in Canada has not decreased (Chapter 6, citing Morissette & Picot, 2005). Similarly, David Howell (1994) found that low-wage workers in the United States increased their skills and education but not their wages. Institutional factors—labor power and minimum wage policy—were deemed more important.

**Women and precarious work.** Even where unemployment is not high, precarious work takes its toll. In Canada, there are more jobs but not necessarily good ones; indeed precarious employment—part-time, temporary and low-wage—has risen in Canada and is both gendered and racialized (Cranford, Vosko, & Zukewich, 2003; Jackson, 2003). Precarious work and high unemployment go together in France, Germany and, for women, in Italy. Japanese women have relatively low unemployment rates, but over half of them are in nonregular work (Chapter 8).

**Lone mothers and employment.** For lone mothers the disadvantages of women workers and mothers are compounded by greater difficulty meshing work and family responsibilities. In some countries, lone mothers are also held back by lower education or qualifications than married mothers.

Several country studies report much higher unemployment or underemployment for lone than partnered mothers. In France, their employment rates are about the same, but lone mothers have almost twice the unemployment rate of partnered mothers (Chapter 3), and the same is true in Germany (Chapter 4; U.S. Bureau of Labor Statistics, 2008, Table 8).

Authors of several of the country studies point out that the labor market status of lone mothers is related to educational deficiencies. Due to their lower level of education than partnered mothers, French lone mothers are more often low skilled or blue collar workers and more likely to have precarious jobs (Chapter 3). The employment rate of U.S. lone mothers with at least a high school diploma is markedly higher than of those with less than high school completion (Table 9.3).

**Employment and welfare regimes.** As predicted by Esping-Andersen's "three world's" typology, the social democratic model does most to encourage women's employment by lessening the familial burden (1999, p. 45). Not only do Swedish women have the highest employment rates among the study countries, but they also have the lowest gender employment gap and next highest ratio of women's to men's wages. One indication of this is Sweden's very low gender gap in employment. The three countries classified as liberal have the next highest employment rates. On average, their employment rates are not much lower than Sweden's, but their employment gender gaps are much higher. In the liberal countries, women's economic independence is weakened by the quality of their jobs, and the paucity of affordable child care is an economic and social burden on employed mothers and their children.

It should also be noted that, in the United States relatively high rates of employment are achieved, not by government's reducing women's responsibilities for family care. Indeed, it is the absence of family benefits, other than those contingent on employment, that pushes less well-off women into the labor market. Better-off women who work pay the high market price of child care while women of modest means often have to settle for the inadequate care they can afford. Formerly, public assistance offered poor women the opportunity to be caregivers, but welfare reform imposed strict work requirements that are tantamount to "forced commodification" (Giddings, Dingeldey, & Ulbricht, 2004). De-commodification or the ability to opt out of the market has been seriously abridged by the repeal of the entitlement to welfare (Holden, 2003). Because employment often fails to lift lone mothers above the poverty line, what U.S. welfare "reformers" refer to as "self-sufficiency" means only that they are off the welfare rolls but not necessarily able to support themselves. Thus, despite the rhetoric of welfare reform, work requirements, do not lead to economic independence or an escape from poverty. What has happened in the United States is happening in milder forms in Canada and Britain, the two other study countries classified as liberal.

In the remaining countries, all classified by Esping-Andersen as conservative, women's employment rates range widely. In Germany, both high unemployment and lack of alternatives to family care hold down women's employment, and probably related to both is the high rate of part-time employment. In France the availability of child care does not overcome the effects of chronic, high unemployment.

Italy is the outlier among women in the study countries. Italian women have the lowest employment rate, 26% under the average for the eight counties. Whereas the unemployment rates of men and women are similar in most countries and more often higher for men than women, the unemployment rate of Italian women is 60% higher than men's. Further, its employment gender gap is by far the highest. Based on women's employment, one would be inclined to categorize Italy differently from Esping-Andersen—not as a conservative regime but rather, as an example of the Mediterranean model (Ferrera, 1996, cited by Morlicchio, Pugliese, & Spinelli, 2002) or as a Latin rim or Southern regime (Leibfried, 1993; Bonoli, 1997; Arts & Gelissen, 2002). Leibfried, in comparing the Latin rim to the Scandinavian countries, pointed out that the former do not have a full employment tradition—"in particular, one that also fully applies to women" (1993, p. 142).

Although the employment rates of Japanese women are not far below those of French and German women, Japan's gender gap in employment is much greater. Japanese lone mothers, like U.S. single mothers, are commodified or forced to be in the labor market because of the paucity of social benefits. To conclude, women's employment levels in the social democratic and liberal countries are predicted by the three worlds model, but there is considerable variety among the countries classified as conservative and great enough divergence on the part of Italy to suggest that it belongs to another regime type.

### States, Markets, and Poverty

**Lone mothers.** Market income alone leaves lone mothers with high poverty rates in all the study countries for which there are reliable data. Leaving aside the anomalous group of Italian lone mothers,[19] the pre-transfer poverty rates of single mothers ranged from just over half in France to 85% in the United Kingdom. This is not to say that employment is unimportant, for employed lone mothers have much lower poverty rates than those who are not active. In their earlier, multi-country study, Kilkey and Bradshaw (1999) found that in every country the poverty rate of lone mothers was lower if they were employed. Even though transfers cut the poverty of British solo mothers by nearly 50%, their post-transfer poverty rate is still high because their activity rates and earned incomes are relatively low (Table 10.10, p. 290).

Table 10.10 shows that both market income and social policy matter. Sainsbury and Morissens (Chapter 2) point out that earnings constitute the mainstay of solo mothers' incomes, but they also observe that, without social transfers, the poverty rate of Swedish solo mothers and their children, in the mid-1990s, would have been nearly on a par with the poverty rate of U.S. solo mothers (citing Christopher, England, McLanahan, Ross, & Smeeding, 2001). The same would have been true in 2000 (Table 10.10). Swedish single mothers have one of the lowest rates of market poverty, the highest poverty reduction rate, and consequently the lowest poverty rate among the eight countries. France had a somewhat lower rate of pre-transfer poverty than Sweden, but it expended much less effort in reducing poverty through social policy. Consequently, French lone mothers had double the poverty rate of Swedish lone mothers.[20]

The pre-transfer poverty rate of U.S. lone mothers is average for the study countries. The source of their great disadvantage lies elsewhere: in social policy. Poverty reduction through income transfers was half the average rate in 2000 and the lowest in the group.

TABLE 10.10 Pre-transfer and Post-transfer Poverty Rates[a] and Poverty-Reduction Rates of Lone Mothers, 1994, 2000, and Mid-decade[b]

| | Pre-transfer | | | Post-transfer | | | Poverty Reduction | | |
|---|---|---|---|---|---|---|---|---|---|
| | 1994 | 2000 | 2004 | 1994 | 2000 | 2004 | 1994 | 2000 | 2004 |
| Canada | 55.8 | 59.7 | – | 38.3 | 37.5 | – | 31.4 | 37.2 | – |
| France | 35.5 | 52.0 | – | 12.9 | 27.5 | – | 63.7 | 47.1 | – |
| Germany | 56.8 | 58.2 | – | 40.9 | 34.9 | – | 28.0 | 40.0 | – |
| Italy[c] | – | (32.1) | – | – | (18.2) | – | – | (43.3) | – |
| Sweden | 40.4 | 55.4 | 57.1 | 4.4 | 12.4 | 9.7 | 89.1 | 77.6 | 81.0 |
| U.K.[d] | 73.3 | 78.2 | 75.0 | 31.6 | 41.5 | 30.5 | 56.9 | 46.9 | 59.3 |
| U.S | 52.8 | 57.0 | 57.0 | 45.4 | 44.0 | 43.7 | 14.0 | 22.8 | 23.3 |
| Average[e] | 52.4 | 60.1 | | 28.9 | 33.0 | | 48.0 | 45.3 | |

[a] The poverty standard is <50% of Median Disposable Income (MDI).
[b] 2004 for U.K. and U.S.; 2005 for Sweden.
[c] Not available for 1994.
[d] 1999 for 2000.
[e] Averages are not weighted by population. Italy is not included in averages.

*Sources*: For 1994, Christopher, 2001.
LIS data for 2000 and 2004/2005. Calculations by Ann Morissens.

Sweden and the United States are outliers in poverty reduction—in opposite directions. Indeed, the two prototypes—of the social democratic and liberal regimes—perform as predicted in reducing the poverty of lone mothers. Sweden's anti-poverty effort is more than triple that of the United States and over 60% higher than that of runner-up France. The poverty reduction rate of Canada, though it is the second lowest of the study countries, is nonetheless more than 60% higher than the United States.

Table 10.10 also shows that between the mid-1990s and 2000 the condition of lone mothers deteriorated. Pre-transfer poverty increased, the effect of transfers dropped, and, as a result, the average rate of post-transfer poverty increased. All six countries had higher rates of pre-transfer poverty, and half had lower rates of poverty reduction. The United States alone had a sizeable increase in poverty reduction, perhaps due to increases in its Earned Income Tax Credit, but this was just about enough to overcome the increase in pre-transfer poverty. Germany also increased its effort, and despite somewhat greater pre-transfer poverty, was able to reduce its post-transfer rate considerably.

LIS data for mid-decade show improvements in poverty reduction rates for Sweden and especially the United Kingdom with the former still not as effective in reducing poverty as in 1994, before the effects of its severe economic downturn. The United States, on the other hand, remained virtually the same on all three variables.

What about Japan? Although a breakdown of pre-transfer and post-transfer poverty is not available, Japanese lone mothers do poorly on both counts. They are severely disadvantaged in the labor market (Table 10.8),

TABLE 10.11 Pre-transfer and Post-transfer Poverty Rates[a] of Lone Elderly Women, 2000 and Mid-decade[b]

| | Pre-transfer | | Post-transfer | | Poverty Reduction | |
|---|---|---|---|---|---|---|
| | 2000 | 2004 | 2000 | 2004 | 2000 | 2004 |
| Canada | 76.5 | – | 13.5 | – | 82.4 | – |
| France | 86.4 | – | 12.1 | – | 86.0 | – |
| Germany | 89.6 | – | 18.7 | – | 79.1 | – |
| Italy | 75.6 | – | 22.6 | – | 70.1 | – |
| Sweden | 93.5 | 91.6 | 17.4 | 14.7 | 81.4 | 84.0 |
| UK[c] | 76.3 | 80.1 | 25.6 | 24.3 | 66.4 | 70.0 |
| US | 71.2 | 72.6 | 38.0 | 39.2 | 46.6 | 46.0 |
| Average[d] | 81.3 | | 21.1 | | 73.1 | |

[a] The poverty standard is <50% of Median Disposable Income (MDI).
[b] 2004 for U.K. and U.S.; 2005 for Sweden.
[c] 1999 for LIS 2000.
[d] Averages are not weighted for population.
*Source*: LIS data for 2000 and 2004/2005. Calculations by Ann Morissens.

but nevertheless the Japanese government refuses to support the care-giving role of "parted mothers" or those who deviate from a "normal" family model that no longer holds sway. The vast majority of solo mothers work, earn low wages, and get less than 10% of their income from the state (Chapter 8).

**Lone elderly women.** Without income transfers the vast majority of lone elderly women would be poor (Table 10.11). In fact, on average, four of five were poor prior to transfers. The U.S. had the lowest pre-transfer rate which was nonetheless 71%. The other liberal countries, as might be expected from their greater dependence on the market, were also relatively low, but both Canada and the United Kingdom exceeded the United States in poverty reduction. Canada was among the countries with the highest poverty reduction whereas Britain's, though much higher than the U.S. rate, was nonetheless second lowest. Here, too, the United States stood alone with an anti-poverty effort much below average.

Pre-transfer poverty was over 85% in France, Germany, and Sweden. Owing to the highest rate of poverty reduction among the study countries, France had the lowest poverty rate, and Sweden and Germany were close in both respects.

Mid-decade data show improvements for Sweden on all three counts and for the United Kingdom which offset a rise in pre-transfer poverty with an increased reduction effort. Between 2000 and 2004, the United States made no progress, leaving lone elderly women at virtually the same high risk of poverty.

## Summary

This chapter assessed and compared the ability of lone women to achieve an acceptable standard of living, as measured primarily by a relative poverty standard of less than 50% of median disposable income. At the turn of the century, none of the eight countries in this study achieved a poverty rate for lone mothers below 12%. The averages were one-third for lone mothers and about one-fifth for the older women. Although country data were more optimistic, the overall picture is one in which many lone women in most, if not all these countries, are unable to escape poverty, and many partnered women would be poor if they were to support themselves.

Countries differed widely and, in the case of the elderly women, did not cluster according to regime type. The prototype social democrat and liberal countries, Sweden and the United States, did perform predictably in the case of lone mothers, and that was also true of the United States in regard to lone elderly women. The countries with low poverty rates for lone elderly women included all three regime types. Countries classified as conservative did not form a distinct cluster with respect to the poverty of either group of lone women.

Poverty is clearly feminized among older lone women and is indeed an international phenomenon. Lone mothers have higher poverty rates than older lone women, but, being a minority among families with children, are less likely to predominate among the poor. Yet, they are sizable minorities of the poor in most countries and pass the 50% mark in some countries at one or more of the three LIS poverty standards. Surprisingly, LIS data showed family poverty at the turn of the century to be less feminized in the United States than in some other countries, but U.S. government data cast some doubt on those findings. Some findings pertaining to the heterogeneity of lone women were also summarized, and their poverty was found to differ by marital status, race/ethnicity, and nativity.

The labor market conditions of women, generally, and lone women, particularly were presented. Whether gender gaps in activity rates, extent of part-time employment and wages were related to welfare regimes was also explored. When it came to the labor market, the social democratic regime stood out: Swedish women had higher activity and employment rates, a much lower gender gap in employment, the latter probably owing partly to the universality of child care, and low incidence of low wages. The Swedish wage gap is low but wider than that of France.

LIS data make it possible to isolate the effects of both market income and income transfers on the poverty of lone women. The market left both groups with high poverty rates: on average, three-fifths of lone mothers and four-fifths of lone elderly women were poor prior to transfers. The escape from poverty for lone women is highly dependent on government income support. Indeed, women need the state if they are to achieve an acceptable standard of living independent of family relationships. The relative disadvantage of U.S. lone women is not a function of poor market outcomes but of very deficient income support.

The second of these concluding chapters identifies the social and economic policies that contribute to the outcomes presented in this chapter and calls attention to the changes in policy that would reduce the economic vulnerability of women. It probes the opposite types of exceptionalism of Sweden and the United States and, finally, ventures a look at the future for lone women in this time of mounting uncertainty.

## Appendix to Chapter 10

Cross-national data both facilitate and complicate cross-national comparisons. There are problems in coverage, differences in poverty standards and differences in calculating poverty rates even when the poverty standard is the same. Further, because it takes some time to acquire data from a number of countries and to make them comparable, statistics may be somewhat out-of-date.

The OECD includes all the countries in the study whereas the LIS does not cover Japan. Eurostat covers only Europe. OECD data sometimes differ from the national measures, for example, in the age ranges of the working population. Both OECD and Eurostat are quite current. However, Eurostat does not provide household data by gender (e.g., single mothers) and reports poverty rates for only one standard, less than 60% of MDI. LIS data are available by gender, and poverty rates can be broken into pre-transfer and post-transfer, but the latest LIS figures available for the seven countries covered by LIS are for the year 2000. For some of the countries, however, there are LIS data for 2004 or 2005, and these were cited where relevant.

Added to comparability problems is the fact that equivalence scales (i.e., adjustment for family size) may differ from country to country and between the international agencies. The comparability of the Eurostat data for 2000 and 2005 is seriously in question because of a change in data sources and of some variables. Figures for the year 2000 are based on ECHP (European Community Household Panel) data, a longitudinal survey between 1994 and 2000, whereas 2005 figures are based on the ECHP successor, EU-SILC (European Community Statistics on Income and Living Conditions). The majority of variables are defined in the same way, but there are differences in total gross household and disposable income and income composition (European Commission, 2005). Thus, differences in Eurostat data for 2000 and 2005 may reflect differences in these variables rather than true changes.

For a variety of reasons, even at the same proportions of median income, LIS poverty rates are generally higher and present a more pessimistic picture than Eurostat or the country data. A reason for some of the difference is that while LIS figures are for lone mothers only, those of Eurostat and some of the country data pertain to lone parents, thus including a small group of single fathers whose poverty rates are generally lower. Probably more important are differences in the equivalence scales or adjustments for family size used by the various sources. Further, there may be differences in how the individual countries define households and disposable income. Because of the discrepancies between country data and the international data sets, Appendix tables 10.1 and 10.2 provide country data for the two groups of lone women.

APPENDIX TABLE 10.1 Poverty Rates of Lone Mothers Using Government Data from Study Countries, Selected Years and Poverty Measures[a]

| | <50% | <60% | Other |
|---|---|---|---|
| Canada | 36.3 (2000) | | |
| | 29.1 (2005) | | |
| | 23.6 (2007) | | |
| France | 12.2[b] (2004) | | |
| Germany | | 35.4[b] (1998) | |
| | | 35.4[b] (2003) | |
| Italy | 12.1[b] (1997) | | |
| | 13.8[b] (2006) | | |
| Japan | 53.0[c] (2001) | | |
| Sweden | 9.2 (2000) | | |
| | 7.2 (2004) | | |
| U.K. | | 57[b] (1999/00) | |
| | | 48[b] (2005/06) | |
| | | 50[b] (2007/08) | |
| U.S. | | | 33.0 (2000) |
| | | | 35.8 (2004) |
| | | | 37.0 (2007)[d] |

[a] Note that in different countries the same standards (proportions of median disposable income) may differ, for example, in equivalence scales and in the components of income that are counted. The figures for Italy are for <50% of mean expenditures. The figures for Canada are based on consumption patterns but produce results broadly similar to 50% of median income. For the United Kingdom, they are for <60% of the median, after housing expenses. For more on the derivation of poverty standards, see the country chapters.

[b] Lone parents.

[c] This is the rate given by the Japanese Ministry of Health, Labour and Welfare. A panel study for the years 1994–2002 found that 53.9% of single-mother households were continually under a poverty line set at 60% of median consumption and that the figure was 92.4% when those temporarily under the poverty line were included (Iwata & Hamamoto, 2004).

[d] The offical U.S. poverty standard for a family of three consisting of one adult and two children was $13,874 in 2000, $15,219 in 2004, and $16,705 in 2007. In 2004, the poverty rate for lone mothers was 43.6% at 125% of the official standard, 51.0% at 150% of the standard, and 58.2% at 175% of the standard.

*Sources*: Country Studies in this book; U.S. Census Bureau, 2001, Table POV04; 2005, Table POV04; 2008, Table POV04.

APPENDIX TABLE 10.2 Poverty Rates of Lone Elderly Women Using Government Data from Study Countries, Selected Years, and Poverty Measures[a]

| | <50% | <60% | Other |
|---|---|---|---|
| Canada | 21.7 (2000)<br>20.3 (2005)<br>14.3 (2007) | | |
| France | 6.7[b] (2001) | | |
| Germany | | 13.5[b] (2003)<br>14.2[b] (1998) | |
| Italy | 12.6[b] (2006)<br>14.9[b] (1997) | | |
| Japan | 43.0[b] (2001) | | |
| Sweden | 4.6/8.4[c] (2000)<br>2.6/6.2[c] (2004) | | |
| U.K. | | 37 (1999/00)<br>20 (2005/06)<br>23 (2007/08) | |
| U.S. | | | 20.8 (2000)<br>19.6 (2004)<br>19.9 (2007)[d] |

[a] Note that in different countries the same standards (proportions of median disposable income) may differ, for example, in equivalence scales and in the components of income that are counted. The figures for Italy are for <50% of mean expenditures. The figures for Canada are based on consumption patterns but produce results broadly similar to 50% of median income. For the United Kingdom, they are for <60% of the median, after housing expenses. For more on the derivation of poverty standards, see the country chapters.
[b] Both men and women.
[c] Rates are for ages 65–74 and 75+.
[d] The official U.S. poverty standard for one person 65 and older was equal to $6259 in 2000, $9060 in 2004, and $9944 in 2007. In 2004, the poverty rate for a lone elderly woman was 32.9% at 125% of the official standard, 47.2% at 150% of the standard, and 57.9% at 175% of the standard.

*Sources*: Country studies in this book; U.S. Census Bureau, 2001, Table POV01; 2005, Table POV01; 2008, Table POV01.

## Notes

1

The countries included by Esping-Andersen (1999) in each of the three regime types are:

| Liberal | Conservative | | Social Democrat |
|---|---|---|---|
| Australia | Austria | Italy | Denmark |
| Canada | Belgium | Japan | Finland |
| New Zealand | France | Netherlands | Norway |
| United Kingdom | Germany* | Portugal | Sweden* |
| United States* | Spain | | |

* Considered the quintessential example of its regime type.

2 The LIS rate is somewhat lower for lone mothers and higher for lone elderly women:

| | U.S. Official Poverty Rate | LIS Rate for U.S. <40% MDI |
|---|---|---|
| Lone mothers | | |
| 2000 | 33.0 | 31.0 |
| 2004 | 35.9 | 33.0 |
| Lone elderly women | | |
| 2000 | 21.3 | 25.0 |
| 2004 | 19.6 | 24.7 |

3 At the time this was written, LIS data for mid-decade (2004 or 2005) were available for only three of the countries in this study: Sweden, the United Kingdom, and the United States. Because they give some indication of trends and can be compared with the country data, which are usually from that time or later, they are included in the tables, where relevant.

4 Using data from Istat, the Italian Statistical Office, Morlicchio and Spinelli (Chapter 7) point out that Italian single mothers have lower rates of poverty than two other family groups: couples with two or more children and cohabiting families, but, according to Eurostat, which was using a larger and presumably reliable sample of lone parents, this was not the case at the 60% level in 2005 except for two-parent families with three or more children. Support for the high poverty rates of Italian partnered families with children comes from LIS; they have the highest poverty rates among the seven study countries covered by LIS (Table 10.3).

5 The French statistical office reported lone parent poverty rates nearly 50% lower than LIS figures. Swedish country rates for solo mothers were 25% lower, and German official data were about one-third lower. (Compare Table 10.1 and Appendix Table 10.1.)

6 Japanese data are given separately for couple families with one, two, or three or more children. The ratios are 6.2, 7.6, and 8.5, respectively (Table 8.2).

7 Whether or not Italy is included in the average of lone elderly persons makes little difference in this comparison.

8 As shown in note 2, LIS rates were higher than on the comparable, official U.S. standard. Compared to LIS, government data reflected larger declines in the early years of the twenty-first century for Sweden (50% level) and for the United Kingdom (60% level).

9 There is some evidence from the United States that the gender gap in life expectancy may be shrinking because men are smoking less and retiring earlier (Miller & Gerstein, 1983, cited by Ghilarducci, 2008).

10 For example in Appendix Table 10.2 German women have lower poverty rates than their British counterparts, even with the latter's great improvement in the first 5 years of the century (13.5% in Germany [2003] and 20% in the United Kingdom [2005/2006]). Further, Canada's rate at the 50% level was about like that of the United Kingdom at the 60% standard but not the much higher LIS rate for the United Kingdom. According to LIS there was virtually no improvement for the United Kingdom between 1999 and 2004 (28.7%–28.0%) at the 50% level and a much smaller change at the 60% level

than that reported by the British government (a drop of about 9% compared to 46%). LIS data for Canada and Germany at mid-decade were not available

11 See Chapter 11, for a discussion of similarities among social democratic or Nordic countries.

12 For instance, Shirahase's (2006) cross-national study of single elderly women reported a rate of 43.7% for Japan and 45.5% for the United States (2000), whereas Morissen's calculation for the United States, based on LIS data for the same year, was lower, 38%. The data for Japanese lone mothers are for 2001 and are derived from a Japanese government source. Although the poverty standard is also less than 50% of MDI, the methods of calculating the poverty standard may have differed.

13

Feminized Family Poverty[a] in the United States According to Different Sources and Standards, 2004.

| Luxembourg Income Study | | | Percent of U.S. Poverty Standard | | | |
|---|---|---|---|---|---|---|
| <40% MDI | <50% MDI | <60% MDI | 100% | 125% | 150% | 175% |
| 57.8 | 51.8 | 46.3 | 60.0 | 55.6 | 52.0 | 48.8 |

[a] Lone-mother families as percent of all poor families with children.

*Sources*: LIS data for 2004. Calculations by Ann Morissens
For U.S. poverty standard, U.S. Census Bureau, 2005, table POV04.

14 In the United States, separated single mothers have poverty rates higher than those who are divorced or widowed and only somewhat less than the never-married mothers. Divorced and separated women are sometimes treated as a single category of divorced-separated, but the adage that separation is a poor man's divorce seems to hold. The official U.S. poverty rates in 2005 were 22.3% for divorced single mothers, 36.8% for widows, 43.4 for separated mothers, and 47.5% for never-married mothers (Chapter 9, Table 9.8).

15 See Chapter 4 for advantages and disadvantages of each status, p. 113.

16 The other shift, according to Chapter 4, is from the poverty of older people to that of children.

17 Wage data were not available for Italy.

18 The OECD bases the wage gap on median gross earnings of 15–64-year-old full-time wage and salary workers, whereas the U.S. gap which is based on year-round workers, 15 and older, is higher. The U.S. Census Bureau's figure in 2005 was 0.77, compared to the OECD's 0.81. Canadian national statistics are also less optimistic: 0.72 in 1995 and 0.71 in 2003, instead of the 6.6% gain reported by the OECD.

19 See Chapter 7.

20 However, French data for 2001 show a lower pre-transfer poverty rate than LIS, a higher poverty reduction rate, and a post-transfer poverty of 13.9%, half the LIS rate for the previous year; the rate for 2004 was 12.9% (Algava, Le Minez, Bressé, & Pla, 2005). According to data from both governments, French lone mothers had a poverty rate 50% higher than their Swedish counterparts, a much smaller difference than between the LIS rates.

## References

Algava, E., Le Minez, S., & Bressé, A. P. (2005). Les familles monoparentales et leurs conditions de vie. *Études et Résultats, 389,* Avril, 1–12.

Arts, W., & Gelissen, J. (2002). Three worlds of welfare capitalism or more? A state-of-the-art report. *Journal of European Social Policy, 12, 2,* 137–158.

Axinn, J. (1990). Japan: A special case. In G. S. Goldberg & E. Kremen (Eds.), *The feminization of poverty: Only in America?* (pp. 91–106). New York: Praeger.

Bardasi, E., & Gornick, J.C. (2007). *Women's part-time wage penalties across countries.* Working Paper No. 467. Luxembourg: Luxembourg Income Study. http://www.lisproject.org/php/wp/wp.php#wp. Accessed July 29, 2009.

Bimbi, F. (1997). Lone mothers in Italy: A hidden and embarrassing issue in a familist welfare regime. In J. Lewis (Ed.), *Lone mothers in European welfare regimes: Shifting policy logics* (pp. 171–202). London: Jessica Kingsley Publisher.

Blau, F. D., & Kahn, L. M. (2006). The gender pay gap: Going, going ... but not gone. In F. D. Blau, M. C. Brinton, & D. B. Grusky (Eds.), *The declining significance of gender?* (pp. 37–66). New York: Russell Sage.

Bonoli, G. (1997). Classifying welfare states: A two-dimension approach. *Journal of Social Policy, 26, 3,* 351–372.

Christopher, K. (2001). *Welfare state regimes and mothers' poverty.* Luxembourg Income Study Working Paper No. 286. Luxembourg: Luxembourg Income Study. http://www.lisproject.org/publications/liswps/286.pdf. Accessed May 24, 2009.

Christopher, K., England, P., McLanahan, S., Ross, K., & Smeeding, T. M. (2001). Gender inequality in poverty in affluent nations: The role of single motherhood and the state. In K. Vleminckx & T. M. Smeeding (Eds.), *Child well-being, child poverty and child policy in modern nations: What do we know?* (pp. 199–219). Bristol: The Policy Press.

Cranford, C., Vosko L. & Zukewich, N. (2003). Precarious employment in the Canadian labour market: A statistical portrait. *Just Labour: A Canadian Journal of Work and Society, 3,* 6–22.

Daly, M., & Rake, K. (2003). *Gender and the welfare state: Care, work and welfare in Europe and the USA.* Cambridge, UK: Polity Press.

Department of Work and Pensions. (DWP) (2007). *Households below average income 2005/06, Supplementary Tables.* Leeds: Corporate Document Services. http://www.dwp.gov.uk/asd/hbai/hbai2006/pdf_files/supplementary_tables/full_suptables_hbai07.pdf. Accessed July 29, 2009.

Esping-Andersen, G. (1990). *The three worlds of welfare capitalism.* Princeton, NJ: Princeton University Press.

Esping-Andersen, G. (1999). *Social foundations of post-industrial economies.* New York: Oxford University Press.

Esping-Andersen, G. (2002). A new gender contract. In G. Esping-Andersen, D. Gillie, A. Hemerijck, & J. Myles (Eds.), *Why we need a new welfare state* (pp. 68–95). Oxford: Oxford University Press.

Eurostat. (n.d.). *At-risk-of-poverty rate after social transfers, by household types.* http://epp.eurostat.ec.europa.eu/tgm/refreshTableAction.do;jsessionid=9ea7974b30e9df7065ea224948cfaee3fb3217a39206.e34SbxiOchiKc40LbNmLahiKaNyNe0?tab=table&plugin=1&init=1&pcode=tsdsc240&language=en. Accessed July 7, 2009.

European Commission. (2005). *The continuity of indicators during the transition between ECHP and EU-SILC.* Luxembourg: Office for Official Publications of the European Communities. http://epp.eurostat.ec.europa.eu/cache/ITY_OFFPUB/KS-CC-05-006/EN/KS-CC-05-006-EN.PDF. Accessed July 30, 2009.

Gallie, D. (2002). The quality of working life in welfare strategy. In G. Esping-Andersen, D. Gallie, A Hemerijck, & J. Myles (Eds.), *Why we need a new welfare state* (pp. 96–129). Oxford: Oxford University Press.

Ghilarducci, T. (2008). *When I'm sixty-four: The plot against pensions and the plan to save them*. Princeton, NJ: Princeton University Press.

Giddings, L., Dingeldey, I., & Ulbricht, S. (2004). The commodification of lone mothers' labor: A comparison of US and German policies. *Feminist Economics, 10, 2,* 115–142.

Hartmann, H., Rose, S. J., & Lovell, V. (2006). How much progress in closing the long-term earnings gap? In F. D. Blau, M. C. Brinton, & D. B. Grusky (Eds.), *The declining significance of gender?* (pp. 125–155). New York: Russell Sage.

Holden, C. (2003). Decommodification and the workfare state. *Political Studies Review, 1,* 303–316.

Howell, D. (1994). The skills myth. *American Prospect,* Summer. http://www.prospect.org/cs/articles?article=the_skills_myth. Accessed August 11, 2009.

Iwata, M., & Hamamoto, C. (2004). Defure jokyoka no hinkon keiken [Experiences of poverty during deflation]. In Y, Higuchi, K. Ohta., Kakei Keizai Kenkyusho (Eds.), *Joseitachi no Heisei fukyo [The Heisei recession for women]* (pp. 203–234). Tokyo: Nihon Keizai Shimbun-sha.

Jackson, A. (2003). *Is work working for women?* Research Paper No. 22, May. Ottawa: Canadian Labour Congress.

Kesselman, M. (2002). The triple exceptionalism of the French welfare state. In G. S. Goldberg & M. G. Rosethal (Eds.), *Diminishing welfare: A cross-national study of social provision* (pp. 181–210). Westport, CT: Auburn House.

Leibfried, S. (1993). Toward a European welfare state? On integrating poverty regimes into the European Community. In C. Jones (Ed.), *New perspectives on the welfare state in Europe* (pp. 133–156). London: Routledge.

Levy, L. (1998). France in a globalizing economy: The shifting logic of welfare reform. Paper presented at the workshop, *The Adjustment of National Employment and Social Policy to Internationalisation*. European University Institute, Florence, October 19–20.

McDonald, L., & Robb, A. (2004). The economic legacy of divorce and separation for women in old age. *Canadian Journal of Aging, 23,* S83–S97.

Miller, G. H., & Gerstein, D. R. (1983). The life expectance of nonsmoking men and women. *Public Health Reports, 98, 4,* 343–349.

Morissette, R. (2002). Pensions: Immigrants and visible minorities. *Perspectives, 6, 3,* 13–18.

Morissette, R., & Picot, G. (2005). *Low-paid work and economically vulnerable families over the last two decades*. Ottawa: Statistics Canada, Business and Labour Market Analysis Division, cat no: 11F0019MIE-No. 248.

Morlicchio, E., Pugliese, E., & Spinelli, E. (2002). Diminishing welfare: The Italian case. In G. S. Goldberg & M. G. Rosenthal (Eds.), *Diminishing welfare: A cross-national study of social provision* (pp. 245–270). Westport, CT: Auburn House.

Mosisa, A., & Hippie, S. (2006). Trends in labor force participation in the United States. *Monthly Labor Review, 129, 10,* 35–57.

OECD. (2006). *OECD in figures 2006–2007*. Paris: Author.

OECD. (2007). *OECD employment outlook 2007*. Paris: Author.

OECD. n.d. *What are equivalence scales?* Paris: Author. http://www.oecd.org/dataoecd/61/52/35411111.pdf. Accessed July 30, 2009.

Rosenthal, M. G. (1990). Sweden: Promise and paradox. In G. S. Goldberg & E. Kremen (Eds.), *The feminization of poverty: Only in America?* (pp. 129–156). New York: Praeger.

Sainsbury, D. (1999). Gender, policy regimes, and politics. In D. Sainsbury (Ed.), *Gender and welfare state regimes* (pp. 245–276). London: Oxford University Press.

Shirahase, S. (2006). Widowhood later in life in Japan: Considering Social Security System in aging societies. Working Paper No. 444. Luxembourg: Luxembourg Income Study. http://www.lisproject.org/publications/liswps/444.pdf. Accessed August 22, 2009.

U.S. Census Bureau. (2001a). *Data Ferrett, Current Population Survey, March 2001.* Washington, DC: Author.

U.S. Census Bureau. (2001b). *Detailed poverty tabulations from the Current Population Survey.* Washington, DC: Author. http://www.census.gov/hhes/www/poverty/detailedpovtabs.html. Accessed July 29, 2009.

U.S. Census Bureau. (2005). *Detailed poverty tabulations from the Current Population Survey.* Washington, DC: Author. http://pubdb3.census.gov/macro/032005/pov/toc.htm. Accessed July 29, 2009.

U.S. Census Bureau. (2007). *Detailed poverty tabulations from the CPS.* Washington, DC: Author. http://pubdb3.census.gov/macro/032007/pov/toc.htm. Accessed July 29, 2009.

U.S. Census Bureau. (2008) *Detailed poverty tabulations from the CPS.* Washington, DC: Author. http://www.census.gov/hhes/www/macro/032008/pov/toc.htm. Accessed July 29, 2009.

11

# SUMMARY, SYNTHESIS, A… PART 2: GOVERNMENT POLICIE… LONE WOMEN

*Gertrude Schaffner Goldberg*

This chapter identifies the economic, social, and equal opportunity policies that facilitate women's achievement of an acceptable standard of living or an escape from poverty independent of family relations. Following discussion of policies conducive to this goal of de-familiailization, two policies are highlighted: minimum-income guarantees and full employment. After considering economic and political resources for reducing the poverty of women, the discussion compares Sweden and the United States, two study countries that differ widely in social policies and the achievement of de-familialization. Finally, notwithstanding the difficulty of foreseeing the future in a time of crisis, there is an attempt to look ahead.

## Policies to Improve Market Outcomes for Women

Policies with the potential of reducing gender gaps include laws that forbid discrimination, promote integration of the labor force or achieve pay equity, but they can also include policies like the minimum wage or full employment that are not specifically gendered but benefit women disproportionately. Child care is also treated as an equal opportunity policy because it reduces an important barrier to women's employment.

**Equal opportunity laws.** For a time, various types of equal opportunity policies offered hope of overcoming gender gaps. Once promising policies like affirmative action and pay equity are being dismantled in Canada, and both have lost ground in the United States. Their lapse is particularly cause as Misra, Moller, & Budig (2007) point out, in these coun- le major, noncoercive state policies to engage women in the work have been those to remove gender discrimination rather than to ress work-family balance.

In Japan, the effect of equal opportunity policies is blunted because they benefit regular, full-time female workers but not single mothers who work mainly as low-wage or part-time workers. Kimoto and Hagiwara also point out that "deregulatory employment measures pushed forward by business are limiting the effect of gender equality policies in Japan" (Chapter 8).

With many women working part-time and usually at considerable disadvantage, equal opportunity would be served by measures like Britain's "Part-Time Workers Directive" (2000) that extends the same occupational pension rights, pay, and training opportunities to part-time as to full-time workers. However, there are limits to this policy—that part-timers can only claim the same rights as full-timers if there is a full-time colleague with whom they can make a direct comparison (Chapter 5).

**Minimum or solidarity wage policies.** These class strategies disproportionately benefit women and minorities. When Britain adopted a national minimum wage for the first time in 1999, two-thirds of those directly aided were women (Chapter 5, citing Bellamy & Rake, 2005). Similarly, women were 60% of the beneficiaries of the U.S. minimum wage hike in 2007 (Mishel, Bernstein, & Allegretto, 2007).

**Unionization.** The Swedish labor movement has contributed significantly to women's economic independence. Seventy-eight percent of the Swedish labor force is unionized (2003) (Visser, 2006), and women are even more highly represented than men. Membership of part-time workers is high. Solo mothers are well represented in Swedish unions, and union women champion issues that benefit them (Chapter 2).

Unionization also improves the conditions of U.S. women, particularly minorities, but the country's very low union density severely limits its reach. Only about 14% of men and 11% of women belong to unions (Visser, 2006). President Barack Obama has indicated his support for the Employee Free Choice Act that would make it easier for workers to join unions and harder for employers to block unionization, but its passage is nonetheless dubious.

**Child care.** Unlike other equal opportunity policies that are basically regulatory, subsidized child care is a social welfare benefit-in-kind. Affordable child care that accommodates a wide range of work schedules is an important way to increase mothers' presence in the labor force, particularly solo mothers who lack partners with whom to share care in the home and the cost of nonparental care.

According to Sainsbury and Morissens, municipal child care in Sweden has promoted the high labor force participation of lone mothers, and in a period of general retrenchment, child care has become nearly universal.[1] Feminists, however, are concerned about a policy adopted in 2008 that gives municipal governments the option to provide allowances for home care of very young children. They fear that this could erode funding of child care, have a negative effect on women's careers, and reinforce the traditional gender division of labor.

Since the 1970s, child care has been an important component of French social policy, particularly for young, solo mothers. Nearly all French children between ages three and six have access to free child care as do just over one-third of two- and three-year-olds. Recent French policy, however, includes a move comparable to Sweden's child-care allowance. According to Morgan and Zippel (2003), some countries are finding it cheaper to pay mothers to stay home than to subsidize child care, but this could limit their occupational mobility. Such a policy seems to go against the prevailing current of activation but is quite consonant with budgetary restraint.

What about the other countries? Child care has increased in Germany, the United Kingdom, the United States, Canada, and Japan, but substantial deficiencies persist, especially for very young children and during hours that accommodate irregular work. Limits are related to cost, preference for a market approach, and reluctance to make child care a right.

Important as child care is, high unemployment reduces the liberating potential of generous state provision. France, for example, has abundant child care (albeit to a lesser extent for children under age three) However, with women's unemployment consistently in the 10% range, French women have a below average activity rate and an especially low employment-to-population rate. East Germany is another case in point: high unemployment, abundant child-care resources and a *surplus* of child-care slots. Klammer (Chapter 4) points out that because the majority of German solo mothers are not caring for a child under 10 years, lack of public child care cannot be regarded as the main cause of their poverty (citing VAMV, 2006, p. 7). What has to be seen as a major cause is that German women have an unemployment rate in the 10% range and about two-fifths of those who work are employed part-time. The latter could be related to child-care deficiencies, but it is doubtful that a labor market with such high unemployment would provide full-time jobs for these part-timers, even if their children were cared for.

As an explanation for the very low labor force participation of Italian women and the consequent disincentive for independence, limited employment opportunity seems more important than limited child-care resources. Publicly-subsidized child care is available for 95% of Italian children ages three to five (90% in the South) (OECD, 2001); yet Italian women have the lowest activity and employment-to-population rates of the study countries. It is true that child care is deficient for very young children in Italy but no less than some other study countries (Esping-Andersen, 2002). Of course, extensive provision of social services, including child and elder care, can create employment opportunities for women as it has in service-rich Nordic countries.

Misra, Moller, & Budig (2007) found that work-family policies are related to poverty rates of both single and partnered mothers. In the United States, Canada, and Britain where mothers are expected to work and where the approach to child care is market-driven, lone mothers had the high poverty rates that were also found in this study (Table 10.1). In discussing the importance of work-family policies, Misra and colleagues also recognize the importance of income transfers. However, they appear to leave the availability and quality of employment out of the equation.

Recent Swedish experience shows that abundant child care cannot compensate for employment opportunity and cash family benefits. Following Sweden's economic crisis in the 1990s, unemployment rose and some family benefits declined. The poverty of Swedish lone mothers rose nearly three-fold from 1994 to 2000; it fell by 2005 but was still more than double the 1994 rate (Table 10.10). This occurred even though public provision of child care was increasing.

## Social Policy for Lone Mothers

Publicly subsidized child care enables mothers to work outside the home, if jobs are available, and to be relieved of the high price of market care. However, the problem of a low, woman's wage and a single wage often necessitates other types of government income support. The high pre-transfer poverty rates of lone mothers—ranging from 56% in Sweden to 85% in Britain in 2000—attest to this need (Table 10.10).

**Child support.** Single-earner families are at an economic disadvantage in economies where many partnered families have two earners. Economist Steven Pressman (2003) has shown that the gender poverty gap between "female-headed households" and all other nonelderly households would virtually disappear if the former had the same number of workers as the latter. However, the gap would narrow but probably not disappear if the comparison were between lone-mother and two-parent families with children.[2]

In theory, child support from the noncustodial parent could reduce the economic losses of separation, divorce, or nonmarriage. However, child support is often minimal or missing if it is not guaranteed by the state—unless it is a public rather than private income transfer. Even when governments step in to help mothers collect it, child support is deficient. This is the case in Canada, the United States, and the United Kingdom. Child support deficiencies are one facet of the high poverty rates in the regimes classified as liberal.

Unlike these Anglo-Saxon countries, other nations provide child support and then collect from the noncustodial parents the amount that they are deemed able to pay. Government-assured child support or advance maintenance policies vary in length and breadth of coverage. In Germany, advance maintenance is limited in duration and by children's age so that many lone mothers do not get support from absent fathers or the state. Formerly a basic minimum for Swedish lone mothers, advance maintenance was de-indexed in 1997 and is serving one-third fewer children than formerly. By contrast, the number of French lone parents receiving guaranteed child support increased five-fold from 1994 to 2004. This policy is especially important where deteriorating economic conditions reduce fathers' ability to provide child support or to marry the mothers of their children (for the latter, see Wilson, 1997).

**New directions in cash benefits for lone mothers.** The thrust of social policy in a number of countries has been to move economically dependent people into paid work—with varying degrees of coercion and often without the assurance of living wage jobs or in some cases child care. The terms activation, welfare to work, and workfare have been used interchangeably, but the latter sometimes has a specific meaning—that recipients are required to work in exchange for their welfare and without customary workplace benefits. Workfare in this form has been more characteristic of U.S. policy than of most other countries in this study. Workfare in the more general sense has been viewed as an international movement by Peck (2001), although his emphasis was on the United States and Canada. The "carrot" of activation policies in Britain and the United States is a tax credit to supplement the incomes of the working poor or to make work pay.

In France, minimum-income benefits have become more employment oriented in recent years. There is apprehension among some French experts that a program implemented in 2009, the *revenu de solidarité active-RSA* is a move in the direction of workfare. Whereas the United States has placed primary emphasis on the Earned Income Tax Credit, the universal family allowance that is not contingent on earnings is still an important anti-poverty policy in France. German policy has moved in two directions: support for some mothers who leave the labor market and for the unemployed as well as an effort to encourage employment through income supplements.

The disadvantages that Italian women suffer from a patriarchal labor market are compounded by a "meritocratic-occupational" welfare system that restricts family benefits to fully employed or retired workers. The result is a virtual "catch 22" in which neither employment nor social policy facilitates the economic independence of women.

"Before other developed countries made the transition from welfare to workfare in the 1990s, Japan had steadily established a 'workfare system'" (Chapter 8; Uzuhashi, 1997). Increasingly strict limits on public assistance essentially created a "work only system" for lone mothers.

In contrast to coercive activation initiatives that require women to work, Swedish policy facilitates women's employment by making work and family life compatible: through nearly universal child care and generous paid leave for new parents and those with sick children. It also attempts to reduce inequality of both gender and class in the workplace. At the same time, it provides a national minimum income to those who either do not work or do not earn enough. Sweden, however, has not been immune to retrenchment. In addition to the change from advance maintenance to maintenance allowances, replacement rates are lower in parental, sickness and unemployment compensation, and family and housing allowances have been reduced.

**In-kind benefits.**[3] In all the study countries but the United States, public provision for health care is taken for granted. In the earliest weeks of his administration, President Obama extended health coverage to more children as a "downpayment" on universal coverage which is still on the agenda, despite the economic crisis.

Only a third of financially eligible families get housing assistance in the United States, but it is not alone in insufficient benefits to offset the high costs of shelter. Of considerable loss and hardship for Canadian solo mothers is the steep decline in social housing, and in Sweden, housing allowances were among the largest cuts in the 1990s. On the other hand, France seems to have held the line on housing allowances which, according to the French government, cut the poverty rate of lone mothers in half. It has been argued that the French welfare state neglects those who are most needy (Smith, 2004), but French social policy ranks second among the study countries in the prevention of poverty of lone mothers and perhaps first in the case of lone elderly women.

## Policies for Lone Elderly Women

There is reason to expect that with rising employment rates, women will enter old age with more market income, along with better pensions in their own right, both private and public. Yet, the growth of precarious work militates against the increases in current and future income that would otherwise result from women's more continuous presence in the labor market. Canada is a case in point. Poverty rates of older women have fallen to historic levels, but even with increasing rates of employment, women's ability to save for retirement will continue to be compromised if patterns of paid and unpaid work remain unchanged. A report released by the German government in 2007 is also pessimistic forecasting that people with low income, discontinuous careers, and who do not save for old age will be at increasing risk of poverty.

**Government money.** For the vast majority of lone elderly women, economic security depends on government money. Their major source of income is public pensions based on their own earnings and/or their spouses, but these are often too low to prevent poverty. Targeted benefits are playing a role in filling the poverty gap for the elderly in some countries.

Pensions based on earnings during their working lives leave women at a substantial disadvantage. France has the lowest gender wage gap in this study; nonetheless, the median older women's pension based on contributions was less than half that of men of the same age. One reason is women are more than twice as likely to have interrupted working lives (Chapter 3).

Welfare regimes have various ways of compensating women for low and interrupted earnings that leave them with inadequate pensions in their own right. Each of these reflects different conceptions of gender roles. Some pension systems combine more than one of these with women's direct pensions or benefits based on their own earnings.

An approach that reflects the male breadwinner model is to provide benefits to women as dependents or survivors of their spouses. Variants of this policy exist in all the countries in the study except Sweden. This is the case, even though the breadwinner model itself is either a minority pattern or has been succeeded by the "modified breadwinner model" in which women or mothers work part-time and men, full-time. Yet, older women have often lived by the male breadwinner model and have relatively low pensions in their own name. Even if they work continuously, the wage gap means lower pensions. Thus, they need some means of making up for lost income. Obviously survivors' benefits are helpful to widows and, in some countries, divorcées married for specified lengths of times also get derived benefits. On the other hand, in some regimes survivors' or derived pensions do not carry the same right as one's own pension.

Although the U.S. Social Security system compensates low-wage workers with a higher ratio of benefits to contributions, this is not enough to prevent the poverty of many older women. According to pension specialist Teresa Ghilarducci (2008), U.S. Social Security benefits are among the world's lowest in comparison to average wages. A major deficiency is the lack of a minimum benefit. And the U.S. social assistance program for the elderly does little to fill the poverty gap or to serve as an adequate, guaranteed minimum for the elderly.

An ominous trend in the United States and one experienced particularly by low-wage workers is forced employment in old age owing to "the collapse of retirement income" (Ghilarducci, 2008, esp. pp. 26–57). Loss of an important right gained during the twentieth century—to opt out of the labor market in old age and to maintain an adequate standard of living—is a form of re-commodification that could occur in other countries where declines in private and, particularly, public pensions are reducing the length and security of retirement.

In some countries pensions acknowledge the economic toll of caregiving. For example, in Britain the Home Responsibilities Protection allows a person caring for a dependent child or adult receiving disability benefits to deduct the number of years of such care from the years required to qualify for the basic state pension. In addition to derived benefits, Germany grants credits for child and elder care.[4] However, Germany's recognition of the penalty for caring is overshadowed by severe general cuts in the state pension system.

It should be noted that privatized pensions have no such recognition of the costs of caring. Indeed, based on their study of increased reliance on privatized pensions, Ginn and Arber conclude that: "The individualistic ideology on which pension privatization is based may lead to a society in which no one can afford to care for others" (2008, p. 149).

The Swedish system, in keeping with its emphasis on decreasing women's dependence on the family, is based on individual entitlement to a pension regardless of sex, marital status, labor market participation, or income. Instead of a benefit derived from a spouse, Sweden provides some benefits, including a special income supplement, to compensate women and those with only a few years of earnings. In spite of these compensatory policies, Sweden's retrenchment in old age insurance—from a defined benefit to a defined contribution—threatens the pension levels of future retirees.

**Services for the elderly.** Problems in quality and quantity of community and institutional care abound. The under-served are disproportionately lone women. The burden of their care falls on family members, typically middle-age women who suffer economic loss and stress from a difficult role. This is a feminist issue on both counts.

During the last two decades, in response to the aging of populations and the burden of family care, even conservative, familist regimes have eased the burden of family responsibility. Germany added Long Term Care Insurance to its contributory social insurance system in the mid-1990s, but most long term care continues to be given by family members at home (Garaedts, Heller, & Harrington, 2000). Japan's system is modeled on the German approach and was designed to socialize care, but subsequent cost cutting still leaves the burden on families. In recent decades, Italy, despite its familist orientation, has added benefits to its social security system to pay for elder care, but it remains deficient in public provision of home and institutional care (Chapter 7).

Often harder to categorize than other regimes France had formerly been regarded as a country relatively rich in child but not elder care (Martin, Math, & Renaudat, 1998). In 2002, the Socialist government created services for anyone determined to be in need of support with tasks of daily living, but the dramatic increase in the cost of this progressive measure is likely to lead the conservative government to cut it back. This is another example of good news and bad—expanded coverage undermined by cost-cutting.

What of the countries categorized as liberal? Like child care, home care in Canada is minimally developed. In the United States some elder care is available through the health care programs for the elderly and disabled, but the vast majority of care is provided by family members; and many elderly women, particularly, are forced into nursing homes where care is often deficient. In the United Kingdom the responsibility falls to local government, and although community services have increased, they still fall short of need.

Sweden is a leader in child but not elder care. Privatization of services has resulted in reduced resources and increased fees. Where Sweden stands in relation to other countries that have increased their commitment to elder care in recent years is not clear, What is clearer is that need goes unmet in all the countries of this study to a varying but unmeasured extent and at a cost to older women and their typically female caregivers.

According to Daly and Lewis (2000) the concept of social care tells us much about welfare state variation and welfare state change and development. In the case of child care we gathered enough information to be able to say that the social democratic and liberal regimes clearly vary, with the former promoting de-familialization and the latter doing much less in this respect despite the expectation or requirement that single mothers work. Differences among the conservative countries were noted with France closer to the social democratic approach to child care.

In our investigation of elder care we found, along with earlier research (Anttonen & Sipilä, 1996), that countries may differ in the two domains of care, that is, for children and the elderly. However, more research on elder care is required in order to permit accurate cross-national comparisons. This assessment is complicated, as it is in the case of child care, because of retrenchment or forward and backward motion—expansion of provision in response to increased need and retreat from this commitment on account of budgetary constraints and regime change.

## Minimum-Income Guarantees

Policy logic, even if universal, can be a skeleton without flesh. Unless benefits are adequate, neither forms of liberation—de-commodification or de-familialization—will occur. In fact, both require an adequate income or escape from poverty. As Kenneth Nelson (2008) points out, Rawlsian conceptions of social justice cannot be reached when nations fail to establish a basic minimum income above the poverty line. According to British historian Asa Briggs, one of the three attributes of a welfare state is: "Guaranteeing individuals and families a minimum income irrespective of the market value of their wealth and property" (1961, p. 29). This is close to Esping-Andersen's concept of de-commodification. Most, if not all, the study countries fall short of guaranteeing an adequate minimum income to lone mothers and lone elderly women, albeit to very different extents.

Several countries attempt to fill the poverty gap for the elderly with minimum-income measures that need not be fraught with the stigma and indignity traditionally characteristic of programs for the poor. This is not to overlook the political disadvantages of selectivism that can ultimately weaken support for social policies as it did for the U.S. social assistance program for poor, single mothers.

Minimum-income measures are used, not only by a liberal state like Canada that is associated with means-tested programs but by one like Sweden that features universalism. Myles (2002) has distinguished traditional means and assets testing in programs from "modern variants" that are less pauperizing and demeaning of the elderly. For example, income testing measures income but not assets so that recipients are not forced to spend themselves into poverty.

Tax credits, as noted, can supplement wages of the "working poor." They are not stigmatized, and, if they are refundable tax credits, as they are in the United States, they are essentially public assistance for the great majority of claimants who do not pay federal income taxes. The U.S. Earned Income Tax Credit is free of stigma because it is administered, not by a welfare department, but by a universal agency, the Internal Revenue Service that collects taxes from all income receivers. Further, it is referred to as a tax credit and is for the "worthy," working poor. Nonetheless, compared to minimum-income guarantees, there are disadvantages to these credits: they omit persons who are unemployed or not in the labor market, often those who are most economically disadvantaged. Not to mention the possibility that this subsidy may deter efforts to raise wages.

Social assistance levels provide some indication of minimum-income guarantees, if, indeed, they are available to all in need. Using data from the Luxembourg Income Study (LIS) and the Minimum Income Protection Interim Dataset (SaMip), Nelson (2008) found that social assistance benefits for lone parents in 17 countries in Europe and North America ranged from 26% of median disposable income in the United States to 65% in Germany with a 17-country, unweighted average of 49.7%—comparable to the 50% poverty standard. The German social assistance level is somewhat above the highest of the three poverty standards used in this study. Yet, according to the German government, at least one-third of lone mothers had incomes below this amount, and LIS puts their poverty rate at over 50%. The problem could be one of take-up, of eligible individuals not using the benefit for reasons of stigma or deterrence. Unless public assistance is adequate and absent of demeaning conditions so that all who need it avail themselves of it, a minimum benefit level does not amount to a minimum-income guarantee.

## Full Employment

Once an important component of the welfare state, full employment is nowhere in sight. In a number of countries, including France, West

Germany, Sweden, and the United Kingdom, full employment was national policy in the decades following World War II and considered a vital part of the welfare state, perhaps more important than income support (Beveridge, 1945; Ginsburg, 1983; Goldberg, 2002; Korpi, 1978). In his typology of welfare states, Leibfried described the Scandinavian regime as one of "full employment" with the welfare state as "*employer of first resort* and compensator of last resort" (italics in original) (1993, p. 142). Since the 1970s, France, Germany, and the United Kingdom have abandoned full employment. Sweden gave up its signature full employment policy in the 1990s after it joined the European Union which "had firm rules against inflation but none against unemployment" (Ginsburg & Rosenthal, 2002, p. 111). Japan had very low unemployment rates until the 1990s although this policy was not a welfare state component but a means of avoiding one.[5] Japan's unemployment rate, under 2.5% from 1960 until 1994, began climbing thereafter although not to European levels (U.S. Bureau of Labor Statistics, 2008, table 8).

Even when unemployment rates are relatively low, there is much "hidden unemployment," and, in addition, many who work remain poor.[6] Yet, activation policies are in vogue. As one French observer puts it, the goal is to promote a society of "full activity" but not full employment (Castel, 2006; Chapter 3). Women, especially, are expected to work at low wages, supplemented by tax credits or some form of public assistance that still may not provide an escape from poverty. Activation policies, moreover, are anti-feminist in implying that the work women do in the home is *in*activity.

Unemployment is not only a problem of current and future income. The architect of the British welfare state, William Beveridge, emphasized the noneconomic attributes of work: "Idleness is not the same as Want, but a separate evil, which *men* do not escape by having an income. They must also have the chance of rendering useful service and of feeling that they are doing so" (emphasis added) (1945, p. 20). This was a male full employment ideal based on a male breadwinner model, but recent reinterpretations of full employment encompass a fully employed population of women and men as well as an emphasis compatible with an earner/carer model (Collins, Ginsburg, & Goldberg, 1993).[7]

Employment is sometimes seen as promoting social integration and unemployment as leading to social exclusion, although more in some countries than others. Anthony Atkinson (1998) who heads the London School of Economics, holds that marginal work will not lead to social integration.[8] As sociologist Ruth Levitas points out, emphasis on paid work as the mechanism of integration devalues unpaid work and "overlooks the fact that the positions into which people are 'integrated' through paid work are fundamentally unequal" (1996, p. 18). Advocates of full employment, however, define it broadly, in terms of both availability and quality of work or as rights *at* work as well as rights to a job (Goldberg, Harvey, & Ginsburg, 2007). They are cognizant, too, that loose labor markets contribute to declining and stagnant wages. Living wages are just one of the essential components of full employment. "Decent work" is a concept promoted by the International Labour Organization (Undated) and one that resembles this broad definition of full employment.

Employment, particularly in precarious labor markets, may fail to achieve social integration, but unemployment, according to economist and Nobel laureate Amartya Sen, leads to many social ills, including social exclusion:

> There is plenty of evidence that unemployment has many far-reaching effects other than loss of income, including psychological harm, loss of work motivation, skill and self-confidence, increase in ailments and morbidity (and even mortality rates), disruption of family relations and social life, hardening of social exclusion, and accentuation of racial tensions and gender asymmetries (1998, p. 94).

Before Sweden witnessed mass unemployment in the 1990s, Esping-Andersen (1990) wrote that the social democratic regime was as fully committed to the right to work as to the right to income protection. Interestingly, though, Esping-Andersen made the right *not* to work or de-commodification—instead of the right to living-wage work—the criterion by which welfare states should be classified (1990, p. 22).

Employment is important to de-commodification and to de-familialization. In the case of the latter, freedom from family dependence requires services like child care that enable women to work continuously, but we have argued that without employment opportunity, child care cannot accomplish that purpose. De-commodification addresses the right to opt out of the market at certain times in the life course, but the assumption is that one will be employed the rest of the time. Reductions in work time are part of the full employment package. Spreading employment and facilitating leisure are particularly beneficial for women and men who assume dual roles.

With full employment, as defined here, work itself becomes de-commodified, for workers are not treated as commodities, forced to work for any job at any wage and with little or no autonomy in the workplace. Thus, it seems that full employment, the right to a non-commodified job, should be a criterion for welfare regimes. During the period covered by this research, none of the countries in this study met this criterion that was once integral to the very conception of the welfare state.

Without full employment, the social democratic regime falls short of its anti-poverty and egalitarian objectives. This is the case in Sweden, even though it continues to surpass other types of regimes. Those categorized as liberal had relatively low unemployment rates during the time of the study but many jobs of dubious quality, and regimes classified as conservative have high unemployment and a growing number of poor-quality jobs with a disproportionate amount of precarious employment for women. In Italy, where women's rate of employment is low, Morlicchio and Spinelli conclude that "for Italian women employment at a living wage is fundamental for escaping poverty," and that includes not only divorced and widowed women but many with partners as well (Chapter 7, p. 195).

Thanks to income-support policies, the return of mass unemployment has prevented a commensurate rise in poverty in continental European countries (Atkinson, 1998; Kleinman, 2002). But poverty has nonetheless increased with a consequent strain on social budgets—lower tax revenues and more spending to compensate the unemployed and probably some of the problems increased by unemployment. How much longer France will continue generous social policies in an economy that is creating more need for them is a big question. Substantial cutbacks have been threatened in France but averted by mass resistance. For how long? This is a problem for Germany, too, although its policies toward lone mothers are less than generous. It is harder for Sweden to maintain its level of income support and services without full employment. High unemployment also threatens the financial stability of public pensions based on payroll taxes.

Prior to the recession economists and other social scientists on both sides of the Atlantic had crafted job creation proposals that are at the same time public investments in social housing, restructured transportation systems, urban refurbishment, renewable energy, and vital social services such as child and elder care (EuroMemorandum Group, 2007; National Jobs for All Coalition, 2007; Pollin, 2007). Public investment in a sustainable economy and a better quality of life is an anti-poverty strategy that would have created the foundation for greater and shared prosperity for these rich nations, for all their inhabitants, and especially the excessive number of poor women in their midst. It is particularly important for women that such proposals include development of the social infrastructure—education, child care, and other service jobs in which they are likely to be employed and that are as important to the future prosperity of nations as physical infrastructure. Current proposals to stimulate flagging economies are raising this question. In Canada, for example, there is some concern that the focus on physical infrastructure is directed more to traditional forms of male employment and that, as a result, women will do especially badly in the current environment (Chapter 6). Similar concerns are voiced over economic stimulus legislation in the United States (Chapter 9; Garza, 2009; Goldstein, 2009).

With more people working and paying taxes and fewer requiring compensation for unemployment and its attendant social problems, meeting other social needs becomes more affordable. The availability of decent work, along with the socialization of family care, would not only facilitate the economic independence of working-age women but would mean as well that more older women would have adequate income in their own right. Job creation that would at the same time improve the physical and social infrastructure is undertaken as a stimulus to economies during periods of recession. However, the proposals cited above are proposed as permanent solutions to chronic unemployment, not only as temporary measures to reduce joblessness during economic downturns.

## Rich Countries, Poor Women

Amidst the affluence of these eight, rich countries many single mothers and lone elderly women have been living in poverty at much higher rates than their married or partnered compatriots and the general population. Between 1990 and 2005 the national output per person of these already rich countries had grown on average by almost one-fourth (U. S. Department of Labor, 2008).[9] Yet, millions of lone women and their children did not share this prosperity. And lone minority and immigrant women are at greater risk of poverty than lone women, generally. (See Chapter 10 for a discussion of the heterogeneity of lone women.)

In the period covered by this research—if less so since the financial meltdown of 2008—the eight study countries had the economic resources to prevent the high unemployment in some of them and the chronic unemployment and underemployment that was characteristic of all. And they certainly had the wherewithal to offset the inequality of market incomes with more adequate social policies. Yet, social policy became more restrictive, even as market conditions deteriorated, and perversely, work requirements were tightened in tandem with precarious employment, increased unemployment, or both. Although there are examples of expansion, these were often qualified by budgetary restraints, and the general impression is of regress in both employment and income support. Arguably, increased inequality, particularly in the United States, is an important factor in the economic crisis. In this case economic injustice and economic collapse go hand in hand!

## Political Prospects

Most of the authors of the country studies commented on the political resources of women. On the one hand, in Sweden, "The range of resources is wide, and so is societal attention to women's problems" (Chapter 2). Solo mothers' membership in organizations was above average, and they were primarily involved in unions, housing associations, and parents' organizations This was not sufficient organizational and political strength to prevent the deterioration of their economic condition but may well have limited the damage.

Findings are different for the other countries. In France, neither public debate nor academic research is focused on women's poverty, even though the precariousness of both groups of lone women increased in recent years and the financial crisis is likely to exacerbate their already fragile condition. Lone mothers are neither of political or scholarly interest in Italy, probably because their poverty is hidden in larger family units or they are a small group owing to the barriers against women's economic independence. Yet, it is a responsibility of social science to make latent problems manifest.

In several countries, notably Germany and the United Kingdom, women are the indirect focus of concern with childhood poverty and what it augurs for these nations. "It is the growing concern about child poverty and its potential impact on the future development of the country" writes Klammer, "that has helped single mothers to receive a lot of attention and some support from different political parties and interest groups" (Chapter 4, p. 116). With elderly poverty likely to rise in the future, there may be more public concern about it than in the recent past. Millar, along with other scholars, is concerned "that the focus on child poverty will make it more difficult to press claims for gender equality and the needs of women as women, and not only as mothers... [and there is] a risk that the child poverty focus will reinforce, rather than challenge, gender divisions in work and care" (Chapter 5, p. 146). Similarly, Evans writes that "the emphasis on child poverty may serve to obscure further the challenges that the mothers of poor children face" (Chapter 6, p. 168).

In Japan, the rise of nonregular work is thought to have triggered public concern over poverty and social disparities, including the once latent poverty of women. A declining birthrate became a major source of policy debate in Japan in the 1990s and, as a result, there was some increase in child-care and work-family harmonization programs. Here, too, women benefited, not primarily because of concern over their inequality, but rather because of the problems that their disadvantages were causing. Demographic changes or the rise of the "longevity society" also led to some societal concern and policy change in regard to the care of the elderly. When the problems of women became problems for the nation, action was taken but not necessarily on behalf of women or primarily because women were mobilized.

Women's issues are hardly at the forefront in the two North American countries in this study. The dismantling of equal opportunity organizations in Canada has already been cited. Dependence on government funding, even of the major women's advocacy organization that was once seen as a powerful defender of the welfare state, left these organizations vulnerable to successive governments that cut back their resources. "Funding for women's issues was rolled back during a time when Canada was never better positioned to afford them" (Chapter 6, p. 154).

The poverty of women is not a focus of public policy in the United States. The women's liberation movement, once concerned with a broader range of issues, has been preoccupied with the need to protect the constitutional right to abortion from constant battering, not least by the conservative, "pro-life" women's movement. Government-provided child care that would aid the majority of working women who are burdened by the high cost of private services has not been a priority of the National Organization for Women.

Granted that the countries in this study represent a range of resources concerned directly or indirectly with women's poverty, the overall picture is not one of substantial political clout or societal concern with the problems of women or of activism on the part of women in behalf of gender equity Moreover, in most of the countries, the poverty of one or more of these groups—children, minorities, and immigrants—takes precedence over that of women—even though the poverty of women cannot be separated from that of their children, and they are often especially beleaguered as immigrants or minorities.

## Exceptionalism Probed

Among the eight countries in this study, neither Sweden nor the United States is completely alone at the top or bottom of poverty prevention and the policies related to it. Still, they both stand out. Just how exceptional are they, and, more importantly, how can their differences be explained?

**Other Nordic countries.** Had this study included other Nordic countries, Sweden might have been less exceptional. In the mid-1990s, Anttonen and Sipilä (1996) found that Denmark exceeded Sweden in social care services for both children and the elderly. Two other Nordic countries, Norway and Finland, as well as the Netherlands which is classified as conservative, did better in elder care. Although Esping-Andersen refers to Sweden as an exemplar of the social democratic regime (1990, 1999), Denmark was the major model for work-family balance policies in his proposal for "a new gender contract" (2002). As for the poverty of lone parents, Eurostat (2007) reported similar rates for Denmark, Finland, Norway, and Sweden in the early years of the twenty-first century.

It is really on behalf of solo mothers that Sweden stands alone in this study, reducing their poverty more than three times as much as the United States and at least 65% more than any other country (Table 10.10). Although its own official data put Sweden ahead of the other study countries in prevention of the poverty of lone elderly women (at the 50% level), there is evidence from LIS that Canada and France do better at the lower two standards and that Sweden is closer to the United States than to those other countries at the highest level. Nor is Sweden a leader in elder care which has contracted at the same time that child care has expanded.

**U.S. exceptionalism.** Since Alexis de Tocqueville, the term "American exceptionalism" has been used to describe what is uniquely good, bad, or different about the United States. In their study of family policy and its consequences in 12 relatively similar countries, Janet Gornick and Marcia

Meyers concluded that "Although the challenges of balancing work and family life are not uniquely American, many of the resulting problems are particularly acute in this country" (2003, p. 82).

In a study of gender, liberalism, and social policy in four Anglo-Saxon nations, O'Connor, Orloff, and Shaver (1999) recognized why the United States is dubbed a "welfare state laggard" but pointed out that it is comparatively progressive on such issues as occupational segregation and women's entrepreneurial and professional achievements. Nonetheless, U.S. women still predominate in low-wage work. As McCall found in her research on regional labor markets, "anti-discrimination policies have been more effective for highly educated women than for women at the bottom end of the labor market" (2001, p. 170).

If not exceptional in all gender comparisons, the US is nearly always less generous in social policy—in health care, housing, child support, child care, parental leave, sick leave. In addition to leaving millions of its inhabitants without an entitlement to health care, it is the only one without paid parental leave. It also stands alone, not only among the countries in this study but all those in the European Union, in measuring poverty by a low, absolute standard. Relative standards are not inherently higher than absolute standards but differ conceptually in being concerned with inequality or how far an individual or family can fall from the standard of the community without being considered poor. A low standard like that of the United States both reflects and reinforces a lack of societal concern about the problem of poverty.

The United States is seen as an "archetypical" example of the liberal model of the welfare state, along with Canada and Australia (Esping-Andersen, 1990). This research has revealed differences among the three countries in the study that are classified as liberal, differences wide enough to question their being lumped together. During the long reign of Prime Minister Margaret Thatcher, the United Kingdom came closer to the liberal model, but it has changed course after several decades of neo-liberalism—setting targets for reduction of child poverty and making strides toward reducing elderly and lone mother poverty. Further, it holds itself to a poverty standard of less than 60% of median income after housing costs. Canada, the third study country classified as liberal, has made significant progress in reducing the poverty of the elderly. Although it had pulled back from a national child-care initiative, its largest province, Ontario, despite the economic climate, will make full-day child care available to all 4- and 5-year-old children by 2010. The United States, however, never had such an initiative. Canada has two poverty standards, roughly equal and both higher than the U.S. threshold.[10] The United Kingdom and Canada may be edging toward work requirements for lone mothers, but neither has gone as far in that direction as the United States.

Japan may have a higher rate of lone mother poverty than the United States. Japanese policy toward lone mothers has become increasingly restrictive and is akin to the U.S. approach. The poverty rate of lone elderly women, a large group in Japan and growing with the decline in three-generation households, may exceed the U.S. level. Although Japan is viewed as a much more patriarchal society than the United States and women generally have much lower activity rates, the two groups of lone women who are the focus of this study may be at comparably high risk of poverty although we lack harmonized data for the two countries.

Stimulated by a very low fertility rate that it was unlikely to mitigate by means of mass immigration, Japan has deviated from a familism extreme enough—combined with worsening labor market conditions—to discourage marriage and motherhood. It began dealing with a problem that could threaten its existence as a nation by increasing child care provision and enacting Long Term Health Insurance, but it has moved toward privatization of child care and undermined elder care through cost cutting. Nevertheless, the move away from familism in Japan and in Germany as well raises questions about the force of "path dependency." Important exigencies can lead countries to deviate from previous courses. For example, economic and social crises led to significant changes in U.S. policy in the 1930s and again, in the 1960s.

The reluctance of the U.S. government to use the power of the state on behalf of middle- and lower-income groups could be taken for an important path dependency. A different interpretation of U.S. history is given by Arthur Schlesinger, Jr: that periods of affirmative government alternate with the individualism, rampant self-interest, and limited government that predominated in the years covered by this study. Perhaps it is this cycling—expansion in response to an economic or social crisis, followed by retrenchment and roll backs under normal conditions—that helps to account for what Harold Wilensky has famously dubbed "a reluctant welfare state."[11]

According to Edwin Amenta and Theda Skocpol (1989), one explanation of the distinctiveness of American public policies in the last century was an "erratic pattern"—in contrast to Western Europe where development was halting but in a unilateral direction.[12] Just as a demographic "crisis" led to a departure from path dependency in Japan, a financial crisis could once again change the direction of U.S. policy.

In stark contrast to the erratic pattern of the United States, Sweden stayed on a path that joined full employment to generous, universal social welfare benefits for over 60 years. Amidst financial crisis in the early 1990s, Sweden deviated from the full employment policies that were integral, if not more important, to its welfare state than social policies, and it cut back some of those as well. Nonetheless, women's activity rates remain high, and its employment gender gap is much lower than any of the other study countries.

It is true that Sweden's current record in prevention of poverty and inequality is less stellar than in the 1980s and early 1990s. Nonetheless, Sweden's achievements, like that of the other Nordic countries, remain admirable. As Ginsburg and Rosenthal (2006) point out, this may be because other welfare states have been weakened. They further conclude that "despite extensive cutbacks and restructuring in the 1990s, Sweden's welfare state has not been dismantled, though it has been and continues to be changed—sometimes in perilous ways, for instance pension reform, elder care, and the lack of full employment" (p. 77).

**Political contrast.** Politically, Sweden presents a very different picture from the United States. Sainsbury and Morissens argue that because poverty rates have been low, equality, not poverty, has been a major source of political mobilization, and that has led to broader coalitions that include rather than isolate disadvantaged groups.

Neither poverty nor equality has been on the U.S. political agenda in the period covered by this research. Since the mobilization of poor women of color in the Welfare Rights Movement that flourished for about a decade, beginning in the mid-1960s, poor women have not been well organized or well-represented in more powerful organizations. Selectivism left single mothers without powerful allies in defending their entitlement to welfare which was repealed in 1996 under Democrat Bill Clinton.

Sweden's labor movement is both powerful and, especially in earlier years, ideologically committed to a strong and equalizing welfare state (Ginsburg, 1983; Meidner, 1980).[13] According to power resources theory which has focused on variations in the development and growth of welfare states, the success of parties of the left depends on a well-organized and powerful labor movement. The powerful Swedish labor movement has been closely allied to the Social Democratic Party that has led Sweden alone or in coalition through most of the years since 1932. It is, however, important to point out that Sweden's Social Democratic Party, like left-of-center parties elsewhere, itself turned toward neo-liberalism in the 1990s (Ginsburg & Rosenthal, 2002).

The U.S. labor movement is both weak and, particularly since the purges of its more progressive leadership in the 1950s, more representative of its declining membership than the working class as a whole. It has not, for example, been a strong advocate of full employment. It is supportive of the Democratic Party, but the latter has adopted policies such as the North American Free Trade Agreement that were opposed by organized labor and that largely ignore their rights.

Political representation of women in the two countries is also quite different. Nearly half the members of the Swedish parliament are women, and solo mothers particularly have had strong advocates in the seats of government. Women's political representation has increased in the United States, but by 2008, only 18% of Senators and 22% of members of Congress were women.

The United States has been deeply divided by race from its earliest days. Successive waves of immigration have added to this basic cleavage a wide range of ethnic groups and ethnic divisions that capital has manipulated to its advantage. The result is a divided working class with an extremely low rate of union density and, notwithstanding periods of crisis and temporary downgrading, an unusually strong capitalist class.[14]

Deep cleavages based on race, ethnicity, and class make it difficult to build unified reform movements, including movements on behalf of women's rights. Particularly in recent years, the U.S. women's movement has been more representative of privileged white women than of minority and working-class women. The movement suffers from gender essentialism or "the notion that there is a monolithic 'women's experience' that can be described independently of other facets of experience like race, class, and sexual orientation" (Harris, 2003, p. 34). In Canada, Evans observes that despite the likelihood that visible minorities will increasingly be represented in the ranks of low-income lone mothers, gender and its intersection with race receive diminishing attention from Canadian governments. In the country studies included in this volume, the intersection of gender with race, ethnicity, nativity, or social class has had an important, albeit varying effect on the poverty of women.

Gender essentialism can lead an organization to assume it speaks for all women when in fact it represents one class or race. Its failure to make government subsidized child care a high priority is a strong indication that the National Organization for Women, the major women's organization in the United States, represents constituents who can pay the high price of private child care and not those disadvantaged by the absence of a universal service.

Gender essentialism on the part of a women's movement can lead to disaffection and separate organization by women of color and poor or immigrant women who do not see their experiences and needs represented by a gender essentialist vision or organization. An integrated approach, based on intersectionality or the interactions among different forms of inequality (McCall, 2001), could be the basis for overcoming the divisions that undermine U.S. movements for social reform. The United States may suffer more than other countries from divisions based on race, ethnicity, class, and national origin, but an intersectional strategy could build strong and unified women's movements in other countries as well—particularly as immigration increases diversity in these nations.

## The Future

It is always risky to predict the future, even in normal times. Had a global economic crisis not occurred just as this study was nearing completion, its findings would have led one to anticipate these future developments:

*Labor Market*

- Increasing and less interrupted employment of women, sometimes encouraged and sometimes required by social policies;
- Continuance and likely growth of precarious work in most countries, women's disproportionate share of it, and the likelihood

that it will undermine the potential benefits to current and future income of their increased and more continuous labor force participation;

- Continued mass unemployment in some countries and substantial chronic unemployment and underemployment, even where it is lower;
- Reduction of the bargaining power of labor as a result of chronic, high unemployment and underemployment;
- Decline of the male breadwinner model and its replacement with either a modified breadwinner (part-time work for women) or dual earner model (sometimes aspiring to dual carer) that disadvantages single-parent (single-earner) families;
- A perverse combination of high or moderate levels of unemployment and of activation policies that increase the number of job seekers;
- With a rise in precarious work for men as well as women, parity with males is becoming a less desirable goal, making a focus on class strategies such as unionization, increases in minimum wages, or full employment important, along with a continuing focus on gender.

*Child and Elder Care*

- Increased recognition of the need to reduce women's burden of family care but with varying degrees of public support, ranging from near universal government subsidies for child care in some countries to minimal coverage and largely private responsibility in others, including those where single mothers are expected or required to work;
- Some indication of a trend toward child-care allowances as cheaper alternatives to public child care that could lead to reduction in women's employment and reinforcement of traditional gender roles;
- A growing need for publicly supported elder care, some evidence of expansion in response to increasing need but limited by budgetary restraint and regime change to conservative government, hence the likelihood of continuing shortages;
- Concurrent with cutbacks, expansion in some countries, as well, for example, of nursing home insurance, elder care, and child care.

*Income Support: Lone Mothers*

- Continued whittling away of income support in some, though not all countries, even as unemployment and underemployment increase the need for it;

- Restructuring of income support through work-incentives—tax credits or increased retention of earnings—with consequent neglect of the neediest families who have no employed member;
- Continued deficiency of child support, a critical resource for lone mother families—except where it is guaranteed by government and covers children of all ages and at poverty-prevention or adequate levels.

*Income Support: Elderly Women*

- Cutbacks in pensions—increases in the retirement age, lower replacement rates, and defined contributions instead of defined benefits—despite increasing need to compensate for deteriorating labor conditions and declines in private pension coverage (in countries where these were more important components of retirement income);
- Extension of the working years to compensate for declining public and private pensions and a consequent reduction of freely chosen retirement, thus the potential re-commodification of the elderly;
- Owing to limited employment opportunities, even for pre-retirement-age workers, little likelihood that employment can fill the income gap created by pension cutbacks for those elderly workers who want to work and are able to do so;
- Continuing need in public pension systems to compensate older women for gender gaps in continuity of employment and earnings;
- Greater emphasis on nontraditional forms of targeting to reduce elderly poverty but not without the political liabilities of selectivism.

*Differences and Similarities among Countries*

- Persistence of wide differences among welfare regimes and the continuance of better poverty prevention and more economic autonomy for women in some countries (especially Sweden and France in this study);
- Ongoing U.S. exceptionalism, as manifested in its combination of the most abundant economic resources and the highest poverty rates among the eight study countries (with the possible exception of Japan);
- Continued high rates of lone women poverty in Japan with some recognition of the need to relieve their burden of family care but ambivalence over public assumption of responsibility;
- Persistence in Italy of "hidden" single motherhood as long as the combination of a very patriarchal labor market and insufficient family policies severely limit women's economic independence.

*Feminized Poverty*

- Likely continuation of high rates of lone-mother poverty in most countries and, where lone motherhood is frequent and at high risk of poverty, feminized family poverty as well;
- Continuance of feminized poverty among the lone elderly—clearly an international phenomenon.

*Political and Scholarly Interest in Women's Poverty*

- Relatively little scholarly or political interest in the poverty or inequality of women in most, but not all, study countries;
- Diminished or limited agency of women on behalf of their economic and social rights in most countries, particularly in support of poor women, Sweden being a prominent exception;
- Increased societal interest in the poverty of some other groups, notably children and youth, that could, on the one hand, eclipse interest in women's poverty or, on the other hand, lead to policies that benefit women, but possibly at the expense of gender equality;
- The need to approach research on the condition of women as well as advocacy and policies on their behalf from the perspective of intersectionality or the interaction among the inequalities of gender, race, ethnicity, nativity, and social class;
- Societal indifference to the poverty of lone elderly women owing partly to the perception that the poverty of the elderly as a group has been eradicated and the failure to recognize the continuing disadvantage of the lone elderly, especially women;
- Increasing importance of immigration as a source of inequality and poverty in most study countries and the need for it to be integrated more fully into research on the condition of women as well as advocacy on their behalf.

## Crises as Opportunities

Crises, aside from the dangers they pose, can also be opportunities for positive change in societal values and public policies. Recovery could mean reconstruction, not simply a return to pre-crisis conditions of inequality, poverty, and chronic, high unemployment. The collapse of financial sectors has dealt an ideological blow to neo-liberalism but one of unknown magnitude and duration. The reigning ideas of the last quarter century have not been buried. Amidst collapse of the U.S. financial system in the Great Depression, President Franklin Roosevelt declared:

> The money changers have fled from their high seats in the temple of our civilization. We may now restore that temple to the ancient truths. The measure

of the restoration lies in the extent to which we apply social values more noble than mere monetary profit (1933).

Perhaps this is written too early in the current crisis for a change in values to be evident. It is possible that this crisis will cast doubt on the concomitants and consequences of neo-liberalism: on the deregulation that has contributed to the financial collapse, on the dysfunctional effects of extreme economic inequality on consumption, unsustainable borrowing, and speculation; on restrictive monetary policies that have kept unemployment high in some countries; on the tight limits on government spending for income support and social services; and on the derogation, particularly in the United States, of the capacity of government to play a positive role in the economic and social life of ordinary people. In an analysis of what led to economic collapse in the United States, Nobel laureate in economics Joseph Stiglitz (2009) concluded: "most of the individual mistakes boil down to just one: a belief that markets are self-adjusting and that the role of government should be minimal."

The expenditure of billions of dollars to repair financial sectors might well serve as an excuse for cutting social spending in order to hold down budget deficits. Welfare for the financial sector could crowd out welfare for less powerful groups. The problem of crowding coupled with the increased unemployment wrought by deep recession could mean an intensification of some of the problems that were predicted prior to the crisis, particularly where lone women have limited political resources.

Another, more sanguine possibility is that middle- and lower-income groups who stand to lose jobs and savings will organize and demand that their governments focus on *their* needs. As this study has shown, women would gain from government policies to reduce unemployment and increase wages as well as from social policies that provide more generous cash benefits and services.

Government spending to create jobs and improve both infrastructure and vital human services, including those that reduce the burdens of family care, is not only a means of decreasing poverty and inequality. In times of deep recession, it is also an essential component of economic recovery.

## Notes

1 Sainsbury and Morissens (Chapter 2) report that three-fourths of Swedish school children, ages 6–9, have some form of after-school child care. That only 16% of children ages 6–9 are served is seen as a major problem! This is in contrast to near total lack of concern over care for school-age children of working parents in the United States. This study did not give sufficient attention to that problem. For a discussion of the needs of school-age children of working parents, see Heymann (2006).

2 "Female-headed households" and all other households with adults under 60 years of age include households with and without children. The poverty

rates for both types of households are likely to be lower than those of either type of household with children. One would expect that a single-earner in a two-parent family would be less hampered in the labor market than a single earner in a single-parent family. The more telling test for the effect of number of workers would be between single-mother and two-parent families with children.

3 Child care, discussed in the section on equal opportunity policies, is an in-kind benefit that is of special relevance to the employment of mothers and to the reduction of gender inequality. It has been treated separately from the other in-kind benefits included in this section.

4 Since passage of compulsory care insurance in 1995, periods of elder care are taken into account only if care givers suffer actual loss of income and insurance entitlements.

5 Labor economist Masami Nomura (2000) has argued that Japan had "total employment" rather than full employment because many people, especially women, worked but at low wages.

6 A U.S. unemployment rate of 4.8% or 7.4 million people in February 2008 concealed "hidden unemployment" of 9.7 million and another 17.7 million "working poor." "Hidden unemployment" includes those who want full-time work but are forced to work part-time (4.9 million) and those who want jobs but aren't looking (4.8 million). The working poor are those who earn less than the four-person poverty level for year-round, full-time work ($24,200 in 2008). The U.S. Department of Labor conducts monthly job vacancy surveys. In January 2008, there were four officially unemployed workers for every job opening (National Jobs for All Coalition, 2008, using figures from the U.S. Department of Labor and U.S. Bureau of the Census). The methods of calculating unemployment in other countries do not differ markedly from U.S. concepts. For monthly figures on hidden unemployment and other more comprehensive measures of unemployment, see the website of the National Jobs for All Coalition: http://www.njfac.org/jobnews.html.

7 British sociologist Rosemary Crompton (1999) has identified a continuum of gender division of labor ranging from the traditional male breadwinner to a "dual earner/dual carer" model. With state-supported child care this is the prevailing model in Sweden and other Nordic countries.

8 Atkinson (1998), however, cites no evidence to support his claim that marginal work will not lead to social integration. And, it might be noted that the title of a French social program intended to encourage employment by subsidizing low-wage jobs implied that such work is integrating: *Revenu minimum d'insertion* (RMI). The RMI was replaced in 2009 by another activation policy, *revenu de solidarité active* whose name also implies integration. Welfare reform studies in the United States find that former welfare recipients, often in marginal jobs, seem to prefer being off welfare and to have higher qualities of life, better self-respect, more personal autonomy, and more optimism about the future. Perhaps it was not so much that life off welfare was better but that life on was worse. The price, for these gains, however, seems too large and unnecessary (Altman & Goldberg, 2007).

9 The range was from 16.9% in Germany and Japan to 36.4% in the United Kingdom.

10 According to Canada's absolute poverty standard (Low Income Cut-offs or LICOs) about 34% of lone mothers were poor in 2006, whereas its relative

poverty standard, less than 50% of median disposable income adjusted for family size and composition (Low-Income Measure or LIM) leaves about 36% of lone mothers poor (Chapter 6).

11 Wilensky coined the epithet, "reluctant welfare state," in 1965 even though the United States adopted Medicare and Medicaid and declared a "war on poverty" at this time.

12 Amenta and Skocpol cite Peter Flora and Jens Alber (1981) for this model of welfare state development in Western Europe.

13 Rudolf Meidner, one of the architects of Swedish full employment policies, has emphasized that power alone is not enough to accomplish the kind of welfare state that Sweden has. As Meidner put it,. "Organizational strength without ideology is form without content" (cited in Ginsburg, 1983, p. 226).

14 As the white populist leader Tom Watson put it to racially mixed meetings of Southern farmers at the end of the nineteenth century, "You are kept apart that you may be separately fleeced of your earnings. You are made to hate each other because upon that hatred is rested the keystone of the arch of financial despotism which enslaves you both" (Goldman, 1953, citing Woodward, 1938).

## References


Altman, J. C., & Goldberg, G. S. (2007). The quality of life paradox: A study of former public assistance recipients. *Journal of Poverty, 11*, 4, 71–90.

Amenta, E., & Skocpol, T. (1989). Taking exception: Explaining the distinctiveness of American public policies in the last century. In F. G. Castles (Ed.), *The comparative history of public policy* (pp. 292–333). New York: Oxford University Press.

Anttonen, A., & Sipilä, J. (1996). European social care services: Is it possible to identify models? *Journal of European Social Policy, 6*, 2, 87–100.

Atkinson, A. B. (1998). Social exclusion, poverty and unemployment. In A. B. Atkinson & J. Hills (Ed.), *Exclusion, employment and opportunity*, CASE/4 (pp. 1–20). London: Centre for Analysis of Social Exclusion, London School of Economics. http://sticerd.lse.ac.uk/dps/case/cp/Paper4.PDF. Accessed July 30, 2009.

Bellamy, K., & Rake, K. (2005). *Money, money, money, is it still a rich man's world? An audit of women's economic welfare in Britain today*. London: The Fawcett Society.

Beveridge, W. (1945). *Full employment in a free society*. New York: W. W. Norton.

Briggs, A. (1967). The welfare state in historical perspective. In C. Schottland (Ed.), *The welfare state: Selected essays* (pp. 25–45). New York: Doubleday.

Castel, R. (2006). Au-delà du salariat ou en deçà de l'emploi? L'institutionnalisation du précariat. In S. Paugam (Ed.), *Repenser la solidarité: L'apport des sciences sociales* (pp. 415–433). Paris: PUF.

Crompton, R. (1999). Discussion and conclusions. In R. Crompton (Ed.), *Restructuring gender relations and employment* (pp. 201–214). Oxford: Oxford University Press.

Daly, M., & Lewis, J. (2000). The concept of social care and the analysis of contemporary welfare states. *British Journal of Sociology, 51*, 2, 281–298.

Esping-Andersen. G. (1990). *The three worlds of welfare capitalism*. Princeton, NJ: Princeton University Press.

Esping-Andersen. G. (1999). *Social foundations of post-industrial economies*. New York: Oxford University Press.

Esping-Andersen. G. (2002). A new gender contract. In G. Esping-Andersen with D. Gallie, A. Hemerijck, & J. Myles (Eds.), *Why we need a new welfare state* (pp. 68–95). Oxford: Oxford University Press.

EuroMemorandum Group. (2007). *Full employment with good work, strong public services, and international cooperation.* Bremen: University of Bremen. http://www.memo-europe.uni-bremen.de/euromemo/indexmem.htm. Accessed July 29, 2009.

Eurostat. (2007). At-risk-of-poverty by household type. Luxembourg: Author. http://epp.eurostat.ec.europa.eu/tgm/refreshTableAction.do?tab=table&plugin=0&init=1&pcode=tsdsc240&language=en. Accessed January 2, 2008.

Flora, P., & Alber, J. (1981). Democratization and the development of welfare states in Western Europe. In P. Flora & A. J. Heidenheimer (Eds.), *The development of the welfare state in Europe and America* (pp. 37–81). New Brunswick, NJ: Transaction Books.

Gallie, D. (2002). The quality of working life in welfare strategy. In G. Esping-Andersen with D. Gallie, A. Hemerijck, & J. Myles, *Why we need a new welfare state* (pp. 9–129). Oxford: Oxford University Press.

Garza, I. (2009). Concerns about the draft American Recovery and Reinvestment Act. *Feminist Law Professors,* January 27. http://feministlawprofs.law.sc.edu/?cat=41. Accessed July 30, 2009.

Geraedts, M., Heller, G. V., & Harrington, C. A. (2000). Germany's long-term-care insurance: Putting a social insurance model into practice. *The Milbank Quarterly, 78,* 3, 375–401.

Ghilarducci, T. (2008). *When I'm sixty-four: The plot against pensions and the plan to save them.* Princeton: Princeton University Press.

Ginn, J., & Arber, S. (2008). The generational contract and pension privatization. In S. Arber & C. Attias-Donfut (Eds.), *The myth of generational conflict: The family and state in ageing societies* (pp. 133–153). London: Routledge.

Ginsburg, H. (1983). *Full employment and public policy: Sweden and the United States.* Lexington, MA: Lexington Press.

Ginsburg, H. L., & Rosenthal, M. G. (2002). Sweden: Temporary detour or new directions? In G. S. Goldberg & M. G. Rosenthal (Eds.), *Diminishing welfare: A cross-national study of social provision* (pp. 103–148). Westport, CT: Auburn House.

Ginsburg, H. L., & Rosenthal, M. G. (2006). The ups and downs of Sweden's welfare state: General trends, benefits and caregiving. *New Politics, 11,* 1, 70–78.

Goldberg, G. S. (2002). Introduction: Three stages of welfare capitalism. In G. S. Goldberg & M.G. Rosenthal (Eds.), *Diminishing welfare: A cross-national study of social provision* (pp. 1–32). Westport, CT: Auburn House.

Goldberg, G. S., Harvey, P., & Ginsburg, H. L. (2007). A survey of full employment advocates. *Journal of Economic Issues, 41,* 4, 1161–1168.

Goldman, E. F. (1953). *Rendezvous with destiny.* New York: Knopf.

Goldstein, D. (2009). Pink-collar blues. Does the recession provide an opportunity to remedy occupational segregation? *The American Prospect,* June 8. http://www.prospect.org/cs/articles?article=pink_collar_blues. Accessed July 29, 2009.

Gornick, J. C., & Meyers, M. K. (2003). *Families that work: Policies for reconciling parenthood and employment.* New York: Russell Sage Foundation.

Harris, A. P. (2003). Race and essentialism in feminist legal theory. In A. K. Wing (Ed.), *Critical race feminism: A reader* (2nd ed.) (pp. 34–47). New York: New York University Press.

Heymann, J. (2006). *Forgotten families: Ending the growing crisis confronting children and working parents in the global economy.* Oxford: Oxford University Press.
International Labour Organization. (undated). Decent work: The heart of social progress. Geneva: Author. http://www.ilo.org/decentwork.
Japanese Special Survey on Employment Trends, more than half of Japanese women were in non-regular work (2002).
Kleinman, M. (2002). *A European welfare state? European Union social policy in context.* Houndmills, Basingstoke, Hampshire: Palgrave.
Korpi, W. (1978). *The working class in welfare capitalism: Work, unions and* politics *in Sweden.* London: Routledge and Kegan Paul.
Leibfried, S. (1993). Toward a European welfare state? On integrating poverty regimes into the European Community. In C. Jones (Ed.), *New perspectives on the welfare state in Europe* (pp. 133–156). London: Routledge.
Levitas, R. (1996). The concept of social exclusion and the new Durkheimian hegemony. *Critical Social Policy, 16,* 5–20.
Martin, C., Math, A., & Renaudat, E. (1998). In J. Lewis (Ed.), *Gender, social care and welfare state restructuring in Europe* (pp. 139–174). Aldershot, UK: Ashgate.
McCall, L. (2001). *Complex inequality: Gender, class, and race in the new economy.* New York: Routledge.
Meidner, R. (1980). Our concept of the third way: Some remarks on the socio-political tenets of the Swedish Labour Movement. *Economic and Industrial Democracy, 1,* 3, 343–369.
Mishel, L., Bernstein, J., & Allegretto, S. (2007). *The state of working America 2006/2007.* Ithaca, NY: ILR Press.
Misra, J., Moller, S., & Budig, M. (2007). Work-family policies and poverty for partnered and single women in Europe and North America. *Gender & Society, 21,* 6, 804–827.
Morgan, K. J., & Zippel, K. (2003). Paid to care: The origins and effects of care leave policies in Western Europe. *Social Politics, 10,* Spring, 49–85.
Myles, J. (2002). A new social contract for the elderly? In G. Esping-Andersen with D. Gallie, A Hemerijck, & J Miles (Eds.), *Why we need a new welfare state* (pp. 130–172). New York: Oxford University Press.
Nomura, M. (2000). Full employment or "all employment?" Japan's labor market structure for low unemployment. Paper presented at the *Third Latin American Congress on the Sociology of Work,* Buenos Aires, May 17–20.
National Jobs for All Coalition (2007). *Shared prosperity and the drive for decent work.* New York: Author. http://www.njfac.org/sharedpros.pdf. Accessed July 29, 2009.
Nelson, K. (2008). *Adequacy of social minimums: Workfare, gender and poverty alleviation in welfare democracies.* Working Paper No. 474. Luxembourg: Luxembourg Income Study. http://doc.politiquessociales.net/serv1/474.pdf. Accessed August 11, 2009.
O'Connor, J. S., Orloff, A. S., & Shaver, S. (1999), *States, markets, families: Gender, liberalism, and social policy in Australia, Canada, Great Britain, and the United States.* Cambridge: Cambridge University Press.
OECD. (2001). *Early childhood education and care policy in Italy: OECD country note.* Paris: Author. http://www.oecd.org/dataoecd/15/17/33915831.pdf. Accessed July 30, 2009.
Peck, J. (2001). *Workfare states.* New York: Guilford Press.
Pollin, R. (2007). A people's economy is possible. *New Labor Forum, 16,* 3&4, 8–17.

Pressman, S. (2003). Feminist explanation for the feminization of poverty. LIS Working Paper No. 351. Luxembourg: Luxembourg Income Study. http://www.lisproject.org/publications/liswps/351.pdf. Accessed July 30, 2009.

Roosevelt, F. D. (1933/1938) Inaugural address. In S. I. Rosenman (Ed.), *The public papers and addresses of Franklin D. Roosevelt*, vol. 2 (pp. 11–16). New York: Random House.

Sen, A. (1998). *Development as freedom*. New York: Anchor Books.

Smith, T. B. (2004). *France in crisis: Welfare, inequality and globalization since 1980*. Cambridge: Cambridge University Press.

Stiglitz, J. (2009). Capitalist fools. *Vanity Fair*, January, 48–51. http://www.vanity-fair.com/magazine/2009/01/stiglitz200901. Accessed July 29, 2009.

U.S. Bureau of Labor Statistics. (2008). *Comparative civilian labor force statistics, 10 countries, 1960–2007*. Washington, DC: Author. http://www.bls.gov/fls/flscomparelf.htm. Accessed July 29, 2009.

Uzuhashi, T. (1997). *Gendai fukushi kokka no kokusai hikaku [Comparative study of the modern welfare states]*. Tokyo: Nippon Hyoron-sha.

VAMV (Verband allein erziehender Mütter und Väter Bundesverband e.V.) (2006). *Schwarzbuch Hartz IV und Alleinerziehende*. Berlin: VAMF. www.vamv.de. Accessed July 29, 2009.

Wilson, W. J. (1997). *The truly disadvantaged: The inner-city, the underclass and public policy*. Chicago: University of Chicago Press.

Visser, J. (2006). Union membership statistics in 24 countries. *Monthly Labor Review, 129*, 1, 38–49. http://www.bls.gov/opub/mlr/2006/01/art3full.pdf—92K. Accessed July 29, 2009.

Woodward, C. V. (1938). Tom Watson and the Negro in agrarian politics. *Journal of Southern History, 4*, 2q, 14–33.

# INDEX